WHAT PEOPLE ARE :
WEAPONISING AN

"For those puzzled by the extravagant claims of anti-Semitism in the Labour party, this book is essential reading. It is a comprehensive answer to right wing propagandists who endorse this manufactured campaign. The truth will out, and Asa Winstanley begins to tell it. Every bookshop should sell this book, and everyone should read it."

— Ken Loach

"Extremely important. This informative page-turner is full of intrigue. A great source for anyone who wants to understand how anti-Semitism is cynically weaponised by people who don't actually care about combatting anti-Semitism."

— Katie Halper, *The Katie Halper Show*

"A much-needed comprehensive (and meticulously documented) dissection of one of the most scandalously misreported and misrepresented episodes in recent British politics, including important insights into the workings and influence of Israel's lobby in the UK and its ruthless stifling of critics."

— Abdel Bari Atwan, author of *A Country of Words*

"Regardless of whether you consider yourself engaged in UK politics or not, everyone should read *Weaponising Anti-Semitism*. The same cynical methods Winstanley lays out here will be used against any groundswell that questions the politics of empire."

— Felix Biederman, *Chapo Trap House*

"Asa Winstanley has done a masterful job, painstakingly documenting a McCarthyite campaign of political arson aimed at sabotaging Britain's most popular left-wing leader in decades. This enthralling text chronicles crimes against democracy, committed in a modern-day witch hunt whose cynical exploitation of false accusations of anti-Semitism has set the actual anti-racist movement back decades."

— Ben Norton, *Geopolitical Economy Report*

"Jeremy Corbyn ... so terrified the British establishment that it launched a vigorous campaign to demonise Corbyn personally and crush his effort to democratise British politics. The weapon used was claims of anti-Semitism, wielded with endless deceit and slander, and powerful backing. This revealing record of the sordid story provides much insight not only into the ugly tactics of supporters of Israel's crimes but also into the deep fear of democracy in dominant elite British culture and their media and other institutions."

— Noam Chomsky

"An excellent, easy to read, factual account of the unprincipled witch hunt against Corbyn, the left and supporters of Palestine. A must read."

— Helen Marks, Jewish Voice for Labour and
Liverpool Friends of Palestine activist

"Jeremy Corbyn's political movement was a threat to the UK establishment ... [which] cynically exploited the history of anti-Semitism to smear Corbyn and his followers with fabricated allegations. Asa Winstanley has written a definitive account of this tragic farce."

— Aaron Maté

"A must-read, authoritative reference source for the use of researchers, journalists, and all who are concerned about the demise of a once-proud British political party, brought down by the deliberate weaponisation of anti-Semitism in the service of a foreign power. Highly recommended."

— Ghada Karmi, co-founder of the European Centre for
Palestine Studies at the University of Exeter

"Because the rest of the British press colluded with apartheid agents to destroy Corbyn, it was left to Asa Winstanley to document their malign plot in painstaking detail. An authoritative and shocking history."

— Max Blumenthal

"Asa Winstanley's investigative work in exposing the bogus nature of the anti-Semitism smear campaign in the Labour Party has been outstanding journalism."

— John Pilger

"An arresting account of the sordid saga of political subversion which dashed the hopes and dreams of millions in this country and beyond."

— Lowkey, musician, activist and scholar

"Winstanley dissects the disinformation that portrays opposition from the left to Israel's oppression of the Palestinians as stemming from anti-Semitism. It is an important intervention, documenting the political calculations and manoeuvres that have turned this spurious argument into a mainstream orthodoxy."

— Paul Kelemen, Manchester University academic
and author of *The British Left and Zionism*

"Unfounded smears and allegations became received wisdom and facts, even in liberal papers like *The Guardian* and especially throughout BBC news and current affairs. The lies worked: Corbyn was crushed; Labour was rendered back to Israel-supporting, neoliberal Blairism. Asa Winstanley tells this story vividly in all its shocking and depressing detail."

— Tim Llewellyn, former BBC Middle East Correspondent

"A detailed insight into the deliberate sabotage of a democratic project to elect a political leader who prioritised social justice, brought hope to millions of people and championed Palestinian rights."
— Huda Ammori, co-founder of Palestine Action

"Few people have paid closer attention to the still-unfolding 'Labour anti-Semitism crisis' than Asa Winstanley . . . a clear and urgently needed account of how anti-Semitism was and is being weaponised to destroy the Corbyn movement and to silence criticism of Israel's oppression of the Palestinian people."
— Heather Mendick, Complaints on a Podcast

"Asa Winstanley has left no stone unturned with this utterly compelling and detailed account of the manufactured Labour anti-Semitism crisis and the organised campaign to stop Jeremy Corbyn at all costs."
— Rachael Swindon, *BuzzFeed's* "Woman leading Corbyn's Twitter army"

"An invaluable forensic account of how the Israeli lobby provided the British establishment and the Labour Party right-wing with the ammunition of false accusations of 'anti-Semitism,' deployed in a witch-hunt against the Labour Party left. It has indispensable lessons as a case study of the British sector of a world-wide campaign against the left's support for Palestinian rights."
— Moshé Machover, academic and Israeli dissident

"In his outstanding new book, Asa Winstanley lays out the whole wretched story for the first time—not only providing the definitive account of one of the most intense propaganda campaigns in British history, but also, crucially, giving future generations a guide for how to fight back better should the opportunity for a decent prime minister ever present itself again."
— Matt Kennard, co-founder *Declassified UK* and author of *The Racket*

"This solid investigative journalism provides essential reading to anyone who is concerned about how our democratic process is subverted by a powerful elite influenced by the interests of an apartheid state."
— Mnar Adley, editor-in-chief of MintPressNews.com

"No reporter has covered the weaponisation of anti-Semitism in British politics as rigorously and courageously as Asa Winstanley . . . This book is essential for anyone trying to understand the Israel lobby's role in the downfall of Jeremy Corbyn and serves as a warning for the left in other parts of the world."
— Rania Khalek, Breakthrough News

"A riveting and candid account of the civil war that erupted in Britain's Labour Party after Jeremy Corbyn became its leader . . . *Weaponising Anti-Semitism* is essential reading for anyone interested in this tumultuous and intriguing chapter of British politics."
— Daud Abdullah, director of Middle East Monitor and author of *A History of Palestinian Resistance*

"Proves once again that Asa Winstanley is one of the most talented and necessary journalists of his generation."
— Kerry-Anne Mendoza, founder of *The Canary*

"Asa Winstanley has done more than any other journalist to expose what really lay behind the anti-Semitism smear campaign against Corbyn and his supporters in the Labour Party. His new book sets out in stark and disturbing detail how this assault on democracy was engineered."
— Jonathan Cook, author of *Disappearing Palestine*

"Thanks to Asa Winstanley's incisive investigative journalism we now have the definitive version . . . After reading Winstanley's book it's quite clear that while Israel holds the Palestinians under a brutal occupation its supporters hold Keir Starmer's Labour under a political occupation."
— Yvonne Ridley, author of *In the Hands of the Taliban*

"One of the timeliest analyses of how the pro-Israel lobby in the UK manipulated claims of anti-Semitism as a tool to undermine the Corbyn project and its support towards the issue of Palestine."
— Zaher Birawi, chair of the Palestinian Forum in Britain

"A must read. With his brilliant writing Asa Winstanley captures the tragedy of the deliberate and successful Zionist campaign to bring down Jeremy Corbyn."
— Miko Peled, author of *The General's Son*

"In all the protracted, manufactured 'Labour antisemitism crisis' used against Jeremy Corbyn and the left, Asa was the most fearless and consistent voice calling it what it was: a scam. If you're going to read any book about it, make it this one."
— Steve Walker, The Skwawkbox

WEAPONISING ANTI-SEMITISM

WEAPONISING ANTI-SEMITISM

How the Israel Lobby Brought Down
Jeremy Corbyn

ASA WINSTANLEY

OR Books
New York

© 2023 Asa Winstanley

Published by OR Books, New York
Visit our website at www.orbooks.com

All rights information: rights@orbooks.com

All rights reserved. No part of this book may be reproduced or transmitted in any form or by any means, electronic or mechanical, including photocopy, recording, or any information storage retrieval system, without permission in writing from the publisher, except brief passages for review purposes.

First printing 2023

Library of Congress Cataloging-in-Publication Data: A catalog record for this book is available from the Library of Congress.
British Library Cataloging in Publication Data: A catalog record for this book is available from the British Library.

Typeset by Lapiz Digital.

paperback ISBN 978-1-68219-381-5 • ebook ISBN 978-1-68219-382-2

For B.

Rise, like lions after slumber
In unvanquishable number!
Shake your chains to earth like dew
Which in sleep had fallen on you:
Ye are many—they are few.
　　　—Jeremy Corbyn quoting a Shelley poem to a crowd of
　　　　120,000 at Glastonbury music festival, June 2017

England in modern times has always been a centre of subversion—known as such to others, but not to itself.
　　　—W. J. M. Mackenzie, *History of the Special*
　　　　Operations Executive, 1948

The Israeli ambassador made a very full apology . . . the diplomat in question no longer seems to be a functionary of the embassy in London. Whatever that person might exactly have been doing here, his cover can be said to have been well and truly blown, and I think we should consider the matter closed.
　　　—Boris Johnson to Parliament, 10 January 2017

CONTENTS

1. A History of Hostility	5
2. Workers of Zion	43
3. The Oxford Crisis	72
4. The Lobby	97
5. Nazi Comparisons	129
6. The Crucible	166
7. Jews and Un-Jews	195
8. The Turning Point	223
9. Fallout	248
Afterword	303
Appendix	305
Acknowledgements	308
Bibliography	313
Index	315

ABBREVIATIONS USED IN THIS BOOK

ADL	Anti-Defamation League
AIPAC	American Israel Public Affairs Committee
BDS	Boycott, Divestment, Sanctions
BICOM	Britain Israel Communications and Research Centre
CAA	Campaign Against Antisemitism
CLP	Constituency Labour Party
CST	Community Security Trust
EHRC	Equality and Human Rights Commission
EI	The *Electronic Intifada*
EUMC	European Union Monitoring Centre
FDD	Foundation for Defense of Democracies
IHRA	International Holocaust Remembrance Alliance
JLC	Jewish Leadership Council
JLM	Jewish Labour Movement
JVL	Jewish Voice for Labour
LFI	Labour Friends of Israel
NEC	Labour's National Executive Committee
PRC	Palestinian Return Centre
PSC	Palestine Solidarity Campaign
TIP	The Israel Project
ZVfD	*Zionistische Vereinigung für Deutschland* (Zionist Association for Germany)

A NOTE ON SOURCES

This book is the product of seven years of reporting on the Labour Party and its alleged anti-Semitism crisis, during and after the leadership of Jeremy Corbyn. As a journalist who by now has been reporting on both the UK's Palestine solidarity movement and the UK's pro-Israel lobby for 15 years, I was almost uniquely positioned to cover this story. At the *Electronic Intifada* we felt that nobody else was covering the issue properly, so we did our best to meet a need as felt by our readers. My articles from 2015 onwards covered the Corbynist movement and the Israel lobby's war against it extensively. Our coverage was so enthusiastically devoured that eventually even the Community Security Trust (whose pro-Israel activities are explained in this book) had to admit that *EI* had achieved "narrative dominance" on the subject of Palestine, Israel, and Labour anti-Semitism smears.[1]

This book contains entirely new material based on my own reporting, but it also draws extensively from my *EI* articles. As far as possible, I have indicated sources in the text. If sources are unclear you can refer back my contemporary reporting as cited in the footnotes. I have taken this approach to aid readers who wish to learn more detail. You can often also read the primary documents on the original article at www.electronicintifada.net. Every article we publish is rigorously fact-checked by professional editors and we always explain our sources, linking to them online where possible.

---

1   Asa Winstanley, "Why I just quit the Labour Party," *Electronic Intifada*, 7 February 2020.

CHAPTER ONE

A HISTORY OF HOSTILITY

Jeremy Corbyn was livid. "You're trying to trivialise the whole discussion about how you bring about a long-term peace process," he steamed at the journalist. It had been a rocky interview, even before they reached the topic of armed Palestinian and Lebanese resistance. Channel 4's Krishnan Guru-Murthy asked a series of robust questions right out of the gate. But Corbyn wasn't playing by Westminster's usual rules. It was the summer of 2015, and Corbyn's unexpected popularity had electrified a dull leadership contest.

"So you've got no problem with somebody coming from abroad as a migrant with five kids," Guru-Murthy said, "and claiming five lots of child tax credits, five lots of child benefits, housing benefit, no limit on their benefits at all." It was more of a statement than a question. "Why do you think people who voted Conservative in 2015 would suddenly vote for a socialist in 2020?" And: "Would there be no super-rich people in Britain if you were prime minister?" Guru-Murthy repeatedly interrupted the MP, refusing to let him finish his sentences. But it was not until halfway that the journalist really pounced. And Corbyn—probably the most left-wing candidate ever to run for the leadership of the Labour Party—lost his cool.

"Let's briefly talk about foreign affairs," the journalist said. "Why did you call Hamas and Hizballah your friends?" Corbyn's people must have known this was likely to come up. Newspapers had been sniffing around. Corbyn began to answer, but Guru-Murthy interrupted again. "I asked you a question and you're ignoring it," he objected.

"If you'd give me a minute I'll answer it," Corbyn replied, clearly frustrated. Finally, he got out a full sentence: "I spoke at a meeting about the Middle East crisis in Parliament. And there were people there from Hizballah. And I said I welcomed our friends from Hizballah to have a discussion and a debate. And I said I wanted Hamas to be part of that debate." He continued to explain but was stopped again.

"So are they your friends or not?"

"Can I finish?" Corbyn said, exasperated.

"Well you can't if it's a long answer."

Corbyn then accused the presenter of not taking the issue seriously. "Hamas and Hizballah are part of a peace process," he argued. Even the former head of Israeli spy agency Mossad concedes that peace talks should include Hamas, he said. But the journalist seemed fixed on a particular word: "You calling them 'friends.'" It went against everything the British media's conventional wisdom stood for: Lebanese and Palestinian combatants cannot be brave resistance fighters; rather they are evil terrorists. The word "friends" was tantamount to heresy. "To bring about a peace process you have to talk to people with whom you may profoundly disagree," Corbyn explained.[1]

A maverick candidate for Labour leader, Corbyn had fought his corner. The next week, Corbyn would cause disbelief as a shock YouGov poll of Labour activists eligible to vote in the election gave the left-winger a massive lead.[2] But the Channel 4 interview hadn't gone very well. Guru-Murthy's hostile questioning clearly touched a raw nerve. Corbyn seemed genuinely angry. Years later, the former Labour MP reflected bitterly that the anti-Semitism smears against him had been "foul, dishonest and utterly disgusting . . . [it was] designed to be very isolating and distract from our policies."[3]

---

[1] "Jeremy Corbyn on Hamas, the Middle East and the super-rich," Channel 4 News YouTube channel, 13 July 2015.

[2] Peter Kellner, "Comment: Corbyn takes early lead in Labour leadership race," YouGov.co.uk, 22 July 2015.

[3] Matt Kennard, "Exclusive: Jeremy Corbyn on the Establishment Campaign to Stop Him Becoming PM," *Declassified UK*, 22 June 2022.

The terrorist hobgoblin repeatedly came back to bite Corbyn. It was a powerful political weapon that would contribute heavily to his ultimate downfall. The interview was a signal that Corbyn was vulnerable on the issue. The left-wing MP had seemed hurt at the implication he was an anti-Semite. Hostile media were onto something. This was a bone they'd continue gnawing for the next five years, successfully demonising the Labour leader. On the video of the full Channel 4 interview, YouTube comments dating from soon after Corbyn's December 2019 leadership downfall give only a taste of the hatred the media had stirred up.

"Didn't the UK dodge a bullet by rejecting this Hamas Communist four years on from this interview?" said one. The propaganda of the right-wing backlash against the Jeremy Corbyn phenomenon ultimately cut through to mainstream voters during that final general election. "The very sight" of Corbyn "fills me with rage," another YouTube user posted.

"An absolute traitor! I hope he has a horrible death," came one posting, from YouTube user Avi Oleg, who raged that Corbyn was "a cancer cell in a healthy body." But vicious online comments were the least of it.

Corbyn had barely arrived as Labour leader in September 2015 before a senior serving general in the British Armed Forces warned the *Sunday Times* that there would be a mutiny if Corbyn were elected prime minister. "There would be mass resignations at all levels and you would face the very real prospect of an event which would effectively be a mutiny," the general said. "Feelings are running very high within the armed forces. You would see a major break in convention with senior generals directly and publicly challenging Corbyn," he said. "The army just wouldn't stand for it . . . I think people would use whatever means possible, fair or foul to prevent that."[4]

Years later, in an interview with journalist Matt Kennard, Corbyn reflected that this had been "a sort of shot across the

---

4 Tim Shipman, "Corbyn hit by mutiny on airstrikes," *Sunday Times*, 20 September 2015.

bows, a warning to me." When a snap election was expected in the winter of 2018, two conservative papers reported that Corbyn had been "summoned" for a "facts of life" talk with the head of MI5 and an "acquaintance" meeting with the head of MI6. The meetings were supposed to have been completely confidential, but were soon leaked by the two spy agencies—deliberately, Corbyn told Kennard. "It was leaked by them and it was leaked in a way to undermine," said Corbyn, "that somehow or other I'd been summoned and given a dressing down." He denied the spooks' demeaning characterisation of the meeting, and complained that civil servants had spread rumours that he was mentally unstable.[5]

An investigation by Kennard concluded that during his leadership Corbyn had been the target of 34 major national media stories openly sourced by former or current officials in the UK's intelligence and military establishment, including MI5 and MI6. The stories all cast him as a danger to British security.[6] Other governments were involved too. US secretary of state and former CIA director Mike Pompeo hinted in a private meeting with Israel lobby leaders that the US government could stage its own intervention to stop Corbyn becoming prime minister. "It could be that Mr. Corbyn manages to run the gauntlet and get elected," he said in a leaked audio recording obtained by the *Washington Post*. "It's possible. You should know, we won't wait for him to do those things to begin to push back. We will do our level best. It's too risky and too important and too hard once it's already happened."[7]

---

5   Kennard, "Exclusive." See also Tim Shipman and Richard Kerbaj, "MI5 head Andrew Parker summons Jeremy Corbyn for 'facts of life' talk on terror," *Sunday Times*, 2 September 2018, and Con Coughlin, "Jeremy Corbyn meets head of MI6 for first time amid snap election fears," *Daily Telegraph*, 9 November 2018.

6   Matt Kennard, "How the UK military and intelligence establishment is working to stop Jeremy Corbyn becoming prime minister," *Declassified UK*, 4 December 2019.

7   John Hudson, "Pompeo pledges not to wait for Britain's elections to 'push back' against Corbyn and anti-Semitism," *Washington Post*, 8 June 2019.

Over the years there was a constant stream of alarming headlines about the alleged threat Corbyn posed to Jews—despite his decades of anti-racist campaigning. In July 2018, three pro-Israel, British Jewish newspapers published identical front-page editorials[8] claiming that a Corbyn-led government posed an "existential threat to Jewish life in this country" due to the "Corbynite contempt for Jews and Israel."[9] A month later former chief rabbi and BBC radio personality Jonathan Sacks accused Corbyn of "the most offensive statement made by a senior British politician since Enoch Powell's 1968 'Rivers of Blood' speech" (a reference to a criticism Corbyn had made of pro-Israel heckler Richard Millett, as we'll see later in this chapter).[10]

During the 2019 general election campaign, right-wing columnist Simon Heffer claimed on live radio that Corbyn "wants to reopen Auschwitz"—the most notorious Nazi death camp where Jews were systemically murdered on an industrial scale during the Holocaust.[11] Prominent Israel lobbyists also spat venom at Corbyn. "I think we should sacrifice him for all the trouble he has caused," said Lionel Kopelowitz, pointing out the verbal similarity of Corbyn's surname to the Hebrew word for the victim of a sacrifice.[12] Kopelowitz was a 92-year-old former president of the Board of Deputies of British Jews, whose meeting he was addressing at the time. The Board claims to represent all British Jews. Yet it also admits in internal documents to having a "close working relationship with the Embassy of Israel

---

8   "Jewish newspapers unite against Labour 'threat,'" BBC News, 25 July 2018.

9   "Voice Of The Jewish News: United We Stand," *Jewish News*, 25 July 2018.

10 George Eaton, "Corbyn's 'Zionist' remarks were 'most offensive' since Enoch Powell, says ex-chief rabbi," *New Statesman*, 28 August 2018.

11 David Edwards and David Cromwell, "Reopening Auschwitz—The Conspiracy to Stop Corbyn," Media Lens, 3 December 2019. Video of Heffer's comments can be viewed on LBC's Twitter account, timecode 42:48: https://twitter.com/LBC/status/1149031265569390592.

12 James Wright, "Watch the former Board of Deputies president call for Jeremy Corbyn to be 'sacrificed,'" *Canary*, 28 May 2019.

in the UK" and strong links to Israel's semi-covert Ministry of Strategic Affairs, as well as the Israeli military spokesperson.[13]

"Labour MUST kill vampire Jezza," *Mail on Sunday* columnist Dan Hodges implored.[14] Serving British Army soldiers later filmed themselves using Corbyn's image for target practice.[15] Increasing incitement against Corbyn had inevitable results. An attempt on his life came in June 2017.

Darren Osborne, a 48-year-old Islamophobe from Cardiff, tried to murder a group of Muslims in Finsbury Park (an area in Corbyn's constituency). He deliberately drove a hire van into the crowd, killing Makram Ali, a 51-year-old grandfather. But it emerged in court that Osborne's original target had been Jeremy Corbyn himself. Osborne admitted he had planned to mow down demonstrators at an annual Palestine solidarity demonstration. "Another reason for [attacking] the Al-Quds [Day] march was that Jeremy Corbyn would be in attendance," he said. When security roadblocks thwarted his plan, he drove to Finsbury Park and rammed into a group of Muslims gathered outside on the first day of Ramadan. Osborne was given a 43-year minimum sentence. "This was a terrorist attack. You intended to kill," judge Parmjit Cheema-Grubb concluded.[16]

Visiting Finsbury Park Mosque, Corbyn became the victim of an unprovoked assault. CCTV footage showed right-winger John Murphy punching the Labour leader in the head, reportedly

---

13   Board of Deputies Charitable Foundation, Trustees' Report for the year ended 31 December 2020, filed with the Charity Commission for England and Wales, 25 May 2021, page 5.

14   Dan Hodges, "Labour MUST kill vampire Jezza," *Mail on Sunday*, 26 June 2016. After complaints, the online version of the article was altered to read "dump" instead of "kill."

15   Conrad Duncan, "Soldiers who used photo of Jeremy Corbyn for target practice disciplined but not sacked, MoD says," *Independent*, 5 July 2019.

16   "Finsbury Park attacker Darren Osborne jailed for minimum of 43 years," BBC News, 2 February 2018. Lizzie Dearden, "Finsbury Park terror trial: Darren Osborne only targeted mosque after planned attack on Jeremy Corbyn failed, court hears," *Independent*, 30 January 2018.

shouting pro-Brexit slogans.[17] Murphy was swiftly sentenced to 28 days in jail. But the media downplayed the worrying attack as an "egging" (Murphy had held an egg in the hand he used to punch Corbyn).

In December 2019, Corbyn announced he would step down as Labour leader, after losing the general election. Keir Starmer succeeded him in April 2020 and intensified the party's purges of Corbynites, saying he wanted to support "Zionism without qualification."

Then in October 2020 Corbyn was suspended from the party altogether. He had made an objectively factual statement that the scale of anti-Semitism in Labour had been exaggerated by his political enemies.[18]

How did it come to this?

* * *

Long before Jeremy Corbyn took the Labour leadership, his campaigning had made him many enemies. Among the most vociferous were those in the Israel lobby. To understand the reasons for this, we need to look at Jeremy Corbyn's pre-leadership career.

Corbyn was a backbencher, deeply involved in Britain's social movements. He was a campaigner, an activist—an experienced public speaker and organiser. He was dedicated to left-wing and anti-imperialist causes. Tory MP William Hague—once himself the leader of a party in opposition—warned Corbyn that he would face multiple knives in the back. "I have a confession to make," he wrote, "as foreign secretary I always respected and made time for Jeremy Corbyn. He was an inveterate campaigner on many issues, from the return of the Chagos Islanders to nuclear disarmament. Consistent and predictable, he asked

---

17 Nadeem Badshah, "Brexit supporter who assaulted Jeremy Corbyn jailed for 28 days," *Guardian*, 25 March 2019.

18 Asa Winstanley, "Israel lobby slaughters Corbyn again," *Electronic Intifada*, 20 October 2020.

his own questions in the Commons without paying the slightest attention to his front bench."[19]

Corbyn got his start in the trade union movement. Elected MP for the London constituency of Islington North, he dove headfirst into just causes—even if they made him deeply unpopular in his own party. He spoke against racism and fascism and for immigrants' rights. He opposed privatisation, cuts and austerity. He campaigned against wars and military occupations, and supported people's liberation struggles from Ireland to South Africa to West Asia. A black-and-white photo from the 1980s—later popular on social media—showed Corbyn being dragged away by police from the South African embassy wearing a sign reading: "Defend the right to demonstrate against apartheid: join this picket." He and his comrades had been protesting the white supremacist regime in that country, known in Afrikaans as *apartheid*, or "separateness."

Corbyn had also opposed British occupation in the north of Ireland. One of his more controversial moves as backbencher was to invite Sinn Féin leaders Gerry Adams and Martin McGuinness to a meeting in the House of Commons to argue the case for British withdrawal from the six counties forming the British statelet known as Northern Ireland. This was at a time when the Irish Republican Army (effectively Sinn Féin's military wing) was leading an armed struggle against the British Army in Ireland. The campaign spread to a series of bombings on the UK mainland. The IRA was considered a terrorist group in Britain, but was popular among Irish republican communities in the north, and bitterly opposed by sectarian Ulster loyalists.

In 2001, when Tony Blair threw Britain's armed forces into President George W. Bush's war against Afghanistan in the wake of the 9/11 attacks, Corbyn marched against it. Not only did he march, but he was a leading voice in the anti-war movement: both against that war, and against the war in Iraq soon after. He helped found the Stop the War Coalition, which succeeded in mobilising one of the biggest demonstrations ever recorded. In February 2003 as many as two million people protested against

---

19   William Hague, "There are countless sworn assassins waiting to knife Jeremy Corbyn in the back," *Daily Telegraph*, 15 September 2015.

the invasion of Iraq, in London and all over the UK.[20] Corbyn was one of the few MPs who addressed these demonstrations.

While the British establishment is savvy enough to tolerate such a dissident on the Parliamentary backbenches, the thought of an avid leftist and anti-war campaigner leading the main opposition party (let alone the country) must have set off warning sirens in Whitehall and in Langley, Virginia. Afghanistan and Iraq were not the only internationalist causes Corbyn committed himself to. Islington, where Corbyn lives and which he represents in Parliament, is much parodied by the right-wing press as a well-heeled, upper-middle-class enclave of "champagne socialist" elites. But, in fact, the North London borough contains extreme poverty as well as extreme wealth. It ranks third nationally on the income deprivation indicator for children, and fifth for income deprivation affecting older people. And Islington North is home to a diverse set of peoples. According to council statistics, 39 percent of residents were born outside of the United Kingdom compared to 14 percent nationally.[21] Corbyn met constituents from all over the world and heard their concerns and needs. He was embedded in their struggles.

But probably more than anything else, Corbyn was known among activists for his involvement in the Palestine solidarity movement. After decades of struggle, the Palestinian cause has made big strides on the British left. Even in the Labour Party, some of the more right-wing MPs (like Wes Streeting and Lisa Nandy) find themselves having to pay lip service to the issue.

At one Palestine Solidarity Campaign conference in early 2015, I was asked to run a workshop; the keynote speaker was *Guardian* columnist Owen Jones. This was before May's general election, and Ed Miliband was still Labour leader at the time. I remember thinking how bland Jones's talk was. Instead of rallying the activists to campaign harder for the Palestinian cause, and encouraging BDS, the boycott, divestment, and sanctions movement, Jones pushed his political party. He told us

---

[20] "5 Photographs From The Day The World Said No To War," Imperial War Museum website, undated (accessed 9 June 2022).

[21] State of Equalities in Islington: Annual Report 2019, Islington Council, page 19.

we should "vote for a Labour government" so that they could recognise the "Palestinian state." This event stuck in my mind, because it was just the sort of shallow, self-interested electioneering that Jeremy Corbyn would *not* have done. As a reporter in London focused on the issue of Palestine, I must have heard Corbyn speak at dozens of anti-war and Palestine solidarity events over the years, long before he was Labour leader. Never once do I recall him urging the assembly to vote Labour—not that he didn't want us to.

Corbyn saw a Labour government as a means to an end, rather than as power for power's sake. He is still, as of this writing, a patron of the Palestine Solidarity Campaign. But unlike most MPs, for whom such a position would have been an entirely symbolic posting, Corbyn's involvement in the Palestine solidarity movement was a nuts-and-bolts activist one. He led demonstrations against Israeli wars. He spoke at rallies against Israeli racism. And instead of insisting on his own voice being heard before others, he chaired conference sessions and panels. Corbyn had a genuine, grassroots connection to the popular movements, and especially to the Palestine solidarity movement.

Just as the warning bells were going off in British and US intelligence circles, so too were they sounding in Tel Aviv. The prospect of Corbyn entering Number 10 Downing Street represented Israel's worst nightmare. It would have to be stopped at all costs.

* * *

The British media's attitude to Jeremy Corbyn was one of implacable opposition from the outset. The interview with Guru-Murthy was only one of the earliest signs of what was to come. The media, conservative and liberal alike, did everything they could to stop Corbyn becoming leader. When they failed in that, they tried to overturn the election result. When that too was unsuccessful, they did everything they could to stop him being elected prime minister—and that succeeded. British journalists, editors, and politicians showed extreme dedication to reversing the Labour membership's democratic selection of the party's most left-wing leader since it was founded.

But despite his strong progressive leanings, the policies Corbyn proposed in his 2015 campaign for Labour leader were anything but the "hard left" of media mythology. There was very little in his platform that would have been out of place in even some Conservative manifestos prior to the 1979 rise of Margaret Thatcher and the Western neoliberal consensus. Thatcher and her later, Labour, successor as prime minister Tony Blair are perhaps the key to understanding the British establishment's utter rejection of Corbyn's moderate programme for change. Thatcher's libertarian, free-market-obsessed governments imposed successive waves of privatisation, resulting in the utter decimation of Britain's industrial economy and public sector. Coal mines were shut down and the country's railways were sold off. So too were water, steel and practically anything else they could ram through Parliament.

Meanwhile, the Labour opposition moved increasingly to the right—slowly at first, but later at breakneck speed. In the 1980s Labour fought a vicious civil war to expel and marginalise the left. The head of this witch hunt was party leader Neil Kinnock, the notoriously gaffe-prone Welshman who had once been a young star of the Labour left. But after assuming the leadership he did an about-face, demanding the expulsion of socialists such as Militant—a Trotskyist group with a serious power base in Liverpool. The Labour left resisted this push, naming their campaign "Labour Against the Witchhunt," and Corbyn was a leading part of it.[22] The same name would be adopted by a new group in 2017, formed to push back against false anti-Semitism allegations.

Tony Benn himself (once a Labour government minister, and later the doyen of the party's few remaining left-wing MPs) was opposed to the expulsion of Militant. Labour's civil war was decisively won by the right. Benn remained as an MP, but was a marginalised backbencher for the rest of his career. He was joined there by newer comrades who arrived in Parliament in the 1980s, including John McDonnell, Diane Abbott, Bernie

---

22   Dominic Kennedy, "Jeremy Corbyn's hard-left blueprint revealed," *The Times*, 6 July 2019.

Grant, and Jeremy Corbyn. Apart from Grant (a parliamentary giant hailing from Guyana who passed away in 2000), all would later be appointed to Corbyn's shadow cabinet. Benn died only months before the Corbyn phenomenon took off in 2015. He would have been ecstatic, having called the younger man "My favourite MP." According to Special Branch whistle-blower Peter Francis, Benn, Corbyn, Grant, and Abbott, along with Ken Livingstone (the former leader of the Greater London Council, who also arrived in Parliament in 1987), were all spied on by Britain's secret political police.[23] In the 1980s and 1990s, Jeremy Corbyn becoming leader of the party seemed a wildly unlikely scenario. Labour had a slick new corporate image, first pioneered by Kinnock in the hyper-capitalist 1980s. This later reached its apex under Kinnock's protégés Gordon Brown and Tony Blair.

Margaret Thatcher herself gave a retrospective endorsement of Blair's legacy. She was asked in retirement to name her greatest achievement. From the perspective of the Tory hard right, she could have listed any number of successes. But instead she replied: "Tony Blair and New Labour. We forced our opponents to change their minds."[24] Thatcher correctly understood that her right-wing legacy couldn't be cemented using her own Conservative Party alone. She did so by cajoling the Labour Party establishment into aping her.

Blair continued privatisation using Private Finance Initiatives (PFI) and so-called "Public-Private Partnerships." These schemes allowed profit-making companies to build public infrastructure projects such as hospitals and schools, while burdening public bodies with onerous long-term financial payments. The payments to these private investors provided massive profits to their shareholders: up to 60 percent in some cases. Always unpopular with unions, PFIs became increasingly

---

23 Rob Evans, "Police face questions over covert monitoring of Jeremy Corbyn and other MPs," *Guardian*, 2 October 2015. Asa Winstanley, "Britain's secret political police," *Declassified UK*, 16 March 2021.

24 Conor Burns, "Margaret Thatcher's greatest achievement: New Labour," *ConservativeHome*, 11 April 2008.

unpopular with the public and proved to be more costly than the publicly funded alternative.[25]

But Blair quickly developed his most lasting legacy with his wars, especially in the post 9/11 world. After the shocking and deadly attacks against the United States on 11 of September 2001, Blair stood "shoulder to shoulder" with his friends in Washington, DC. He became a regular visitor at the Crawford, Texas ranch of the US president, former oil man George W. Bush, where they plotted wars of invasion. It's unlikely the US president would have succeeded in pulling his country into the violent quagmire that their troops were about to impose upon the people of Iraq without Blair's support. "I will be with you, whatever," Blair told Bush in a secret memo, revealed by a UK government inquiry some years later.[26] He dragged the UK into Iraq. The result was up to a million dead Iraqis, two decades of chaos, and the genesis of ISIS—a new Wahhabi terrorist force even more fierce and destructive than al-Qaida, the violent fundamentalist network that carried out 9/11.[27]

Tony Blair's headlong pursuit of power came at the cost of long-term terminal decline in the party base. Labour slowly haemorrhaged millions of voters, who increasingly stayed at home in successive elections. The party was hollowed out internally by Blair's lackeys, and increasingly centralised around the leader. Labour's annual conference was reined in. Policy making was taken over by a "national forum" strongly under the leadership's influence. Party membership plunged from 400,000 in 1997 to 190,000 by the time of Blair's forced exit in 2007. It continued to slide further under Gordon Brown, Blair's right-hand man and once his chosen successor. Membership increased slightly under new leader Ed Miliband in 2010, who was seen as "soft left" and a break with Blairism. But 200,000 was still a

---

25 Iqbal Khadaroo and Ekililu Salifu, "PFI has been a failure—and Carillion is the tip of the iceberg," *Conversation*, 24 January 2018. Matt Weaver, "PFI: the issue explained," *Guardian*, 15 January 2003.

26 Asa Winstanley, "A year after Chilcot, Tony Blair is still not in jail. He should be," *Middle East Monitor*, 23 July 2017.

27 See Max Blumenthal, *The Management of Savagery* (London: Verso Books, 2019), especially chapters 3-5.

pale shadow of the one million members Labour had had at its 1954 peak.[28] Miliband failed to make much headway, and lost the 2015 general election. He quit with immediate effect, triggering a leadership election. The Miliband leadership did, however, achieve something of great significance: he revised Labour's rules governing who could vote in party elections.

The party's leader had once been chosen by Labour MPs alone. But the rules were changed in the 1980s, after a mammoth struggle for democratisation led by Tony Benn. An electoral college of MPs, members, and affiliated trade unions were then allowed a vote. After protracted negotiations within the Labour movement, Miliband did away with the electoral college system. Leadership elections would henceforth be voted on by Labour members and supporters only, with MPs being given the same vote as ordinary members. Members of affiliated unions would have a right to vote, but only as individuals. No longer would trade union bloc votes have such a decisive impact. The choice was put into in the hands of the membership. But Labour MPs were still given a collective veto, since a percentage of their nominations would be required for a candidate to get onto the ballot.[29]

In retrospect it seems obvious that this more democratic arrangement would result in disaster for the Labour right. But at the time they didn't see it that way. In fact some in Progress (a Blairite faction) argued for open primaries, allowing *any* member of the public to vote in Labour leadership elections. It was thought this would bring the party more into line with the US Democratic Party and split Labour from the trade unions. Ignorant of just how genuinely unpopular Blair had become, Progress assumed that more democratic elections could only mean victory for "moderate" Labour leaders—i.e., right-wing, corporate-friendly politicians. The popular movement that helped Jeremy Corbyn win the leadership of the UK's main opposition party in the summer of 2015 was to prove a stark awakening.

---

28 Figures compiled by Stan Anson.

29 Alex Nunns, *The Candidate: Jeremy Corbyn's Improbable Path to Power* (New York: OR Books, 2016), pages 20-43.

Corbyn led Labour to far better results in 2017's general election than anyone predicted—the greatest increase in Labour's vote share since 1945. This caused Conservative prime minister Theresa May to lose her majority. It was a hung parliament. She quit and was replaced by right-wing former journalist and TV celebrity Boris Johnson. John McTernan, a former speechwriter for Blair, candidly admitted the historical significance of the 2017 election. It was "not just the end of Blairism, but the end of Thatcherism. It's the end of an entire moment in British politics. [Corbyn's] appeal is too wide and too deep to be ignored."[30]

It could no longer be ignored. So instead it was fought.

* * *

The vast preponderance of the press in Britain has always been hostile to Labour, right from the party's inception in 1900. For British press barons, the Labour movement represented the threat of proletarian democracy. In their textbook *Power Without Responsibility*, James Curran and Jean Seaton note that among the newspapers, "the only consistent supporter of the Labour Party for over a half a century" was the *Daily Herald*. But even this ended when Australian press baron Rupert Murdoch bought the paper for a song in 1969, relaunching it as the *Sun*. It was "converted into a paper which stood for everything that the old *Daily Herald* had opposed." The new paper "greatly increased its entertainment coverage" and "shrank its coverage of public affairs." In many ways it "anticipated the Thatcherite era by expressing new right arguments before Thatcher herself."[31] As the *Sun* went, so others followed. The tabloid remains the country's highest circulation newspaper, thanks in large part to its sports and entertainment coverage. Under Tony Blair, press attitudes towards Labour shifted. New Labour represented the

---

30   "Jeremy Corbyn: A profile by Stephen Bush," *BBC Newsnight*, 6 July 2017, available on YouTube (timecode 00:34).

31   James Curran and Jean Seaton, *Power Without Responsibility: Sixth Edition* (London: Routledge, 2003), page 90.

co-optation of the party by Thatcherism so the *Sun* endorsed Blair for prime minister in 1997's general election.

British media opposition to Labour was therefore nothing new. But the evidence indicates that their campaign against Corbyn was totally unprecedented. The Media Reform Coalition found in 2015 that "the press set out to systematically undermine Jeremy Corbyn during his first week as Labour leader with a barrage of overwhelmingly negative coverage." Their study found that, out of 494 articles on Corbyn that week, 60 percent were negative, with only 13 percent positive. This was not confined to opinion pieces either, with the news sections being even more likely to have "expressed animosity or ridicule; [they] chose to focus on negative events; or were dominated by overt criticism."[32]

The most successful attack vector against Corbyn would prove to be the narrative of a "crisis" of anti-Semitism within the Labour Party. It wasn't a new strategy. Ed Miliband had been attacked with milder—but equally false—insinuations of "anti-Semitism" in the party after he began to be perceived as critical of Israel. The smears were partly motivated by the fact that he had mildly condemned Israel's devastating 2014 attack on Gaza. Miliband scolded then–prime minister David Cameron for not condemning that attack and said that Israel was "losing friends in the international community day by day."[33] In total 2,251 Palestinians were killed by Israel during that war—most of whom were civilians, including 551 children.[34] Miliband forced his MPs to vote for a motion against the government (the motion had been sponsored by Jeremy Corbyn).

Television actress Maureen Lipman scored some headlines when she said Miliband's policies on Israel meant she

---

[32] *Corbyn's First Week: Negative Agenda Setting in the Press* (London: The Media Reform Coalition, 26 November 2015).

[33] Oliver Wright, "Labour funding crisis: Jewish donors drop 'toxic' Ed Miliband," *Independent*, 9 November 2014.

[34] Ali Abunimah, "'Balance' in UN Gaza report can't hide massive Israeli war crimes," *Electronic Intifada*, 22 June 2015.

would no longer vote for Labour as she had done under Blair.[35] She also insinuated that Miliband's policy was tantamount to anti-Semitism: "Just when the anti-Semitism in France, Denmark, Norway, Hungary is mounting savagely . . . in steps Mr Miliband to demand that the government recognise the state of Palestine," she complained, improbably describing criticism of Israel's assault on the civilian population of Gaza as "virulence against a country defending itself."[36] Lipman managed to repeat the trick of "abandoning" Labour for a second time several years later under Corbyn, even acting in an anti-Corbyn television ad during the 2019 election campaign.[37] Miliband had said he would recognise the Palestinian Authority as a state immediately after a Labour government was elected—a policy Corbyn later continued.

Lipman's attacks on Miliband as supposedly fomenting "anti-Semitism" in Labour were ironic—the former Labour leader is Jewish himself. But this inconvenient fact proved no obstacle to the crisis-mongers. The Israel lobby makes a habit of smearing Jewish critics of Israel as "self-hating." "The moment Israel was under pressure and under fire, the first thing he did was to dump on Israel," *Jewish Chronicle* editor Stephen Pollard complained to the *New York Times*. Miliband however insisted he was a "friend" to Israel.[38]

Ed Miliband is the son of Marion Kozak and late Marxist academic Ralph Miliband. Miliband Senior was for decades an intellectual doyen of the Labour left. A teenager in 1940, he had fled Belgium as the Nazis invaded, later served in the Royal

---

35   Press Association, "Maureen Lipman drops long-standing support for Labour party," *Guardian*, 29 October 2014.

36   Maureen Lipman, "Labour has Lost Me," *Standpoint Magazine*, 28 October 2014.

37   Emily Apple, "Maureen Lipman using The Sun to promote an anti-Corbyn smear is utterly vile," *Canary*, 22 November 2019.

38   Stephen Castle, "British Labour Chief, a Jew Who Criticizes Israel, Walks a Fine Line," *New York Times*, 23 October 2014.

Air Force and became a prolific writer and pamphleteer.[39] The concluding paragraph of his seminal 1961 book, *Parliamentary Socialism*, read decades later during the Corbyn era, seemed to accurately prophesy both the frenzied media campaign against Corbyn and the stark reality of the situation facing the party:

> If the Labour Party were to become such a party [a genuine socialist opposition], it would be subject to attacks infinitely more fierce than it has had to endure for many a day, both from Conservative interests [and press] . . . and also from former [Labour] members who would feel impelled to turn against it and denounce its policies and deeds. But against this, it would elicit and enlist the kind of devotion and support which a consolidating Labour Party now finds it increasingly difficult to engender. It is well to resist the urge to prophesy. But it does not seem unduly rash to suggest that the alternative to its becoming such a party is the kind of slow but sure decline which—deservedly—affects parties that have ceased to serve any distinctive political purpose.[40]

Before the summer of 2015, the party's fortunes did indeed seem to be inexorably headed towards oblivion—"Pasokification," as Corbyn's supporters argued.[41] Pasok, once Greece's social-democratic party of government, collapsed from 44 percent in 2009, to a 5 percent wipe-out in 2015, thanks to its embrace of austerity programmes dictated by the European Commission. It was part of a European trend of "moderate left" parties facing long-term decline after their embrace of neoliberalism. Labour was headed down the same path. The Corbyn years were an attempt to stem this tide. Partly because of his left-wing parents, and partly because he—very timidly—attempted to move

---

39 Tariq Ali, "Ralph Miliband, 1924-1994," *Against the Current*, issue 52, September-October 1994.

40 Ralph Miliband, *Parliamentary Socialism* (London: Merlin Press, 1964), page 349.

41 Gary Younge, "Jeremy Corbyn has defied his critics to become Labour's best hope of survival," *Guardian*, 22 May 2017.

Labour's policies away from the Blairite legacy, the tabloids dubbed the younger Miliband "Red Ed." In a feature-length hatchet job, the *Daily Mail* smeared Ralph as "the man who hated Britain." Some of the press coverage of Miliband and his father even veered into outright anti-Semitic attacks against the Jewish intellectual.[42]

But Miliband had decisively broken with the Marxist heritage of his father, working as a special adviser for Chancellor Gordon Brown in the Tony Blair years. Miliband's "anti-Semitism crisis" was nothing compared to what was to follow under Corbyn. But the very fact it happened at all showed there were vested interests dedicated to preserving the Labour Party status quo.

* * *

One reason that the Jeremy Corbyn phenomenon took the entire media and political establishment by surprise in the summer of 2015 was that, at first, many mainstream journalists just didn't know who he was. The popular movements, however, did know.

After his years of campaigning, almost everybody at the grassroots activist level immediately got involved in the push to get Corbyn onto the Labour leadership ballot. "He talks our language," Dave Prentis, general secretary of public service union Unison told Channel 4 News.[43] Support for Corbyn from Britain's main trade unions represented a tipping point in the 2015 leadership race. The first to endorse Corbyn was BFAWU, a small, left-wing baker's union. But Britain's two biggest unions (Unite and Unison) soon backed him as well. This gave Corbyn's campaign much needed funding and resources. But it also gave the campaign some institutional credibility. It began to look like he could actually win. The big unions had been thought likely to endorse Corbyn's rival Andy Burnham. So for the leader of a

---

[42] Boyd Tonkin, "Is criticism of Ed Miliband a coded form of anti-Semitism?" *Independent*, 26 November 2014.

[43] "Unison leader: Jeremy Corbyn speaks 'the language of hope,'" Channel 4 News website, 29 July 2015.

more conservative union like Unison to back Corbyn signalled a sea change.

Until July's shock YouGov poll lead, Corbyn had been thought to stand little chance. The political-media establishment's reaction was sheer denial, while the grassroots left dared to dream. Activists from the anti-war movement, the trade unions, the anti-austerity movement, the movement against racism, the Palestine solidarity movement, and many others, flowed freely into the Labour Party. They already knew Corbyn—he had spoken on their platforms for years, signed their petitions, led their rallies and demonstrations, and been one of the tiny group of MPs who gave their campaigns even a modicum of parliamentary endorsement. Seeing a once-in-a-lifetime opportunity, they declared their intent to vote for Corbyn. Miliband's rules changes meant that ordinary members of the public could now pay a one-off fee of £3 to register as Labour "supporters," enabling them to vote in leadership elections. Labour's membership soared.

The corporate media usually reported this as "entryism" from the "hard left." It is true that some small communist factions have long had the strategy that their members should enter the Labour Party in order to argue for their own policies from within. This has sometimes been done in a clandestine fashion—as in the case of the Alliance for Workers Liberty (a bizarrely pro-Israel Trotskyite cult).[44] But the media's obsession with this marginal phenomenon was out of all proportion with reality. What journalists too often missed was the far more exciting, organic process of the popular movements joining the Labour Party in the hope of turning it into a genuine, mass movement for change.[45]

*　*　*

Although Corbyn had made many enemies over the years on the British right, he was not usually seen as significant enough

---

44　Tony Greenstein, "No longer part of left," *Weekly Worker*, 14 March 2019.

45　See Nunns, *The Candidate*, chapter 7.

a figure by the media to demonise. But in the specific areas he campaigned on, the vested interests he pushed up against often pushed right back. Right-wing activists and corporate or state-backed lobbies can be extremely well funded. The general phenomenon of the British media's stifling establishment groupthink can also lead to intense demonisation against anyone deviating from the perceived norm. These factors all intertwine. There's often crossover between all three, with the media's sources being heavily biased towards the right and the lobbies.

Nowhere were the factors of right-wing activists and lobbies more at play against Corbyn than when he campaigned against Israeli mistreatment of the Palestinian people. Anti-Palestinian activists and lobby groups knew Corbyn almost as well as the left-wing activists—albeit as their enemy. They had been attacking Corbyn for years. Long before the *Sun* was smearing Corbyn as a "Marxist extremist" supposedly unfit for high office, the *Jewish Chronicle* had already long painted him as one of the "extremists" on the "radical fringe" of Labour.[46] In 2012 one of the paper's more strident columnists (right-wing historian Geoffrey Alderman) baselessly accused Corbyn of plotting "a very public, officially sanctioned witch-hunt against British citizens of the Jewish persuasion."[47]

* * *

The Palestinian Return Centre is a small organisation based in London, run by Palestinian refugees, which campaigns for the Palestinian right of return. The year 1948 marks the expulsion of more than half of the Palestinian people from their native land. This is known as the *Nakba*, Arabic for "Catastrophe." Nakba is the term used by Palestinians to refer to the traumatic act of ethnic cleansing which inevitably accompanied

---

46   "Miliband's foolish flirtation," *Jewish Chronicle*, 14 October 2014.

47   Geoffrey Alderman, "OK, Corbyn, let's have an inquiry," *Jewish Chronicle*, 3 May 2012. The online version of this article now only lists the byline as "The JC." But on his website geoffreyalderman.com under "Publications," Alderman still claims the article as his own (accessed 9 June 2022).

Israel's 1948 foundation. The forerunner militias of the Israeli army expelled roughly 800,000 Palestinians between 1947 and 1949, directly leading to the foundation of Israel as a Jewish supremacist state.[48] Since then, Israel has systematically barred these Palestinians and their ancestors from returning to their homeland—solely because they are not Jewish. Yet Israel's "law of return," established in the early 1950s, allows anyone in the world who is Jewish (or who has at least one Jewish grandparent) to migrate to historic Palestine and automatically become an Israeli citizen. This means that a Jewish person born in New York, London, Baghdad, Buenos Aires, or Paris has a right under Israel's apartheid laws to citizenship, housing, and health care, while an Indigenous Palestinian born in Jerusalem, Nablus, or Hebron has no such right under Israeli law. But the right to return is enshrined in international law, including most notably in UN General Assembly Resolution 194 of December 1948. It states that in Palestine, "the refugees wishing to return to their homes and live at peace with their neighbours should be permitted to do so at the earliest practicable date." Israel rejected this resolution and has remained in defiance of it ever since.

As dissident Israeli historian Ilan Pappé documented in his seminal book *The Ethnic Cleansing of Palestine*, the Zionist armed groups Haganah, Irgun, and Lehi began illegally expelling Palestinians from their villages the day after the United Nations advised a partition of Palestine into a Jewish state and an Arab state in November 1947. Only after months of atrocities, with a quarter of a million Palestinians driven from their homes, 200 villages destroyed and scores of towns emptied, did armies from the neighbouring Arab countries belatedly intervene in the areas the UN had allocated for a Palestinian state.[49]

---

48 Ilan Pappé, *The Ethnic Cleansing of Palestine* (Oxford: Oneworld Publications, 2007). On Israel as a Jewish supremacist state, see "A regime of Jewish supremacy from the Jordan River to the Mediterranean Sea: This is apartheid," B'Tselem position paper, 12 January 2021, and Maureen Clare Murphy, "Top Israeli rights group breaks 'apartheid' taboo," *Electronic Intifada*, 13 January 2021.

49 Pappé, *The Ethnic Cleansing of Palestine*, page 118.

Even then, the Arab governments did so on strictly limited terms and in line with their own interests. The Jordanian monarchy, for example, even before the war had secretly struck a deal with the Zionist movement to send their forces only into the areas designated by the UN as the "Arab state." Apart from in Jerusalem, which the Zionist forces attempted to seize in full (in violation of the UN partition plan), Jordan's army did not fight the new Israeli army.[50]

Realising the Palestinian right to return has therefore been the top priority of the Palestinian national liberation movement ever since. Millions of Palestinians still live in refugee camps today, in the West Bank, the Gaza Strip, and in surrounding Arab countries, mostly in Jordan. The right of return is *the* unifying issue for the Palestinian liberation movement still today. This is agreed on by all Palestinian armed and political factions, and by all Palestinian civil society groups, charities, and unions. Even the Palestinian Authority (whose ageing leader Mahmoud Abbas once said he would decline his right to return to the city of Safed in present-day Israel from which he was expelled as a child in 1948) has to pay lip service to the issue.[51]

So the Palestinian Return Centre was formed in 1996 and carries out its work in London. It received formal UN special consultative status in 2015. It is a moderate political campaign group that lobbies the British government for Palestinian human rights. The PRC generally favours putting on meetings, panels, and discussions rather than holding protests and tends to seek supportive MPs. These are few and far between, but Jeremy Corbyn was one such supporter. Years later, as part of the manufactured 2018 anti-Semitism crisis, one PRC meeting, which had taken place in 2013, would be revisited as part of a major media offensive against Corbyn.

Almost anyone who has attended a public meeting on the subject of Palestine in London will be familiar with the dreary inevitability that a small circle of anti-Palestinian hecklers are likely to disrupt it. The two most notorious pro-Zionist activists

---

50 Pappé, *The Ethnic Cleansing of Palestine*, page 119.

51 Ali Abunimah, "Mahmoud Abbas: collaboration with Israeli army, secret police is 'sacred,'" *Electronic Intifada*, 30 May 2014.

are Jonathan Hoffman, a retired economist, and blogger Richard Millett (son of the late founder of the Millets chain of outdoor clothing stores).[52] Both use similar disruptive tactics. They aggressively heckle speakers, stand outside the venue harassing attendees and generally attempt to derail the meeting. In Hoffman's case especially, in at least one instance (that of the writer and composer Tom Suarez) this escalated to the point of standing up in front of the audience screaming and talking over the speakers—a hijacking of a meeting which was supposed to have been in solidarity with the Palestinians.[53]

In 2019 Hoffman was finally convicted of harassment and threatening behaviour.[54] The victim was Sandra Watfa, a Palestinian member of a group that had mounted protests calling for a boycott of a Puma store in London over the company's sponsorship of the Israeli football league. In negotiations with the Crown Prosecution Service, police dropped an initial assault charge after Hoffman agreed to plead guilty to the others. Hoffman and Millett were also among four anti-Palestinian activists who gate-crashed a Palestinian Return Centre event in 2017, and were subsequently ejected by Parliamentary police on the orders of chair Mark Hendrick MP. According to the PRC, the four had caused "immense disruption to the meeting by engaging in verbally abusive behaviour towards the audience, the speakers, and the chairman."[55]

Millett often works in tandem with Hoffman. He has not to my knowledge been accused of assault. But in 2012 he infiltrated a memorial wake for Hanna Braun, a Jewish anti-Zionist who had recently passed away. With no apparent shame he

---

[52] Dominic Kennedy, "We are all scared, says Richard Millett, blogger in Corbyn 'Zionist' row," *The Times*, 25 August 2018. Kathryn A. Morrison, "Multiple Multiples: Disentangling the Story of Millets," Building Our Past blog, 16 December 2020.

[53] David Cronin, "The warped logic of pro-Israel bully Jonathan Hoffman," *Electronic Intifada*, 26 August 2017.

[54] Asa Winstanley, "Anti-Palestinian activists guilty of harassment," *Electronic Intifada*, 19 June 2019.

[55] "Four Disruptive Anti-Palestinian Activists removed from House of Commons," PRC press release, 27 April 2017 (accessed 9 June 2022).

began filming attendees, including Braun's daughters. He was confronted and ejected, protesting he had been there to "record anti-Semitism."[56]

In 2013 Millett was already notorious as a usual suspect. Organisers of Palestinian events in London often go out of their way to prove their democratic free-speech credentials. Unfortunately, this has sometimes allowed their opponents to disrupt their meetings. At a 15 January 2013 Palestine Solidarity Campaign meeting chaired by Corbyn, Millett did just that. Although police wanted to eject Millett from the meeting (which was being held in Parliament with Palestinian Authority representative Manuel Hassassian as one of the speakers), Corbyn allowed him to stay, despite the fact that he and another pro-Israel activist were being "incredibly disruptive," as the Labour leader later explained to the BBC's Andrew Marr. A few days after, at the later-controversial Palestinian Return Centre conference, he made reference to the PSC meeting with Hassassian. The PA representative had made what Corbyn told the PRC audience was a "passionate and effective speech about the history of Palestine." Corbyn then said Hassassian's speech had been recorded by the "Zionists who were in the audience on that occasion." Years later, Millett confirmed that he was one of these Zionists.[57]

Corbyn explained that the Zionists had approached Hassassian after his speech and berated him. "There's clearly two problems," he continued. "One is they don't want to study history and, secondly, having lived in this country for a very long time, probably all their lives, they don't understand English

---

56 "UK Zionist Federation Activist and Blogger—Richard Millett—Harassed Mourners," London BDS Group blog, 27 August 2012. Diane Langford, "Open Letter to Rosie Duffield MP," Diane Langford blog, 13 August 2019 (both accessed 9 June 2022).

57 "The text of that speech by Jeremy on the Palestinian ambassador to the UK, English irony and certain Zionist critics," *Labour Briefing* website, 14 September 2018 (accessed 9 June 2022). See also point 4 of "Briefing for canvassers: Challenging false allegations of antisemitism," Jewish Voice for Labour website, 30 October 2019, and Jonny Paul, "Palestinian envoy to Britain dismisses two-state solution," *Jerusalem Post*, 20 January 2013.

irony either. Manuel does understand English irony and uses it very effectively so I think they needed two lessons which we can perhaps help them with." Hassassian had ironically commented that God must be a real estate dealer, since the Israelis rely on the Bible for their exclusivist claim to the land: "You know I'm reaching the conclusion that the Jews are the children of God, the only children of God and the Promised Land is being paid by God! I have started to believe this because nobody is stopping Israel building its messianic dream of Eretz Israel [Greater Israel] to the point I believe that maybe God is on their side. Maybe God is partial on this issue."[58]

During a 2018 upswing in the anti-Semitism campaign against Corbyn the media revisited this event. But the context of the attacks by Millett and friends was entirely missing and it was misreported by almost the entire national press. One paper used a headline containing a fabricated quote: "John McDonnell leaps to defence of Jeremy Corbyn over 'Zionists don't understand English irony' remark," it read.[59] This was typical of the media's dishonesty on the issue. As even the selectively edited video showed, Corbyn never said "Zionists don't understand English irony." As the full quote above proves (based on video of the event) Corbyn had actually said that two *particular* Zionists didn't understand Hassassian's irony.

The effect of the misreporting—and seemingly its intention—was to imply that Corbyn was using the word "Zionists" as a code word for "Jews." Such misrepresentations were common during the confected crisis. The media did its best to conflate Zionism with Jewish identity and religion. Such conflation has always been a key goal of the Israeli government. It is also a common tactic of the Israel lobby, used to discredit critics of Israel and Zionism. To his credit Corbyn defended his previous

---

[58] Richard Millett, "Palestinian Ambassador to the UK: 'I've started to believe that the Jews are the only children of God,'" Richard Millett's blog, 16 January 2013 (accessed 21 June 2022).

[59] Mikey Smith, "John McDonnell leaps to defence of Jeremy Corbyn over 'Zionists don't understand English irony' remark," *Daily Mirror*, 24 August 2018,

comments, saying he had used the term Zionist in an "accurate political sense and not as a euphemism for Jewish people."[60]

Tellingly, Millett himself didn't seem bothered about Corbyn's remarks back in 2013. The blogger wrote about the comments by Hassassian soon after.[61] But he chose not to report on Corbyn's comment about Millett not understanding irony, which took place only a few days later. An index page on his blog shows that he wrote no other posts mentioning Jeremy Corbyn for the rest of 2013.[62] A few months before the 2019 general election (during a period of political upheaval in the country when an election was expected to take place at any time), Millett sued Corbyn over an interview with the BBC's Andrew Marr in which the Labour leader defended his remarks. On the live Sunday morning show the year before, Corbyn had accused the Zionist of being "incredibly disruptive."[63] But in September 2022 Millett settled the case out of court, only two weeks before it would have gone to trial. Corbyn was preparing to defend his words about Millet on the grounds that what he said was true. Thirty-one independent witnesses agreed to give evidence on Corbyn's behalf, and gave witness statements about Millett's conduct at twenty separate meetings. Corbyn paid no damages and made no apology or undertaking not to repeat his comments.[64]

These usual suspects were part of a small but dedicated network of anti-Palestinian activists in the UK. Blogs like Millett's do not have much of an audience beyond their own circles. But at times, they managed to reach outside their clique, pushing their narratives into the national press. They have also received support from Israel's anti-BDS Ministry of Strategic Affairs, with

---

60 "Jeremy Corbyn defends 'British Zionist' comments," BBC News, 25 August 2018.

61 Millett, "Palestinian Ambassador to the UK."

62 "Tag Archives: Jeremy Corbyn," RichardMillett's Blog (accessed 21 June 2022).

63 "Corbyn Being Sued in High Court by Zionist 'Lacking Irony,'" Guido Fawkes, 13 June 2019.

64 "Right-winger Millett who featured in Al Jazeera documentary drops legal case against Corbyn," *Skwawkbox*, 27 September 2022.

David Collier (another blogger) flying out to speak at Israeli government conferences.[65] Millett has often recorded audio, or taken photos and video while infiltrating Palestine solidarity meetings. Decontextualised clips of the speakers can then be published online or leaked to the national press in the hope of creating a media scandal—especially for politicians.

The most effective exponent of the tactic of recording and releasing decontextualised clips of Palestine solidarity meetings is David Collier. An anti-Palestinian blogger and activist who emphatically denies the fact that Israel is an apartheid state, Collier is self-appointed chief researcher for the UK's Zionist movement. Throughout Corbyn's leadership Collier was the source of many of the smears later appearing in the mainstream British media. Collier once wrote of an "invasion" of British universities by Palestinians, and happily spoke on a panel with journalist Melanie Phillips, a fierce and regular critic of Muslims.[66] Unlike Hoffman and Millett, Collier does not disrupt meetings. He describes his own strategy as "going undercover" in the Palestine solidarity movement, to expose alleged anti-Semitism.[67] During the Corbyn years he intervened in the Labour Party, joining as a party member and attending its annual conference. He also seems to have joined as a member of the Jewish Labour Movement, attending and tweeting from an Emergency General Meeting that was open to members only.[68]

The Western left often fails to understand the nature of the Zionist movement. Although by and large supportive of the Palestinians in theory, Western liberals too often view their plight as part of a "conflict" and a "complicated" story with valid arguments on all "sides." What they fail to understand is

---

65 Asa Winstanley, "How Israeli spies are flooding Facebook and Twitter," *Electronic Intifada*, 25 June 2019.

66 Asa Winstanley, "Palestinians win damages over 'Labour anti-Semitism' libel," *Electronic Intifada*, 19 June 2020. Asa Winstanley, "How racist blogger David Collier infiltrated the Labour Party," *Electronic Intifada*, 6 November 2017.

67 David Collier, "After years going undercover . . ." Twitter, 12 July 2018.

68 David Collier, "Ok. Will sit at the @JewishLabour . . ." Twitter, 6 March 2019.

that Zionism is not an ethnicity or an "identity," it is a concrete political ideology. A racist, inherently right-wing ideology with a base of dedicated, fanatical followers scattered throughout Western countries. Over the last decade, many of Zionism's ideologues have increasingly begun to concede that they have lost the argument, especially among liberals and the left, and especially in Europe. That assessment seems to be shared by Israeli government officials.

"Our view and the view of the [Israeli] Ministry of Strategic Affairs is that Europe is lost," Jacob Baime of the US group Israel on Campus Coalition said in 2016. His candid remarks were exposed by an undercover Al Jazeera reporter (see chapter 4). Baime had been talking up the prospect of Israeli government support for his organisation's covert activities in the US. He boasted that his group "coordinates" its activities with and provides "intelligence" to Israel's Ministry of Strategic Affairs—a semi-covert government agency. The ministry's mandate is to sabotage and attack Palestine solidarity groups, especially those involved in BDS, the boycott, divestment, and sanctions movement.

Zionist ideologues like Millett, Hoffman, and Collier, however, were not willing to admit that Europe was lost for Israel. They wouldn't go down without a fight. If they could help remove Jeremy Corbyn as leader of the Labour Party, so much the better. At the very least they could cause him problems.

* * *

One key factor driving the Labour Party's alleged anti-Semitism crisis was the reporting of two vehemently anti-Palestinian national newspapers—the *Jewish Chronicle* and *Jewish News*. Krishnan Guru-Murthy's hostile questions about Hamas and Hizballah being Corbyn's "friends" did not come from nowhere. A Factiva database search showed that the first newspaper to report this story was the *Jewish Chronicle*.[69] Both newspapers are close supporters of the Zionist movement in the UK. Without

---

69 "Corbyn candidacy branded 'disgraceful,'" *Jewish Chronicle*, 18 June 2015.

fail, both follow the general line of Israel and its lobby, while covering opposing sides when there is an internal dispute between factions (usually coming down on the side of the Zionist right). They attack both Palestinians and Palestine solidarity campaigners, habitually smearing both as anti-Semites.

But it wasn't always like this. The *Jewish Chronicle* commenced publishing in 1841, long before the Zionist movement was formally founded. Under the ownership of Israel Davis between 1878 and 1906, the paper was actively hostile towards Zionism—in line with the vast majority of British Jews at the time.[70] This later changed and, eventually, under right-wing owners, in 2008 the paper brought in new editor Stephen Pollard. A *Daily Express* columnist, Pollard gave the paper a campaigning right-wing Zionist orientation. On his blog only two years earlier, Pollard had revealed just how far to the right he was, posting a "manifesto" written "to preserve Western civilisation" from the threat of "Islamists." In it he stated that "the Left, in any recognisable form, is now the enemy."[71] Emblematic of its anti-Palestinian bent, one *Jewish Chronicle* article in 2015 downplayed the infamous Deir Yassin massacre, describing it as an "alleged killing."[72] In fact, the 1948 massacre at the village of Deir Yassin by Zionist militias is probably the single most well-attested atrocity of the Nakba. At Deir Yassin, the right-wing Irgun and Lehi militias—supported by the "Labour Zionist" fighters of the Haganah—slaughtered about 100 Palestinians, including unarmed men, women, and babies. Word spread of the massacre quickly amongst neighbouring Palestinian communities, leading many to flee rather than stay and risk being

---

70   David Cesarani, *The Jewish Chronicle and Anglo-Jewry, 1841-1991* (Cambridge: Cambridge University Press, 1994), pages 67 and following.

71   Stephen Pollard, "The Maida Vale Manifesto," StephenPollard.net, 18 April 2006 (original deleted, but copies available at the Internet Archive's WayBack Machine).

72   Marcus Dysch, "Don't vote for Jeremy Corbyn, urges new Labour Friends of Israel chair Joan Ryan," *Jewish Chronicle*, 10 August 2015. After complaints by this author, the online version of the article was later edited to remove the word "alleged."

blown up, shot dead, or knifed.[73] In 2014 the commercial arm of the *Chronicle* printed a Disasters Emergency Committee charitable appeal for Gaza after Israel's war that summer there. But Pollard actually apologised, stressing that he and his paper were "entirely supportive" of Israel's war and smeared "many" of Gaza's civilian victims as "terrorists."[74] Israel killed 2,200 Palestinians during that war, most of whom were civilians, including 551 children.

Jewish News likewise has an obsessive focus on demonising both Palestinian cultural expression and pro-Palestinian campaigning. Probably the most emblematic example of their anti-Palestinian editorial line was the front page they ran after the Labour Party's conference in 2018. "One state of mind," the headline read. It showed a photo of Labour delegates waving Palestinian flags in the conference hall. The Palestine Solidarity Campaign had given out thousands of flags the day of a debate on Palestine. Delegates passed a motion in favour of ending the arms trade with Israel almost unanimously. The anti-Semitism "crisis" had been raging for more than three years, creating a climate of fear, which meant that everyone from ordinary members up to MPs and shadow ministers had found it difficult to talk about their support for Palestinian human rights.

PSC's canny conference intervention successfully challenged this unsavoury situation, breaking the embargo of fear. One of the most successful tactics of the manufactured crisis, as we will see later, had been to pick off "high-profile cases of anti-Semitism." Individuals were either misquoted or had their words rendered shorn of necessary context, leading to more headlines about "Labour's anti-Semitism crisis." These activists were then swiftly kicked out by the party's faceless bureaucrats, who suspended their membership, or in some cases "auto-excluded" them—expelled. In this short-sighted way, the party hoped to damp down the bad publicity. Sometimes that worked in the short-term—but only at the price of exacerbating the crisis in the long-term. PSC's day-of-the-flags short-circuited

---

73   Pappé, *The Ethnic Cleansing of Palestine*, pages 90-1.

74   Roy Greenslade, "Jewish Chronicle editor apologises for running Gaza appeal advert," *Guardian*, 15 August 2014.

this vicious cycle, by ensuring that no single person had to stick their neck out.

None could be picked off, because Labour would have had to expel almost the entire conference hall. It was a moving display of solidarity with the Palestinian people. British-Palestinian activist Huda Ammori said that it was the first time in living memory a motion on Palestine would be heard at a Labour conference and that the waving of the flags was "such a powerful moment . . . Palestine will be free."[75] Palestine's BDS National Committee called it great news that was "rekindling hope that Israel's South Africa moment is getting closer." However, for some, the flags were anything but a sign of hope. "The Palestinian flag was being used by Labour Party delegates as a weapon against Jewish people," Labour Friends of Israel's chairperson Joan Ryan said.[76] "Many people," the *Jewish News* wrote, had found the Palestinian flags at a debate about Palestine a "chilling display."

The *Jewish News* and the *Jewish Chronicle* describe themselves as the communal newspapers of Britain's Jewish communities—similar to other sectional media like Black community newspaper *New Nation* and the Asian weekly *Eastern Eye*. All have a national circulation, and are sometimes carried in newsagents and supermarkets in areas with significant populations of their target demographic. In that regard they have a valid role. But for both, their anti-Palestinian agenda has become the single most overriding concern. Years before Jeremy Corbyn was elected leader of the Labour Party, both papers already had him in their sights. For the national press, Corbyn at the time seemed like an insignificant backbencher. But the Israel lobby aims to quash all dissenting voices. They understand things in much the same way as the US empire during the Cold War understood the threat of independent leftist governments in Latin America. Central to this anti-communist ideology was the "Domino Theory"—small examples that could nevertheless set off a long chain of events. Likewise, Corbyn for the Israel lobby was the threat of a "bad example."

---

75 Asa Winstanley, "Defying Israel lobby, Labour votes for arms freeze," *Electronic Intifada*, 26 September 2018.

76 *Forced Out*, YouTube, 5 December 2019, timecode 17:25.

Unwittingly speaking to an undercover Al Jazeera reporter, one manager of US pro-Israel lobby group The Israel Project (or TIP) explained that the Israel lobby relies on a bi-partisan consensus for political hegemony when it comes to policy on Palestine and the Israelis. But, alarmingly for the lobby, that hegemony is in long-term decline. "The foundation that AIPAC stood on is rotting," said TIP's fundraising director Eric Gallagher in the undercover footage, referencing the American Israel Public Affairs Committee (probably the richest and most influential Israel lobby group in the world).[77]

The *Jewish Chronicle* in 2018 had a circulation of only 20,000 (compared to the million-plus copies sold by some of Britain's top tabloids and the 360,000 sold by *The Times*, the leading broadsheet).[78] Its readership was also in stark decline, down from almost 33,000 a decade earlier. But what the paper lacked in readers it made up for in being loud—and influential. Unlike the national news media's journalists, who were largely unfamiliar with Corbyn and his record, the *Chronicle* by the summer of 2015 had already done years of negative reporting on Jeremy Corbyn. They wrapped all this up in a package and tied it up in a proverbial bow, on an infamous front page of 13 August 2015: "The key questions Jeremy Corbyn must answer." Among other things, the article questioned Corbyn on his comments about Hamas, as later picked up by Channel 4.[79] It also asked about his links to one particular Palestinian Muslim.

* * *

---

[77] Al Jazeera Investigations, *The Lobby - USA*, episode 4, timecode 48:00. Available at "Watch final episodes of Al Jazeera film on US Israel lobby," *Electronic Intifada*, 6 November 2018.

[78] Charlotte Tobitt, "Cash donors save Jewish Chronicle from 'grave' closure threat," *Press Gazette*, 20 June 2019. Freddy Mayhew, "National newspaper ABCs: Daily Mail closes circulation gap on Sun to 5,500 copies," *Press Gazette*, 19 March 2020.

[79] "The key questions Jeremy Corbyn must answer," *Jewish Chronicle*, 12 August 2015.

A Palestinian citizen of Israel and former mayor of the town of Umm al-Fahm, Raed Salah is a popular Muslim preacher and a non-violent activist against Israeli occupation. In 2011 he was invited to the UK by Palestine solidarity campaigners. As the only MP deeply involved in the Palestine Solidarity Campaign's work, Corbyn naturally got involved. Despite entering the country openly and legally, a few days into his visit Salah was arrested. The government then briefed the press that he had been banned from entry yet had somehow evaded authorities at Heathrow airport. This tale later fell apart in court. Meanwhile Salah spent the best part of a year under house arrest.

Despite Israel's attempt to portray Salah as a radical Islamist, the topic of his speaking tour was anything but. It called simply for human rights. He held several such talks in London with the aid of a translator. Corbyn was involved in hosting one talk in Parliament. Salah had entered via Heathrow airport in the usual fashion. Taking legal advice after his arrest a few days later, he refused voluntary deportation, since that would have been a confession of wrong-doing that could have been used against him by Israeli authorities on his return. Salah was ultimately vindicated, with the High Court ruling that there was no lawful basis for the government's deportation order and that Home Secretary Theresa May had been "under a misapprehension as to the facts" about Salah.[80] Only then did he return home to Palestine.

The court case, which I reported on in detail for the *Electronic Intifada* throughout 2011 and 2012, was an illuminating experience. It shed particular light on the skulduggery employed by the UK Border Agency, an especially cruel and vindictive government department. Documents revealed in court detailed the intimate relationship between the UK's Home Office, the Israeli government, and the British pro-Israel lobby group Community Security Trust. They showed that the CST often works as an intermediary between the Home Office and Israel, and that the CST passed Israeli intelligence about Salah onto the British government. Most of this information was deeply misleading and in

---

80   Asa Winstanley, "Court victory for Raed Salah deals blow to UK 'anti-terror' policy," *Electronic Intifada*, 9 April 2012.

some cases it was outright fabricated. In perhaps the most egregious example, a poem that Salah was supposed to have written in Arabic contained a starkly anti-Semitic statement: "You Jews are criminal bombers of mosques / Slaughterers of pregnant women and babies. Robbers and germs in all times." Much of the Salah media coverage focused on these alarming lines. But they were a fabrication.

Court documents revealed the original poem in Arabic, as well as the CST's English translation (which was quite different from the version that made it in to the papers).[81] I also published parts of the expert opinion of a School of Oriental and African Studies professor, Stefan Sperl, a specialist in Arabic poetry who examined the original poem for the defence. The misquotations relied on by the UK Border Agency had seriously misrepresented Salah—crucially, the word "Jews" did not appear anywhere in the text. In fact the poem was addressed to "the oppressors" and seemed to be alluding to the abuses of Israeli occupation forces against Palestinians, comparing them to Quranic and Biblical stories (including the tale of Pharaoh persecuting the Israelites). A judge ruled that the Home Secretary had been "misled as to the terms of the poem." Who had been responsible for the doctoring of the poem was never made explicit. But it had the hallmarks of an Israeli intelligence disinformation campaign.

The CST is a British charity whose remit is to combat anti-Semitism. But a secret report on Salah's supporters the group passed on to the Home Office demonstrated the lobby group's anti-Palestinian agenda. Under the heading "Support for Raed Salah from Various Quarters," the document denounced anti-Zionist Jews who'd called for Salah to be released as "extremists"—a dangerous epithet during the "War on Terror" era.[82]

The campaign to free Read Salah received a wide range of support. Palestinian politician Haneen Zoabi had also become a national hate figure for many Israelis, so naturally supported Salah, despite political differences. Jeremy Corbyn was another of Salah's backers. "His is a voice that must be heard," Corbyn said,

---

81 Asa Winstanley, "Documents prove the UK used fabricated anti-Semitism to ban Raed Salah," *Electronic Intifada*, 12 October 2011.

82 Winstanley, "Documents prove the UK used fabricated anti-Semitism."

describing the former mayor as "a very honoured citizen" during a press conference celebrating his court victory and release from house arrest. He invited him to parliament for meetings. "I look forward to giving you tea on the terrace, because you deserve it," he said before adding wryly: "The Home Secretary will probably not be in attendance." He also called for an inquiry into how May had come to her decision (making no mention of Israel or its lobby). The *Jewish Chronicle* and the notoriously pro-Israel blog *Harry's Place* then covered this in a particularly hostile and misleading fashion. The blog falsely claimed the Labour MP had called "for [a] public inquiry into Jewish influence in the Conservative Party." Apparently taking its cue from this, a piece by *Jewish Chronicle* correspondent Martin Bright ran with the false headline claim: "Jeremy Corbyn calls for inquiry on 'pro-Israel lobby.'" The quote by Corbyn in the text of the article did not support the headline, and video of the press conference still available on YouTube at the time of writing this book confirms Corbyn did not mention Israel or the pro-Israel lobby, and certainly not "Jewish influence."[83] Bright later admitted that he had not even bothered to contact Corbyn for comment before publication.[84]

It was Corbyn's stand against the injustice done to Salah—and by extension to the Palestinian people as a whole—that would be brought back by the British media as another example of Corbyn's "extremism" after he'd entered the leadership race in 2015. Further interrogations by Channel 4 News repeatedly brought up the issue of Salah. Instead of questioning British and Israeli disinformation about their Palestinian enemy, the liberal channel took these governments' claims at face value.

---

83 "Labour MP Corbyn hails hate preacher Raed Salah," YouTube channel "habibi," 10 April 2012. The channel appears to be run by the anonymous Harry's Place blogger going by the name "habibi" (Arabic for "beloved"). Harry's Place is a notoriously Islamophobic website set up to promote the 2003 invasion of Iraq from the "left." The title of the video reflects the blogger's anti-Muslim bias. But the video itself exonerates Corbyn entirely.

84 Ben White, "How the Jewish Chronicle is trying to smear Jeremy Corbyn MP," *Liberal Conspiracy*, 23 April 2012.

After harassing Salah through the courts for years, and unable to tolerate the role he played leading Palestinian freedom marches in Jerusalem, the Israeli state eventually banned the Islamic Movement. In August 2020 Salah was jailed for more than two years on a charge of belonging to an "illegal organisation" and a trumped up "incitement" allegation. The court claimed he had encouraged armed Palestinian attacks on Israeli occupation forces in Jerusalem. Jamal Zahalka, former Joint List Knesset member, said that Salah's jailing was "another milestone in his political persecution. The Islamic Movement has been outlawed, now the right to speak is also outlawed."[85]

For the British establishment's media, Palestinian voices do not seem to matter. Salah is still described today as an extremist that Corbyn alone had foolishly—or maliciously—supported. The damage had been done. The Guru-Murthy interview set the tone of the sheer aggression and irrationality of the British media's long campaign against Corbyn that was to follow in the years ahead.

* * *

But five years before the Corbyn leadership raised the hackles of MI5, British generals, and the UK's corporate media, another country's intelligence agencies already had the future Labour leader in their sights—Israel's.

In 2010 Corbyn took part in a small Parliamentary delegation to Palestine organised by the website Middle East Monitor and the Palestine solidarity group Friends of al-Aqsa. Corbyn and his soft-left Labour colleague Andy Slaughter were joined on the trip by journalist and future senior Corbyn leadership adviser Seumas Milne (then one of the *Guardian's* few remaining prominent socialists) and local journalist Jenny Ousbey (who would go on to be an adviser for Liberal Democrat MP Paul Burstow). The delegation visited Palestinians living under the Israeli apartheid regime's military occupation, including the El-Kurd family in

---

[85] "Islamist firebrand preacher Raed Salah begins prison term for inciting terror," *Times of Israel*, 16 August 2020.

East Jerusalem, facing down the prospect of violent eviction by state-backed Jewish fundamentalists who believe God gave them the land (often settlers from the United States). They also met with elected Palestinian politicians from the opposing Fatah and Hamas political factions. Only a few years before that, Hamas had been overwhelmingly elected to lead the Palestinian Authority. But the democratic result was rejected by Israel, the US, and the European countries, which soon set about trying to reverse it.[86]

A decade later, after Corbyn had been removed as Labour leader, *Middle East Eye* editor David Hearst uncovered an extraordinary fact. The Shin Bet (Israel's secret police) had hauled the delegation's local fixer (a Palestinian citizen of Israel) in for a five-hour interrogation at a Haifa police station. Shin Bet told her they "would not tolerate her campaigning inside the Houses of Parliament in the UK," Hearst reported. "If she did not heed the warning, she would spend the rest of her days in prison as an enemy of the state. Her lawyer told her that such a charge could indeed be fabricated against her and that an Israeli court would send her to prison if this happened."

Hearst, a former senior *Guardian* journalist concluded: "The warnings given to Corbyn's fixer confirm that Israel's security services had set their sights on the MP at least five years before he became Labour leader and long before anti-Semitism in Labour became a newsworthy issue."[87]

---

86 Ali Abunimah, "The Palestine Papers and the 'Gaza coup,'" *Electronic Intifada*, 27 January 2011. David Rose, "The Gaza Bombshell," *Vanity Fair*, 3 March 2008.

87 David Hearst, "Suspension of Corbyn will define Starmer as Iraq defined Blair," *Middle East Eye*, 2 November 2020. See also Eylon Levy, "Exclusive: Jeremy Corbyn's secret trip to Israel to meet Hamas," i24 News website, 21 August 2018. Levy (a British former Union of Jewish Students activist who later became media adviser to the Israeli president) and Israeli satellite channel i24 appear to have been fed their "exclusive" by Israeli spy agency the Shin Bet. He also neglects to mention the fact that Corbyn's "secret" trip was widely publicised at the time.

CHAPTER TWO

WORKERS OF ZION

"Thank you all for coming," said a diminutive young man with a patchy beard. "This is definitely the first Young Jewish Labour Movement event in 32 years."

It was September 2016. Labour's anti-Semitism "crisis" had been raging for more than a year. The Jewish Labour Movement had been at the forefront of sounding the alarm about anti-Semitism in the Labour Party—coinciding with the rise of Corbyn. Publicly, the group claimed that it had been affiliated to Labour for a century. But from what the young speaker, Liron Velleman, was saying, the JLM's youth wing at least, had been inactive for decades. Several key figures on the right of Labour's student movement were present that evening: Labour Friends of Israel's Michael Rubin, youth representative on Labour's ruling national executive Jasmin Beckett, and Ella Rose, the JLM's new staffer. There was also Rebecca Filer, a student who would become the Union of Jewish Students officer responsible for running a "Bridges Not Boycotts" anti-BDS conference.

But one of these young Labour members (known to the others as "Robin") was an undercover Al Jazeera journalist. He had been posing as a pro-Israel activist for several months and was secretly recording video.

Velleman despaired of what he saw as Labour's anti-Semitism crisis: "We've been hit with many an incident," he told the group as they tucked into a barbecue. But "it's really great that over the last eight, nine months we've had a huge increase in membership of young people into the Jewish Labour Movement." There was a new leadership election on. Corbyn was facing a challenge from Owen Smith, a minor MP who had been propelled to the forefront of the Labour right's battle against the left-wing leader, after a failed coup attempt that summer. JLM's guests spoke of Corbyn's leadership in euphemistic terms: "this difficult time of the party," as Jasmin Beckett put it. She offered the assembled group a chance to put questions to him at the National Executive Committee meetings she attended. "These issues cannot just be swept under the rug," she said.

But the main speaker that evening was a rotund man with a smooth face—the JLM's chairperson Jeremy Newmark. "He works tirelessly to get us into the position we're in today where we now have a staff member," gushed Velleman. Newmark had become a regular media presence over the previous year. Always good for a quick quote, he was sought out by journalists keen to put across the view that there was a serious Labour anti-Semitism problem. But they never seemed to mention a basic fact of Newmark's career: he is a veteran professional Israel lobbyist.

Newmark was downbeat on Labour's prospects under Corbyn: "I'm not going to reflect on the state of the Labour Party today because that would be too bloody depressing." In what seemed to be a reference to the new leader, Newmark condemned the "growth and the mutation of a new form of anti-Semitism at the heart of our party." He thanked Beckett for her attendance. "You've been here tonight for the ... inaugural relaunch meeting of JLM," he said.

By "relaunch," Newmark may have been referring to Young JLM, rather than JLM as a whole. But it was a telling slip: the reality was that, before Corbyn arrived as leader, JLM had been (at best) a dormant group. Newmark proceeded to explain to his private audience why the JLM was not quite the ancient, foundational Labour Party group it was publicly claiming to be. "There was an interview actually that Tony Blair gave over the summer," he recalled. Newmark's idol had been giving his analysis of the state of the world and why "he doesn't get it anymore." Blair discussed "the rise of Jeremy Corbyn, Bernie Sanders in the States" and how "things have moved on" now that there was a "new generation" in politics. "A lot of it is for the worse," explained Newmark. He then laid out his vision for the new JLM.

"When a bunch of us sat in a coffee shop in Golders Green—we were talking about this before—a year ago, to talk about—just under a year ago—talk about re-forming the JLM, and to do something with it." This new guard wanted to "util[ise] the rights and privileges [the JLM] enjoys as a socialist society under the constitution of the Labour Party." A moribund Labour Party group was being reactivated to fight Corbyn. Newmark's admission was revealing, one which was not made public until I reported it three years later.[1]

Who was doing this "re-forming"? Israel was not openly mentioned by any of the speakers that evening. But at least two Israeli embassy staff (past and present) were in attendance. And Newmark himself has a long history of ties to the embassy. Also present was Michael Rubin, an employee of Labour Friends of Israel which, as we'll see later, is an embassy front group.

Another attendee was an Israeli embassy employee who told "Robin" that he "worked with Shai" at the Israeli embassy (this was a reference to Shai Masot, an embassy agent whose activities would soon be exposed). This exchange is viewable in Al Jazeera's 2017 undercover investigative series *The Lobby* (although the employee's name was not divulged).[2] A transcript of the unedited sequence reveals that his name was Theo Robertson-Bonds. Robin later confirmed his name to me. According to a LinkedIn profile under the name of Theo Bonds, he continued to work for Israel's Ministry of Foreign Affairs in London as a Policy Adviser until 2021 (the profile doesn't reveal that the "MFA" in question was Israel's).[3]

Ella Rose followed Newmark. A young woman with curly brown hair, Rose was the new JLM staffer people seemed so excited about. She chatted amiably about flipping burgers and said little of substance. Newmark's introduction was more telling. He predicted Rose would be at the forefront of "a struggle

---

1   Asa Winstanley, "Jewish Labour Movement was refounded to fight Corbyn," *Electronic Intifada*, 7 March 2019.

2   Al Jazeera Investigations, *The Lobby*, episode 1, timecode 09:18. Available at Winstanley, "Jewish Labour Movement was refounded."

3   Theo Bonds, LinkedIn profile (accessed 10 June 2022).

and a battle we will all be engaged in for months and probably years ahead of us." Newmark recalled how JLM had made the decision to hire her. "Ella was by no means the person on that pile of CVs that had the most Labour Party and political experience . . . But there was something we felt on the JLM executive as trustees mattered far more, which is that she's one of you," he said to the assembled young people. "We think she's gonna go on and play an incredibly critical role at the lead of the struggle against anti-Semitism in the Labour Party." Newmark wanted to establish politically committed young cadres who could influence Labour from within. With the leadership election looming, Newmark looked forward to a time after Corbyn, a time where they could "have a year or two in the party—whoever the next leadership is—in which we're not consumed with struggling and battling anti-Semitism."

But there was one detail Newmark didn't mention. He'd hired Rose out of the Israeli embassy. Unbeknownst to most, the main group promoting the idea there was a "Labour anti-Semitism crisis" was run by someone who had represented a human-rights–abusing foreign state—which also happened to be actively seeking the overthrow of the leader of the British opposition.

* * *

We only know all this happened because it was caught on camera by Al Jazeera, the ground-breaking TV channel based in the tiny Gulf Arab nation of Qatar. Led by Clayton Swisher and Phil Rees, the channel's investigations unit ran two undercover journalists for six months in 2016: one inside the UK's pro-Israel groups and another in the US. The resulting UK series made international headlines when the first clips were released in January 2017. The Israeli embassy offered an apology to the British government and sent Shai Masot, a "senior political officer," on a plane home. Masot had been the main focus of the film. Almost certainly an agent of Israel's anti-BDS Ministry of

Strategic Affairs, Masot was caught on camera calling then-foreign secretary Boris Johnson "an idiot." More seriously, he had been exposed plotting with a civil servant to bring down MPs and ministers deemed even mildly critical of Israel (see chapter 4). The Jewish Labour Movement was also at the centre of the film.

The JLM is in some ways typical of the Labour Party's undemocratic structures. An inside source—its secretary Peter Mason—once admitted to the JLM's lack of democracy. "Delighted to have been 'elected' to the JLM executive," he posted on Twitter. Another user responded that the quote marks suggested Mason's "election" to the group was "something other than truly democratic."

"Something like that!" Mason replied. The comments were lighthearted, but they did give an insight into how the JLM operates in practice.[4]

Conversation at the barbecue showed that the JLM had not been active for the entire century it later claimed. As Newmark unwittingly admitted, the JLM needed "re-forming." He explained how they had revived the defunct group in that coffee shop in Golders Green around September 2015—the same month Corbyn was first elected leader. The Israel lobbyist's plan to use "the rights and privileges" that the JLM "enjoys as a socialist society" within Labour was key to the "battle" ahead. JLM's status as a formal affiliate of Labour meant that it could reach areas of the party denied to more openly pro-Israel groups, such as Labour Friends of Israel. The JLM could demand membership of key committees and obtain meetings with MPs and Corbyn himself, as well as lodge formal complaints and send delegates to conference.

I obtained transcripts of Al Jazeera's undercover footage and, based on un-broadcast portions of the barbecue, in March 2019 I revealed for the *Electronic Intifada* how the JLM had been revived. Little more than an on-paper group by September 2015, the JLM had required a massive shake-up and reorganisation to make it fit for the "battle" against Corbyn.

---

4 Peter Mason, Twitter, 12 February 2013. The tweet has now been deleted. Screenshot on file.

They began immediately after Jeremy Corbyn's unexpected 2015 victory. Newmark and his friends seized the JLM, and restructured it into a more effective anti-Corbyn organisation. The JLM then attempted to revise, re-invent, and cover up its history. A major part of this was the claim they had been in Labour for almost a century. The group planned a centenary celebration for 2020. There was a membership drive, promoted by Labour bigwigs like Gordon Brown and Tony Blair. The JLM is an integral part of Labour, the story went, now under threat from Corbyn's "anti-Semitism." They seeded a defeatist narrative, calling Labour's elections chances under Corbyn into doubt. JLM spokespeople constantly claimed Labour had "a problem with anti-Semitism." This eventually mushroomed into Labour supposedly being "institutionally anti-Semitic." JLM members overwhelmingly voted against Corbyn and openly called for him to be deposed, even suggesting that its members would not vote Labour as long as he were leader. In elections, JLM activists campaigned only for right-wing MPs that supported their agenda.

For Newmark (who took over as the JLM's new chairperson in February 2016) all this was the application of a familiar strategy to a new battlefield. As a veteran Israel lobbyist, he'd been involved in a similar defamation campaign against another part of the labour movement—the University and College Union, the trade union for academics and other university staff. A campaign of legal harassment (or "lawfare") was launched by the Israel lobby in 2008 against the UCU for allegedly being "institutionally anti-Semitic." In a purely legal sense, the case spectacularly failed, with a judge in 2013 ruling against it on all counts.[5] But in another sense it succeeded, generating years of negative headlines for the union, and making it much harder for grassroots activists to discuss Palestinian human rights and the proposed boycott of Israeli academic institutions.

Where did the JLM come from? Is it accurate to describe it as an "emanation of the Israeli state in the Labour Party" as

---

5 Asa Winstanley, "Crushing defeat for Israel lobby as anti-boycott litigation fails in UK," *Electronic Intifada*, 26 March 2013. See also "Why Newmark and Mann's past (failed) attempt to equate anti-Zionism with antisemitism is relevant now," Free Speech on Israel blog, 3 June 2016.

campaign group Free Speech on Israel once put it?[6] To answer these questions, it's necessary to explain the JLM's history.

* * *

The JLM itself ties its story to Poale Zion, a far older group which was committed to what it described as a left-wing form of Zionism (the state of Israel's official ideology). *Poale Zion* is a Hebrew name usually translated as "Workers of Zion." Zion is a Biblical name for a hill in Jerusalem, and by extension a name for the city itself. It's also a term for the ideal society envisaged in Judaism. The word was adopted by Christians, particularly millenarian evangelical Protestants, for whom it has a dual meaning, also standing for heaven. In one famous hymn they envision themselves "Marching to Zion . . . the beautiful city of God." Zionism therefore sometimes portrays itself as utopian. But in practice Zionism has always been a brutal colonial project, whose realisation depends on the expulsion of the Indigenous people of Palestine.

Founded in Russia at the end of the nineteenth century, Poale Zion groups were later established in the Austro-Hungarian Empire, the United States and Britain. The movement began helping to colonise Palestine at the start of the twentieth century. By 1906, the group in Palestine had formally abandoned any pretence of class struggle. By 1920, the movement was solidly anti-communist, with its pro-Soviet faction breaking away to form the Palestine Communist Party. The right-wing faction became "the mainstream of the Zionist labor movement."[7] Poale Zion leader David Ben-Gurion led the 1948 expulsion of 800,000 Indigenous Palestinians, becoming Israel's first prime minister. His political party Mapai was Israel's nearest equivalent to the UK's Labour Party. The British Poale Zion group was founded

---

6 "What is the Jewish Labour Movement?" Free Speech on Israel leaflet, 2017.

7 "Po'alei Zion," *Encyclopedia Judaica*, as cited by the Jewish Virtual Library, 2008.

in London in 1903.[8] It was considered the "left wing" of the Zionist movement. In 1920, the group affiliated to the Labour Party. Labour itself had by that stage only been in existence for twenty years.

The concept of a "left wing" Zionism today seems a contradiction in terms. The tendency is in long-term decline, with the list led by the Israeli Labor Party relegated to a paltry seven seats in the 2020 Knesset election. Successive governments have led Israel on such an extreme rightward trajectory that the far-right government of Benjamin Netanyahu could one day be viewed as "moderate" in the Israeli context. But Labour Zionism is a faction with a long history. Until 1977, every Israeli government was led by the Labor Party or its forerunners. The worst crimes of the Zionist movement and the Israeli state were carried out by the Labour Zionist tendency—most notably the 1948 Nakba and 1967's invasion, occupation and illegal colonisation of the West Bank and Gaza Strip (as well as Syria's Golan Heights and Egypt's Sinai Peninsula).

Zionism's left wing is just as colonial and racist as its right wing. It actively sought alliance with the British empire. Labour Zionism's settler-colonialism was viewed favourably by many non-Jewish British Labour leaders. And the same British Labour leaders so enamoured of Zionism were also often strident anti-Semites. Leading party intellectual Sidney Webb delighted in the lack of Jewish members of Labour, explaining there was "no money in it." He said that, "French, German, Russian socialism is Jew-ridden. We, thank heaven, are free!"[9] Party leader Herbert Morrison was an ardent anti-communist and fervent Zionist. He viewed Zionism as a way to transform Jewish people into "first class colonisers" who would "have the real, good, old, Empire-building qualities."[10]

---

8 Andrew Sargent, "The British Labour Party and Palestine 1917-1949" (PhD thesis, University of Nottingham, 1980), pages 4-5.

9 Paul Kelemen, *The British Left and Zionism: History of a Divorce* (Manchester University Press, 2012), page 20.

10 Hansard, Volume 341, Column 2005, 24 November 1938: *Palestine.*

Ramsay MacDonald (Britain's first Labour prime minister) heaped praise on "the Jewish colonisers in Palestine."[11] He had visited Palestine in 1922, and the resulting pamphlet was published by Poale Zion. The Zionist group was unfazed by its anti-Semitic contents. MacDonald attacked anti-Zionist Jews (who at the time were vastly in the majority) as having "the blindness and the stiff-neckedness of the proud tribe of Judah at its worst." Some of the pamphlet was so extreme that it wouldn't have been out of place over in Germany in a Nazi party publication of the time. It condemned "the rich plutocratic Jew" as those "whose views upon life make one anti-Semitic. He has no country, no kindred. Whether as a sweater or a financier, he is an exploiter of everything he can squeeze. He is behind every evil that Governments do."[12]

From 1945, when Britain began reneging on its pledge to hand Palestine over to the Zionist movement in order to found a Jewish state, the two allies violently fell out (just as the British and the Boers had done in South Africa). While initially trying to restrain the right-wing, fascist-oriented Zionist terror groups (the Irgun and Lehi), Labour Zionism's armed wing (the Haganah) joined their right-wing allies in launching armed attacks on British soldiers.[13] Neither three armed factions had any hesitation about launching terrorist attacks on Palestinian civilians.

Fiercely anti-communist, Labour Zionism later became an important tool for American imperialism. CIA defector Philip Agee revealed in 1975 that the Histadrut (the Labour Zionist trade union federation in occupied Palestine, which barred Arabs as members until 1959)[14] was "used by the CIA in labour

---

11   Hansard, Volume 245, Column 116, 17 November 1930: *Palestine*.

12   J. Ramsay MacDonald, *A Socialist in Palestine* (London: Poale Zion, 1922), pages 5-6.

13   See, for example, Christopher Mayhew and Michael Adams, *Publish It Not: The Middle East Cover-Up* (Oxford: Signal Books, 2006), page 37. Former Labour minister Christopher Mayhew relates an incident in which a pro-Israel British Labour MP and a British Labour minister conspired to approve an armed Haganah attack on British soldiers operating in Palestine at the time.

14   Tony Greenstein, "Histadrut: Israel's racist 'trade union,'" *Electronic Intifada*, 9 March 2009.

operations."[15] According to the renowned whistleblower, the Histadrut was used by the agency "for specialised training within the social-democratic movement" as part of the agency's infiltration of trade union groups in the "free world."[16]

Poale Zion argued that it was a natural ally for the British Labour Party. It had a point. Not only did Labour have pro-imperialist policies, but Labour governments up until the 1960s actually *ran the British empire itself*. Labour's imperialism led to it being generally in favour of settler-colonial movements like Zionism. Going into the 1945 election, Labour's official policy was to promote a (European) Jewish state in Palestine—a country whose Arab Indigenous people were overwhelmingly Muslim and Christian. In 1944, Labour's National Executive Committee issued a party policy document on global issues and the "colonies." Jews from Europe should "enter this tiny land in such numbers as to become a majority," the document argued. After more than 50 years of Zionist colonisation under the tutelage of the British empire, Jews in Palestine were still vastly outnumbered by the Indigenous Palestinians. To achieve a majority, the document argued, there should be a mass expulsion of Palestinians. There was a necessity in Palestine "for transfer of population. Let the Arabs be encouraged to move out, as the Jews move in."[17] That's what happened only three years later—800,000 Palestinians were "encouraged" by Zionist militias to flee from their bombs, guns, and knives as the state of Israel was established on the rubble.

The principal author of the policy was Hugh Dalton, chancellor in the 1945 Labour government (the same government that founded the NHS and the modern welfare state). Dalton was a particularly fanatical example of UK Labour Zionism. His policy called for the Jewish state to expand its borders into

---

15   Philip Agee, *Inside the Company: CIA Diary* (London: Penguin, 1975), page 610.

16   Agee, *Inside the Company*, pages 74-76.

17   *The International Post-war Settlement: Report by the National Executive Committee of the Labour Party to be presented to the annual conference to be held in London from May 29th to June 2nd, 1944* (London: Labour Party, 1944?), page 7.

Egypt, Syria, and Jordan. According to Dalton's biographer, this "Zionism plus plus" vision fell short of an earlier draft in which Dalton had advocated "throwing open Libya or Eritrea to Jewish settlement, as satellites or colonies to Palestine."[18]

Dalton also held anti-Semitic views. According to one biography of Labour chairperson Harold Laski (who was Jewish), Dalton had a habit of referring to him as an "under-sized Semite" with an extreme "yideology." He routinely used such racial slurs, calling Africans "niggers" and Arabs "wogs."[19] Dalton's support for Zionism was motivated by his disdain for the Indigenous Palestinians he hoped the Zionists would expel. But it's likely he also viewed Zionism as a convenient method to remove Jews from Britain. Were British Jews to become settlers in Palestine and Libya, they would be leaving Britain—away from him. Dalton was by no means the only Labour Party politician to share such attitudes.

Richard Crossman was for many years a leading MP and minister aligned with the Labour left. His attitude towards Palestine and its native inhabitants verged on the genocidal. In a 1959 lecture in Israel, Crossman discussed Zionism in the context of other settler-colonial movements—favourably. Referring to European settlers ("the white man") in Africa and the Americas, he argued that, "No one, until the twentieth century, seriously challenged their right, or indeed their duty, to civilise these continents by physically occupying them, even at the cost of wiping out the aboriginal population." He wrote that the Palestinian "intelligentsia began to regard the Middle East as the classic pattern of Leninist 'imperial exploitation,'" and lamented that the Jewish settlers in Palestine had not "achieved their majority before 1914," and that the Palestinians "regarded them as 'white settlers,' come to occupy the Middle East."[20]

---

18 Ben Pimlott, *Hugh Dalton* (London: Harper Collins, 1995), page 390.

19 John Newsinger, "The Labour Party, anti-Semitism and Zionism," *International Socialism*, Issue 153, 3 January 2017.

20 Richard Crossman, *A Nation Reborn: The Israel of Weizmann, Bevin and Ben-Gurion* (London: Hamish Hamilton, 1960), page 58. See also Asa Winstanley, "When Israel's friends in Labour advocated genocide," *Electronic Intifada*, 25 July 2017.

In his 1975 book *Publish It Not*, former Labour minister Christopher Mayhew recounted what he over-optimistically described as the zenith of Zionism's influence in Labour. At a dinner to celebrate the group's anniversary in 1970, leading Poale Zion MP Ian Mikardo attacked the civil servants at the Foreign Office. Mayhew had worked with them as a junior minister in the late 1940s, at a time when Zionism's armed wings in Palestine were at war with Britain. Mikardo scorned them using both racism and homophobia, saying the officials were "public school boys who share with the Arabs a tendency towards homosexuality, romanticism, and enthusiasm of horses." A group of Labour MPs complained to the National Executive Committee about these remarks. But the complaint went nowhere: Mikardo himself chaired the committee, and Labour Prime Minister Harold Wilson (himself enamoured of Zionism) had been at the dinner.[21]

The Jewish Labour Movement was re-founded in 2015 to resist the rise of Corbynism. Or as Newmark had put it, the idea was to "do something" with the JLM's privileges under Labour rules. The JLM's status as a constituent organisation also meant that they could use the threat of leaving the party as a form of political pressure if they were not appeased. This manufactured a sense of crisis and moral panic.

From 2016 onward, the new JLM began to portray itself as having been affiliated to Labour for almost a century. But in a now-deleted page on their website, the group had described itself as having been first "founded in 2004 in a meeting at the House of Commons attended by the Israeli ambassador." Mentions of this version of history remained on the JLM's website well into 2016, before Newmark's new guard scrubbed it away with a new website.[22]

---

21   Mayhew, *Publish It Not*, pages 29-30.

22   Winstanley, "Jewish Labour Movement was refounded." For a contemporary account of the launch of the "new" organisation by Louise Ellman in Westminster, see Bernard Josephs, "New Labour battle against racists," *Jewish Chronicle*, 30 July 2004. The paper reported that Israeli ambassador Zvi Heifetz was at the launch. Prior to that Heifetz spent seven years in Israeli military intelligence (Barak Ravid, "Israeli

A 2019 pamphlet published by the JLM to promote this new revisionist history is mostly a history of Poale Zion. Its author breezily claims that the 2004 founding of JLM was merely a "change [of] name" for Poale Zion, though that was not claimed by JLM at the time.[23] The pamphlet is so strongly anti-Palestinian that it doesn't even call the Indigenous people by their own name, repeatedly smearing "the Arabs" instead. It puts forth the long-debunked Israeli myth that the Palestinians left in 1948 due to threats from their own political leaders, rather than being driven out by Zionist militias (as has been agreed by all credible historians for decades).

There's no doubt that the JLM and the version of Poale Zion which affiliated to Labour in 1920 represented similar political tendencies—the contradiction in terms that is "left-wing" Zionism. But the claim that the two groups were one and the same (or that JLM has had a century of uninterrupted activism) is doubtful at best.

* * *

In Al Jazeera's series *The Lobby*, Ella Rose, the JLM's new director, is seen telling Robin that a "new guard" had arrived at JLM, hired her out of the Israeli embassy, "and then all the anti-Semitism stuff kicked off." Some of this new guard were well-established figures in the Israel lobby. They would soon emerge as the bitterest public enemies of the popular movement backing Jeremy Corbyn.

Beginning at that September 2015 Golders Green café meeting which Newmark had described, it took a few months to

---

Envoy to U.K. Zvi Heifetz Likely to Advise Blair on Mideast," *Haaretz*, 9 November 2007).

23 Derek Taylor, *Solidarity and Discord: A brief history of 99 years of affiliation to the Labour Party* (London: Jewish Labour Movement, 2019). Interestingly, Taylor on page 6 gets the year of the foundation of the British Poale Zion wrong, claiming it was 1902. Andrew Sargent (on pages 4-5 of his PhD) says the two 1902 groups in Leeds and East London (relied on by Taylor) had in fact "soon collapsed" and the British Poale Zion was a separate group founded in London the "following year."

complete their takeover. But after a 2 February 2016 meeting, the group formally announced a "new structure" to increase its influence "inside Labour Party structures on a local, regional, and national basis." In the accompanying statement, the new guard announced its executive committee. Newmark gave himself the rather grand title "National Movement Chair"—a new position. Former JLM chairperson Louise Ellman was to enter "retirement."[24]

A right-wing Labour MP, Ellman became one of Corbyn's bitterest foes in her own right. Having been active in Labour Friends of Israel for years, she'd go on to become the lobby group's chair before quitting the party. The new JLM executive featured many other prominent opponents of Corbyn. Coinciding with the February 2016 relaunch, Newmark wrote an opinion piece claiming that "Labour's bonds with the Jewish community have been strained recently," due to Corbyn's reference to the political wing of a Palestinian resistance group as friends.[25] In the JLM's relaunch statement, Newmark said that his "new team" was committed to strengthening links with the Labor Party in Israel. He spoke of wanting to "develop a cadre of younger political activists" to do so.

Ella Rose was hired as JLM director in July 2016. She ran the JLM's daily business until the winter of 2018. Rose's career path seemed set. She had begun her pro-Israel career while still in school, doing work experience for Luciana Berger (then the director of Labour Friends of Israel, Berger became a Blairite Labour MP and a key Corbyn opponent). At university Rose became president of the Union of Jewish Students, a pro-Israel lobby group which claims to speak on behalf of Britain's Jewish students (as *The Lobby* series revealed, the UJS is also funded by Israel).[26]

---

24 "JLM Elects New National Executive Committee," Jewish Labour Movement website, 3 February 2016 (accessed 10 June 2022).

25 Jeremy Newmark, "Why does Labour find it so hard to weed out antisemitism?" *Daily Telegraph*, 17 February 2016.

26 Asa Winstanley, "Israeli government cash to UK's Union of Jewish Students exposed," *Electronic Intifada*, 12 January 2017.

In 2017, Rose was selected for Labour's Jo Cox Women in Leadership Programme.[27] The JLM's leaders, it seemed, were attempting to groom Rose as a future MP. But there was a setback when she ran for councillor in May's local elections and came third.[28] She ultimately went on to win a council seat in Barnet, North London in 2022's local elections. For Newmark, Rose's dedication to the state of Israel and Zionism was her main asset.

The *Electronic Intifada* revealed in September 2016 that the JLM's new director had been an Israeli embassy officer.[29] A few weeks later, Rose responded to the story by tweeting a photo of herself and Newmark posing with ambassador Mark Regev, saying she was "proud" to have worked there.[30] But in private, Rose had actually been upset her secret was out. As seen in the undercover footage, she wept to Al Jazeera's reporter "Robin" that "*Electronic Intifada* released that I worked at the embassy before JLM."[31] Some days later, in conversation with Robin, she regained her composure enough to say of this author (the reporter who'd broken the story) and certain left-wing Labour activists: "as far as I'm concerned they can go die in a hole." Rose later faced a cursory Labour Party probe after these comments were exposed by Al Jazeera.[32] The probe led nowhere, and was described as a "whitewash" by the members who had complained. Rose remained active in the group after 2018, joining their executive committee as its "equalities

---

27 Asa Winstanley, "Jewish Labour Movement director investigated for violent threat," *Electronic Intifada*, 15 February 2017.

28 Election results for Bushey South (30) County Council, Thursday 4 May 2017, Hertfordshire County Council website (accessed 10 June 2022).

29 Asa Winstanley, "New Jewish Labour Movement director was Israeli embassy officer," *Electronic Intifada*, 21 September 2016.

30 Asa Winstanley, "Jewish Labour Movement worked with Israeli embassy spy," *Electronic Intifada*, 12 April 2018.

31 Al Jazeera Investigations, *The Lobby*, episode 2, timecode 21:36. Video available at Ali Abunimah, "'Die in a hole,' Israel lobbyist tells critics," *Electronic Intifada*, 13 January 2017.

32 Winstanley, "Jewish Labour Movement director investigated."

officer." The undercover transcripts show that she maintained her close ties to the Israeli embassy even after becoming JLM director.[33]

But for most of the UK's media the public face of the JLM was Jeremy Newmark. It's likely he was often the "senior Jewish Labour source" so beloved of the *Jewish Chronicle*. Although unfamiliar to most on the Labour left, for many active in the Palestine solidarity movement, Newmark was already well known as an Israel lobbyist. He has been involved in at least two known attempts to sue unions in the UK for policies opposing the Israeli occupation of Palestine—and particularly for allowing debate on BDS, the boycott, divestment, and sanctions movement. As part of these "lawfare" efforts, Newmark repeatedly deployed dubious allegations of anti-Semitism.

As CEO of Israel lobby group the Jewish Leadership Council, Newmark played a key role in a lawsuit against the University and College Union, giving hours of evidence to tribunal hearings. The lawsuit was initiated in 2011,[34] and was finally thrown out on all counts by a judge in 2013.[35] But it managed to generate years of negative publicity about alleged anti-Semitism in the union. It was a very similar smear campaign to that which would later be utilised against Labour, and was just as mendacious. In September 2015 (as Corbyn was elected leader), Newmark wrote describing the "trench warfare-like campaign to oppose boycotts inside the University and College Union" that he had helped to lead.[36] The lawfare effort was intended to bankrupt

---

33 Winstanley, "Jewish Labour Movement worked with Israeli embassy spy."

34 "Ronnie Fraser takes legal action against the anti-Semitism of the University and College Union (UCU) in the UK," Scholars for Peace in the Middle East website, 14 March 2012 (accessed 10 June 2022). Despite its name, SPME is actually a right-wing, Islamophobic group set up to harass Palestine solidarity activists on campus. See Ali Abunimah, "Anti-Palestinian group to 'monitor' boycott activists on campus," *Electronic Intifada*, 1 August 2013.

35 Asa Winstanley, "Crushing defeat for Israel lobby as anti-boycott litigation fails in UK," *Electronic Intifada*, 26 March 2013.

36 Jeremy Newmark, "Now is not the time to walk away from the Labour Party," *Jewish News*, 16 September 2015.

the academics' union after its members called for debate on the Palestinian-led academic boycott of Israeli institutions.

When judge Anthony Snelson threw the case out, he denounced it as "wreckage" and, devastatingly, "an impermissible attempt to achieve a political end by litigious means." In his ruling the tribunal judge singled Newmark out for particularly harsh criticism.[37] Newmark had claimed in his testimony that Jewish academic (and pro-Israel activist) Ronnie Fraser had been "booed, jeered, and harassed" at a UCU conference.[38] But Newmark's testimony had been untrue. Transcript and recorded audio evidence flatly disproved his claim.

Essentially calling him a liar, the judge insisted that Newmark had given "untrue" evidence. His accusation that stewards at a UCU congress had stereotyped him in anti-Semitic terms was rejected as a "preposterous claim." Finally, Newmark's striking allegation that the Israel boycott debate meant the union was "no longer a fit arena for free speech" was said by the judge to be "not only extraordinarily arrogant but also disturbing." Newmark had responded during cross-examination by essentially accusing UCU lawyer Antony White QC of anti-Semitism, having made a "disturbing assumption" about him. After the ruling he insinuated that even the judge was guilty of anti-Semitism, describing his ruling as "extreme."[39] For Newmark, it seemed, anyone disagreeing with him was by definition an anti-Semite.

A second key witness in the case against the UCU would also become one of Corbyn's bitterest opponents. This was John Mann, the right-wing Labour MP who would be responsible for the political assassination of leading Labour left-winger Ken Livingstone (see chapter 5). In September 2019, after four years of open sabotage from the backbenches, he announced he would

---

[37] Winstanley, "Crushing defeat." The full judgment is linked to from that article and available directly from the Courts and Tribunals Judiciary, *Mr R Fraser v. University & College Union*, Case Numbers: 2203390/201, 25 March 2013.

[38] Asa Winstanley, "UK lawsuit challenges college union's right to boycott Israel," *Electronic Intifada*, 21 December 2012.

[39] "UCU judgment 'is a travesty,' says JLC chief," *Jewish Chronicle*, 15 April 2013.

stand down as MP. He took a job advising the Conservative government on the "most effective methods to tackle antisemitism."[40] Bizarrely, the position was dubbed the "anti-Semitism tsar" by the press. "Tsar" is a common term used in the British media for an unelected government official. But it seemed particularly inappropriate in this case, considering the Russian tsars' history of violent anti-Semitism.

Mann had also come in for criticism from the judge. He "seemed more disposed to score points or play to the gallery rather than providing straightforward answers." Union leaders had met with Mann, then chairperson of the All-Party Parliamentary Group Against Antisemitism. The judgment relates that Mann launched into "a somewhat hostile display" against the trade union leaders. He claimed the UCU was anti-Semitic and that they needed to do something about it. "He did not explain what the anti-Semitic behaviour was supposed to have consisted of besides referring to the boycott debate and characterising any boycott of Israel or Israeli institutions as itself anti-Semitic," the judge wrote.

Judge Snelson also reflected on the woeful nature of Mann's evidence. He presented no evidence that he had witnessed *anything* at a UCU event, let alone anti-Semitism. Mann "clearly enjoyed making speeches . . . [but] seemed [ill] at ease with the idea of being required to answer a question not to his liking," Snelson concluded.

Having lost the case, the Jewish Leadership Council ended up having to repay the UCU's court costs, thought to amount to as much as half a million pounds.[41] But the case achieved a sort of victory for the Israel lobby. Discussion of the academic boycott of Israel was severely chilled in the trade union movement. The case was a harbinger of things to come in the Labour Party. Paul Mackney, one of the two joint UCU leaders, "argued that defenders of Israel had used the charge of anti-Semitism as a tactic to smother democratic debate and legitimate censure,"

---

40 "John Mann appointed as independent adviser on antisemitism," Prime Minister's Office press release, 23 July 2019.

41 "Union seeks to reclaim costs after tribunal win," *Jewish Chronicle*, 12 September 2013.

the judge explained. This was the very same weaponisation of anti-Semitism which was to prove so effective a tactic against Corbyn's Labour.

Although unique in its scale, the UCU case was only one of many such assaults on the Palestine solidarity movement led by Newmark. He told Israeli newspaper *Haaretz* in 2012 that he was "liaising closely with the government of Israel" to help an Israeli army colonel sue both Unison and a local NHS trust.[42] Lt. Colonel (res.) Moty Cristal sought damages amounting to tens of thousands of pounds, complaining of "indirect discrimination." Union members had declined his "offer" to run a workshop on negotiations. The case was dropped in 2014 when it became clear it would fail.[43]

Not long after his 2013 dressing down by the tribunal judge, Newmark left his JLC position under mysterious circumstances which wouldn't be explained for years. For the time being, Newmark quietly stepped down. He briefly returned to the world of public relations. Then in September 2015 he reinvented himself as the public face of the JLM. In 2017's general election, he ran as Labour's candidate for Parliament in Finchley and Golders Green—narrowly losing. Ironically, he benefited from a Corbyn-era vote swing to Labour. But a few months later he won a consolation prize, becoming a local councillor in an October by-election and was appointed leader of the opposition Labour group.[44]

In his new JLM role Newmark was often called to comment when journalists wanted to promote Labour's "anti-Semitism crisis." The JLM's chosen weapon was slinging false allegations of anti-Semitism. Newmark was a past master of this dark art. Although the right tried many different attack strategies against Corbyn, none was more persistent or effective than

---

42 Asa Winstanley, "Israeli colonel sues UK National Health Service and union for 'indirect discrimination,'" *Electronic Intifada*, 22 September 2013.

43 Asa Winstanley, "Lawfare in retreat as Israeli colonel drops case against union,'" *Electronic Intifada*, 30 May 2014.

44 "Councillor Jeremy Newmark," Hertsmere Borough Council website, accessed 30 August 2022. Ben Weich, "Newmark re-elected as Borehamwood councillor," *Jewish Chronicle*, 3 May 2019.

the "anti-Semitism crisis." In February 2016, only days after the JLM's "new guard" publicly announced its takeover, the Israeli embassy saw evidence that this weapon could be used to impressive effect.

Although Corbyn had been targeted with insinuations of anti-Semitism even before he was elected Labour leader, so far nothing had really stuck. The *Jewish Chronicle* attacks had been picked up by the mainstream media. But these were soon debunked, and the popular left-wing movement that swept Corbyn into his new leadership position mostly turned the other cheek. It was only from the Spring of 2016 that the issue began to cause real divisions on the left. In a disturbing and paranoid atmosphere, reminiscent of the US McCarthy era, the issue would turn comrade against comrade, causing even former Corbyn allies to denounce him as anti-Semitic, or at least "tolerant" of anti-Semitism.

At a secret meeting behind the scenes at Labour's 2016 conference filmed by Al Jazeera, Newmark met with Israeli ambassador Mark Regev and with Shai Masot, the Israeli spy who would later be sent home. Newmark gleefully described his strategy as "wheels within wheels" and a plan that had "created a bit of division within Momentum" (the Labour grouping founded to support Corbyn). That same sequence in the undercover series shows that Newmark also told Regev of "intelligence" he had received about Clive Lewis, a pro-Corbyn Labour MP who had allegedly been censured by Momentum for speaking at a JLM event.[45] In a 2015 opinion piece written for the *Jewish News* the month Corbyn was first elected leader, Newmark explained his emerging strategy and the history of lobbying he had built it on. In the fight against the trade union boycott of Israeli academic institutions, "we built a robust political discourse, *rooted in the politics of the left* and deployed it in *their* own backyard" (my emphases). Some activists will want to resign because of Corbyn, wrote Newmark. "I understand that. But if we walk away, Israel's case will be lost by default." He instead advocated staying inside the party to push the case for Israel, writing: "We can't have that

---

45 Al Jazeera Investigations, *The Lobby*, episode 3, timecode 04:33. Video available at Asa Winstanley, "Labour's top Israel lobbyist accused of defrauding Jewish charity," *Electronic Intifada*, 9 January 2018.

debate from a position of influence if we all resign . . . While the assault upon Israel's legitimacy is happening in civil society and trade unions, the stance of the Labour Party will matter."[46] Newmark's use of a third-person pronoun to refer to the left's backyard as something external to himself was a tell. Newmark didn't think of himself as a leftist. He was a supporter of Tony Blair and a Zionist. After spending years as a professional Israel lobbyist, Newmark's efforts to reinvent himself as a Labour Party politician was both an attempt to halt the party's leftward, pro-Palestinian drift from within and a way to carve out another niche for himself.

Newmark had advocated such a strategy as long ago as 2011, at a conference addressing fellow Zionist activists. Ironically, he called for use of the strategy of entryism that mass media would later claim was responsible for the rise of Corbyn. "Get active," he urged the conference. "If you're not in a trade union and you're able to join one, join one. When you see these resolutions [against Israel] appear, speak out. If you feel that you're the sort of person that wants to join the local branch of your political party, join the local constituency party association and be that—and engage on the issues and become a voice for Israel."[47]

Newmark certainly became a "voice for Israel" when he entered Labour. As well as his frequent media appearances, he was noted by many Labour activists to be the JLM's most vigorous enforcer. One left-wing Labour councillor even accused him of harassment. At Labour's annual conference in 2017, Newmark filmed and confronted Nikki McDonald, while she and her friends applauded a Palestine solidarity campaigner's speech, saying he found her "deeply offensive." "It was awful," McDonald told me in 2019. "It made me feel really uncomfortable . . . I'm not a delicate little flower but . . . he was really, really quite frightening. I was actually quite shaken." It seemed to be an attempt to intimidate leading Labour activists away from supporting Palestinian rights. (Newmark responded at the time that he "wholly" denied McDonald's account.) McDonald's husband, trade union leader Tosh McDonald, also told me he had

---

46   Newmark, "Now is not the time to walk away."

47   Asa Winstanley, "Jewish Labour Movement harassed Labour activists," *Electronic Intifada*, 4 April 2019.

been filmed or photographed by mysterious activists as he and other union leaders clapped.[48]

* * *

Aside from Newmark, who were this "new guard" of the JLM? In an un-broadcast section of a transcript of Al Jazeera's undercover footage, Ella Rose named some of them. Newmark seems to have brought much of the new leadership over with him from the Jewish Leadership Council.

The JLC is a well-funded charity whose main focus is lobbying for Israel.[49] Established only in 2004, initially it was a competitor to the far older Board of Deputies of British Jews. It represented an attempt by leading Jewish businessmen and financiers to take over the leadership of the organised Jewish community. JLC claims to represent "the major institutions of the British Jewish community."[50] But its list of constituent member bodies overwhelmingly consists of Zionist organisations. The group does not include Britain's sizeable anti-Zionist orthodox Jewish communities, or non-Zionist secular Jews. Secular Zionist organisations, however, are given constituent status giving them, in theory, a say in how the organisation is run. In documents lodged with the Charity Commission, the JLC states that its top aims include promoting "education of the public" about Israel.[51]

Historian Geoffrey Alderman has accused the JLC of planning a hostile takeover of the Board of Deputies. In one column he wryly dubbed them the "mainly male moneyed *machers*"

---

48 Winstanley, "Jewish Labour Movement harassed Labour activists."

49 Its financial data filed with the Charity Commission for England and Wales for the year ending 31 December 2020 shows a total income of £2.45 million (charity number 1115343).

50 "Members," deleted page from the JLC website, available on the Internet Archive's WayBack Machine (latest copy dated 19 April 2022).

51 "Charitable objects," paragraph 6, extract from the JLC's governing document (as amended 19 December 2019), Charity Commission for England and Wales (accessed 10 June 2022).

(Yiddish for fixers) and called for them to be shut down.[52] The Board of Deputies is more dominated by supporters and members of the Conservative Party, with fewer Labour members—although there are some deputies on the Labour right. The situation in the JLC is to some extent different, with its leadership more tilted towards the Blairite, pro-Israel wing of the Labour Party. Despite initial tensions, the JLC and the BoD reached a modus vivendi after the latter ramped-up its lobbying for Israel.

In *The Lobby*, Ella Rose explained to Al Jazeera's undercover reporter that the dormant JLM had been run by Liverpool MP Louise Ellman, "who obviously is great but is also an MP and didn't have time to run the sort of political operation that was needed." Ellman stepped aside in 2015, "and a sort of new guard came in," Rose explained. "Jeremy [Newmark], Peter [Mason], Adam [Langleben], that crowd—and they sort of thought at some point 'Okay, we're gonna hire someone.'"

The JLM's new guard is a veritable Who's Who of Labour's internal Israel lobby. Adam Langleben's professional background is in political lobbying and public relations. He was head of communications and political adviser to the Jewish Leadership Council. Elected as a Labour councillor in Barnet, North London in 2014, he lost his seat in 2018. His declaration of interests statement filed with the council reveals he was also involved with Labour Friends of Israel.[53] He later quit the party, protesting Labour's "institutional anti-Semitism."[54]

When the new JLM announced itself to the world in February 2016, Mike Katz was appointed one of its two vice chairpersons.[55] After an apparent internal power struggle in the wake of Newmark's forced departure, Katz was appointed chairperson

---

52 Geoffrey Alderman, "Moneyed machers with ambition," *Jewish Chronicle*, 15 February 2015.

53 London Borough of Barnet, Part I Form of General Notice, Notification of Members' Interests, General Notice of Registrable Interests, Adam Langleben, signed 27 March 2014 (accessed 23 March 2016).

54 Adam Langleben, "My resignation from the Labour Party," Medium.com, 18 February 2019.

55 "JLM Elects New National Executive Committee."

in 2019. Katz's professional background is also public relations. For a decade he's been a lobbyist for the rail industry, pushing to keep Britain's rail lines in private hands, including his employer FirstGroup. His LinkedIn profile also reveals a stint as a spin doctor for advertising agency Freshwater.[56]

At the JLM's February 2016 "re-forming," Peter Mason was appointed secretary. Mason's resume is similar to others in the JLM leadership: a Labour councillor in Ealing, a former member of Progress,[57] a former executive of the JLC's London Jewish Forum and a former adviser to the Labour group at the London Assembly. He was also office manager for Blairite MP Liz Kendall, who came last in the 2015 leadership election. More than a decade ago, Mason also did a stint working for the pro-Israel Union of Jewish Students.

Ella Rose was only the first of several young Labour right-wingers to become active in the group. While the JLM never seems to have claimed any more than 4,000 members, it is unclear what percentage are actually Jewish and how many are affiliate or "solidarity" members.

JLM's youth cadres later came into their own by appearing in a controversial 2019 episode of the BBC's *Panorama* (see chapter 7).

* * *

Anti-Corbyn from the start, the Jewish Labour Movement was a key advocate of the narrative that there was a Labour anti-Semitism "crisis." In 2016, 92 percent of JLM members voted to endorse Owen Smith against Corbyn in the leadership election.

The JLM's openly stated commitment to Israel (let alone its more covert links to the Israeli embassy via Ella Rose and Jeremy Newmark) was rarely, if ever, reported in the papers.

---

56 Mike Katz, LinkedIn profile (accessed 22 June 2022).

57 Ealing Council, Register of Members' Disclosable Pecuniary Interests, Part 2: Membership of organisations, 13 January 2019. On the most recent register as of this writing (dated 23 June 2020), Progress is no longer listed as one of Mason's memberships.

When the JLM's activities *were* reported they were seen as just "Jewish Labour members" becoming alarmed at increasing levels of anti-Semitism allegedly rocking the party. Left-wing pro-Corbyn group Jewish Voice for Labour received far less coverage. The JLM's primary goal seemed to be manufacturing the appearance of an "exodus" of Jewish members out of the Labour Party for fear of a new, supposedly racist environment under Corbyn.

In the summer of 2018, during one of the worst peaks of the "crisis," the JLM made headlines as it met to consider formally disaffiliating from the Labour Party "after almost 100 years." They repeated this move in April 2019, when members overwhelmingly voted for a motion calling for Corbyn to step down. Former prime minister Gordon Brown spoke at a JLM event and even joined up.[58]

The reason for the new emphasis on the JLM's alleged century of affiliation became clearer. It was an almost identical strategy to that which Newmark had used in his attempt to bring down the University and College Union. The JLM was constructing a myth: that Jewish members were fleeing the Labour Party in fear. It was a powerful and emotive narrative. What did evidence matter compared to feelings? This all contributed to a sense of panic in the Labour Party's top ranks.

The JLM led a successful campaign to have high-profile Corbyn supporters thrown out of the party, with Labour bureaucrats suspending, expelling or otherwise pushing out people like Ken Livingstone, Jackie Walker, and later, the left-wing MP Chris Williamson. At the end of 2018, Ella Rose stepped down from her paid position as JLM director. Her reasons for leaving were not disclosed, and no successor was announced.[59] But in August 2019, a new "national organiser" position was announced, with Rebecca Filer occupying the post (another former leader in the Union of Jewish Students and JLM barbecue

---

58 "Former Prime Minister Gordon Brown joins JLM as affiliate member," *Jewish News*, 1 April 2019.

59 "Director of Jewish Labour Movement to leave post and join HET," *Jewish News*, 25 October 2018.

attendee). Rose remained active in the JLM, and was appointed "equalities officer."

In February 2018 Newmark was forced to step down as the JLM's chairperson. The reasons for his mysterious ejection from the JLC four years earlier became clear. There had been grave allegations of fraud involving tens of thousands of pounds.[60]

The charges were exposed by the *Jewish Chronicle*, indicating an intra-Zionist disagreement about the usefulness of the JLM and the personal behaviour of Newmark. Pollard's *Chronicle* tended to argue that Jews should leave the Labour Party altogether, and that the JLM was a busted flush. There was also the implication that its leaders were out to enrich themselves, building up positions of power and influence. Pollard excoriated Newmark in an opinion piece accompanying his paper's revelations. "I'm not exaggerating when I say that at least ten times a year someone has asked me when we are going to expose his activities," he wrote. "As a result of this community-wide cover-up, Mr Newmark came within 1,657 votes of becoming an MP last June," Pollard continued. The editor also let another truth slip: that the JLM was, in effect, a new group formed to fight Corbyn, and not the century-old Labour Party establishment it made itself out to be: "As Mr Newmark rebuilt himself as a Labour Party figure, using his undoubted skills to *revive* the Jewish Labour Movement, those same people who knew his true measure sat back mutely and watched, saying nothing. Worse, some of them gave the JLM generous donations, while knowing the details of his behaviour" (my emphasis). Pollard didn't name the mysterious donors.[61]

The paper reported that Newmark had billed tens of thousands of pounds in inappropriate expenses to the Jewish Leadership Council, including holidays in Israel and VIP transport for himself and his family. When Newmark stepped down from the JLC in 2013, it had supposedly been for personal health reasons. But a secret internal JLC investigation, obtained by the *Chronicle*, showed that the real reasons related to corruption.

---

60 Asa Winstanley, "Labour's top Israel lobbyist accused of defrauding Jewish charity," *Electronic Intifada*, 9 February 2018.

61 Stephen Pollard, "The long term damage is in the cover-up," *Jewish Chronicle*, 6 February 2018.

The Israel lobby group covered this up, handing him six months' salary as a parting gift. Under Newmark, the report stated, it "appears to be standard practice in the JLC to falsify information relating to finances." Newmark "did not provide honest responses to a number of queries" put to him by auditors.

The report lists several totally inappropriate expense claims, including a lease on a brand-new BMW worth £46,000—to which he even attached his own personalised number plate. He also withdrew thousands of pounds in cash on JLC cards while failing to provide receipts, and artificially inflated project budgets so that he could allegedly pocket the difference.[62]

According to the internal investigation (which the *Chronicle* published in full on their website) one of the channels Newmark used to extract money for these "expenses" was the bank accounts of the Fair Play Campaign Group—a small Israel lobby group he ran to combat the Palestinian-led BDS movement. The report stated that Newmark made "transfers and grant payments amounting to nearly £21,000" into accounts he ran alone.[63]

Newmark responded to the *Chronicle* revelations with typical blustering chutzpah, calling the allegations "politically motivated." Newmark denied any wrongdoing. Yet the facts in the documents spoke for themselves. The JLM's response was to distance themselves from Newmark. While they initially denied a follow-up report by the paper that they had asked Newmark to step down, before long they issued a statement admitting Newmark was toast. He had left to focus on "seeking redress following the publication of historic allegations." The word "redress" seemed to imply that Newmark would be suing the paper, or otherwise seeking to clear his name. Such a move never transpired. But a few weeks after Newmark's departure, the JLM announced to its members that it had "referred certain internal financial matters to the police for investigation."[64] The internal email did not name Newmark, but the implication

---

62 Winstanley, "Labour's top Israel lobbyist."

63 "Jeremy Newmark - the evidence: Read the full report here," *Jewish Chronicle* website, 8 February 2018. See especially pages 7 and 11 of the report.

64 Asa Winstanley, "Jewish Labour Movement reports 'financial matters' to police," *Electronic Intifada*, 26 February 2018.

seemed clear. The *Chronicle* later reported that the investigation had indeed concerned Newmark, and that the City of London Police were looking into the affair. When I contacted the force some months later to check on the progress of the case, I was told they couldn't comment. A year after he stepped down, the *Chronicle* reported that police had dropped the investigation. They had been seriously hampered by missing documents. The *Chronicle* alleged that Newmark personally removed documents from the JLC's office shortly after stepping down (something Newmark denied).[65]

Newmark was gone. For a brief moment, it looked like the JLM was a spent force. But the group's sabotage campaign against the party and its left-wing leadership proved to be relentless. After all, this had been the very reason for its re-foundation. There seemed to be genuine internal disagreement over the efficacy of their strategy. If the aim was to immediately overthrow Corbyn, it seemed to be failing. Corbyn's position as Labour leader at the time looked unassailable. But if the aim was to generally sabotage the party's election chances, causing bad headlines and negative publicity about "Labour anti-Semitism," then it had succeeded with spectacular effect. And Newmark's strategy of "utilising the rights and privileges [the JLM] enjoys as a socialist society" had been a triumph. His group had made much of their status as the party's "only affiliated Jewish organisation," something they increasingly emphasised after the foundation of leftist group Jewish Voice for Labour in 2017 (see chapter 7).

Newmark had used his position of influence to push for changes to Labour's 2017 manifesto, watering down the already muted criticism of Israel in the final document. Reference in a leaked draft to "expansion of Israeli settlements on the Palestinian West Bank" being "wrong and illegal" was removed from the final version. Instead it demanded both "an end to the [Israeli] blockade" of Gaza, its "occupation and settlements" and an "end to [Palestinian] rocket and terror attacks." By doing so, it created a false equivalence between the violence of Israel, a

---

65 Lee Harpin, "Newmark protests his innocence after police drop investigation," *Jewish Chronicle*, 28 March 2019.

highly militarised state backed by the US, and the resistance tactics armed Palestinian guerrilla groups used to respond. *The Times* reported that these changes were made only after Newmark had complained about the draft being an "unbalanced, partisan" text.[66] An anonymous "senior" Labour Friends of Israel source told the *Jewish Chronicle* that the changes were a "difficult win."[67] The source said that Tom Watson, Labour's right-wing deputy leader (and a supporter of Labour Friends of Israel) had also lobbied for the changes.

The JLM was also able to use its affiliate status to propose motions to conference, successfully changing party rules. It put forward a motion at 2017's conference calling for anti-Semitism to be made a specific disciplinary offence. A compromise motion by the Labour leadership (which adopted many of the JLM's demands) was passed by delegates. This set a pattern whereby Labour's rules were repeatedly changed to enable a witch hunt against party members, culminating the following year with Labour's National Executive Committee adopting a pro-Israel "working definition" of anti-Semitism, as we'll see in chapter 6.

The JLM had put itself in a win-win position. Whether it stayed in the Labour Party or quit, it would cause a serious headache for the left-wing leadership, and a new onslaught of negative publicity. Hence the threat by the JLM in 2018 to formally disaffiliate. They ended up staying in "for now." Despite all the problems they had caused for him and for the membership, Corbyn had practically begged them to stay—an organisation which now described its own aims as being to "promote the centrality of Israel in Jewish life."[68] The defenders of an apartheid state were being given immense power inside Labour.

It was by no means the last concession Corbyn made to the Israel lobby.

---

66 Asa Winstanley, "Israel lobby claims 'win' over Labour manifesto changes," *Electronic Intifada*, 17 May 2017.

67 Marcus Dysch, "Labour reveals official manifesto, with some key changes," *Jewish Chronicle*, 16 May 2017.

68 "What is the Jewish Labour Movement?" JLM website, undated (accessed 10 June 2022).

CHAPTER THREE

THE OXFORD CRISIS

Labour activist Max Shanly did not hold back. "Let me be honest about this: I've been suffering quite badly from depression for a long time, really for like the past two years," he said.

It was a rambling episode of his podcast. Shanly and his co-host chatted about football and nationalism, the Parliamentary Labour Party, and debated mandatory re-selection for MPs. A working-class activist in Labour's Bennite wing, Shanly's generous demeanour often endears him to others. He and his interlocutor Matt Zarb-Cousin (a former press officer for Jeremy Corbyn) were friends who had come together to start the podcast in 2017. It was hosted by Novara, a new-media empire founded by grad student former anarchists.[1]

As Shanly opened up about his experiences, his co-host tried to steer the discussion away from the topic that had caused his friend's depression. He had been falsely accused and swept up in Labour's anti-Semitism "crisis." Zarb-Cousin seemed torn between letting his friend open up about this trauma and steering the conversation away from an uncomfortable direction. But Shanly pressed on, and slowly, the true story emerged.

---

1   See "What is Libertarian Communism?" NovaraFM, 16 September 2016. In this episode, Aaron Bastani says "anarchism . . . a libertarian communist or socialist perspective" is "the ideological background from which this show and project originally emerged." Fellow Novara co-founder James Butler says "it's a tradition out of which we both come." This is what Ash Sarkar meant in her viral "I'm literally a communist" comment to Piers Morgan. See also Andrew Neil, *The Backstory* podcast, "Episode 5 - Ash Sarkar," 24 May 2022, in which she says that in the summer of 2015 she was "still a bit of a sulky anarchist."

"You wake up of a morning and you just want to go back to sleep," he said. "I was in a very bad state for a very, very, very long time . . . I was stuck in my parents' house, in my childhood bedroom, because I was ill from like, February 2016 when all the OULC stuff kicked off." As a student at Oxford's Ruskin College, Shanly had been involved in the Oxford University Labour Club. Clearly something had happened there that caused him great distress. Shanly said he was "stuck in my room [for] days on end, not leaving, not talking to anyone . . . For two years I tried to make out like I didn't have a problem at all."

Shanly had been an activist in Young Labour, the party's official youth wing, and had developed a reputation as a leftist agitator even before arriving on campus. Traditionally a working-class institution, Ruskin is not a college of the University of Oxford, although it does have affiliate status. "There were already rumours about me going around before I arrived," he revealed. Left-wing union leader "Len McCluskey was paying my tuition fees, apparently," scoffed Shanly. "And Tony Benn was training me up to destroy the Labour Party."

With the election of Corbyn in 2015, Shanly was excited for the possibilities. But he cautioned that the right would not take things lying down. On the podcast he recalled how he had predicted that if Corbyn should win the leadership, "the MPs are going to revolt, the party staff are not going to work with us, and the entire British press will unite with them to make Corbynism a non-starter to try to kill it off before it's even had a chance to grow. And that is exactly what happened." In an interview at the time he had warned that the Parliamentary Labour Party would "have to be brought into line, some members of party staff will need to be pointed towards the exit, and the entire party structures would, in my opinion, need to undergo a comprehensive and thorough review."[2] A staff and MPs' revolt against the new leadership was indeed what happened. The right in Labour's often vicious student politics battlefield was also deeply unhappy. Shanly's exposure of looming realities was unwelcome.

---

2   "Understanding the Corbyn campaign: an interview with Max Shanly," rs21, 13 July 2015.

In February 2016 a national scandal broke out when the co-chairperson of Oxford's student Labour club resigned. Alex Chalmers claimed his club was anti-Semitic. Chalmers's statement named no names, but anonymous allegations soon made their way into the papers. They named Shanly and a second pro-Corbyn student activist, James Elliott. This represented a dangerous new escalation targeting the wider pro-Corbyn left. The results for Shanly were devastating, as he recalled on the podcast. "I was under investigation for two years. The party refused to meet with me in those two years, despite numerous attempts of my lawyer," he said.

Chalmers's allegations were suspiciously timed. They came only days before Young Labour gathered to elect its representative to Labour's ruling National Executive Committee (NEC). Shanly's friend Elliott was the left's candidate for the NEC seat. But after the negative press coverage, he lost to right-wing candidate Jasmin Beckett by a single vote. As we've seen, Beckett was a strong supporter of the Jewish Labour Movement and an opponent of Corbyn. The smear campaign was victorious. "All that OULC stuff, for me, it was all about party stuff," recalled Shanly. "It all kicked off the weekend before the election for NEC youth rep," he said. The Labour student right wanted "to try to influence the NEC youth election of which James was the left's candidate . . . and the candidate backed by the unions."

But it wasn't over. The Labour investigation continued. "Two years," Shanly remembered bitterly, "and then the day before the next set of youth elections, they dropped the case and go, Oh well, we actually don't have any evidence. But they leaked all my information to the press, so everybody thinks I'm guilty as sin. But the truth is, is that the allegations that were made against me were all false. There was no evidence." Shanly recounted a disturbing experience. A man at a night club recognised Shanly, told him as much and spat in his face. "The media is also an authority," Shanly explained. "When people read these things, they read them as: Oh then, well it must be true." Shanly explained his depression was caused by how the press reporting endangered his employment chances. But "they never found any evidence that anybody at Oxford had said anything anti-Semitic." Years later, Shanly was proven correct. But by then the damage had been done.

Events at Oxford University Labour Club had only been the latest salvo in the decades-long campus war by the Labour right against the left. But it was also the opening of a major new front: "Labour anti-Semitism."

* * *

Max Shanly's account of events at Oxford was enlightening. His podcast is titled *All The Best*—a playful, sarcastic sign-off addressed to right-wing antagonists. But unlike the rest of the show's archive, you won't be able to find this particular episode on the Novara website or Apple Podcasts. Soon after release it was deleted without explanation.[3]

Shanly's retelling had been years in the making. I long tried to persuade Max to go public with his account, but it's unclear whether or not my entreaties had any effect. It always seemed he would tell his story when the time was right. It was odd then, now he'd finally done so, that the episode was deleted under mysterious circumstances. But it wasn't entirely surprising. Shanly is a close friend of Tony Benn's former aide Jon Lansman, then leader of Momentum, a Labour faction established in 2016 to back Corbyn. But, as we'll see in a later chapter, Lansman is sympathetic to Zionism, and ultimately came to strongly oppose all attempts to fight back against the smear campaign.

As the witch hunt against "Labour anti-Semitism" escalated, asking for evidence of anti-Semitism *in itself* became "evidence" of anti-Semitism. It was a Catch-22 which meant that, for the weaker side of the Corbynist movement led by Lansman, that episode of Shanly's podcast was impolitic in 2018.

Shanly had long been something of a scapegoat for the Labour right. On his Twitter profile, he wryly describes himself as an "underground avant-garde hate figure." He was despised by the right-wing partisans of Labour's civil war and the more openly

---

3   "It's Coming Home?" *All the Best*, Novara Media, 5 July 2018. As of this writing (22 June 2022) a copy is still available at the Internet Archive.

conservative right alike. Far-right libertarian blog Guido Fawkes made Shanly one of the targets of its long-running anti-Labour campaign, describing him as a "Leninist Momentum fixer" and "Lansman's protégé."

An internal Labour report, leaked in April 2020, shows anti-Corbyn party staff mocking Shanly's mental health problems. "I hope Max Shanly dies in a fire," wrote Sarah Mulholland in a leaked 2017 group chat. "Wish there was a petrol can emoji."[4]

In 2016 he was even targeted by reporters. Channel 4's *Dispatches* programme had sent undercover reporter Gesbeen Mohammad, who went by the name Gesh, into the group's headquarters looking for dirt on the pro-Corbyn group. But they found little of substance. Contrary to the narrative the corporate media had been trying to establish of a "hard-left" Momentum purge targeting "moderate" Labour MPs, the film actually showed Shanly *discouraging* Momentum activists keen to replace right-wing Labour MPs with left-wingers. The *Mail on Sunday* also sent an undercover journalist, Abul Taher, who infiltrated Momentum under the name "Mohammed," and published an article using the byline "Omar Wahid." Taher has a reputation for scare-mongering reporting about the "jihadis next door."[5] While undercover in Momentum, he asked Shanly silly, leading questions like "Are we Trotskyists, Max?" Shanly told me he had never trusted "Mohammed" and warned others away. The resulting *Mail on Sunday* piece had nothing of substance to back up its headline about the "cult of Corbyn" and the "hard-line left-wing" group Momentum.

But Shanly also made enemies on Labour's left. Some I spoke to who had known him were displeased by his uncritical attitude towards his friend Jon Lansman. One prominent Labour leftist told me they were irritated by how Shanly would act as if he was

---

4   Harry Hayball et al., *The work of the Labour Party's Governance and Legal Unit in relation to antisemitism, 2014 - 2019,* (London: The Labour Party, 2020), page 56. See also Asa Winstanley, "Leaks show how Labour sabotaged Corbyn," *Electronic Intifada,* 17 April 2020.

5   Abul Taher and Michael Powell, "Identified for the first time . . . the jihadis next door: The eight men who stood in prayer behind ISIS flag in London," *Mail on Sunday,* 15 June 2019.

the only person on the left who had known "my mate Tony"— the late Tony Benn MP, who had been a friend to so many on the Labour left. "Max has his good sides," another source (an aide to a left-wing Labour MP) told me. "He's a funny bloke and I do think he's got this Bennite side to him, because he was close to Benn before he died and he used to go round [to] his house."

But Shanly's life was changed by events at Oxford. The smears caused a mental health breakdown culminating in a serious psychotic episode. "I had my mental health destroyed entirely," he revealed on the deleted podcast episode. As the Israel lobby's latest major assault on the Labour Party over allegations of anti-Semitism erupted in the summer of 2018, Shanly was hospitalised. "I had a breakdown this summer and was hospitalised for six weeks," he wrote on Facebook a few months later. "I am currently taking some time out from political activism and everything else I do whilst I try to recuperate from what has been to be quite honest a hellish few years marred by depression and self-doubt."[6]

Had this really all been caused by the anti-Semitism smears? In the podcast, Shanly spoke of underlying mental health issues that had always been with him, the kind of problems typical for many young men in the UK today. But there was no doubt in his mind that events at the Oxford University Labour Club had taken those problems to a whole new level.

Factional Labour warfare at Oxford had got dirty, erupting into Alex Chalmers's resignation from the student Labour club over what he claimed was endemic anti-Semitism there and in the Oxford student left generally. The resignation made international headlines. Anti-Semitism tolerated and embraced at one of the world's most prestigious universities! The Israeli embassy accused Oxford students of "disgraceful activity." Former Labour leader Ed Miliband cancelled a speaking event, and the government's minister for universities Jo Johnson demanded Oxford investigate.[7] The JLM's newly appointed "national chair" Jeremy Newmark opined that the club had "national

---

6   Asa Winstanley, "This is the bogus anti-Semitism report that sank Jeremy Corbyn," *Electronic Intifada*, 24 August 2020.

7   Winstanley, "This is the bogus anti-Semitism report."

significance . . . as a breeding-ground for future Labour MPs" and that the resignation was an example of how Corbyn's Labour was supposedly finding it "so difficult to weed out antisemitism."[8]

But it was clear even at the time that Chalmers's allegations were baseless. The main "evidence" he gave for his wildly generalised claims that the club (and the wider student left) discriminated against Jews was that they had earlier that evening voted to endorse Israeli Apartheid Week. IAW is an annual series of talks held by the Palestine solidarity movement the world over. For right-wingers like Chalmers, expressing solidarity with Palestinians amounted to "anti-Semitism" almost by definition.

Shanly and his left-wing comrades were attacked by Chalmers and his friend David Klemperer—both from the Progress wing of the party. Progress is a Blairite faction which for many years was bankrolled by supermarket magnate Lord Sainsbury. Founded in 1996, its main goal was to keep Labour on the path set by Tony Blair: regressive on both foreign and domestic policies.[9] Chalmers typified the sort of right-wing careerist student activist that dominated groups like Labour Students (known and despised among left-wingers as NOLS—after its older title the National Organisation of Labour Students). NOLS imposed a toxic environment of perpetual warfare against the left on the entire student politics scene. It was a reactionary vanguard.

Chalmers burst onto the national stage not through any personal merit, but because of his high-profile attack against the Labour left. Due to Elliott and Shanly's proximity to Corbyn, Chalmers's attack was seen as an offensive against the new leader. The media ate it up. Chalmers had been co-chair of the Labour club. "The entire student left has some sort of problem

---

8   Jeremy Newmark, "Why does Labour find it so hard to weed out antisemitism?" *Daily Telegraph*, 17 February 2016.

9   "About," page deleted from progressonline.org.uk but available on the Internet Archive's WayBack Machine (copy archived 25 July 2017, accessed 13 June 2022).

with Jews," he wrote in a public Facebook posting.[10] Such explosive accusations would surely need to be backed up by evidence. But the lack of established facts didn't bother the mainstream media—Chalmers's claims were trumpeted without question. And they got around the world. They were repeated in the Israeli media and even made it into a piece by prominent *New York Times* columnist Roger Cohen.[11]

But where was the evidence? There were no named individuals accused of anti-Semitism in the Facebook posting, only vague allegations and rumours. Chalmers's comments about Israeli Apartheid Week made his agenda clear: it was a classic smear campaign of the type habitually launched by the pro-Israel lobby. Flying in the face of all mainstream human rights groups, Israeli and pro-Israel propagandists have for years claimed that using the word "apartheid" for Israel is anti-Semitic.[12]

The similarity was no coincidence. It turned out that Chalmers had worked for the Israel lobby itself, as an intern for BICOM, the Britain Israel Communications and Research Centre. He wrote in more detail about his claims in BICOM's journal, *Fathom*, soon after his resignation.[13] Founded in 2000, BICOM's original mission was "to bring about a significant shift in opinion in favour of Israel amongst the general public, opinion-formers, and the Jewish community."[14] A 2011 BICOM conference was titled "Winning Britain Back for Israel"—a tacit admission of its failure to shift British public opinion. They later dropped the goal of influencing the general public in favour of

---

10   Asa Winstanley, "How Israel lobby manufactured UK Labour Party's anti-Semitism crisis," *Electronic Intifada*, 28 April 2016.

11   Roger Cohen, "An Anti-Semitism of the Left," *New York Times*, 7 March 2016.

12   For the recent history of international human rights groups finally conceding the long held Palestinian position that Israel is an apartheid state, see Maureen Murphy, "What makes Amnesty's apartheid report different?" *Electronic Intifada*, 3 February 2022.

13   Alex Chalmers, "Antisemitic anti-Zionism and the scandal of Oxford University Labour Club," *Fathom*, Spring 2016.

14   Asa Winstanley, "Is Israel lobby UK quitting battle for public opinion?" *Electronic Intifada*, 27 November 2013.

focusing on elites and "opinion-formers." BICOM takes journalists on propaganda trips, leading guided tours and taking them to Israeli institutions to hob-nob with politicians, spies, and soldiers.

One of BICOM's leaders was Lorna Fitzsimons, a former Labour MP. At "The Big Tent for Israel," a 2011 Israel lobby conference, Fitzsimons ran a panel titled "Every Jew is an ambassador for Israel"—a classically anti-Semitic statement.[15] This was far from the first time that such anti-Semitism had emanated from a Zionist (in this case a gentile Zionist). But Fitzsimons's bigotry was ignored and tacitly condoned by both other Zionists and the political-media establishment. Too often anti-Semitism that serves Israel is given a free pass. As James Baldwin once put it, "In order to be a Zionist, it is not necessary to love the Jews. I know some Zionists who are definitely anti-Semitic. And to be a Jew is not necessarily to be a Zionist."[16] Years later, it emerged that Chalmers's ally at Oxford, David Klemperer, allegedly attacked another student in horribly anti-Semitic terms: "You're exactly the sort who should've died in the Holocaust."[17]

For Chalmers and the other right-wing-Labour partisans at Oxford, Israel and Zionism were important weapons against the left. For the student left at Oxford, which did not support Israeli war crimes, the allegation of anti-Semitism (no matter how baseless) was a source of great fear. Ironically, it was powerful precisely because the left *really is anti-racist* and does take such allegations seriously. They were cowed into silence. Instead of condemning Chalmers's obviously anti-Palestinian smear campaign, the student club's remaining executive issued a statement

---

15 Asa Winstanley, "Paul Flynn, BICOM and the nexus between Zionism and anti-Semitism," *Electronic Intifada*, 10 January 2012. For a copy of the conference's now-deleted programme, see Asa Winstanley, "The Electronic Intifada barred from reporting inside UK 'delegitimization' conference," *Electronic Intifada*, 26 November 2011.

16 "James Baldwin on Black-Jewish Relations, Israel and the United States," Tony Greenstein's Blog, 28 August 2020.

17 Winstanley, "This is the bogus anti-Semitism report."

taking his baseless claims seriously and saying they would "fully co-operate" with an investigation.[18]

This was a sign of things to come. No credible evidence had been offered—yet the false anti-Semitism allegations were taken seriously anyway. This set in motion a chain of events that would have repercussions for years to come—one which would ultimately lead to Corbyn's political demise. The media pressure on Labour to "do something" led to the party launching various internal disciplinary processes.

Labour Students launched an immediate "inquiry" into Chalmers's claims. It took less than a week, and it was never published (although, as we'll see in the next chapter, I did eventually get my hands on it). Students in Oxford, who had seen portions of the resulting report, told me it was the culmination of a local campaign by Chalmers and his allies against the student left. This included an alleged "dossier" compiled by Chalmers of allegations against Shanly and other leftists, which was apparently relied on by the Labour Students report.

One of the main claims was that Shanly had been "disciplined for anti-Semitic bullying" by Ruskin College for supposedly following a female Jewish student around campus and harassing her as a "filthy Zionist." But this scurrilous claim was totally denied by the principal of his college. In an email I obtained, college principal Chris Wilkes wrote that he had "looked into the allegations made against Max Shanly" and had "found no evidence of any allegations being made" against him at the college "involving anti-Semitism, or indeed anything else." A spokesperson for the college confirmed to me that the email had been written by Wilkes (who had passed away by the time I was reporting).[19] The idea that people would take this lie seriously deeply shook Shanly. "This was the worst thing," he said on the podcast. "This is why I've been so fucking depressed . . .

---

18 "Statement on Allegations of Anti-Semitism," Oxford University Labour Club website, 17 February 2016. Website deleted, but copies available at the Internet Archive's WayBack Machine (oldest copy of page archived 25 February 2016, accessed 13 June 2022).

19 Winstanley, "How Israel lobby manufactured."

they present it as if it is just a fact, with no evidence at all. No one's ever come forward to say that they are the girl—the girl doesn't exist!"

The media jumped on the Oxford allegations. To them, it was proof that Jeremy Corbyn had unleashed a tsunami of anti-Semitism. They didn't care about the dearth of actual evidence. It was a potent weapon in the anti-Corbyn media campaign and that was all that mattered. The *Daily Telegraph* was the first paper to leak allegations against Shanly and Elliott. It was pitched as evidence of Corbyn's supposed anti-Semitism. A year later the *Jewish Chronicle* claimed to have seen the Labour Students report, and published some of its allegations. But notably the paper didn't publish the document itself. When I eventually obtained it, the document confirmed my suspicions that this lack of disclosure came mainly because it contained a series of libellous statements against named individuals. The *Telegraph* reporting hinted at this too: it was carefully worded, and quoted extensively from Martin Howe, the lawyer representing Shanly and Elliott.

Labour's NEC commissioned a new investigation into the affair, one which they hoped would be more credible than the Labour Students hatchet-job. Enlisted for the inquiry was Janet Royall, Labour's former leader in Britain's unelected upper chamber the House of Lords. Debating the issue in an NEC session, it was reported that left-wing union representative Jennie Formby (who would later advance to the rank of Labour's general secretary) had questioned whether Royall was the right candidate. Royall had been on a Labour Friends of Israel delegation to occupied Palestine, Formby pointed out. This was only one of many such propaganda trips the group organises for lawmakers. But the mere asking of this question was enough to send the Israel lobby and its media allies into a frothing rage, making Formby briefly a target of the lobby. They smeared her as an anti-Semite, but her union employer Unite aggressively combatted this campaign and it was swiftly crushed.[20]

The Royall report ultimately concluded that there was no evidence of widespread or institutional anti-Semitism at Oxford

---

20   Winstanley, "How Israel lobby manufactured."

University Labour Club.[21] But instead of feeling relief at a happy conclusion, in a blog post on the Jewish Labour Movement's website soon after, Royall wrote of her "disappointment and frustration" that the headline conclusion of her report had been that there was no institutional anti-Semitism at the university. She nonetheless claimed that there was a "cultural problem" at the club and that some Jewish students did not "feel welcome."[22]

Including the Labour Students inquiry, so far there had been two internal Labour reports into "anti-Semitism" at Oxford. While the former was so libellous that it was never published, the NEC agreed to publish Royall's executive summary. But all this did nothing to ease demands by anti-Palestinian and right-wing groups to investigate "anti-Semitism" in the party. Corbyn was feeling the pressure in all sorts of ways. In the early part of 2016, around about the same time all this was happening, Labour MPs were plotting his ouster. Large numbers of them had never accepted the leadership election result and wanted him removed by almost any means necessary. Daily headlines agitated against Corbyn and talked up a Labour coup. Hostile briefings abounded. Even some of those MPs who had only "loaned" Corbyn their nominations to ensure a wider field of candidates were now regretting their choice. Former foreign minister Margaret Beckett effectively described herself as a "moron" for having nominated Corbyn. "At no point did I intend to vote for Jeremy myself," she lamented in a BBC Radio 4 interview.[23]

Like a CIA-sponsored opposition targeting a left-wing foreign government, Labour's MPs seemed poised to overthrow their socialist leader. An anti-Semitism scandal was the last

---

21 Asa Winstanley, "Instigator of anti-Semitism scam kicked out of Labour," *Electronic Intifada*, 20 May 2016.

22 Jan Royall, "Blog: Baroness Royall on her report: 'There is too often a culture of intolerance where Jews are concerned and there are clear incidents of antisemitism,'" JLM website, 17 May 2016 (Internet Archive Wayback Machine copy, 21 June 2016, accessed 13 June 2022). For context and analysis, see Asa Winstanley, "Defeating Labour's manufactured anti-Semitism crisis," *Electronic Intifada*, 26 August 2016.

23 "Margaret Beckett: I was moron to nominate Jeremy Corbyn," BBC News, 22 July 2015.

thing the leadership needed. Corbyn relented to pressure to "do something." He commissioned human rights lawyer and campaigner Shami Chakrabarti to launch an investigation into the whole issue, which concluded that Labour was "not overrun by antisemitism" (see chapter 6).

Labour's third inquiry into anti-Semitism, published in full, did nothing to defuse the growing crisis of allegations. If anything, it only seemed to keep the issue alive. Despite a passing reference by Royall to "at least one case of serious false allegations of anti-Semitism," neither the Royall nor Chakrabarti reports got to grips with the real crisis which would grip the party for the next few years: exaggerated and fabricated allegations of anti-Semitism for right-wing, anti-Palestinian, political ends. Both seemed to have accepted in general terms the smears put forward at Oxford by the right-wing, pro-Israel factions. These had been laundered into the party via the Labour Students report, which had clearly influenced Royall (who was also the vice-chair of the Chakrabarti inquiry).

Increasingly, the claim against Labour was inflated from a "crisis" of anti-Semitism under Corbyn's leadership into something new—that Labour as a whole had become "institutionally anti-Semitic." As time went by, this was especially heard from the Jewish Labour Movement.[24] That the claim of "institutional anti-Semitism" was identical to that which had been deployed against the University and College Union some years earlier was no coincidence—Newmark was leader of both of the groups that pushed these false claims.

The phrase was meant to invoke the Macpherson report, the result of a public inquiry led by retired high court judge William Macpherson. In 1999 he famously concluded that London's Metropolitan Police were guilty of institutional racism. The inquiry was triggered by the police's failure (many say refusal) to solve the 1993 murder of Stephen Lawrence, a Black teenager killed by an organised gang of white racists. The fact that the largest police force in Britain was guilty of racism on a systematic scale was exhaustively detailed by Macpherson, and

---

24 "Document lists 9 instances of anti-Semitism by Corbyn among thousands in Labour," *Times of Israel*, 5 December 2019.

the phrase "institutional racism" gained widespread public currency. "Institutional anti-Semitism" was an attempt to piggyback off of this public acceptance. It was a common theme from pro-Israel lobbyists: anti-Semitism was "the real racism."

Chalmers, Klemperer, and especially the author of the Labour Students report had set the Labour Party on a ruinous course. But who had been behind that document?

In an email I obtained in 2016, Chalmers and Klemperer were described by a senior Labour Party staffer (Mike Creighton, a right-winger) as the "two who instigated the anti-Semitism row" at Oxford. Chalmers resigned from the party a few days after he quit the club, party officials confirmed when I asked them for comment. Klemperer was suspended after it emerged that he had nominated a Liberal Democrat candidate in May 2016's local elections. Since it's against party rules to nominate a candidate for another party, Klemperer was given 14 days to appeal before being expelled from the party.[25] Chalmers also nominated the same Liberal Democrat candidate as Klemperer, a friend of theirs named Harry Samuels. All three had been Oxford delegates to the National Union of Students. And all three were involved in a campaign for Oxford to disaffiliate from the NUS. This was part of a wider right-wing campaign against the NUS, which was often viewed by the neoliberal establishment as being on the "loony left" for supporting left-wing causes and campaigning on international issues, such as the Palestinian movement for boycott, divestment, and sanctions against Israel.

* * *

Unlike Shanly, James Elliott had been involved in Palestine solidarity activism on campus. "I had literally no interest in it when I was at Oxford," Shanly explained on his podcast. He had been "too busy running around with Jon Lansman trying to change the Labour Party."

In a 2014 student newspaper article, Elliott defended his Palestine student society against a smear campaign. "Opposition

---

25 Winstanley, "Instigator of anti-Semitism scam."

to racist colonisation of Palestine is the root of the struggle," he wrote, implicitly affirming his opposition to anti-Semitism: "opposition to all forms of racism is what Palestinian solidarity is about." He also wrote that "Anti-Semitism is a tired old accusation from Zionists, retreating behind mendacious slurs when losing the arguments."[26] This latter quote would be used against him by right-wing rival Jasmin Beckett to scupper his election to the NEC in 2016. It was clumsy wording, but viewed in context it was certainly not anti-Semitic. Elliott's main point was certainly true: the pro-Israel lobby has a long history of exaggerating and even fabricating allegations of anti-Semitism to attack Palestinians and their supporters.

To help secure the 35 nominations needed to get Corbyn onto the ballot paper, left-wing activists launched a grassroots campaign to pressure their Labour MPs. Elliott played a small but crucial part in this. He had been one of two members of the Oxford University Labour Club to propose nominating Corbyn as Labour leader. The successful nomination raised the campaign's profile. More importantly, it helped convince the local Oxford East Labour MP to "lend" his nomination to Corbyn. Andrew Smith duly became the thirty-fifth Labour MP to nominate Corbyn, pushing him over the line—a crucial victory that ensured Corbyn could stand in the leadership election.[27] Smith told a student newspaper that the club's decision to nominate Corbyn had influenced his nomination, with students being "an important part" of his constituency. The victory lent momentum to the campaign, empowering the grassroots. But it also made the student left enemies. After years of New Labour hegemony in the party, a right-wing backlash against the newly emerging Corbynism was inevitable.

It came only a few months later. With Corbyn now leader, the left was seeking to entrench itself. Shanly planned to take over Young Labour for the left, something he later revealed in the deleted Novara podcast. Elliott played his role in this too, by

---

26 James Elliott, "Israel's defendants [sic] have questions to answer," *Oxford Student*, 24 January 2014.

27 Luke Mintz, "'OULC Wot Won It?' Labour Club praised for helping Jeremy Corbyn's leadership bid," *Oxford Student*, 16 June 2015.

running for the NEC seat. The National Executive Committee is Labour's key decision-making body. It writes and interprets Labour's rule book. The NEC was delicately balanced, with only a very slim majority of support for Corbyn. There was a very real prospect that, should there be a leadership challenge, a right-wing NEC would simply interpret the party's rule book in such a fashion that would drop Corbyn from the ballot paper, excluding him from even the possibility of reelection. He would once again have needed the nominations of MPs to get back on the ballot—which the "morons" like Margaret Beckett would certainly not lend him a second time. Once bitten, twice shy. It was therefore vital that a left-wing majority be secured on the NEC. Labour's right-wing MPs, acting like aggrieved CIA puppets who had lost an election in some former US client state, utterly refused to recognise the results of Corbyn's landslide leadership victory. A coup attempt seemed inevitable.

On 18 February, left-wing candidates swept the board in elections to Young Labour's national committee. Shanly gained a seat. "The left did well because we organised the unorganised," he told the *Guardian*. "We intend to continue doing so as representatives of Young Labour so as to fulfil Labour's historic role as a vehicle for the liberation of working people and their families."[28] Bennite group Campaign for Labour Party Democracy said it was "the first time in 30 years the left have taken control of Young Labour."[29] Chalmers had made his allegations only four days before the conference, but Shanly and Elliott had yet to be named in the press.

At a Young Labour conference one week later, Elliott was the left's candidate for the youth seat on Labour's NEC. He had secured endorsements from the Unite and GMB trade unions and seemed poised to win easily. The right's candidate, backed by Labour First and Progress, was Jasmin Beckett (who, as we saw in chapter 2, later attended the JLM's re-founding barbecue). But only two days before the conference the *Daily Telegraph*

---

28   Oliver Milne, "Momentum sweeps board at Labour party youth elections," *Guardian*, 19 February 2016.

29   "CLPD: Yes to a Labour Party for members," CLPD press release, 8 April 2016.

published a hit piece attacking Shanly and Elliott.[30] The article hinged on Chalmers's resignation as co-chair of the Oxford University Labour Club as its crucial background. He had quit only one week earlier. Although the piece was carefully worded so as not to directly allege the pair were anti-Semites, it strongly implied as much, saying they were being investigated by Labour Students.

The *Telegraph* piece set off a chain of events that was to destroy Shanly's mental health. Other media outlets spoke darkly of alleged anti-Semitism at Oxford, but only the *Telegraph* and Guido Fawkes actually named the pair. *The Times* also got in on the action in the days before the Young Labour conference. "Corbyn backers seize control of party's youth wing," the piece wailed.[31] So called "party moderates" were being displaced by the "hard left," the paper alleged. They had managed to "seize control" through the dastardly authoritarian method of winning an election. The piece did not report on Shanly, but it did target Elliott, whom it claimed had been "embroiled in controversy" over anti-Semitism. The short article was carefully worded, and insinuated, rather than directly alleged, that Elliott had been responsible for the anti-Semitism alleged by Chalmers.

It later emerged that Beckett and a group of her supporters had carried out a campaign against Elliott in order to influence the election in her favour.

Communist newspaper the *Morning Star* obtained logs from a Facebook group chat run by Beckett. Titled #TeamJB, the right-wing student Labour activists used the chat to plan a smear campaign against Elliott. "At the end of the day do you actually want an anti-Semite as NEC rep?" Beckett asked. "[I] think people need to know." Amid debate over whether or not to share the negative articles about Elliott on their social media, Beckett instructed her followers to go ahead: "Yes share it." But she warned them to distance themselves so that the source of the smears would be harder to detect. "Can we do it away from this

---

30 Camilla Turner, "Momentum activists investigated over alleged anti-Semitism at Oxford University," *Daily Telegraph*, 23 February 2016.

31 Michael Savage, "Corbyn backers seize control of party's youth wing," *The Times*, 20 February 2016.

campaign," she asked. She encouraged them to lobby the unions to revoke their endorsements of Elliott. One friend revealed the cynicism at the heart of their campaign. Josh Woolas (son of former Labour MP Phil Woolas) cautioned that it "needs to look like a genuine complaint about racism and not a smear campaign!" Woolas's father knew a thing or two about smears, having run an openly Islamophobic election campaign back in 2010.[32]

"Team JB's" faux-outrage was focused on Elliott's 2014 article defending the student Palestine society. Inherent in what Elliott wrote was a condemnation of genuine forms of anti-Semitism. He expressed "opposition to all forms of racism." But by taking the next sentence (about anti-Semitism being a tired accusation) out of context, they insinuated that Elliott was denying that anti-Semitism existed *at all*. Yet no fair-minded reading of the article could possibly have come to that conclusion.

There were other figures in the group chat who would become important in the intersection between the Labour right and the Israel lobby over the next few years, helping to manufacture the "anti-Semitism crisis." These included Robbie Young, a National Union of Students officer who—as revealed in Al Jazeera series *The Lobby*—worked tirelessly to undermine left-wing NUS President Malia Bouattia, who was vocally active in the Palestine solidarity movement. Two other such figures were Jewish Labour Movement activists Liron Velleman and Miriam Mirwitch. Both would later be appointed to positions on the JLM executive committee (Mirwitch would two years later become chairperson of Young Labour).

"As the Jewish Labour Movement delegate I find it incredibly upsetting that someone like that can even be on the ballot paper," wrote Velleman to the rest of Team JB, apparently advocating for Elliott's candidacy to be terminated by executive fiat. Others wanted Elliott reported. One chat participant suggested writing an official letter of complaint about Elliott to Labour official Stephen Donnelly. "That sounds good," wrote Mirwitch. "Maybe the letter could be sent to Iain McNicol rather than Stephen," she continued, referring to Labour's general

---

32 "Phil Woolas defends 'extremist vote' election claim," BBC News, 15 September 2010.

secretary.[33] The practice of complaining to party officials about supposed anti-Semitism by left-wing pro-Corbyn members would become wearyingly familiar.

The smear campaign worked. James Elliott narrowly lost the election to Labour's NEC. Jasmin Beckett was elected to the seat by a single vote, amid allegations of procedural irregularities. The manipulated vote for the youth seat was the first time the party saw "organised smears of anti-Semitism," left-wing NEC member and union activist Martin Mayer later recalled. As well as the smears, his union, Unite, also found "evidence of manipulation of the conference and ballot process by Labour officials." Mayer wrote that he had "little doubt that the witch-hunt, including many false charges of anti-Semitism, is part of a wider strategy to undermine Jeremy's leadership, engineered by those who firmly believe he and his supporters have no right to be in control of 'their' party."[34] Whether or not the election was directly rigged, there seems little doubt that Elliott would have won were it not for the anti-Semitism smear campaign.

Beckett used her position on the NEC over the next few years to advocate for what she claimed were "moderate" policies. In other words, she was trying to drag Labour back to the days of privatisation, war, hostility to migrants, and friendliness to Israel.

She also advocated against the Palestine solidarity movement. In a 2018 NEC report Beckett wrote that she had been on a delegation to occupied Palestine with a pro-Israel group, including "on the Lebanese and Syrian borders," presumably in the company of Israeli soldiers. "We must steer away from the BDS movement as boycotts only serve to create further divisions," she claimed—a typical Israel lobby talking point.[35] A few months after her election, Corbyn would come within a

---

33 Luke James, "Labour NEC entrant in smear scandal," *Morning Star*, 26 February 2016. For a link to a PDF file showing the entire group chat, see Winstanley, "How Israel lobby manufactured."

34 Martin Mayer, "How Labour's Right Wing Tried to Fight Back: an Eye-Witness Report," *Labour Briefing*, 27 June 2018.

35 "NEC Report -January 2018," Jasmin Beckett -Labour NEC [blog], 31 January 2018 (accessed 13 June 2022).

hair's breadth of being removed as party leader by an administrative coup of party bureaucrats. In the end, the NEC only very narrowly voted to interpret party rules in the incumbent's favour, putting him back on the ballot paper during the 2016 leadership campaign.

What happened at Oxford University Labour Club in February 2016 should not be underestimated. As with the Israel lobby's years of "lawfare" against the University and College Union, the idea was to portray the Labour Party as "institutionally anti-Semitic." Although Corbyn had been attacked with false allegations of anti-Semitism right from the moment he announced his leadership campaign in 2015, Oxford represented something far bigger.

Before Oxford, the media and the Israel lobby were smearing Corbyn by association, attacking his willingness to bring political representatives of Hamas and Hizballah to the negotiating table in the UK (as he had done with Irish republicans in the 1980s). But the campaign at Oxford against the Corbyn project ramped up the attacks to a whole new level. It was about more than Corbyn—it was a battle for the very soul of the party. Would Labour continue to be a business-led, right-wing party run by an alliance of technocratic and neoliberal elites, or would it transform itself into a mass movement of the socialist left? To the establishment, the Corbyn phenomenon that erupted unexpectedly in the summer of 2015 represented the threat of change. Even worse for the Blairites and their allies, Corbyn represented the spectre of a left-wing *government*. Despite their misleading cant about "electability," that was the real fear. Blair himself at one point was candid: "I wouldn't want to win on an old-fashioned leftist platform. Even if I thought it was the route to victory, I wouldn't take it."[36]

Such a popular, socialist government would not be a natural ally of the state of Israel—especially if led by a patron of the Palestine Solidarity Campaign. Israel and its UK propagandists, then, were natural partners for the Labour right's long campaign of sabotage against Corbyn. And several key right-wing Labour

---

36 Jon Stone, "Tony Blair says he wouldn't want a left-wing Labour party to win an election," *Independent*, 22 July 205.

activists were also Israel lobbyists at the same time. This was the case with the leader of Labour First, Luke Akehurst—a former arms industry lobbyist and the director of a BICOM spin-off candidly titled "We Believe in Israel."

The manufactured crisis at the Oxford student Labour club was a conscious attempt to avert the twin catastrophes represented by the threat of Corbynism—popular, mass movement socialism and an end to the Labour Party's historic support for the state of Israel and its crimes against the Palestinian people. Labour was to be portrayed as anti-Semitic through and through. This smear campaign won many successes. Most importantly, it meant that Corbyn lost the media initiative. Instead of focusing on his socialist policies (which polls repeatedly showed were popular) he was far too often on the defensive, apologising for anti-Semitism, promising investigations and acquiescing to the expulsion of high-profile socialists who had actually said nothing anti-Semitic.

Oxford also represented a turning point for Shanly's mentor Jon Lansman. A key influence on Corbyn's leadership, Lansman began to capitulate to the anti-Semitism narrative. Lansman initially put up a defence of Shanly and Elliott—albeit a weak one. This was unsurprising given that the smear campaign against the pair threatened to tar him by association. Writing in a *Jewish Chronicle* opinion piece soon after Beckett's questionable NEC victory, he attempted damage control. "Knowing two of the individuals at the centre of the current row," Lansman wrote, he regarded "neither of them as being in any way anti-Semitic." Lansman did not name the pair, but it was clear from the wider media coverage he was talking about Shanly and Elliott. "Within the Labour Party," Lansman continued, "some people have factional reasons for stoking the flames of the bandwagon that [Israeli newspaper] *Haaretz* called the 'Oxford firestorm.' Oxford University Labour Club, it turns out, is a key battle ground between the Corbynistas and the Blairites for control of Labour's youth section."[37]

---

37 Jon Lansman, "My doubts about Oxford Labour antisemitism claim," *Jewish Chronicle*, 25 February 2016.

Lansman also argued on his blog that "a frenzied witch-hunt is not the way to combat anti-Semitism or any form of racism."[38] But Lansman was prepared to make such arguments only for a select few. He soon set about throwing others under the bus at the first allegation of anti-Semitism. He later argued that the left should stop using the word Zionism altogether. Conveniently for Zionists, Lansman's moratorium on the words "Zionism" and "Zionist" only seemed to apply to anti-Zionists, and not to pro-Zionists—or to Lansman himself.[39]

Shanly and Elliott also seemed cowed. I first wrote about what happened in Oxford in April 2016, in a long article about the whole anti-Semitism witch hunt then erupting. I revealed the evidence that Alex Chalmers had—completely ignored by the corporate media—worked for pro-Israel lobby group BICOM. In the course of writing that article, I asked Shanly and Elliott to comment. Neither felt able to do so on the record. Elliott cited Janet Royall's inquiry, which was then in progress, saying that he couldn't comment until after that.[40] But the situation didn't change after she'd released her conclusions.

Over the next few years, I periodically attempted to persuade both to tell their story, with no success. Shanly said he just wanted to forget about it. But at other times he said he would tell his story when the time was right. The right time never seemed to come—until that episode of his podcast.

Why was it deleted? Given Shanly's proximity to Lansman, often defending him from the criticisms of the left, it seems likely it was Lansman who advised him to take it down. The admission that Shanly was involved in a planned attempt to "take over" Young Labour was probably embarrassing to the Momentum leader, who was then on a charm offensive towards the Labour right, trying to persuade them that he was not leading an army

---

38   Jon Lansman, "A frenzied witch-hunt is not the way to combat antisemitism or any form of racism," *Left Futures*, 9 May 2016.

39   Jon Lansman, "Why the Left must stop talking about 'Zionism,'" *Left Futures*, 2 May 2016.

40   Winstanley, "How Israel lobby manufactured."

of "hard left infiltrators," as some of the more shrill headlines about his group claimed.

Shanly revealing what had really happened at Oxford was probably embarrassing to Lansman too. It would not be the last time Shanly departed from Lansman's "correct line." In 2018 Shanly publicly supported Marc Wadsworth, after the veteran Black anti-racist was expelled from the Labour Party on entirely spurious grounds (see chapter 6). Shanly said the expulsion "brings the Labour Party into disrepute more than his offending comment ever did" and that Wadsworth had been subjected to "trial by media." But the tweet was soon deleted. And by the following year he'd changed his tune altogether. In another episode of *All The Best*, he castigated Wadsworth in rather patronising terms as having spoken "out of turn," called the anti-racist activist a "tit" and suggested that Labour had been right to expel him, even if what he'd said was not anti-Semitic.[41]

Despite acknowledging in the *Jewish Chronicle* that the Labour right had deliberately stoked the flames at Oxford, Lansman also wanted to put the episode behind him. As we'll see in more detail in chapter 7, Lansman began working closely with the Jewish Labour Movement. By 2018, he had made a very public about-face, deciding that Labour had a "major" problem with anti-Semitism. When I challenged him on Twitter in early 2019 about why he was ignoring the fact that the "crisis" was actually started by Chalmers and other pro-Israel activists, Lansman responded that "whatever its origins Labour's anti-Semitism crisis is real now," and threw in a smear of his own for good measure: "Deny it and you're part of the problem."[42] He gave no evidence for his claims. The publicly available figures of *allegations* of anti-Semitism reported to the party at the time showed that even these (often spurious) allegations concerned tiny numbers: amounting to 0.06 percent of the party's membership.

* * *

---

41 "All The Best: Solidarity Forever," Novara Media, 4 July 2019.

42 Jon Lansman, Twitter, 26 February 2019.

What became of Elliott, Shanly, Chalmers, and Klemperer?

James Elliott went on to train as a lawyer.

Alex Chalmers seemed to disappear from public life after joining the Liberal Democrats. Defection to that party would prove to be the fate of many such promoters of the "Labour anti-Semitism crisis" smear.

David Klemperer got a job with something called the Institute for Government, a think tank funded by Progress-backer Lord Sainsbury (among the institute's minor donors was the Israeli embassy in London, which gave as much as £6,000 in speakers' fees and training). Although he had been told that he would be expelled from Labour due to his nomination of a Liberal Democratic candidate for the council elections, by 2019, Klemperer was back in the party. It's unclear on what basis he was readmitted after so flagrantly breaking party rules—especially considering that left-wing Labour members had been suspended for far less (such as posting on social media about the Green Party).

Saddest of all was Max Shanly. As one of the very first people in the Labour Party after Corbyn to be publicly smeared as an anti-Semite, it is particularly tragic that Shanly seemed to have followed his idol Lansman in capitulating to the witch hunt. In one online posting defending Lansman from a left-wing Twitter user who criticised his unelected control of Momentum, Shanly replied with an anti-Semitism smear of his own. "No one owns Momentum," he claimed, "it's a membership association and the staffing company is a company limited by guarantee (which has no shares or owners). The whole 'Lansman is the owner of Momentum' schtick very much plays into anti-Semitic tropes in my opinion."[43] But, as records filed with Companies House showed at the time, Lansman was indeed the sole owner of Jeremy For Leader Limited, the company to which Momentum members sent their membership dues.[44] Zombie-like, the witch hunt seemed to consume its targets and change them utterly, blackmailed into capitulation.

---

43 Max Shanly, Twitter, 12 August 2019.

44 Asa Winstanley, "How Jon Lansman joined Labour's witch hunt," *Electronic Intifada*, 7 October 2019.

Who had really been responsible for the genesis of the witch hunt at Oxford University? Was there more to it than just the usual right-wing student politics? Who wrote the mysterious Labour Students report? Beyond the involvement of the Israel lobby, was there a more direct role played by the Israeli state itself in manufacturing the anti-Semitism crisis?

I eventually managed to obtain a key document which, taken alongside Al Jazeera's revelations, proved that, indeed, there was.

CHAPTER FOUR

THE LOBBY

The Labour Students report was written by none other than Michael Rubin, a young right-wing Labour activist with close ties to the Israeli embassy.

Rubin was rewarded for his efforts. Concluding his term as chairperson of Labour Students, he stepped right into a paid Parliamentary Officer position for Labour Friends of Israel. He was subsequently caught on camera admitting that LFI and the Israeli embassy "work really closely together . . . behind the scenes."

Janet Royall later made reference to Rubin's investigation in her own report, describing it as an "internal investigation" by Labour Students. Royall explained she'd had "full access" to the Rubin report. But Labour's general secretary advised that "publication of their report might compromise my work," Royall wrote. "Labour Students, helpfully, agreed not to publish their own report," she explained. Publication might have exposed just how ridiculous the "anti-Semitism crisis" really was.

After years of effort, I managed to obtain the Rubin report, publishing selected extracts. The document was an obviously partisan attack on the left. Its main weapon was trumped-up allegations of anti-Semitism, including straight-up fabrications. Max Shanly and James Elliott were its primary targets.

One former student attacked in the report, who asked not to be named, told me that an anti-Semitic quote the report had attributed to them was inaccurate. According to the student, someone had falsely inserted the word "Jewish" into a statement the student had made about the influence of the wealthy over elections. "What I actually said was that there is 'influence wielded over elections by high–net-worth individuals.' I would never blame this on Jewish people," the former student said. "The sections of the report on me are false. Labour Students never even contacted me to get my side of the story." Asked at the time to address the allegation that he had fabricated this anti-Semitic quotation, Rubin did not reply to my request for comment.[1]

As Shanly explained on his deleted podcast episode, the allegations in Rubin's Labour Students report were little more than rumours. "It all comes down to Michael Rubin's report where people say, 'I heard so and so, I heard Max did this from so and so.' It's no fucking proof, it's just fucking hearsay!"

Another student named in the report (who asked not to be named) told me it had "ruined" their life. The document set a toxic precedent, with the false story making it into international press. As Rubin himself later privately admitted, the Oxford University Labour Club affair was the first major claim of anti-Semitism against Corbyn's Labour.[2]

Rubin's ties to the Israeli embassy predated his hiring by Labour Friends of Israel. In the undercover Al Jazeera footage, he admitted to prior contact with Shai Masot, the embassy spy exposed in the documentary. "I knew Shai in my role at Labour Students, we did a couple of things together," he said.[3] This showed that Rubin had been working closely with an Israeli spy during the same period he had written the original "Labour anti-Semitism" report that had caused so much damage. Was the report one of the "couple of things" he had done together with Masot? Rubin did not answer my request for comment at the time of my original report.

Israel seemed to be blurring the lines between its allied pro-Israel lobby groups overseas and its own espionage

---

[1] Asa Winstanley, "This is the bogus anti-Semitism report that sank Jeremy Corbyn," *Electronic Intifada*, 24 August 2020.

[2] Al Jazeera Investigations, *The Lobby*, episode 1, timecode 18:15. Rubin calls it "kind of a first instance of anti-Semitism" in Labour.

[3] *The Lobby*, episode 1, timecode 15:30.

operations. It was developing a network of front groups in the UK and passing them off as "Jewish community" organisations.

* * *

Another such proxy was the Jewish Labour Movement. One month before Newmark and the "new guard" met to plan their takeover of the JLM, it was all change at the Israeli embassy in London. Netanyahu imposed his own spokesperson Mark Regev as the new ambassador. The day before voting began in the Labour Party leadership election, an Israeli TV channel reported that Regev would be replacing career diplomat Daniel Taub.[4]

Born in Australia as Mark Freiberg, in the early 1980s Regev volunteered for the Israeli army, settled in a kibbutz near the Golan Heights (a Syrian territory illegally occupied by Israel since 1967) and picked a new Hebrew surname. Regev's native English made him a natural choice as Israeli propagandist in the UK. He was already a familiar face on international TV screens, having served eight years in the prime minister's office. "What Regev brings is the ability to hold the line when there is bad publicity," gushed one anonymous British diplomat. "He does this relentlessly."[5]

Regev defended Netanyahu during some of Israel's most devastating wars against the Palestinian people in Gaza. In 2014 he gave a quite brazen performance in defence of the killing of the Bakr boys—four young Palestinian children killed by Israeli shelling on a Gaza beach, in full view of the world's television cameras (international journalists had been staying at a nearby hotel).[6] "I don't believe the person—if it was an Israeli—who fired and killed those four boys knew that they were children,"

---

4 "Labour leadership: Cooper and Burnham bids ahead of September election," BBC News, 13 May 2015. "PM's spokesman said tapped as new ambassador to UK," *Times of Israel*, 14 August 2015.

5 Kim Sengupta, "Mark Regev: The one-man Israeli defence force who is set to become ambassador to Britain," *Independent*, 14 August 2019.

6 Ali Abunimah, "Children die playing football, in taxi with grandma, as Israel bombs Gaza for tenth day," *Electronic Intifada*, 16 July 2014.

Regev claimed, to the incredulity of Channel 4 News anchor Jon Snow.[7] Due to such associations with a right-wing prime minister, Regev is often thought of as being on the right of Israeli politics. But in fact he grew up in Zionist groups that describe themselves as left-wing. This confusion is a sign of how meaningless the distinction is between the Zionist right and the Zionist "left."

In Australia, the young Mark Freiberg was part of the Ichud Habonim,[8] a Zionist group which recruited Jewish teens to the kibbutzim—collective, but racist, Israeli settlements which did not have a single Arab member until 2008.[9] With his knowledge of the left, Regev was well placed to impose a divide-and-rule style strategy to sabotage the British left. He explicitly articulated as much in Al Jazeera's undercover video, as a transcript of unused footage shot for the series shows.

"In Britain and much of Western Europe . . . if you are young and left-wing, you automatically adopt an anti-Israel position. That is the fashion," he lamented. "You wear these sort of jeans and you don't like Israel because that's part of your milieu." The fashion was "why it's important to come here [to Labour conference], because we want to try and change that milieu." But the Israeli government's strategy abroad should not be openly pro-Israel, Regev argued. Instead, they would try to muddy the water. "We want people to think more nuanced. That it's not black and white. It's not like the Israelis are devils and the Palestinians are saints, there is a more complex reality."

The undercover series shows him speaking at a private meeting behind the scenes at Labour's 2016 conference in Liverpool. Some of this footage was used in Al Jazeera's series, showing Regev urging the small group to "say *in the language of social democracy*, these people are misogynistic, they are anti-women,

---

7   "Gaza: Mark Regev interviewed by Jon Snow about IDF attacks," Channel 4 News YouTube channel, 28 August 2014.

8   Greer Fay Cashman, "Israel's man in London: Ambassador Mark Regev will go anywhere," *Jerusalem Post*, 14 October 2017.

9   "Kibbutz admits Arab as member," *Jewish Chronicle*, 13 June 2008. Ben Sales, "First Arab Muslim accepted as kibbutz member," *Jerusalem Post*, 12 June 2008.

they are homophobic, they are racist, they are anti-Semitic, they are reactionary. What is progressive about these groups? ... Why are people who consider themselves progressive in Britain supporting reactionaries like Hamas and Hezbollah? I think that's what we need to say. It's an important message" (my emphasis).

Regev's use of the phrase "in the language of social democracy" is telling, much like when Jeremy Newmark had written about his pro-Israel strategy of deploying "a robust political discourse, rooted in the politics of the left" in "their own backyard." Both ostensible leftists seemed to think of the left as something external. The similarity is no coincidence. Sitting next to Regev while he made those remarks was none other than Newmark himself. The JLM leader proceeded to explain the advantage of his "intelligence" gathering for Regev and relate the "wheels within wheels" intrigue he had fomented within Momentum, as we saw in chapter 2. This approach was not unique to Regev and Newmark. It was part of a wider Israeli strategy articulated since 2010, one specifically advocated by Israel's anti-BDS Ministry of Strategic Affairs, and before that by the Reut Institute, an Israeli-government-endorsed think tank, as we'll see later in this chapter.

Regev had a wide network of groups to help him implement this strategy in the UK: the Israel lobby.

* * *

The Israel lobby remains influential and well-funded. But it does not have full control of British or American foreign policy and its influence is not as hegemonic as it once was. Yet Israel lobby cash still has a significant effect. In the sense that it uses propaganda to lobby governments and influence the media, Israel is little different from other Middle Eastern countries. There are multi-million-dollar lobbies to influence US policies in favour of Saudi Arabia, the United Arab Emirates, and Qatar, for example. Especially in the case of the former two, these interests very often align with Israel's—increasingly so over the last decade. Israel's natural alliances in the region are with other repressive, violent dictatorships aligned with US imperialism.

Israel and its lobby have always used anti-Semitism as a political weapon. They deploy false allegations of anti-Semitism as a way to defame, smear, and distract their critics. Most people involved in campaigning for Palestinian rights in the West have stories of being falsely smeared with anti-Semitism.

But as the global movement for justice in Palestine has slowly grown in size and influence over the past two decades, so have more and more people grown alert to this tactic. The Israel lobby even recognises as much.

"Anti-Semitism as a smear is not what it used to be," Jonathan Schanzer, an American pro-Israel lobbyist, privately conceded in 2016. Schanzer's comments were revealed in a leaked, never-broadcast Al Jazeera series titled *The Lobby—USA*, the sequel to the UK series. Schanzer is a senior vice president of the Foundation for Defence of Democracies, a leading neoconservative pro-Israel think tank in Washington, DC. The undercover footage also revealed that the FDD effectively operates as an unregistered agent of a foreign state—Israel—potentially in violation of US law. *The Lobby—USA* was at first delayed by the Qatari TV channel, and later indefinitely shelved after a massive censorship push by the very same Israel lobby it exposed. At the *Electronic Intifada*, we managed to obtain all four parts of the series, releasing them online in 2018.[10]

The footage caught a senior Israeli official stating unambiguously that "This is something that only a country, with its resources, can do the best. We have FDD, we have others working on this."[11] What the FDD and other cut-outs are doing on behalf of Israel amounts to intelligence operations against US civilian targets: "We've got the budget, we can bring things to the table that are quite different . . . Data gathering, working

---

10   "Watch the film the Israel lobby didn't want you to see," *Electronic Intifada*, 2 November 2018 (for episodes one and two). "Watch final episodes of Al Jazeera film on US Israel lobby, *Electronic Intifada*, 6 November 2018.

11   *The Lobby - USA*, episode 3, timecode 29:12. For context and analysis, see Asa Winstanley, "What's in Al Jazeera's undercover film on the US Israel lobby?" *Electronic Intifada*, 5 March 2018. This piece was released before the film itself, based on an interview with a source who'd seen it. It proved to be entirely accurate.

on activist organisations, money trail."[12] Sima Vaknin-Gil, the official, was director of Israel's anti-BDS Ministry of Strategic Affairs, and previously a high-level Israeli intelligence officer with two decades' experience.[13]

Israel's Ministry of Strategic Affairs is the key to understanding much about how the Israel lobby has operated since 2015.

* * *

Vaknin-Gil's tacit admission should not be underestimated. In effect she was stating that the operations of FDD and other pro-Israel lobby groups amounted to the actions of "a country, with its resources"—i.e., the actions of Israel. She made her unguarded comments at a conference of the Israeli American Council, an Israel lobby group bankrolled by late right-wing casino mogul Sheldon Adelson and his wife Miriam.[14] Vaknin-Gil probably thought it safe to speak in a more candid fashion among friends. Under US law, foreign lobbyists are required to register under the Foreign Agents Registration Act, known as FARA. But in practice the Israel lobby seems to be largely exempt from this provision.

After *The Lobby*, the UK series, aired in 2017, some of its subjects realised that one sequence of footage had been filmed in the US, and that Al Jazeera must also have had an undercover journalist in the US. It would have been clear from the camera angles who had filmed the undercover footage, so the gig was up for their undercover journalist "Tony," Al Jazeera's James Kleinfeld.

The investigative unit perhaps underestimated the Israel lobby's ability to bring political and financial pressure to bear on the channel. So too, they overestimated the Qatari government's willingness to hold out to such pressure. In April 2018,

---

12   *The Lobby - USA*, episode 3, timecode 28:33.

13   Asa Winstanley, "Meet the spies injecting Israeli propaganda into your news feed," *Electronic Intifada*, 24 February 2018.

14   Asa Winstanley, "Miriam Adelson now leads Sheldon's pro-Israel empire," *Electronic Intifada*, 29 January 2021. Miriam Adelson's husband Sheldon died that month.

the Zionist Organisation of America claimed that it had successfully convinced the Emir of Qatar, Tamim bin Hamad Al Thani, to cancel the series altogether.[15] The ZOA's Morton Klein made this claim after a trip to the capital Doha. Al Jazeera denied it, and the head of the investigative unit, Clayton Swisher, called Klein's claim that the series was anti-Semitic a "shameful fabrication" (Klein had of course not watched it).

Despite the channel's protestations, the reality was that the series still hadn't seen the light of day. It was indefinitely shelved. But director general Mostefa Souag denied this, after the *Electronic Intifada* and Max Blumenthal's the Grayzone both released excerpts. Responding to reporters' questions at the National Press Club in Washington, DC, Souag denied the Emir had interfered. He also dismissed Klein's claim to have persuaded the Emir to bury the series: "The decision about this documentary was done long before that visit." Souag claimed it would still air once minor legal issues could be straightened out, saying that the series "has never been cancelled. It is delayed. And pending."[16]

But our sources told a very different story. The series had already been thoroughly vetted by lawyers, they said. More stringent US laws around undercover filming than in the UK made this important. But this thorough legal process had been completed. The only remaining issues were political. Another source, who had been briefed by a top-level figure in Doha, told me that the real reasons for the film's shelving were "national security" fears.

As unbelievable as it sounds, it was being rumoured in Doha that broadcasting the series could start a war. The fear was that the broadcast of the new series would lead the US to withdraw its massive Al Udeid air base—facilitating an invasion by hostile neighbours. Qatar paid more than $1 billion during the 1990s to construct the base, now the largest US air base

---

15 Asa Winstanley, "Al Jazeera denies it canceled US Israel lobby film," *Electronic Intifada*, 24 April 2018.

16 Asa Winstanley, "Al Jazeera denies Qatari emir censored Israel lobby film," *Electronic Intifada*, 10 October 2018.

in the region.[17] But with the endorsement of Donald Trump in 2017, Saudi Arabia, the UAE, and Egypt imposed an embargo on Qatar, fingering it as a major funder of "terrorism" in the region. Qatar was already being squeezed by its regional competitors. And it seemed to fear that the release of *The Lobby—USA* could be the final straw. There were reports of a planned mercenary invasion from the Emirates.[18]

The Saudis and the UAE were already very much in bed with the Israelis. A new Israeli embassy was opened in the UAE capital Abu Dhabi in June 2021.[19] Now, with the Israel lobby breathing down their necks, the Qataris decided to get in on the action. Washington lobbyists working for Qatar began a charm offensive—specifically targeting the Israel lobby. In late 2017 and early 2018, the country ploughed a quarter of a million dollars' worth of donations to the most extreme right-wing Zionist organisations. The Zionist Organisation of America was gifted $100,000—possibly explaining Mort Klein's visit to Doha. Nick Muzin, one of the lobbyists hired by Qatar to work on this supposed "dialogue with the Jewish community," was given a monthly retainer of $50,000—later increased to an eye-watering $300,000.[20] It was only after all this came to light that Al Jazeera's director general Mostefa Souag explicitly denied that Al Jazeera had cancelled the US series. The financial ties made his claim particularly unbelievable.

After being the first outlet to publish details of the series's revelations, the *Electronic Intifada* became the first to release clips from the series itself.[21] Finally, we released the entire four-part

---

17 Brad Lendon, "Qatar hosts largest US military base in Mideast," CNN, 6 June 2017.

18 Asa Winstanley and Ali Abunimah, "'National security' cited as reason Al Jazeera nixed Israel lobby film," *Electronic Intifada*, 4 June 2018.

19 Tamara Nassar, "UAE, Israeli leaders embrace over dead Palestinian bodies," *Electronic Intifada*, 29 June 2021.

20 Tamara Nassar and Ali Abunimah, "Qatar funded Zionist Organization of America," *Electronic Intifada*, 10 July 2018.

21 Winstanley, "What's in Al Jazeera's undercover film." Asa Winstanley and Ali Abunimah, "Censored film names Adam Milstein as Canary Mission funder," *Electronic Intifada*, 27 August 2018.

documentary online in November 2018, alongside France's *Orient XXI* and Lebanon's *Al-Akhbar*, which subtitled the episodes into French and Arabic.

What the UK and US series revealed together was explosive: Israel lobby groups on both sides of the Atlantic run covert operations against US and British citizens in order to sabotage Palestinian human rights campaigns. Many ostensibly American and British groups—some of which claim to represent the "mainstream" Jewish community—are in effect arms of the Israeli state.

* * *

One episode of the UK series makes these ties explicit. In part two, Al Jazeera's undercover reporter "Robin" went deep into the pro-Israel lobby groups that specifically target the Labour Party. He was so thoroughly embraced that the Israeli embassy's "senior political officer" Shai Masot recruited him to found a new youth wing for Labour Friends of Israel. Robin spoke to Michael Rubin, Labour Friends of Israel's parliamentary officer. In the footage, Rubin spells out the nature of their relationship with the Israelis.

"The embassy helps us quite a lot. When bad news stories come out about Israel, the embassy sends us information so we can still counter it," he explained. The Israeli embassy no doubt sends lots of people information, but that doesn't necessarily mean those groups are cut-outs or fronts. But what Rubin described was much more intimate. LFI and the embassy "work really closely together," he said. "But a lot of it is behind the scenes." The reason for this secrecy? "We've got to be careful, because I think there are some people who would be happy to be involved in a Young LFI but wouldn't necessarily be happy if it was seen as an embassy thing."

LFI wants to broaden its base of support beyond the ultra-Zionists like Louise Ellman and Ian Austin. There are others who give more equivocal support for LFI, dressing it up as "dialogue" between "both sides." That would be harder if Young LFI was openly "an embassy thing." Rather than advertising the links between the embassy and the prospective LFI youth wing, Rubin wanted to have "Shai [Masot] helping in the background . . . definitely keeping Shai up to date and let him know what we're doing. I think we just have to be careful not to be seen as Young Israeli Embassy."

But Rubin made it clear that not being "seen" with the Israeli embassy was purely a matter of keeping up appearances. "We do work really closely together, it's just publicly we just try to keep LFI as a separate identity to the [Israeli] embassy because being LFI allows us to reach out to people who wouldn't want to get involved with the embassy."[22]

A "separate identity" from the Israeli embassy is the very definition of a front group. Rubin spelled it out: "We work with the ambassador and the embassy quite a lot." He explained that MP Joan Ryan, then LFI's chairperson, will "speak to Shai [Masot] most days."[23] A group that maintains a working relationship with the agents of a foreign state on a daily basis is far more than simply friendly towards that state.

Who was this man that at least one Labour MP worked with every day? Shai Masot came to public attention thanks only to Al Jazeera. The undercover footage demonstrated that he was at the forefront of the Israeli embassy's covert activities inside the Labour Party. Masot introduced himself as working for the Israeli embassy and his business card stated he was their "senior political officer." When exposed, the Israeli ambassador apologised to the British government and Masot was sent home. He seems to have been thrown under the bus by his superiors. The embassy distanced itself from Masot, claiming that he was only junior, temporary staff and that he was not a diplomat. The latter point was technically true, since Masot did not appear on the diplomatic lists.[24] But that only begs the wider question of why Masot—who had worked closely with the ambassador

---

22   *The Lobby*, episode 2, timecode 5:06. For context and a video cued to the correct position, see Asa Winstanley, "Is Labour Friends of Israel an Israeli embassy front?" *Electronic Intifada*, 12 January 2017.

23   *The Lobby*, episode 1, timecode 16:03.

24   Ali Abunimah, "Who is lying about Israeli embassy agent Shai Masot?" *Electronic Intifada*, 12 January 2017.

himself—was allowed by the embassy to pass himself off as a diplomat when he was not. Documents later exposed by the *Electronic Intifada* show that Masot was likely an agent for the Ministry of Strategic Affairs,[25] Israel's semi-covert global agency dedicated to carrying out sabotage operations against BDS and the wider Palestine solidarity movement.[26]

The series made the front page of the *Mail on Sunday* on 8 January 2017, ahead of the first episode's broadcast. On its front-page splash, the conservative paper went with the angle that would most appeal to its readers: "Israel plot to 'take down' Tory minister." This was arguably the single most explosive revelation in the series.[27]

Masot had been caught by Al Jazeera's undercover journalists conspiring with British civil servant Maria Strizzolo to "take down" a Conservative government minister, and any other MPs deemed even mildly critical of Israel. Their target, Alan Duncan, was at the time a senior minister in the foreign office acting, on occasion, as deputy to cover for then foreign minister Boris Johnson. Duncan was not on board with the Conservative Friends of Israel agenda, and had in the past been critical of West Bank settlements. To Masot and Strizzolo (who was an aide to MP and leading Conservative Friends of Israel lobbyist Robert Halfon), this made him a target for political assassination—part of a "hit list," as she put it. Strizzolo suggested she might orchestrate "a little scandal" for the minister. This seems to have been a particularly sinister allusion to causing problems for him in his private life. In 2002 Duncan had been the first serving Conservative MP to come out as gay.[28]

---

25 Asa Winstanley, "Disgraced Israeli agent Shai Masot attended minister's secret London meeting," *Electronic Intifada*, 8 December 2017.

26 Ali Abunimah, "Leaked report highlights Israel lobby's failures," *Electronic Intifada*, 28 April 2017.

27 Asa Winstanley, "Secret video reveals Israeli plot to 'take down' UK minister," *Electronic Intifada*, 8 January 2017.

28 Asa Winstanley, "Probe into UK civil servant who plotted 'hit list' with Israeli embassy," *Electronic Intifada*, 10 January 2017.

After the *Mail on Sunday* splashed Al Jazeera's revelations, Strizzolo quit her post at the education ministry. The ministry announced it would launch an investigation. In 2019 I asked to see the results of the investigation under the Freedom of Information Act. The response soon came: "There was no investigation into Maria Strizzolo as she resigned the same day as the story was released in the media."[29]

Writing in the *Mail on Sunday*, an anonymous minister who had served in David Cameron's government wrote that "the Conservative Party wants pro-Israel donors' money" and that as a result "British foreign policy is in hock to Israeli influence at the heart of our politics, and those in authority have ignored what is going on." I was told by a reliable source that this mystery minister was in fact Alan Duncan himself, although I was unable to verify this. "Even now, if I were to reveal who I am, I would be subjected to a relentless barrage of abuse and character assassination," the piece explained. It also called for "a full inquiry into the Israeli embassy, the links, access, and funding of the CFI and LFI, and an undertaking from all political parties that they welcome the financial and political support of the UK Jewish community, but won't accept any engagement linked to Israel until it stops building illegally on Palestinian land."[30]

Despite the *Mail on Sunday* headlines, the majority of the series focused on the Labour Party. There was a good reason for this, explained by Masot himself. "For years, every [Labour] MP that joined the parliament, the first thing that they used to do is go to join the LFI. They're not doing it anymore in the Labour Party. [For] CFI they are doing it automatically." Speaking to Robin, Masot gave the bottom line: "Out of the 40 new MPs who just got in at the [2015] elections, all of those ones were in the CFI, Conservative Friends of Israel. In the LFI it didn't happen, obviously. And you need to get more people on board." Masot's recruitment of Robin was an attempt to halt this decline.

---

29 William Brown, the Department for Education, email to author, 5 November 2019.

30 Simon Walters, "Israel plot to 'take down' Tory minister: Astonishing undercover video captures diplomat conspiring with rival MP's aide to smear Deputy Foreign Secretary," *Mail on Sunday*, 8 January 2017.

Al Jazeera's months-long investigation revealed a lot about how the lobby operates. Most infamously, Masot was caught discussing what he said was "more than one million pounds" in funding from the Israeli embassy with LFI's leading MP Joan Ryan. "What happened with the names we put into the embassy, Shai?" asked Ryan. The money was earmarked for government-directed junkets to the country, Masot explained. "I've got the money . . . it's not physical, it's an approval."

"I didn't think you had it in your bag!" Ryan laughed.[31]

Labour Friends of Israel responded to the scandal claiming that the trips were "openly arranged" and "advertised" but did not reply to my request to clarify where and when they were openly advertised. LFI also claimed that the £1 million was not intended for trips for MPs and lawmakers (as Al Jazeera had assumed) but was for "a visit for young people." Regardless of who was to go on the trip, it seems clear this lavishly funded exercise by the Israeli government was intended to influence the Labour Party and British public opinion. Many Labour activists suspected the infamous £1 million was a sort of bribe to bring down Jeremy Corbyn (who at the time of filming had only been Labour's leader for a year).

There's little evidence to support that. While it's likely that the embassy upped its funding for such delegations in response to the threat of Corbyn's leadership, the murky and mostly undisclosed nature of the Israel lobby's funding makes it difficult to know for sure. What we do know is that Israel and its lobby in the UK have funded such propaganda trips for many years. Over £1 million certainly seems like a lot to take a few young people on one trip to Israel. It would have been enough to fly 200 people first-class to Tel Aviv and put them up in luxury hotels for two weeks. That seems an unlikely scenario, as LFI delegations are far smaller. The real destination of the £1 million remains a mystery.

With renewed online interest in *The Lobby* inadvertently triggered by a BBC *Panorama* documentary in 2019, LFI went on the attack again, calling Al Jazeera's series "a combination of lies, insinuations, and distortions" that "attempted to construct

---

31   *The Lobby*, episode 2, timecode 7:45.

a vast conspiracy involving hidden power, money and improper influence—typical anti-Semitic tropes." In a thread of slightly desperate postings to Twitter, LFI distanced itself from the Israeli embassy money, saying Al Jazeera's reporting had been "totally untrue and utterly ridiculous."[32] But Ryan and Masot's conversation had been caught on camera. And in any case, other segments of the undercover footage showed Rubin talking about his ability to get money from the embassy to fund LFI projects.

Robin was asked by Masot to establish a youth wing of Labour Friends of Israel, but to do so in a way that didn't seem obviously manipulated by the embassy. Embassy money and support would go into the project, but Rubin and the others would be allowed to continue believing they were in charge. Later Michael Freeman, another Israeli official, attempted to recruit Robin to a post at the embassy itself. At a gathering to listen to a speech by anti-BDS minister Gilad Erdan, Freeman surprised the undercover reporter by whipping out Robin's fake résumé, and discussing the prospect of working on "the whole BDS piece, doing research into the different BDS movements, who they are, what they are."[33] He declined. But the very fact that the embassy wanted to recruit Robin is highly significant. It demonstrates that—despite the lobby's denials, and disingenuous accusations of anti-Semitism—the line between the state of Israel and the Israel lobby is, at best, extremely fuzzy. It was standard operating procedure for the embassy to recruit from the pro-Israel groups.

Robin first came into contact with Jewish Labour Movement director Ella Rose via Michael Rubin—a sign of the revolving door between ostensibly British pro-Israel groups and the Israeli embassy. "I know there are job openings available quite frequently," Rubin told Robin. "So you should chat to Shai [Masot]. Ella Rose, she was president of the UJS, which is the Union of Jewish Students, a couple of years ago. She works in the [Israeli]

---

32 Asa Winstanley, "Labour Friends of Israel denies funding from Israeli spy," *Electronic Intifada*, 17 July 2019.

33 *The Lobby*, episode 1, timecode 12:05.

embassy. But she's leaving the embassy to work as the Jewish Labour Movement's new staff member."[34]

Apart from a few dissenters like Alan Duncan, the Israel lobby appears to have the Conservative Party in the bag. Before Corbyn, it very much had Labour's leadership on board too. But there was a grassroots rejection of Israel by Labour Party members long before the left-winger became leader. *The Lobby's* revelations only encouraged such outrage. In both 2018 and 2019, delegates overwhelmingly passed motions at the party's conference calling for Labour to adopt the boycott of Israel. While not explicitly mentioning BDS, both motions called for an end to British arms sales to Israel. The 2019 motion even committed the party to recognising the Palestinian refugees' right of return to their homeland. The arms embargo made it into Labour's 2019 electoral manifesto. (Meanwhile, the Tory manifesto pledged to ban public bodies from boycotting.) This was a historic sea change. Labour's 1945 endorsement of a "Zionism plus plus" vision that endorsed the ethnic cleansing of Palestine was part of its traditional commitment to empire and colonialism. The new environment that Corbyn's election had allowed to thrive in the party turned all that on its head. Some delegates were explicitly aware of the brutal reality of this history.

"I'm probably the first Palestinian to address this conference," said Ealing Labour delegate Yousef Qandeel in 2019. "Britain had a main role in creating my Catastrophe. In 1948 my parents fled the village of al-Dawayima, in which 500 people were killed in one night in 29 October 1948, and as a result, we became refugees . . . there is no peace without justice and there is no justice if the Palestinians don't have their rights."[35]

* * *

---

34 *The Lobby*, episode 1, timecode 16:46.

35 "Yousef Qandeel at Lab19," Barnet Socialists Facebook page, 23 September 2019. On the well-documented massacre at al-Dawayima, see Michael Palumbo, *The Palestinian Catastrophe* (London: Quartet Books, 1987), pages xii-xv. On the death toll, Palumbo says, "Estimates vary considerably but probably about 300 Arab civilians were slaughtered in the town."

One of the most revealing incidents in *The Lobby* came in episode three. Joan Ryan and other Labour Friends of Israel activists were caught red-handed actually *fabricating* anti-Semitism. The undercover footage showed the truth behind Ryan's alarming stories about "anti-Semitic incidents" and "attacks" against the Labour Friends of Israel stall at conference.

As part of Robin's cover story, he went to Liverpool for the Labour Party's annual conference and volunteered at the LFI stall. The information stand was situated in a prime location, at the entrance to the exhibitors' hall. There, organisations as varied as the Cuba Solidarity Campaign, Her Majesty's Government of Gibraltar, Islamic Relief, and the Guide Dogs organisation pushed their causes. Delegates on their way to take part in debates and hear speeches had to walk through this hall. Most also had to pass the Labour Friends of Israel stall near the main entrance.

LFI staff and volunteers gave out information and networked. A large poster displayed LFI's deceptive new slogan, "Pro-Israel, Pro-Palestine, Pro-Peace." Several leading Israel lobby and Labour-right figures hovered. These included the JLM's Jeremy Newmark, Israel lobbyist Luke Akehurst, Chuka Umunna (a Blairite who would end up leaving to join the Liberal Democrats), and Angela Eagle—briefly a 2016 leadership challenger to Corbyn. Also frequently present at the stall was Israeli embassy agent Shai Masot. I saw him there myself in conversation with Newmark and others. Al Jazeera's footage reveals that then–deputy ambassador Eitan Na'eh also dropped in at one point.

The footage showed an incident with Joan Ryan in discussion with Jean Fitzpatrick, a Palestine Solidarity Campaign supporter and Labour Party member. Fitzpatrick approached the stall and engaged Ryan in a discussion about what LFI was doing to challenge settlements in the West Bank, since it claimed to be "pro-peace." Israeli settlements are built on stolen Palestinian land, and are a war crime under the Geneva Convention. Israel frequently removes Palestinian families by force from land on both sides of the 1949 "Green Line" ceasefire line so that these modern-day colonies can be built to house Jewish settlers. Fitzpatrick later explained to Al Jazeera: "I heard there was a Labour Friends of Israel stall and I thought this'd be a really good opportunity to have a dialogue with a group I know who have a lot of influence and it'd be very interesting to hear their ideas." But she didn't realise who the woman behind the stall was—the LFI's leading MP. "I was actually seeking some reassurance that a two-state solution, if that's what they were promoting, was still possible," Fitzpatrick told Al Jazeera. The film shows her asking Ryan: "Can I just ask you, if you're very anti-the settlements, what is Labour Friends of Israel doing about that?" Ryan replied with a vague spiel about believing in "a two-state solution" and "coexistence." But the usual LFI platitudes were not doing it for Fitzpatrick, as Robin's footage memorably showed. She wanted a detailed plan.

"What about Israeli occupation?" she asked. Ryan blamed the lack of a "two-state solution" on "a distinct lack of security for Israel." The conversation then took a turn for the worse. "I think we have to be very, very careful not to let our feelings about this morph into anti-Zionism," Ryan said. Fitzpatrick continued to press Ryan for details, but she attempted to end the exchange. "Thank you, Jean, I've enjoyed the conversation, I'm leaving it there," she said.

"But how can [a Palestinian state] come about if the whole of the West Bank is atomised?" Jean countered. "Where will the state be?" Ryan's only reply was to blow her nose into a tissue. Jean persisted, saying LFI could influence things if they had been genuine about wanting a Palestinian state. "You've got a lot of money, you've got a lot of prestige in the world," she said, arguing that LFI is a stepping stone to a good career. "A friend of mine's son's got a really good job at Oxford University on the basis of having worked for Labour Friends of Israel." Ryan then bridled at the notion that her group had access to serious funding. She instantly lashed out: "It's anti-Semitic. It is. It's a trope. It's about conspiracy theorists!" Ironically, Ryan had discussed the £1 million funding with Shai Masot only a few hours earlier.

Ryan then claimed that Fitzpatrick had told a story about a former LFI activist getting a job at a large bank "in the City," London's financial district. Undercover footage of Ryan discussing the incident with her colleagues suggests that she convinced herself she had heard the real phrase "good job at Oxford University" as the fabricated phrase "good job at Oxford *and the City.*" But the footage proves Fitzpatrick did not say this. It unambiguously shows she'd said nothing about "the City" whatsoever. This was not some un-evidenced conspiracy theory, it was a factual statement about the son of a person directly known to her, whose involvement in Labour Friends of Israel, the son said, had helped him get a job at Oxford University.

"At no point did I ever say that Labour Friends of Israel will get people jobs in banking in the City," Fitzpatrick later explained to Al Jazeera. "I did say, which is absolutely true, that I know the son of a friend of mine who, he believed himself that having some connection with Labour Friends of Israel didn't harm his career at all."

That evening, Ryan told a concerned crowd at a Jewish Labour Movement event in a Liverpool pub that "we have also had three incidents of anti-Semitic harassment on our stand to the people who are staffing that stall today. And that, I think, tells you something about why we need to be having this Against Anti-Semitism rally."

The concocted incident was also covered by the *Jewish News*, and there was a small media storm about "anti-Semitism at Labour conference." Ryan and her young Parliamentary aide, Alex Richardson, went on to lodge a formal complaint against Jean Fitzpatrick with the party. Fitzpatrick recounted in the series how this left her shocked and suffering from anxiety. She was investigated by the party over the "serious incident."

The undercover footage shows LFI staffers debating whether or not Fitzpatrick's comments really were anti-Semitic and "where the line" is. But that didn't stop Ryan reporting the incident to party bureaucrats. "I reported that incident with that woman," the footage shows her explaining to her LFI colleagues. "I wrote down all this what she was saying about them being rich and powerful and then the one who went to Oxford and the next minute he's got a big job in banking, you know, and I said—classic anti-Semitic tropes aren't they?" The letter Fitzpatrick received from Labour Party staff some days later shows that the party took Ryan's allegations extremely seriously.

A "member of party staff" (seemingly Ryan) alleged they had been approached by Fitzpatrick at the LFI stand. The letter asserted that Fitzpatrick had "constantly suggested that LFI and such organisations had 'lots of money and power' and were doing nothing to address the 'occupation of Palestine.'"

It is concerning that staff at the Labour Party's disciplinary unit rendered the phrase "occupation of Palestine" in apparent scare quotes, as if the very recognition of the fact of Israeli occupation against Palestinians was inherently anti-Semitic.[36]

* * *

As well as Newmark and Masot, there was another group of regulars hanging around the Labour Friends of Israel stall that year—and these were actually Israelis.

The group came from the Israeli Labor Party. The young delegation was led by Masot and jointly organised by the JLM's Ella Rose. It was an official Israeli delegation, begging the question of who Rose was really working for. Al Jazeera's undercover reporter travelled on the train from London with the group to Liverpool. The undercover footage shows Masot introducing "Robin" to pro-Israel activists as the chairperson of Young LFI—a sign of the Israeli's influence. It also shows one of the group describing Masot as "the head of the delegation."[37] Rose had just been appointed JLM director. But only the month before, she had come straight into that position out of a job at the Israeli embassy. Ostensibly, she was therefore no longer working for the embassy. So what was she doing organising a delegation to Labour conference in cooperation with that same embassy? "I am the delegation," a transcript of an unused part of the footage shows her admitting. It was "a JLM delegation" in her view.

Robin was confused. He thought it had been an Israeli delegation led by Shai. "It was his idea originally," replied Rose, "but he couldn't own it because the embassy can't do it now. I can't

---

36 Asa Winstanley, "How the Israel lobby fakes anti-Semitism," *Electronic Intifada*, 14 January 2017.

37 *The Lobby*, episode 2, timecode 9:47.

remember why." She said JLM had organised the logistics and set up all the Israelis' meetings. "I spent the whole week running after them," she said. Clearly, the Israeli embassy expected the Jewish Labour Movement to, at a minimum, work closely with them and follow their guidance. The JLM was acting as a front group: a proxy executing a plan conceived by the Israeli embassy's man Shai Masot.

The delegation went from meeting to meeting in Liverpool, especially targeting events related to Palestine and "Labour anti-Semitism." I was reporting on conference that year for the *Electronic Intifada* and I myself saw them at three meetings on conference's fringe, including that of the Palestine Solidarity Campaign. That year PSC held its event under the auspices of the *New Statesman*, a Labour-aligned magazine. One of the Israelis interjected during the Q&A, giving a short speech rather than asking a question. He didn't give a name, but wasn't happy with the panellists' support for the BDS movement. "It's not only about being pro-Israeli or pro-Palestinians ... When some of you boycott Israel like I heard it, or deny our right to exist, you put us under siege," he said. "It only creates hatred."

The mysterious Israeli's speechifying was cut off by the *New Statesman*'s Stephen Bush, who was chairing the event. PSC leader Hugh Lanning responded to emphasise that the PSC supports BDS. Soft-left Labour MP Andy Slaughter implied that the Israeli Labor party is "Likud lite." And the then–Palestinian Authority ambassador Manuel Hassassian accused the Israeli of selling "propaganda," saying that Israel's Labor party had been in power for 30 years, building settlements and starting wars. "Everything that we're suffering is from Labor," he said.

The Israeli delegation later made an appearance at Momentum's alternative conference festival, The World Transformed. A group of anti-Zionist Jews had organised a debate between opposing sides in the "Labour anti-Semitism" controversy: JLM leader Jeremy Newmark claimed there was a "crisis," while the anti-Zionists argued that it had been exaggerated. The Israeli delegation was present in the audience and acted as Newmark's allies. One stood up and introduced herself to the audience as "Danielle." The message was similar to that they'd given at the PSC meeting: Support the Israeli Labor party, "the biggest left-wing party in Israel." She also backed her sponsor: "I feel very much connected to what Jeremy [Newmark] said . . . I represent the Labor party, we are the opposition. We need you in Israel to stand with us." She said she wanted to end the "conflict" and said that "creating hostility towards Israel" and "committing anti-Semitism" made things harder for the Israeli Labor party. Nobody challenged her false claim that the Israeli Labor party wants to end the military occupation of the West Bank. She conveniently omitted the fact that it was the Labour Zionist party which in 1967 had been the government that invaded the West Bank in the first place. "I really hope to see you all support us, the Jews in Israel," she concluded. There was no disclosure of the fact that the JLM had paid for their trip or that it had been arranged by the Israeli government.

If the young Israeli was misleading, Jeremy Newmark in his reply was outright dishonest. He gave the impression that Danielle's intervention was a surprise to him, describing her only as "the very passionate young woman from the Israeli Labor party." He claimed that for UK Labour members to "delegitimise Labor in Israel" was to "end up perpetuating the occupation" by providing "fodder to Netanyahu."

The delegation also went along to Labour Friends of Israel's evening reception, where Corbyn himself spoke. They grabbed a selfie with John McDonnell, Labour's shadow chancellor. In the photo, posted by the Jewish Labour Movement to Twitter, McDonnell looks uncomfortable, and the Israeli Labor members smile while wearing T-shirts describing themselves as "Young Labour, Israel" (even the British spelling of the shirts suggests that they were printed by the JLM rather than the Israeli Labor party). In the Al Jazeera footage they debate the utility of the T-shirts with Shai Masot. The embassy agent wanted them to make a bold statement by wearing the garments while at another Palestine event. One demurred, arguing it was too cold for T-shirts. A British LFI volunteer agreed, saying the T-shirts would attract hostility, joking that the Israelis should instead remain incognito as "our spies." One of the Israelis then responded, saying "I was an intelligence officer, a spy. For four years. I can get the intel for you, no worries."

The name of this "spy" was Michal Zilberberg. How serious was her offer to obtain "intel" to benefit a foreign power (a state hostile to Labour's left-wing leader)? There's no reason to doubt Zilberberg's claim to have been an Israeli spy.[38] She later became a lobbyist for the Israeli Labor party in Europe.[39]

What was this "delegation" really doing at Labour conference? The Jewish Labour Movement promoted them as part of Labour's "sister party" in Israel. But they did not act in a very sororal manner. The JLM—a group ostensibly representing British Jews—was acting in a very similar fashion to Labour Friends of Israel. The Al Jazeera transcripts show Ella Rose revealing that her first ever job at 15 had been work experience for MP Luciana Berger and her group Labour Friends of Israel. "LFI had a soft place in my heart ever since," she said. "Please consider me your number one fan," she told Robin, who had explained his plan to start Young LFI.

In his history of the British's left's relationship with Zionism, scholar Paul Kelemen explains how Labour Friends of Israel was founded to rebuild the UK Labour Party's relationship with the Israeli Labor party after 1956.[40] Warm relations had cooled for the first time because of the Suez crisis that year, when Israel invaded Egypt in collusion with the British and French governments.[41] It was a failed attempt to stop Egypt's government nationalising the Suez Canal. The UK Labour opposition opposed President Gamal Abdel Nasser's nationalisation and did nothing to challenge the fundamentally exploitative nature of British colonial control of the canal (Egyptian workers had

---

38 Asa Winstanley, "Jewish Labour Movement worked with Israeli embassy spy," *Electronic Intifada*, 12 April 2018

39 David Cronin, "Israel's Labor never had a moral compass," *Electronic Intifada*, 24 November 2017.

40 Paul Kelemen, *The British Left and Zionism: History of a Divorce* (Manchester University Press, 2012), pages 168-9. See also Derek Taylor, *Solidarity and Discord: A brief history of 99 years of affiliation to the Labour Party* (London: Jewish Labour Movement, 2019), page 18, which says LFI was founded in 1957 by Poale Zion, whose secretary remained LFI secretary "for many years." See also Christopher Mayhew and Michael Adams, *Publish It Not: The Middle East Cover-Up* (Oxford: Signal Books, 2006), page 38, which describes LFI as a "front" group for Poale Zion.

41 Kelemen, *The British Left and Zionism*, pages 140-2.

built it, but the country was denied any revenue until 1937—and even after then received a mere 7 percent of total income). But Labour did oppose the war on the narrow grounds that it would prove to be a disaster for British interests.

So LFI was founded to smooth over the first tensions between the British and Israeli Labour parties. By the early 1970s, LFI claimed 17 branches (mostly in London) and 700 members. Its lobbying brought MPs and party officials on well-funded trips to Israel. But by 1978 the group was in stark decline. Only 250 of its members had paid their dues and it was in dire financial straits. According to Kelemen, LFI's general secretary thought that "some limited assistance could be available from the Israeli embassy."[42]

The decline of LFI's membership led its director, in an internal report, to write that 1992 "came near to seeing the end of LFI as an active body." Its fortunes were revived when Tony Blair took over in 1994. Blair called it "one of the most important organisations within the Labour movement." The following year Blair's deputy, Gordon Brown, spoke at a dinner in Jerusalem in similarly gushing terms: "Labour Friends of Israel has today more support among our 270 MPs than at any time."[43] (Not coincidentally, the LFI's director back then was Reg Freeson. A onetime Poale Zion leader, Freeson was, in 1985, ousted as Labour's parliamentary candidate for Brent East by pro-Palestinian left-winger Ken Livingstone.)[44]

LFI no longer has a membership structure. On their website there's no way to apply for membership or pay dues. Instead, LFI declares MPs and other Labour lawmakers as their "supporters," listing them as such online, and lobbying them to make declarations and speeches.

All this suggests that by the time Corbyn became leader in 2015, LFI was essentially a shell organisation, a front for the Israeli embassy which was easy to manipulate.

---

42 Kelemen, *The British Left and Zionism*, page 169.

43 Kelemen, *The British Left and Zionism*, page 179.

44 Andrew Roth, "Obituaries: Reg Freeson," *Guardian*, 11 October 2006.

Agents for a hostile foreign power were working at multiple levels on a semi-covert influence campaign to sabotage the party. It was in line with years of Israeli strategy. The Israeli presence at 2016 Labour conference must be understood in the context of this strategy, as set out by Israel's Ministry of Strategic Affairs.

* * *

Attacking critics as anti-Semitic is a tried and tested method used by successive Israeli governments, Likud and Labor alike. The threat of being smeared as anti-Semitic was once so powerful that it stopped many from speaking about Israel's crimes against the Palestinians altogether. But this death-grip has slowly lessened over the years as people have become more aware of the strategy.

False allegations of anti-Semitism remain a powerful psychological weapon in the Israeli arsenal. Socialists are aghast to be tarred with that brush and do not want to be associated with a form of racism that has been responsible for some of history's worst atrocities. False allegations by Israel and its supporters are not only wrong in principle, but they are damaging to genuine efforts to fight anti-Semitism.

In *The Lobby—USA* series, one young pro-Israel lobbyist described anti-Semitism allegations as "psychological warfare. It drives them crazy." This was Jacob Baime of the Israel on Campus Coalition, caught on camera boasting about his role smearing young Palestinian students as anti-Semitic. He even admitted to how they "coordinate" such activities with, and pass on "intelligence" to, the Israeli government. The Palestinian students then "either shut down or they spend time responding to it and investigating it . . . That's incredibly effective."[45] This was exactly the same dynamic that blighted Corbyn's Labour for years.

---

45 Al Jazeera Investigations, *The Lobby - USA*, episode 3, timecode 17:09. For context and analysis see Asa Winstanley and Ali Abunimah, "Censored film names Adam Milstein as Canary Mission funder," *Electronic Intifada*, 27 August 2018.

Israel's long war against the global movement for justice in Palestine turned a corner in 2010. That year the Reut Institute, a government-backed Israeli think tank, published a series of reports and presentations advocating a more aggressive approach. Israel, Reut wrote, including its "intelligence establishment" and "intelligence agencies," should move to focus on "attacking" what it called "hubs of delegitimisation"—i.e., solidarity activism in key global cities. The think tank called for Israeli spies to work with the Israel lobby to "sabotage" pro-Palestinian groups it dubbed the "delegitimisation network" in London, Madrid, Toronto, and the San Francisco Bay Area.[46]

The Reut Institute has close links to the state of Israel itself. Its strategy documents were later endorsed by the Ministry of Strategic Affairs. Reut's "sabotage" and "attack" prescriptions were closely followed over the next decade. Understanding these strategies is key to understanding the Labour Party's "anti-Semitism crisis."

A 2010 Reut PowerPoint slideshow (later deleted from their website) called for Israel to respond to the Palestine solidarity movement by "driving [a] wedge between soft and hard critics" of Israel.[47] A January 2017 Reut document—prepared jointly with the Anti-Defamation League—drew on and refined its earlier "wedge" strategy, by aiming to create dissension among progressive groups over the issue of Israel. At the *Electronic Intifada* we managed to obtain a copy of the secret report and published it online.[48] Reut's attempt to conceal the document came after increased international media scrutiny of its published reports—beginning with the *Electronic Intifada*'s Ali Abunimah, who had first exposed their "attack" and "sabotage" strategy back in 2010. In the secretive 2017 document the authors lamented the

---

46 Ali Abunimah, "Israel's new strategy: 'sabotage' and 'attack' the global justice movement," *Electronic Intifada*, 16 February 2010.

47 For the original slideshow, see Asa Winstanley, "How the Israel lobby is using Owen Jones," *Electronic Intifada*, 21 February 2017.

48 Ali Abunimah, "Leaked report highlights Israel lobby's failures," *Electronic Intifada*, 28 April 2017. The full report is attached as a PDF: *The Assault on Israel's Legitimacy*, The Reut Institute and the Anti-Defamation League, January 2017.

fact that Palestine solidarity has "migrated into mainstream left-wing parties in Europe" and "may be gaining traction" in the US.[49] The report developed the "wedge" strategy further. It called for driving a "wedge" between "critics" of Israel and others designated "instigators" against or "delegitimizers" of Israel. "Harsh critics should be intellectually engaged and challenged," the authors wrote, but "the instigators must be singled out from the other groups, and handled uncompromisingly, publicly or covertly as appropriate." It said that "soft critics" of Israel should be targeted by "sophisticated engagement strategies."[50]

It carried a glowing endorsement from Sima Vaknin-Gil, director general of the Ministry of Strategic Affairs. "The correlation between the Ministry's mode of operation and what comes out of this document is very high, and has already proven effective," the former senior Israeli intelligence officer wrote. It's no wonder this correlation was so high. The ministry was reported by veteran Israeli security correspondent Yossi Melman in 2016 to be leading a dirty war against Palestinian and solidarity groups around the world—what he termed a "black ops" campaign. Israeli covert action was almost certainly responsible for a series of death threats against Palestinian attorney Nada Kiswanson and her family in the Hague, which were investigated by Dutch police. Kiswanson had been working for Palestinian human rights group Al Haq preparing the case to try Israel for war crimes in Gaza at the International Criminal Court.[51]

The Reut strategy reflected the long-held practice by ostensibly left-wing Israel lobby figures like the JLM's Jeremy Newmark. Indeed, Newmark is listed in the acknowledgements of Reut's influential 2010 report, *Building a Political Firewall Against Israel's Delegitimisation*. The report said that Israel should be "mobilising Jewish and Israeli diaspora communities" as well as "the local

---

49 *The Assault on Israel's Legitimacy*, page 16.

50 *The Assault on Israel's Legitimacy*, page 26.

51 Ali Abunimah, "Israel using 'black ops' against BDS, says veteran analyst," *Electronic Intifada*, 5 September 2016.

pro-Israel community."⁵² Prefiguring the secret Reut-ADL report by seven years, the document argued for a divide-and-rule strategy to "isolate" harsher critics of Israel—those it characterised as "delegitimisers"—while engaging other critics. Newmark said in 2010 that the Jewish Leadership Council (the Israel lobby group he led at the time) had "contributed heavily to the compilation of the Reut report."⁵³

The Jewish Labour Movement, then, and its 2015 revival to fight Corbyn, was a key part of Israel's "wedge" strategy in the UK—to divide the Labour Party against itself with false accusations of anti-Semitism.

Israeli officials often described their campaign against "delegitimisation" using military language. According to Israeli journalist Barak Ravid, there was even a "war room" at the Israeli embassy in London. Describing a "map of Britain hanging on the wall in the office of Yiftah Curiel, spokesman of the Israeli embassy in London," Ravid wrote that it was like something from "a brigade on the Lebanese border." The map showed "the front" (Britain's universities) as well as "the deployment of pro-Israel activists and the location of 'enemy forces.'"⁵⁴

The aim was to sabotage and divide the left in order to promote Zionist ideology, and to block the rise of democratic socialist governments overseas that would be more likely to loosen ties with Israel. The Reut Institute's president Gidi Grinstein made the strategy explicit. At a 2017 anti-BDS conference hosted by Israel's UN delegation in New York, he argued that "only progressive groups" could "win the fight in the progressive circles for us" against the Palestine solidarity movement. "It's a very, very challenging environment," he said, emphasising that the number of BDS activists was growing "among progressive circles" more than in any other area. Like Regev and Newmark, Grinstein is from the Labour Zionist tendency. He was an

---

52 *Building a Political Firewall Against Israel's Delegitimization: Conceptual Framework*, The Reut Institute, March 2010, pages 7, 17.

53 "London's hub of Israel hate," *Jewish Chronicle*, 2 December 2010.

54 Barak Ravid, "Netanyahu, Lapid Play Politics Over BDS, Stand in Way of Real Fighters," *Haaretz*, 8 May 2016.

adviser to Ehud Barak (the then Labor prime minister of Israel) between 1999 and 2001.[55]

About the same time that Grinstein was making his argument at the UN, his strategy was already being implemented by Newmark and his other allies in London. Over the objections of grassroots solidarity activists, liberal *Guardian* columnist Owen Jones was the main speaker at a special event hosted by the Jewish Labour Movement. By then, the JLM's activities on behalf of Israel had been thoroughly exposed by Al Jazeera's undercover series. But Jones didn't seem to care. On the stage he attacked Jackie Walker, a Black, Jewish anti-Zionist and former deputy-chairperson of Momentum, saying she should be expelled from Labour (see chapter 6). He gave only narrow criticisms of the Netanyahu government and its policy on settlements (to the audible disgust of one apparently right-wing audience member). Inviting Jones to be the star turn at their meeting showed that the Jewish Labour Movement was working perfectly in line with the Israeli strategy of "sophisticated engagement"—and Jones was more than happy to play the role of the "soft critic" of Israel.

* * *

The Lobby was a success. On Al Jazeera's YouTube channel alone, the series has had more than 2.2 million views to date. That's in addition to the viewers watching the live stream, not to mention the millions watching on TV the world over in English and Arabic. It also received significant coverage in the UK's mainstream media. Despite some dismissing it as a conspiracy theory, the undercover footage spoke for itself. And the investigation had concrete results. Shai Masot was ejected from the country. Boris Johnson, then the foreign secretary, sought to draw a line under it by making a statement in Parliament. But in his typical blustering style, he gave away perhaps a little more than intended.

---

55   Asa Winstanley, "BDS is winning, admits top Israeli 'sabotage' strategist," *Electronic Intifada*, 21 April 2017.

"Whoever he was and whatever he was doing," Johnson said of Masot, "his cover can be said to have been well and truly blown." In other words, we regret to announce that the activities of the Israeli spy became too embarrassing and we had to send him packing. Regev himself gave a "very full apology," Johnson announced in Parliament.[56]

Masot's co-conspirator, Maria Strizzolo, stepped down from her civil service job.[57] Alan Duncan also sought to draw a line under the affair, posting a photo to Twitter of himself smiling and posing with Regev, calling it a "friendly encounter."[58] The embassy said it had apologised to the minister.[59] Crispin Blunt, another Tory MP on Masot's hit list, told the website *Middle East Eye* that Masot's activities were "clearly interference in another country's politics of the murkiest and most discreditable kind." Prime Minister Theresa May reiterated the line already expressed by Boris Johnson, with a spokesperson telling *Middle East Eye* that the controversy over Masot's comments about having a political hit list was closed: "The Israeli ambassador has apologised and it is clear these comments do not reflect the views of the embassy or government of Israel."[60] Duncan stepped down from politics in 2019, publishing his candid political diaries in 2021. In the book he revealed that the Israel lobby had been responsible for vetoing his appointment as Middle East minister, and wrote that Conservative Friends of Israel "interfere at a high level in British politics in the interest of Israel, on the back of donor power within the UK." He added that: "A lot of things do

---

56 Hansard, Volume 619, Column 148, 10 January 2017, *West Bank: Illegal Settlements*.

57 Asa Winstanley, "Probe into UK civil servant who plotted 'hit list' with Israeli embassy," *Electronic Intifada*, 10 January 2017. Paul Offord, "Investigation launched after former SFA senior manager embroiled in alleged Israeli plot," *FE Week*, 9 January 2017.

58 Alan Duncan, Twitter, 17 January 2017.

59 "Israel's ambassador sorry over 'take down' Sir Alan Duncan comment," BBC News, 8 January 2017.

60 "UK prime minister rejects call for inquiry into Israeli influence," *Middle East Eye*, 18 January 2017.

not happen in foreign policy, or a government, for fear of offending this lobby."[61]

The initial Labour Party response to Al Jazeera's revelations was outrage. Jeremy Corbyn and his foreign affairs spokesperson Emily Thornberry both called for an inquiry. Thornberry even called it "improper interference in our democratic politics" by Israel; "this is a national security issue," she warned.[62] But this ultimately came to nothing. A senior Jeremy Corbyn leadership aide conceded to me in 2020 that this had been a missed opportunity. Labour's failure to follow up on the affair was likely caused by the fact that a Labour inquiry would have revealed too many uncomfortable truths about the inordinate influence the Israel lobby has on the party. In all likelihood Thornberry only made the call for an investigation in the first place because the initial revelations in the *Mail on Sunday* primarily concerned her party-political rivals. But as soon became clear, the majority of the series itself actually focused on the Labour Party. Her initial response began to look like a sop to placate Labour's activist base.

The most lasting legacy of *The Lobby* was among Labour's grassroots membership base—which rose to half a million at one point. The film spread like wildfire online, with activists making clips and memes of what they thought were the most relevant and incriminating parts. Every time the Jewish Labour Movement and Labour Friends of Israel cropped up with their latest smear, activists were ready to respond. But Corbyn's office failed to capitalise on this energy, and there seemed to be no political will from Labour's left-wing leadership to take on the lobby.

An Al Jazeera source later told me that they had been told by an adviser to the Qatari monarch that the series had been "too successful." Their sources told them that Masot had been dragged across the coals when he got back to Tel Aviv. This, combined with the pressure on Qatar that the Israel lobby was able to bring to bear in the US after they realised they had been

---

61 Asa Winstanley, "'High-level' Israel lobby interference in British politics, says ex-minister," *Electronic Intifada*, 9 April 2021.

62 Asa Winstanley, "Secret video reveals Israeli plot to 'take down' UK minister," *Electronic Intifada*, 8 January 2017.

infiltrated, meant that the second series, *The Lobby—USA*, was too hot to handle. To date it has never been broadcast on Al Jazeera, with only leaked copies appearing online.

The genie was out of the bottle. People were beginning to wake up to the true extent of Israel's covert interference in British politics.

But would it be enough?

CHAPTER FIVE

NAZI COMPARISONS

The former mayor of London walked down the street talking into his phone. A tall, kindly-looking man, Ken Livingstone was a doyen of the Labour left. He'd found himself back in demand by journalists since his friend Jeremy Corbyn had won the leadership election the previous year. But now he was at the centre of a media scrum.

Livingstone was on his way to be interviewed by the BBC's *Daily Politics* television programme and spoke to a radio talk show host while he walked. The phone interview was suddenly interrupted by a ranting man in a suit. "I've got a violent MP threatening me, sorry about that," Livingstone told the host. The interview was cut off.

"Disgusting racist! Disgusting racist! Rewriting history. You're a disgusting racist!" the suit screamed. The ranter was right-wing Labour MP John Mann. He had camera crews and journalists in tow as Livingstone entered the BBC. The episode would appear on TV news bulletins that evening. The whole thing looked suspiciously like a set up.

In another radio interview earlier that day the former mayor had said that, prior to World War II, Nazi Germany had supported Zionism.

The group walked through a set of revolving doors. Another journalist lay in wait. "Are you saying it's not true?" Livingstone replied to Mann.

"Yes! You're a lying racist!" Mann spat back. "A Nazi apologist!"

"Check your history," Livingstone responded calmly. Mann continued to rant, complaining that Livingstone had not read

Hitler's book *Mein Kampf*. "You dare say that Hitler supported Zionism! You've lost it mate, you need help!"

Apparently conscious of the cameras, Livingstone continued his attempt to explain the historical reality of Nazi policy against the Jews in 1932. "His view was to deport all the Jews of Germany to Israel. Is it true or not?"

Mann ignored this challenge, instead hectoring the former mayor and calling his sanity into question: "You've lost it. You have lost it! You have lost it!"

Livingstone persevered. The Nazi dictator "wanted to kill all Jews. But his policy in '32 when he won that election, was to deport Germany's Jews to Israel. And the Zionist movement had secret meetings with this administration, talking about that. It's a historical fact."

Mann couldn't argue with what is actually an established fact, so attempted to change the story into one about how "mad" Livingstone was to question the official ideology of the state of Israel and issued an emotionally manipulative screed about the hurt Livingstone's views were causing. "You're losing it, you're losing it. You're twisting history. You're re-writing history," the MP continued.

One of the journalists in the scrum then intervened, physically pushing the Labour leftist back and blocking his passage. "Ken: You see the anger," he said. "Do you maintain what you said earlier?"

"Just go and check the facts historically."

"But those comments have been described as inexcusable and you should no longer stay in the party."

"It's a fact."

Mann resumed his diatribe. "It's a calculated lie! It's a calculated lie! A calculated lie by conspiracy theorists."

The next day all the papers led with the story on their front pages. From left to right, the media united to condemn Livingstone's "Hitler outburst" along with photos of what they identified as a righteous Mann confronting "Nazi apologist" Livingstone.[1] The CST later wrote of the coverage that, "There

---

1   *Antisemitic discourse in Britain 2016* (London: The Community Security Trust, 2016), cover page.

has been no comparable situation in recent years, when antisemitic discourse has been an issue of such national attention and importance."[2]

For both the Israel lobby and the media, the facts didn't seem to matter. It was the narrative of internal conflict in Labour over anti-Semitism that counted.

* * *

Although it took two years to complete, John Mann's on-camera political assassination of Ken Livingstone was successful. Livingstone was suspended as a Labour Party member within hours of the interview. In May 2018, the former mayor of London was forced into quitting the party to which he'd devoted his life. "The ongoing issues around my suspension from the Labour Party have become a distraction from the key political issue of our time—which is to replace a Tory government," he said in a statement. "I am loyal to the Labour Party and to Jeremy Corbyn. However, any further disciplinary action against me may drag on for months or even years, distracting attention from Jeremy's policies."[3] A leaked Labour document later hinted that Livingstone's exit had been negotiated from the top of the party.

Livingstone's removal was important. From the summer of 2015 onward, he had been one of Corbyn's few heavyweight political Labour allies who could boast any kind of access to mainstream news outlets. He defended Corbyn against allegations that he was unelectable. Crucially, he defended Corbyn when the "anti-Semitism crisis" erupted, when very few others would.

Livingstone was initially suspended for one year. Despite this huge concession, the Israel lobby groups, led from within the party by the Jewish Labour Movement and the Labour Friends of Israel, refused to let the case go, and made Livingstone's total expulsion a primary goal. He was close to Corbyn, and considered more politically vulnerable than the Labour leader.

---

2   *Antisemitic discourse in Britain 2016*, page 2.

3   "Statement from Ken Livingstone," KenLivingstone.net, 21 May 2018.

Livingstone had made many enemies over the years, including on the British left—which is infamous for its splits and ancestral vendettas.

In April 2017, his suspension was extended for another year. For Labour's bureaucrats, and for Corbyn, this was probably seen as a compromise. They did not want to upset anyone. But that was a forlorn hope. The grassroots mostly supported Livingstone. A statement by left-wing Jewish members of Labour argued that the new suspension was "an attempt to protect Israel from criticism, while simultaneously weakening the position of the pro-Palestinian left in the party . . . It is the verdict, not Ken Livingstone, that has brought the Labour Party into disrepute."[4]

The Labour right took the opposite track. The Jewish Labour Movement accused Livingstone of having "revised the history of the Holocaust"—a carefully worded formulation one step away from calling him a Holocaust denier. Their chairperson Jeremy Newmark submitted a 170-page dossier to the hearing, where he was also a witness.[5] Meanwhile, Labour Friends of Israel reacted to the situation with fury, saying it was disgraceful that "Jeremy Corbyn's Labour Party" had allowed Livingstone to remain a member after he had "made Nazi comparisons." The group's chairperson Joan Ryan, despite not being Jewish herself, nevertheless spoke for the community, claiming that Livingstone "appears to take a twisted delight in offending Jews."[6]

When he quit later in 2018, Livingstone said he did "not accept the allegation that I have brought the Labour Party into disrepute—nor that I am in any way guilty of anti-Semitism. I abhor anti-Semitism." But he did "recognise that the way I made a historical argument has caused offence and upset in the Jewish community. I am truly sorry for that."

---

4   Asa Winstanley, "Defeat for Israel lobby as Ken Livingstone beats Labour expulsion," *Electronic Intifada*, 6 April 2017.

5   Jessica Elgot, "Ken Livingstone 'brought Labour into disrepute' with Hitler Zionism remarks," *Guardian*, 30 March 2017.

6   "LFI Officers Call on Jeremy Corbyn to Publicly Call For Ken Livingstone's Expulsion," Labour Friends of Israel website, 5 April 2017.

What was this historical argument? Why did it cause upset? Was the argument valid? Were the calls for Livingstone's expulsion fair?

Understanding the answers to these questions is important because, although—as we have seen—he was not the first in the party to be smeared as an anti-Semite, he was the highest profile and most influential public Labour figure at that time to be accused as such. The Livingstone affair was a key moment in the manufactured anti-Semitism crisis. It was a moment when the whole affair could have been turned around.

Deciding that Livingstone was "not the hill we want to die on," some on the Labour left were quick to abandon him. Immorality aside, this didn't even have the desired effect of sweeping the story under the rug. The party's concession that Livingstone had been "offensive"—strongly implying he was anti-Semitic—set a long-running pattern of concession, retreat, and compromise which would undermine untold numbers of Labour activists in the years ahead. If the Labour left would not defend one of its most heavyweight veterans from politically motivated charges of anti-Semitism, then what chance would anyone else have? Ultimately the throwing of Ken Livingstone under the bus meant that Corbyn's own position was seriously undermined. The right—both outside and inside the party—would henceforth argue, with much justification, that Livingstone was one of Corbyn's few natural political allies. The leader was thus tarred by association. As soon as Corbyn said that "Ken Livingstone's comments have been grossly insensitive, and he has caused deep offence and hurt to the Jewish community" (as he did again in April 2017) he was undermining his own position.[7]

But what is the truth behind Livingstone's comments? If what he said really had been anti-Semitic, then Corbyn's condemnation would have been morally necessary even if it cost him politically.

Was it true, as John Mann claimed, that Livingstone was a "Nazi apologist?" Was it true that Livingstone had said

---

7 "Ken Livingstone: Jeremy Corbyn announces new investigation," BBC News, 5 April 2017.

something anti-Semitic? The burden of proof is on the accuser. It is not down to Livingstone—or anyone else—to prove they are *not* anti-Semitic. That isn't how evidence works.

Nonetheless, to answer these questions it will be necessary to examine both the history and the immediate political context.

* * *

In April 2016, the biggest wave to date of the manufactured anti-Semitism crisis started with the MP Naz Shah. Newly elected in 2015, Shah was by no means on the left of the party. She had regained the seat of Bradford West for Labour from George Galloway, the iconoclastic Scottish lawmaker who had won it in 2012 and had endorsed former New Labour government minister Yvette Cooper in the 2015 leadership election.[8] Despite this, Corbyn's shadow finance minister John McDonnell appointed her as a key aide in February 2016.[9] There would be a long pattern of such concessions by McDonnell to party "moderates." Right-wing media soon proceeded to disinter Shah's social media history. Although she may have been targeted in part due to her new-found proximity to McDonnell—Corbyn's closest political ally in Parliament—it is difficult to escape the conclusion that she was primarily singled out as a prominent Muslim woman in public life.

The originator of the attacks on Shah was Guido Fawkes, a scurrilous right-wing libertarian blog which specialises in Parliamentary gossip and rumours. Guido would prove to be a key part of the long British media war against Corbyn, with its attack lines often being picked up by wider broadcast and print media. Guido had already started attacking Shah in the spring of 2015 when she was selected as Labour's candidate to fight Galloway in the by-election. "Labour select Palestine activist

---

[8] Stephen Bush, "150 women back Yvette Cooper to lead the Labour party," *New Statesman*, 19 August 2015.

[9] Rob Lowson, "Naz Shah to become Parliamentary Private Secretary to Shadow Chancellor John McDonnell," *Bradford Telegraph & Argus*, 9 February 2016.

for Bradford West," Guido's headline read. The article was illustrated by Shah posing in a car convoy decked with Palestinian flags. Guido's hint was clearly understood by the site's readers, who filled the comments section under the blog post with a deluge of poisonous Islamophobic and anti-Palestinian invective, and paranoid conspiracy theories about a Muslim takeover of the UK.

"Mohammedanism is a metastasising cancer," wrote one, with another calling Shah "a fifth column." One commenter threatened that a "civil war [is] coming," with another remonstrating that they'd "prefer a bloodless military coup, but I fear our generals are gutless."[10]

The comments were quite typical of Guido's racist readership. They are the kind of Islamophobic conspiracy theories frequently peddled by the "alt-right" and other fascistic movements. Guido's subsequent obsession with "Labour anti-Semitism," then, is hard to take seriously as anything other than a concerted attempt to depose what it termed the "loony left" Jeremy Corbyn leadership at all costs.

In 2016, Guido was the first site to dig up some of Shah's social media postings from 2014, a time before she was an MP. The site revealed a satirical post Shah had shared on her Facebook page. The meme showed a red-outlined map of historic Palestine located smack-dab in the middle of the United States. "Solution for the Israel-Palestine conflict," its caption read, "Relocate Israel into [the] United States." It argued that "Americans will welcome Israelis with open arms into their homes," that "the transportation cost will be less than three years of defense spending," and that "Palestinians will get their land and life back."[11] It was obviously not intended as a serious proposal, although it made some factual points about the Nakba and about US military aid to Israel.

---

10 "Labour Select Palestine Activist for Bradford West," Guido Fawkes, 2 March 2015 (comments section accessed 11 November 2019).

11 "Labour MP: Israelis Should Face 'Transportation' out of Middle East," Guido Fawkes, 26 April 2016.

But with the media picking up on "Labour anti-Semitism" as an increasingly important attack line since the Oxford affair only two months earlier, they were ready to pounce on Shah.

Guido published no less than seven further blog posts against Shah that day, 26 April, alone. These dredged up her old social media postings and reported on the various MPs denouncing her. The articles drew some viciously Islamophobic responses from readers in the comments section. Guido Fawkes's staff seemed to encourage this the next day, illustrating two of its nine further blog posts on the affair with an image it had mocked up of Shah viewed through a crosshair. The chilling graphic was an incitement for further hateful responses. One reader's comment mused on how to "fill a boat back to Arabia," while a second claimed that "Labour has prostituted itself . . . for the Muslim vote."[12]

The consequences for Shah turned out to be severe. She issued an immediate apology, stepping down as McDonnell's aide. In a statement she said that the 2014 war in Gaza happening at the time of her Facebook postings and the "Middle East conflict" were "no excuse for the offence I have given." She said she would engage in "dialogue with Jewish community organisations." As would prove to be the case so often during the constructed crisis, these "Jewish community organisations" turned out to be exclusively pro-Israel, Zionist organisations.

But Shah's capitulation wasn't enough. She was suspended as a Labour Party member the very next day. She was no longer a Labour MP.

* * *

Ken Livingstone, however, was not having it. English local elections were coming up in days, at the same time as elections to the devolved governments in Wales, Scotland, and Northern Ireland. The bad publicity for Labour seemed deliberately

---

12 "Shadow Cabinet Split: Lisa Nandy Tells Corbyn To Sack Naz Shah," Guido Fawkes, 27 April 2016 (comments section accessed 11 November 2019).

timed. He began publicly defending Shah and the wider party. Livingstone had endorsed Jeremy Corbyn for leader early, in July 2015.

On Sky News that month, Livingstone debated Michael Levy (Tony Blair's former "Lord Cashpoint" and a key pro-Israel financier[13]): "We didn't lose the [general] election this year because we were too left-wing. We went into that election saying we were basically going to be not quite as nasty as the Tories, and take a little bit longer. That didn't inspire." He enthused about raising money for Corbyn's public spending plans from taxing super-rich tech firms like Amazon and Google.[14] He was one of Corbyn's few supporters on the National Executive Committee, Labour's powerful leading body. Livingstone had also been appointed by Corbyn to co-lead a review of the party's defence policies. While it was standard practice to include an NEC member on such reviews, the appointment caused unrest on Labour's right.[15] As well as being anti-war activists, both Corbyn and Livingstone are opponents of Trident, Britain's nuclear weapons system.

Livingstone was the only person willing to speak publicly in defence of Shah, telling the BBC that she was "not anti-Semitic." He explained that "I've heard a lot of people [in the Labour Party] being critical of Israel, but if I was to denounce the South African government, you wouldn't say I was racist." He said that he worried that "this confusion with anti-Semitism and criticising the Israeli government policy undermines the importance of tackling real anti-Semitism."[16]

---

13 See Paul Vallely, "Michael Levy: Lord Cashpoint," *Independent*, 18 March 2006, which notes that Blair was first introduced to Levy at a 1994 Israeli embassy dinner. See also Caroline Wheeler, "Lord Levy fundraising again to help fill Labour's coffers," *The Times*, 3 April 2022.

14 "Ken Livingstone & Lord Levy Discuss Jeremy Corbyn," Sky News YouTube channel, 22 July 2015.

15 George Eaton, "Ken Livingstone to co-convene Labour's defence review," *New Statesman*, 17 November 2015. Nicholas Watt, "Trident opponent Ken Livingstone joins Labour defence review," *Guardian*, 18 November 2015.

16 "Jeremy Corbyn denies crisis as Ken Livingstone suspended," BBC News, 28 April 2016.

He also spoke to talk show host Vanessa Feltz for a fateful BBC Radio London interview. This was the interview that triggered Livingstone's political demise. Feltz has yet to speak publicly about it, but given her public support for Israel there seems little doubt she's pleased with the role she played. In an affectionate 2009 *Jewish Chronicle* piece about the Israeli prime minister visiting the UK ("British Jews on what they would say to Bibi") rather than objecting to the 313 children Benjamin Netanyahu's government had killed in Gaza during their "Cast Lead" offensive of a few months earlier, Feltz instead fretted about negative publicity.[17] "Can't you do something about Israel's image?" she implored in her imaginary meeting with Netanyahu. "It really is imperative that Israel works on ensuring that its PR efforts match its military prowess."[18]

Feltz's 2016 radio interview with Livingstone shows that she was aggressively pro-Israel from the outset (you can read a full transcript in the appendix). Feltz used the common Zionist strategy of deliberately blurring the line between opposition to Israel and anti-Semitism. "Some people will say," she claimed, "there's a double standard operating in the Labour Party. That what's really a flagrant kind of anti-Semitism, a deeply embedded systemic anti-Semitism, is hidden behind a mask of anti-Zionism or criticism of Israeli foreign policy." Feltz quoted Levy as claiming Livingstone "must be living on another planet."

But the crucial part of the interview concerned Adolf Hitler's Nazi government of the 1930s. In the days, months and years to follow, Livingstone would be incessantly berated with the allegation that he had brought the Nazis into the conversation out the blue, even of being "obsessed" by Hitler. But examination of the transcript shows that, in fact, it had been Feltz who had raised the issue of the Nazis.

The interview began with Feltz quoting from a *Daily Telegraph* editorial which claimed people were "furious" about "the

---

17 "Confirmed figures reveal the true extent of the destruction inflicted upon the Gaza Strip; Israel's offensive resulted in 1,417 dead, including 926 civilians, 255 police officers, and 236 fighters," Palestinian Centre for Human Rights press release, 12 March 2009.

18 "A word in your ear, Prime Minister," *Jewish Chronicle*, 13 August 2009.

conduct of Mr Corbyn's friend and ally Ken Livingstone" due to his defence of Naz Shah. "Do you still maintain" that Shah's comments were not anti-Semitic? Feltz demanded to know.

Livingstone repeated his standard defence of Shah, in the same terms as in other interviews. "She's a deep critic of Israel and its policies," he argued. "Her remarks were over the top. But she's not anti-Semitic. I've been in the Labour Party for 47 years. I've never heard anyone say anything anti-Semitic. I've heard a lot of criticism of the state of Israel and its abuse of the Palestinians, but I've never heard someone be anti-Semitic."

Feltz then gave a distorted rendering of Shah's Facebook postings: "She talked about relocating Israel to America. She talked about what Hitler did being legal . . . You didn't find that to be anti-Semitic?"

"Oh it's completely over the top, but it's not anti-Semitic," replied Livingstone. His next two sentences were the crucial ones: "Let's remember that when Hitler won his election in 1932 his policy then was that Jews should be moved to Israel. He was supporting Zionism, before he went mad and ended up killing six million Jews."

It was a passing comment, a reference to a relatively unknown historical incident. But as we'll see in this chapter, Livingstone was essentially correct. It is simply a fact of history that the Nazi government struck agreements in the 1930s with Germany's Zionist movement.

Livingstone then continued his defence of Shah, saying that her Facebook postings were made in 2014, "at a time when there was a brutal Israeli attack on the Palestinians. And there's one stark fact, which virtually no-one in the British media ever reports. In all these conflicts, the death toll is usually between 60 and 100 Palestinians killed for every Israeli. Now, any other country doing that would be accused of war crimes, but it's like we have a double standard about the policies of the Israeli government."

Feltz did not challenge Livingstone on his comment about the historical fact that Hitler had been "supporting Zionism" and it's telling that she didn't raise an objection at the time. It only became controversial in a manufactured media storm after the fact.

What had Feltz meant by Shah having "talked about what Hitler did being legal"? This was the part of her question which promoted Livingstone to answer that Hitler had been supporting Zionism.

It was a reference to another Facebook post unearthed by Guido Fawkes. Was it really true that Naz Shah, now a Labour MP, had endorsed Hitler's genocidal racist regime? The government that systematically murdered millions of people on an unprecedented, industrialised scale simply for being Jewish, Roma, a political opponent, or otherwise *untermenschen* according to the Nazis' twisted ideology? That's how it probably sounded to listeners, had they been taking Feltz's version at face value: "She talked about what Hitler did being legal."

In fact, this related to a Martin Luther King Jr. quote on the importance of disobeying unjust laws. Viewed impartially, the meme Shah posted was obviously a denunciation of the Nazis. The 15 September 2014 Facebook posting showed a famous police mugshot of Martin Luther King Jr. taken during the civil rights struggle which he led in the United States, with a caption quoting him: "Never forget that everything Hitler did in Germany was legal." To this, Shah had added the comment: "#Apartheid Israel."[19] The message was obvious, and accurate: every racist government in history, whether it be the Jim Crow south, Nazi Germany or apartheid Israel, legitimates its own unjust actions through its legal system. The fuller, original quote from King himself made the point far more eloquently than an internet meme ever could: "We can never forget that everything Hitler did in Germany was 'legal' ... It was 'illegal' to aid and comfort a Jew in Hitler's Germany. But I am sure that if I had lived in Germany during that time, I would have aided and comforted my Jewish brothers even though it was illegal."[20]

The original meme as posted by Shah included the attribution of the quote to Martin Luther King, along with the correct

---

19   "Naz Shah Compared Israelis to Hitler," Guido Fawkes, 26 April 2016.

20   Martin Luther King Jr., "Letter from Birmingham Jail," 16 April 1963, as cited in Scott Horton, "King – Letter from a Birmingham Jail," *Harper's Magazine*, 5 April 2008.

citation to the "Letter From Birmingham Jail."[21] But Guido used a cropped version of the image in its first blog posting. The site's bloggers seemingly understood it would have been harder to have made the accusation of anti-Semitism stick had it been more widely understood that the quote came from King himself.

The decontextualised and misquoted way in which Shah's old social media postings were pored over in the mainstream media was to be a common method used against Corbyn's supporters in the years ahead. Time and time again, old Facebook postings would be disinterred. Time and time again, the press would demand that Labour leaders denounce their members, councillors, candidates, and activists. Time and again, Corbyn and his spokespeople responded weakly: denouncing anti-Semitism, but rarely, if ever, calling into question the objective facts of the case, the motives of the accusers, or the fact that, in most cases, the postings were legitimate and not actually anti-Semitic (although sometimes crude).

The most salient point about Shah's old Facebook posting comparing the Nazis' racist treatment of Jews to Israel's racist treatment of Palestinians is simply this: it was Vanessa Feltz who raised the issue of Hitler, *not* Ken Livingstone. This is a vital point, because it was ultimately this radio interview that cost Livingstone his Labour membership. Other charges were added later, but it was Vanessa Feltz who ultimately got Livingstone driven out of the party he had dedicated his entire adult life to. There was absolutely nothing anti-Semitic about what Livingstone had said. It is simply a fact of history that Hitler's Nazi government had extensive links with the Zionist movement in the 1930s. Feltz had specifically asked Livingstone to respond to Shah having "talked about what Hitler did being legal."

When John Mann called the former mayor a "Nazi apologist" he was saying that by stating that Hitler had been "supporting Zionism," Livingstone was implying that the Jews themselves had been responsible for the Holocaust. The problem with Mann's false equivalence is that it rests on the assumption

---

21 Bob Pitt, "'George just means Jew. Vile Jew'—How David Baddiel smeared George Galloway," Medium.com, 3 February 2018. For a copy of the original meme, see https://bit.ly/3eqfWLU.

that all or most German Jews were Zionists. They weren't. In 1933 German Zionism was "a minority, fighting alone against a Jewish world." Membership of the German Zionist federation fell from 33,000 in 1923 to 22,000 in 1925. In 1929 just 8,739 voted in Zionist elections out of more than half a million German Jews. When Hitler took power, Zionists made up about 2 percent of German Jewry.[22]

But as we can see from the transcript, what Livingstone actually said was very different. It was a specific claim: that Hitler had been supporting Zionism before the Holocaust. For any historical claim, it is necessary to judge its factual basis before rushing to judgement over motives. When Holocaust deniers (such as the dishonest "revisionist" historian David Irving) twist the facts in this way, we can see the anti-Semitic motives. Their hatred for Jews and support for Hitler's Nazi ideology leads them into factual contortions in which they deny some of the proven facts of Second World War history: that Hitler's Nazi regime murdered some six million Jews; that from 1941 onwards the Nazis' "Final Solution" aimed at the physical elimination of Europe's Jewish population; that there were gas chambers, and other implements of a mass, industrial-scale genocide targeting mainly the Jewish population.

Recounting the historical fact that in the early 1930s, Hitler's new Nazi government had extensive, and well-documented, links with the German Zionist movement is not anti-Semitic—precisely because it is a fact.

What are the historical facts then? To establish this, it is necessary to take a historical diversion. It should not be necessary to do so: stating historical facts is not evidence of anti-Semitism. But I have chosen to look at this in some depth in the following pages precisely because so much of the destructive, irrational,

---

22 Joachim Prinz, "Zionism Under the Nazi Government," *New Palestine*, 17 September 1937, as cited in Lenni Brenner, *51 Documents - Zionist Collaboration with the Nazis* (New Jersey: Barricade Books, 2002), page 99. Donald Niewyk, *The Jews in Weimar Germany* (Manchester University Press, 1980), pages 139, 156. Klaus Polkehn, "The Secret Contacts: Zionism and Nazi Germany, 1933-1941," *Journal of Palestine Studies*, Vol. 5: 3/4, Spring-Summer 1976, page 56. I am grateful to Tony Greenstein for these references.

downward spiral that the "Labour anti-Semitism crisis" went into over the weeks, months, and years that followed had its roots in the Labour Party's decision—reluctantly led by Jeremy Corbyn—to marginalise and ultimately expunge Ken Livingstone from their ranks. It was to prove a fateful error.

* * *

Was Ken Livingstone right or wrong? Were Hitler and the Nazi government "supporting Zionism" after their 1932 election victories (in Germany's parliament where they formed the largest bloc) with the policy "that Jews should be moved to Israel"? The quote has been frequently deployed as a sort of gotcha moment. It's usually distorted as Livingstone having said "Hitler was a Zionist."[23]

The difference between that misquote and the correct "Hitler . . . was supporting Zionism" may at first seem minor, but it is important. The implication—as shown by John Mann's smears—is that Livingstone was trying to use coded anti-Semitic language to express the idea that Hitler was himself Jewish. This would have been similar to neo-Nazi, "revisionist" myths about the Holocaust having been a Jewish plot to frame the innocent Nazis. It was absolutely clear, however, from Livingstone's actual words that this was not what he meant at all.

What Livingstone said was absolutely correct. He was imprecise in one detail: in 1932, of course there was no such country as "Israel," it was Palestine to which the Zionist movement wanted Jews to migrate. Arguably, he would also have been more correct to point to January 1933, when Hitler was appointed chancellor, as the key date that Nazi rule began, rather than the two inconclusive Reichstag elections of 1932 (in both of which the Nazis were the biggest party, but failed to win an overall majority). But these are minor quibbles. On the general facts, there's no doubt Livingstone was correct, however uncomfortable supporters of Zionism in the present day may find it.

---

23 As only one example among many, see: Nick Cohen, "Why has Labour run the risk of alienating progressive Jews?" *Guardian*, 7 July 2018.

The Zionist response when these facts are exposed is usually to distract attention by making false accusations of anti-Semitism. We can learn much about Nazi-Zionist relations in the pre-war years from the work of American academic Francis Nicosia, who is the Professor Emeritus of History and the Raul Hilberg Distinguished Professor of Holocaust Studies at the University of Vermont. His 1985 book *The Third Reich and the Palestine Question* is a detailed exploration of German, British, US, and Israeli/Zionist archives to shed light on the history of this issue. It is written in a fairly dry academic style and loaded with comprehensive footnotes; nonetheless, the facts it exposes about this hidden history are at times genuinely shocking.

On 30 January 1933, the Nazis came to power in Germany, with their leader Adolf Hitler appointed chancellor. There then followed a series of events by which he soon gained absolute dictatorial power; other political parties were banned and internal enemies were purged. In August 1934, Hitler declared himself supreme leader—the *Führer*. Although the Holocaust didn't begin until the invasion of the USSR in June 1941, Hitler's violent anti-Semitism was evident long before the start of his rule. He had made clear his goal was the complete removal—via emigration or deportation—of Germany's Jewish community. "We will carry on our struggle until the last Jew is removed from the German Reich," he said in an April 1920 speech in Munich.[24]

Crucial to his and the Nazi party's worldview was the idea that there was a vast international Jewish conspiracy for the overthrow of Germany and of European civilisation more broadly. Nazi suspicion of the Zionist movement was predicated on racist ideas about the inferiority of Jews and how they were incapable of building a state. Professor Nicosia summarises Alfred Rosenberg (the Nazi party's main theoretician) when he wrote that "Jews had neither the capability to create a state in the European sense nor the intention of making that an end in itself," and that the Zionists merely wanted to create a "Jewish Vatican" as a base to continue the supposed Jewish world-conspiracy.[25]

---

24   Francis R. Nicosia, *The Third Reich and the Palestine Question* (London: I. B. Tauris, 1985), page 22.

25   Nicosia, *The Third Reich*, page 24.

However, Rosenberg also recognised from early on that Nazi and Zionist strategic goals were not necessarily incompatible. He wrote in 1919 that "Zionism must be vigorously supported in order to encourage a significant number of German Jews to leave for Palestine or other destinations."[26] According to Zionist historian Edwin Black, Rosenberg "intended to use Zionism as a legal justification for depriving German Jews of their civil rights" and eventually their presence in Germany altogether.[27]

During a very public campaign of anti-Semitic speeches in the spring of 1920, Hitler explained the apparent duality of the Nazi policy towards Zionism. In the push to remove all Jews from Germany, all methods were permitted, "even if it means we must cooperate with the Devil himself."[28] Whether or not Hitler considered cooperation with Zionism to be a necessary evil, the Zionist ideology that Jews are a nation apart, utterly alien to European civilisation, certainly had a distinct resonance with the Nazis' twisted racial ideas about Jewishness. In his book *Mein Kampf*, Hitler briefly addressed the issue of Zionism, apparently finding in it a useful justification for the Nazi government's later denial of basic rights to the Jews of Germany. "A part of this race even admits quite openly that it is a foreign people," he wrote. But "while Zionism tries to make the other part of the world believe that the national self-consciousness of the Jew finds satisfaction in the creation of a Palestinian state, the Jews again most slyly dupe the stupid *goyim*. They have no thought of building up a Jewish state in Palestine," he claimed, embarking again on his conspiracy theory that the Jews were out to take over the world.[29] Despite this apparent hostility, there's evidence that Hitler had an accord with Zionist ideology, especially on the idea that Jews are a race apart. During one anti-Jewish speech in July 1920, somebody in the audience objected to Hitler's call

---

26 Nicosia, *The Third Reich*, page 25.

27 Edwin Black, *The Transfer Agreement: The Dramatic Story of the Pact between the Third Reich and Jewish Palestine* (Brookline Books, 1999), pages 172-3. I am grateful to Tony Greenstein for this reference.

28 Nicosia, *The Third Reich*, page 22.

29 Nicosia, *The Third Reich*, pages 27-8.

for the removal of the Jews from Germany with shouts about human rights. According to Nicosia, "Hitler responded that Jews should seek their human rights in their own state in Palestine, where they belong."[30]

But Zionism very much is what it has always stated itself to be: a settler-colonial movement to create a Jewish state in Palestine against the wishes of the majority non-Jewish Indigenous population.[31] The Nazis' suspicion of Zionism's Jewishness was soon tempered: Zionism was another racial movement that could actually be used *against* the Jews. In the first years after Hitler came to power the Nazi government embarked on an extraordinary series of supportive, practical measures to boost the Zionist movement.

On 28 January 1935, Reinhard Heydrich (later the architect of the Holocaust) issued a directive: "The activity of the Zionist-oriented youth organisations that are engaged in the occupational restructuring of the Jews . . . lies in the interest of the National Socialist state's leadership . . . [they are] not to be treated with that strictness that it is necessary to apply to the members of the so-called German-Jewish organisations."[32]

In August 1933, an economic agreement was struck between the Nazi government and the *Zionistische Vereinigung für Deutschland* (Zionist Association for Germany, the ZVfD, often also known in English as the Zionist Federation) with the participation of the Zionist movement in Palestine. This complicated arrangement operated under a limited company titled *Haavara*, the Hebrew word for "transfer." German Jews were given economic incentives to liquidate their property and leave the country "voluntarily," on the condition that they agreed to become settlers in Palestine. The money raised from the sale of this

---

30 Nicosia, *The Third Reich*, page 28.

31 See Joseph A. Massad, *The Persistence of the Palestinian Question: Essays on Zionism and the Palestinians* (New York: Routledge, 2006), chapter 4, especially pages 82-3.

32 Lucy Dawidowicz, *The War Against the Jews 1933-45* (London: Penguin, 1987), page 118. Francis Nicosia, *Zionism and Anti-Semitism in Nazi Germany* (New York: Cambridge University Press, 2008) page 119. I am grateful to Tony Greenstein for these references.

Jewish property was then deposited in a special bank account controlled by the Nazis. The Haavara company in occupied Palestine then placed orders for German equipment and goods which were paid for out of the special account.

By 1933 German Jews needed little encouragement to leave Germany. A pogrom-like atmosphere was being whipped up by Nazi mobs against ordinary Jewish citizens. But most German Jews were still hoping that the Nazi tide would recede and that they could ride out the storm, either remaining in Germany or moving temporarily to neighbouring European states. The Nazi solution prior to the Holocaust was expulsion and the Haavara agreement. The Zionist organisations in both Germany and Palestine pushed for and agreed to these measures. They did so despite the fact that Jews in Germany were already being repressed, only months into Hitler's rule, with boycotts of Jewish businesses organised by a Nazi militia, dismissal of Jews from the civil service, and restriction of Jewish students by quota.

Most Jews leaving Germany had about two-thirds of their assets confiscated. Under the Haavara agreement, Jews electing to go to Palestine (at that time a British occupied "mandate" territory) were permitted to take £1,000 in hard currency with them in order to gain admittance to Palestine without the need for an immigration certificate. Between 1933 and 1939, nearly 52,000 Jewish people departed Germany for Palestine[33]—a minority of the 282,000 Jews who fled Germany during the same period (more than half of Germany's 523,000 Jewish population as of January 1933).[34] Only about 20,000 left via the Haavara agreement. The rest left via emigration procedures.

An estimated 105 to 140 million German marks were transferred under the aegis of Haavara[35] (105 million marks was about

---

33   Nicosia, *The Third Reich*, page 217.

34   "German Jewish Refugees, 1933–1939," Holocaust Encyclopaedia, United States Holocaust Memorial Museum (accessed 14 June 2022).

35   Nicosia, *The Third Reich*, page 213, gives a total of 105 million reichsmarks. Concurring with that total are Raul Hilberg, *Destruction of the European Jews: Vol. I, Third Edition* (Yale University Press, 2003), page 139, footnote 9, and Saul Friedlander, *Nazi Germany and the Jews: The Years of Persecution, 1933-1939* (New York: Harper Collins, 1997), page 26. Estimating that

£8.4 million, or the equivalent of more than half a billion pounds in today's money). Haavara accounted for 60 percent of total capital investment in the Jewish settler-colony in Palestine. By June 1937, Nazi Germany had surpassed the colonial power Britain to become the top exporter to Palestine. Although a small market for German foreign trade overall, the Nazi government provided a crucial boost to the struggling economy of the Zionist settler-colonial project in Palestine.

This was especially the case between 1936 and 1939, when a popular Palestinian insurrection against British rule and Zionist settlement broke out amongst the Indigenous people. A major factor in the outbreak was the growing displacement of Palestinian tenant farmers from their traditional lands. Greater numbers of the Zionist settlers came in, increasingly with the racist ideology of "Hebrew labour," which meant that Arabs were barred from working on the land. This colonialist ideology was also known as the "conquest of labour," and formed one of the three pillars of "conquest" integral to Zionism, along with the "conquest of land" and the "conquest of [Jewish] communities" in the imperial metropoles (see chapter 7). As European Jewish settlers arrived, so the Indigenous population was increasingly forced out, with peasant farmers often now living in shanty towns on the margins of the urban centres. Dispossessed, they were denied access to work. The "Hebrew labour" campaign consisted of protests and physical attacks by Zionist gangs against Palestinian workers, denying them employment in the Jewish settlements built on the very same land those workers had until so recently farmed. As academic Paul Kelemen points out, these clashes, which happened in 1934 and 1935, coincided with the Nazi campaign in Germany to boycott Jewish businesses.[36] For

---

Haavara's value was far higher, the equivalent to 140 million reichsmarks are: Hava Eshkoli-Wagman, "Yishuv Zionism: Its Attitude to Nazism and the Third Reich Reconsidered," *Modern Judaism*, Vol. 19:1, 1999, The John Hopkins University Press, page 29, as well as Klaus Polkehn, "The Secret Contacts: Zionism and Nazi Germany, 1933-1941," *Journal of Palestine Studies*, Vol. 5: 3/4, Spring-Summer 1976, page 66. I am grateful to Tony Greenstein for the latter four references.

36   Paul Kelemen, *The British Left and Zionism: History of a Divorce* (Manchester University Press, 2012), pages 28-9.

these reasons, the centre of gravity of the Palestinian uprising of 1936 was the rural population. The peasants' traditional checked *keffiyeh* scarf became a symbol of the revolutionaries.[37]

The details of Haavara were worked out in a 7 August 1933 meeting in Berlin between the German government and Zionist leaders. In attendance were officials from the Nazi-led Ministry of Economics (minister Kurt Schmitt was a personal friend of SS leader Heinrich Himmler), Zionist representatives from the German ZFvD, and leaders of the settler-colony in Palestine, including Jewish Agency chairman Arthur Ruppin. The appeal of Haavara to the Nazis was two-fold. Firstly, it encouraged Jewish emigration from Europe. In the years before the Nazis embarked on the "Final Solution," encouraging emigration was a crucial step towards the Nazi goal of making Germany *judenrein*, or empty of Jews. Secondly, and perhaps most importantly from the Nazi perspective, Haavara was a crucial tool that helped them to break an anti-Nazi boycott of German goods which had been growing around the world since January 1933 when Hitler was made leader. Led by a loose coalition of non-Zionist Jewish groups, socialist activists, and some business interests, the boycott saw major successes. It made such an impact that by June, "the spectre of collapse was hovering over the Third Reich."[38]

The Zionists, however, opposed the boycott, giving the Nazis a lifeline. At the urging of the Nazi government, leaders from the German Zionist federation, the ZVfD, attended the eighteenth World Zionist Congress in Prague, to push against the boycott and in favour of the "transfer" approach. For the Zionists in Palestine, Nicosia summarises, "the Jews from Germany, along with their assets . . . represented a stimulus for the development of the country."[39]

A 28 August 1933 circular to all currency control offices in Germany from the Ministry of Economics explained the new

---

37 Still the best short study of the 1936 Palestinian uprising is Ghassan Kanafani, *The 1936-39 Revolt in Palestine* (New York: Committee for a Democratic Palestine, 1972).

38 Tony Greenstein, *Zionism During the Holocaust* (self-published, 2022), page 113.

39 Nicosia, *The Third Reich*, page 39.

agreement with the Zionists in a nutshell: "In order to promote the emigration of German Jews to Palestine through the allocation of the necessary amounts without excessive strain on the currency holdings of the Reichsbank, and at the same time to increase German exports to Palestine, an agreement based on the following principles has been concluded."[40] It went on to outline the details. From then until at least 1937, summarises Nicosia, "all agencies in the German Foreign Office in any way responsible for Palestine and the Middle East supported Zionist emigration from Germany to Palestine."[41]

Many Zionists today defend Haavara as the only way for Jews to escape their persecution in the early years of Nazi Germany. However, this is untrue. Only a minority of German Jewish emigrants went to Palestine. In fact, Haavara hurt those who wanted to leave for elsewhere by restricting the capital they could take out.

There was also a more sinister Zionist motive. "The situation in Germany" (Nicosia rather euphemistically states of the Nazi persecution of the Jews) "was also viewed as a positive stimulus to Zionist efforts to Palestine, a chance to interest the traditionally liberal/assimilationist Jewish community in Germany in the Zionist cause." While condemning Hitler's regime in public, Zionist leaders in private were far more cheerful about the opportunities that the Nazi regime presented to them. Only a few months after Hitler came to power, ZVfD chairman Kurt Blumenfeld noted that "there exists today a unique opportunity to win over the Jews of Germany for the Zionist idea." In 1934 the German consul-general in Jerusalem reported on the recognition of "the opportunities for Zionism and the development of Palestine that have emerged from the misfortune of the Jews in Germany."[42]

Although Haavara's defenders today like to claim that it saved lives, the opposite is the case. By undermining the boycott campaign, it actually helped Hitler's regime to stabilise itself.

---

40   Nicosia, *The Third Reich*, pages 46-7.

41   Nicosia, *The Third Reich*, page 51.

42   Nicosia, *The Third Reich*, page 42.

The stark reality is that the German Jews who left the country via the agreement were all relatively wealthy, and most would likely have found another way to leave the country. The real goal of the agreement was to save German Jewish capital, not German Jewish lives.[43]

* * *

Nazi-Zionist collusion was not a simple marriage of convenience. Zionist leaders at times attempted to reconcile their ideology with Nazism, expressing agreement with aspects of its racist ideology. A June 1933 memo to Adolf Hitler from the ZVfD "seemed to express a degree of sympathy for the *völkisch* principles of the Hitler regime," summarises Nicosia. This overture was an attempt to persuade Hitler of the benefits of Zionism and its plan to create a Jewish state in Palestine in terms that would appeal to the explicit racism of Nazi ideology. "Zionism believes that the rebirth of the national life of a people, which is now occurring in Germany through the emphasis on its Christian and national character, must also come about among the Jewish people," wrote the ZVfD in a June 1933 memo sent to Hitler himself.[44] Zionist leaders were explicitly comparing their own movement to Nazism. Such a "Nazi comparison" could have gotten them suspended from the British Labour Party of 2016.

As well as being an arch anti-Palestinian colonist, Jewish Agency leader Arthur Ruppin had also deeply internalised the anti-Semitism of his native German society. "I hate the wild thorns of Judaism," a 17-year-old Ruppin wrote in his diary, "more than the worst anti-Semite." Nor were these repulsive views moderated in later life. In 1942, not long before he died, Ruppin wrote a bizarre study of different types of "Jewish nose" as an indication of racial affinity. He attached to each "type" names of Zionist leaders from Herzl onwards. In a 2008 doctoral thesis, Israeli academic Etan Bloom laid out much of

---

43 Greenstein, *Zionism During the Holocaust*, pages 121-2. Polkehn, "The Secret Contacts," page 54.

44 Nicosia, *The Third Reich*, page 42.

this uncomfortable history. In Ruppin's conception, Zionism demanded "racial purity" among the Jews. His views were partly inspired by anti-Semitic thinkers, including some of the original Nazi ideologists. According to Israeli historian Tom Segev, "not only was Ruppin influenced by the theories that engendered Nazi racism, he also had an impact on their formulation."[45] It seems little wonder that such a figure would be willing to collaborate with Nazi racists.

Bernhard Lösener, the director of the German Ministry of the Interior's "Jewish Department," according to Nicosia, "was an avid supporter of the Zionist option." In a legal journal in November 1935 he wrote:

> If the Jews already had their own state in which the greater part of their people were settled, then the Jewish question could be considered completely resolved today also for the Jews themselves. The least amount of opposition to the underlying ideas of the Nuremberg Laws has been raised by Zionists, because they know at once that these laws represent the only correct solution for the Jewish people as well.[46]

Such frankness shows that there was a degree of ideological affinity between the Nazis and Zionism. The latter was born, after all, in the age of essentialist European nationalism, and was imbued from the outset with pseudo-scientific ideas about race and nation. Rather than challenge racism, Zionism from its inception in the late nineteenth century accepted European anti-Semitism as inevitable, pointless to resist and even as "natural." The founder of Zionism, Theodor Herzl, predicted in his diaries that "The anti-Semites will become our most dependable friends, the anti-Semitic countries our allies." In his 1896 pamphlet *The Jewish State*, he explained that "the governments of all countries scourged by anti-Semitism will be keenly interested in assisting us to obtain the sovereignty we want" and that "not only poor

---

45 Tom Segev, "The Makings of History: Revisiting Arthur Ruppin," *Haaretz*, 8 October 2009.

46 Nicosia, *The Third Reich*, page 53.

Jews" would contribute to an immigration fund for European Jews, but also "Christians who wanted to get rid of them."[47]

As such, the Nazi regime encouraged the Zionist movement throughout the 1930s. Zionist groups in Germany were often exempt from growing Nazi restrictions and bans on Jewish political activities and public life. Throughout 1935 the intelligence arm of the SS (a notorious Nazi paramilitary formation) was active in infiltrating, monitoring, and censoring Jewish meetings. It banned anything encouraging Jews to remain in Germany but, at the same time, encouraged Zionist propaganda activities. In May 1935 the Gestapo secret police issued a general ban on Jewish organisations holding meetings or making speeches. Apart from some sports and cultural activities, the only exemptions to the ban were Zionist organisations.[48] In the anti-Semitic Nuremberg laws of 1935, Jews were banned from flying the German flag. Instead, they were permitted to display a blue-and-white national flag—the same flag which would, in 1948, become the standard of the state of Israel.[49]

In September 1935, leading SS intelligence officer Reinhard Heydrich wrote the following chilling passage in a Nazi newspaper (my emphasis):

> In the context of its *Weltanschauung* [world view], National Socialism has no intention of attacking the Jewish people in any way. On the contrary, the recognition of Jewry as a racial community based on blood, and not as a religious one, leads the German government to guarantee the racial separateness of this community without any limitations. *The government finds itself in complete agreement with the great spiritual movement within Jewry itself, the so-called Zionism*, with its recognition of the solidarity

---

47 Joseph Massad, "Pro-Zionism and antisemitism are inseparable, and always have been," *Middle East Eye*, 15 May 2019. See also Massad, *The Persistence*, pages 148-51.

48 Nicosia, *The Third Reich*, page 55.

49 Nicosia, *The Third Reich*, page 60.

of Jewry throughout the world and the rejection of all assimilationist ideas.[50]

The first thing to note about this disturbing quote is its propagandistic quality. Even though the Holocaust had not yet got underway, the contention that the Nazis had "no intention" of attacking Jews would have been laughable in 1935, were it not so sinister. The second thing to note about this passage identifying Nazi sympathy for the Zionist movement is its author: Heydrich would go on to be one of the primary architects of the Holocaust; he was assassinated in 1942 in Prague by Czechoslovak agents, trained by British forces. But one of the very worst Nazis of all had found himself in "complete agreement" with Zionism. Before the Nazis settled on the "Final Solution" of genocide, Zionism was viewed as a useful tool to help get rid of German Jews.

Almost immediately after Hitler came to power, the German Zionist movement began establishing an extensive network of occupational retraining centres to prepare prospective settlers for their new lives in Palestine. By August 1936, Hechaluz, the youth wing of the ZVfD, had established 40 such *Umschulungslager* (or re-education camps) with the full approval of the Nazi authorities.[51] The Ministry of Labour in 1935 "expressed its unqualified support," Nicosia recounts. It also "referred favourably to the *support* already given to the retraining programme *by Hitler and the Gestapo*" (my emphases).[52] The Nazis considered the programme a useful way of encouraging Jews to leave Germany. Hitler himself had given "support" to this central Zionist activity. Hitler was supporting Zionism. Ken Livingstone was right.

These camps featured in a broad programme of Zionist propaganda among the Jews of Germany, showing films and collecting money, and generally promoting emigration to Palestine. It was part of a wider push for Jews "to cease identifying themselves as Germans and to awaken a new Jewish national

---

50   Nicosia, *The Third Reich*, page 57.

51   For a map of their locations see Nicosia, *The Third Reich*, page 217.

52   Nicosia, *The Third Reich*, page 59.

identity," Nicosia writes.[53] Even while Jews were being removed from state schools, a separate Jewish school system was subsidised by the Nazi government right up until 1939.

The SS spy agency even sent Nazi officers to observe the nineteenth and twentieth sessions of the Zionist Congress.[54] Leopold von Mildenstein went to Lucerne, Switzerland in 1935, attached to the German Zionist delegation. At the next Zionist Congress, in 1937 in Zurich, the Nazis sent Adolf Eichmann himself. A few years later, Eichmann would be one of the leading orchestrators of the Holocaust. Both Mildenstein and Eichmann visited Palestine personally. Mildenstein toured the Zionist settlements in 1933 while Eichmann arrived in 1937 but was expelled by the British within a day.[55] Mildenstein's 1933 tour led to a series of reports in Nazi newspaper *Der Angriff* titled "A Nazi goes to Palestine."[56] The reports portrayed the Zionist settler in Palestine as a "new Jew" far removed from the stereotypes of European anti-Semitism which had been adopted and propagated by the Nazis. German Jews en route to Palestine no longer had the "ghetto look," he wrote. He described one farmer on an agricultural settlement, writing that he "stands before us in the moonlight. He suits the soil. The soil has reformed him and his kind in a decade. This new Jew will be a new people." This nationalist mythology was very much in tune with the mystical Nazi ideology of "blood and soil." In other words, the "blood" purity of a people was determined by its relationship with the "soil" of the country. The anti-Semitic ideology held that Jews were an alien force in Germany and so they could never form a real part of the German people.

Uncomfortable as it may be for Labour Party members to recognise today, such "blood and soil" ethnic chauvinism also

---

53   Nicosia, *The Third Reich*, page 60.

54   Nicosia, *The Third Reich*, page 61.

55   Chen Malul, "Adolf Eichmann's Secret Visit to Palestine," The National Library of Israel website, 6 November 2017 (accessed 14 June 2022).

56   "Why the Head of the SS's Jewish Desk, Baron von Mildenstein and top German Zionist official Kurt Tuchler went [sic] visited and stayed in Palestine together," Tony Greenstein's blog, 3 May 2018.

had its advocates on the British left. Recall pro-Zionist Labour MP Herbert Morrison, whose speech in the House of Commons stressed that Jewish settlers in Palestine were "first-class colonisers" for the British empire. "I have met many Jews in many countries," he wrote in 1935. "I know the London Jews very well, but the [newly settled] Palestinian Jews were to me different; so different that a large proportion of them were not obviously Jews at all." As academic Paul Kelemen explains, Morrison "saw in Jewish agricultural labour a form of purification, redeeming the anti-Semitic projection of the Jew which Morrison took for real."[57] Morrison's conception of the new Jewish settlers in Palestine being "not obviously Jews at all" was almost identical to Nazi leader Mildenstein's ideas of the Jewish settlers becoming "new Jews," mystically redeemed by the soil of Palestine.

Nazi support for Zionism even went as far as arms. Eichmann had a notable Zionist contact by the name of Feivel Polkes, who was an intelligence agent of the Haganah, the main Labour Zionist militia and precursor to the Israeli army. Eichmann brought Polkes to Berlin in 1937 for meetings with SS and Gestapo officials. As well as paying for his stay, Eichmann's spy agency arranged for monthly payments to the Haganah agent "for his news gathering activities" on Jewish organisations in Palestine and elsewhere. According to Nicosia, during his Berlin meetings Polkes boasted to the Nazis of his anti-British, anti-Arab, and anti-communist credentials. He claimed contacts with French, British, and Italian intelligence and offered to expand this circle to include the Nazi government in exchange for any aid they could offer the Zionist cause. Between 1933 and 1935, the Haganah smuggled 300 barrels half-filled with Mauser pistols and ammunition into Palestine from Germany. In Berlin, Polkes expressed his gratitude to the Nazi officials for the guns, which he said had been useful to the Haganah during the recent Palestinian Arab uprising. Nicosia's research in the German archives revealed that Haganah agents were then active in Germany and that, while it is unclear who exactly supplied the guns, "it is certain that somebody in Germany did and that the [Nazi] police authorities were aware of it." Even decades

---

57 Kelemen, *The British Left and Zionism*, page 27.

later, when Nicosia was writing in the early 1980s, the question of the mainstream Zionist movement's collusion with the Nazis remained a closely guarded secret. Nicosia—a sympathiser with Zionism—was denied access to a file on Polkes in the Haganah archives in Tel Aviv.[58]

More well-known than Feivel Polkes is the offer of a right-wing Zionist militia, the Lehi, to collaborate with Hitler during the Second World War. Also known as the Stern Gang, the Lehi was fairly open about its fascistic ideology. In late 1940, they approached Hitler's government offering to form an alliance with Nazi Germany in exchange for recognising their aspirations to create a Jewish state in Palestine. The proposal was ignored. Lehi is notorious for its bloody role in the 1948 Deir Yassin massacre of mostly unarmed Palestinian civilians, and for its assassination of UN peace envoy Count Folke Bernadotte. Decades later, Lehi leader Yitzhak Shamir was elected prime minister of Israel.

The record of Nazi-Zionist collusion during the 1930s is therefore quite extensive. None of these historical facts is seriously contested by anyone. What is contested is their interpretation. Zionists and their sympathisers now say that cooperation with Nazi authorities was an essential method of rescuing Jews from the growing threat of the Nazi regime. But at the time, Zionists had no such illusions. The first Israeli prime minister David Ben-Gurion was absolutely opposed to a British plan to rescue and bring to Britain 10,000 mostly Jewish children after the November 1938 *Kristallnacht* pogroms (the rescue later came to be known as the *Kindertransport*). Ben-Gurion told Labour Zionist leaders: "If I knew that it was possible to save all the [Jewish] children in Germany by transporting them to England, but only half of them by transporting them to Palestine, I would choose the second—because we face not only the reckoning of those children, but the historical reckoning of the Jewish people."

---

58 Nicosia, *The Third Reich*, pages 62-4. The archive's policy seems to alternate between denying access to the file and denying the file even exists. Anti-Zionist historian Lenni Brenner was told "There is no file because it would be too embarrassing." See Stanley Heller, "Isn't it Time for the Truth about Feivel Polkes and His Haganah Chiefs?" *New Politics*, 25 February 2021.

Ben-Gurion worried that "the human conscience" might lead other countries to offer to take these child refugees in, which he saw as a threat: "Zionism is in danger!"[59] Zionist leader Chaim Weizmann (later the first president of Israel) also spoke out against the Kindertransport. Like Ben-Gurion he wanted the children sent to Palestine instead.[60] "I remember at the time that Weizmann's attitude shocked me," Colonial Secretary Malcolm MacDonald recalled. "He insisted on the children going to Palestine. As far as he was concerned it was Palestine or nowhere."[61]

Another Labour Zionist visited Germany in 1933 and crudely laid out the opportunities the Nazi regime provided for Zionism: "The streets are paved with more money than we have ever dreamed of in the history of our Zionist enterprise. Here is an opportunity to build and flourish like none we have ever had or ever will have."[62]

* * *

The immense amount of material support that the German government under the Nazis gave to the Zionist movement is plain from the historical record. The general outline of the facts laid out by Nicosia had already been published two years earlier in another book, *Zionism in the Age of the Dictators*, by Jewish American author Lenni Brenner. Addressing the Labour Party's disciplinary panel, Ken Livingstone cited the latter. But even the mere fact of his reliance on a book by an anti-Zionist author

---

59 Tom Segev, *The Seventh Million: The Israelis and the Holocaust* (New York: Hill and Wang, 1994), page 28.

60 Kelemen, *The British Left and Zionism*, page 59. See also pages 62-3 for details of the history of Zionist efforts in Britain (right through World War II) to prevent German Jewish refugees from being brought to the UK. Polling showed that despite British anti-Semitism, there was popular support for settling Jewish refugees.

61 Nicholas Bethell, *The Palestine Triangle* (London: Andre Deutsch, 1979), page 52.

62 Segev, *The Seventh Million*, page 18.

for his defence got him into trouble. The *Telegraph*'s former editor Charles Moore raged that the former mayor's use of the Brenner book proved that Labour had "embraced an ideology that has race hate at its heart."[63] The *Guardian*'s approach was to red-bait, stating in its headline that Livingstone had cited a "Marxist book" in defence of his comments. The reporter went on, bizarrely, to quote a history professor who admitted to not having read the book.[64] Despite a raft of "Why Ken's comments on Zionism were wrong" –style articles, no-one in the mainstream seriously addressed the historical record of Nazi support for the German Zionist movement in the 1930s.

As the "Labour anti-Semitism crisis" grew, the relevance of this largely forgotten history came to have a modern-day prominence. As decried by Labour Friends of Israel, it became a crime in the party punishable by expulsion, suspension, or censure to make "Nazi comparisons."[65] The most prominent example of this was the renowned Israeli anti-Zionist Moshé Machover, who was expelled from Labour in 2017. In a long article written for a communist newspaper, Machover had analysed the growing party witch hunt in the context of wider Zionist efforts to paint anti-Zionism as anti-Semitic. He argued that Livingstone's point about Zionism and the Nazis the previous year had been "basically correct." He wrote that Labour's witch hunt should be defeated with a full-frontal political counterattack. His words now seem grimly prophetic: "It is correct to expose Zionism as a movement based on both colonisation and collusion with anti-Semitism. Don't apologise for saying this. If you throw the sharks bloodied meat, they will only come back for more. At the moment the left is apologising too much, in the hope

---

63 Charles Moore, "How the Labour Party embraced an ideology that has race hate at its heart," *Daily Telegraph*, 29 April 2016.

64 Ben Quinn, "Ken Livingstone cites Marxist book in defence of Israel comments," *Guardian*, 29 April 2016.

65 "LFI Officers Call on Jeremy Corbyn to Publicly Call For Ken Livingstone's Expulsion."

that the right will let up. They never will."⁶⁶ If the party leadership had taken these words to heart things could have turned out differently.

Machover's article was reprinted by a small left-wing group, Labour Party Marxists, who put it on the front page of a special newsletter they distributed outside Labour conference in September 2017. The headline read: "Anti-Zionism does not equal anti-Semitism," above a photo of Jeremy Corbyn speaking to a Palestine solidarity rally. Although the group had only a handful of members, they reported that their publication was eagerly snapped up by the Brighton delegates. The membership was, as polling evidence showed, overwhelmingly sceptical of "Labour anti-Semitism" claims. At conference that year, powerful pro-Corbyn union leader Len McCluskey (the general secretary of Britain's largest trade union, Unite) spoke for many when he called the smears "mood music created by people trying to undermine Jeremy Corbyn."⁶⁷

But in what was by that point becoming an annual ritual, corporate journalists were stalking around party conference hunting "anti-Semites." And in the Labour Party Marxists newsletter they claimed to have found one such group—a sadly apropos illustration of exactly the argument Machover was making. Ever the "anti-Semitism" hunter, Livingstone's persecutor John Mann, was back on hand to denounce the small group. "The Labour Party Marxists should all be thrown out of the party, every single one of them," he told *The Times*. Deciding the outcome of the trial in advance, he decreed that "we want them investigated and then thrown out. Their scurrilous publication, which contains antisemitic material, is good only for the recycling bin."⁶⁸

---

66 "Anti-Zionism does not equal anti-Semitism," Labour Party Marxists newsletter no. 17, 21 September 2017. For a link to the full newsletter and my report on Machover's expulsion, see Asa Winstanley, "Israeli anti-Zionist expelled from Labour amid anti-Semitism smear," *Electronic Intifada*, 4 October 2017.

67 "Labour: Len McCluskey says party does not have anti-Semitism issue," BBC News, 26 September 2017.

68 Lucy Fisher, "Throw out antisemitic party members now, Corbyn urged," *The Times*, 27 September 2017 (accessed online 23 June 2022).

But the article was not anti-Semitic. In fact, it contained *denunciation* of anti-Semitism, including by "its proponents within the left and the Labour Party." The article was smeared because it denounced both Israeli policy and Zionism, the foundational ideology of Israel. As was also now becoming a long-standing pattern, the press reporting of Machover's case was totally inaccurate on even the most basic facts. The same *Times* article reported that "The leaflet handed out in Brighton discussed the 'commonality between Zionists and Nazis'"—but this alleged quote actually appeared nowhere in the newsletter. At best, this was a journalistic dereliction of duty by *Times* reporter Lucy Fisher, perhaps quoting a critic's distorted summary of the Machover article (if so, that should have been made clear). The paper continued its inaccurate summary of Machover's article by stating it had "quoted Reinhard Heydrich, the Nazi architect of the Final Solution, saying in 1935: 'National Socialists had no intention of attacking Jewish people.'"

If anything, this de-contextualised quote was even more dishonest than the misquote about "commonality" in the previous sentence. Firstly, the context given by the paper strongly implied that the leaflet's author was giving an apologetic for one of the very worst genocidal Nazi war criminals by favourably quoting his own words as a credible source, claiming that the Nazis had no intention of attacking Jews. But, for anyone who had read Machover's article, it was clear that he was quoting Heydrich for exactly the opposite effect: to denounce him. Secondly, and perhaps even more suspect, comparison of *The Times*'s rendering of this quote to the original article shows that, again, the paper had at best mangled the quote. Unlike the previous "commonality" misquote, which was entirely fictional, this was a subtler form of disinformation. Machover's article accurately quoted Heydrich's 1935 article saying, in part, "National socialism has no intention of attacking the Jewish people in any way" (Nicosia's book contains the same, accurate quote, although it capitalises the word "Socialism"). But *The Times* appears to have altered this to incorrectly to read "National *Socialists had* no intention of attacking Jewish people" (my emphasis).[69] Whatever the reason for its

---

69 Fisher, "Throw out antisemitic party members."

misquote, *The Times* ended up making Machover look like he was *approving* of Nazi actions, when in reality his original article had done the opposite. By changing Heydrich's present-tense 1935 quote from "has" to the past-tense "had," an unsuspecting reader not familiar with the article's author may even have reasonably concluded that the quote was his own apologetic for this genocidal Nazi war criminal, rather than a quote from Heydrich himself.

If *The Times* had bothered to name him, anyone familiar with Moshé Machover would have seen through the corporate media's misreporting. Born in British-occupied Palestine, Israeli dissident Moshé Machover is an almost legendary name on the Palestine solidarity scene in the UK. An Israeli dissident, Machover rejected Zionism decades ago and moved to London in 1968. In Israel in 1962 he had been one of the original members of the Israeli Socialist Organisation, an anti-Zionist group. As detailed in Eran Torbiner's 2003 film *Matzpen*, the organisation was focused on their newspaper *Matzpen*—Hebrew for "Compass." According to Torbiner, Matzpen never numbered more than a handful of members, but had an influence far greater. They were some of the first Israeli dissidents to forge links with Palestinians in the West Bank, in Jordan, and overseas in Europe, especially in London. Palestinian author and academic Ghada Karmi formed close relationships with Machover and his comrades, such as the late Akiva Orr. They also began forging ties with the wider emergent New Left of the late 1960s.

But neither the Palestine solidarity movement nor the Labour membership was in control of the party's bureaucratic apparatus. Machover was summarily expelled only days after Mann's demand and the media outcry about "anti-Semitism." This was even harsher than the usual suspension pending investigation.[70] The expulsion letter gave the pretext of his "support" for Labour Party Marxists, but it also cited the "apparently anti-semitic article published in your name."

* * *

---

70   Winstanley, "Israeli anti-Zionist expelled."

Machover's expulsion was met with a huge backlash, a campaign which took on international dimensions. Labour bureaucrats had shown their ignorance. A spokesperson for Jeremy Corbyn told me at the time that the Labour leader would not comment on a disciplinary case. This was strange, since procedural niceties had not stopped Corbyn from criticising his old ally Livingstone's supposed causing of "hurt to the Jewish community." Nonetheless, I was also told by a Labour source inside the leader's office that Corbyn was in fact "looking into" the expulsion of Machover. The campaign to reinstate Machover was successful. The expulsion was reluctantly rescinded less than a month later—party bureaucrats had been embarrassed into a U-turn.[71]

But the issue didn't go away. Supposed "comparisons" of Israel or Zionism to Nazi Germany were deemed to be unacceptable—no matter how historically factual or carefully worded. These were matters for expulsion, suspension, or disciplinary action. Ken Livingstone and Moshé Machover were only the two most high-profile cases. The effect was to keep the "anti-Semitism crisis" in headlines for years. The fact that Corbyn did not protect Livingstone, one of his vanishingly few senior party allies, sent a message to the grassroots that none were safe should they step out of line. It was a fateful choice that would have repercussions for years. By the time Livingstone formally resigned his membership in 2018, the saga had stretched on for two years, a damaging, interminable story for the Corbynite project.

The concocted media outrage over "Nazi comparisons" for the most part only went one way. John Mann, for example, had compared Naz Shah to Adolph Eichmann.[72] For the right, it seemed, Nazi analogies were ok, as long as they were mobilised in defence of Israel.

As for Shah herself, soon after the scandal broke in April 2016, she made a series of grovelling apologies, culminating in a House of Commons statement. "The words I used caused

---

71 Asa Winstanley, "Facing outcry, UK Labour reverses expulsion of anti-Zionist Moshé Machover," *Electronic Intifada*, 31 October 2017.

72 "Labour MP Compares Naz Shah to Eichmann," Guido Fawkes, 26 April 2016.

upset and hurt to the Jewish community and I deeply regret that," she said. At the time of her suspension, the Jewish Labour Movement made clear its intention to re-educate Shah, and the wider Labour membership. Shah "is clearly on a political journey," said Jeremy Newmark. He continued that they expected her to embark on "a programme of education and action that includes standing up to anti-Semitism on the left and within the Palestine solidarity movement."[73] Posting a photo to Twitter soon after, Shah made a public show of meeting with Newmark.[74] The *Jewish News* reported in May that she had held several such meetings.[75] Her campaign paid off, and Shah's suspension was lifted that July, ensuring she could stand as a Labour candidate in future elections. Shah "has proven herself to be a bold and courageous agent of change at a time when strong leadership on this issue is so important," Newmark gushed. She had been made an example of.

Livingstone by contrast refused to bow to the logic of the witch hunt. He knew that the issue was a major attack vector against Labour's left-wing leader. He was proven correct, but for his trouble, he was hounded out of the party.

Unanswered questions remain about the Naz Shah incident, as triggered by Guido Fawkes. Who was the site's source for Shah's Facebook posting of the Martin Luther King quote about Hitler? The Guido screenshot shows that Shah's posting was not set to public, and was only viewable to her Facebook "friends." Did a friend sell Shah out? Why was the posting kept hidden for so many years? And who had doctored the screenshot to remove the quote's attribution to King? Was Guido responsible? Such questions would multiply as the "crisis" unfolded.

Jacob Baime, the US Israel lobbyist caught on camera by Al Jazeera admitting to sending "intelligence" to the Israeli government had also boasted of having "corporate-level,

---

73 "JLM Statement on Naz Shah MP," Jewish Labour Movement website, 27 April 2016 (accessed 14 June 2022)

74 "'Preposterous liar' Jeremy Newmark re-educates Naz Shah MP," Free Speech on Israel blog, 4 May 2016.

75 "Suspended Labour MP Naz Shah to speak at a synagogue," *Jewish News*, 25 May 2016.

enterprise-grade social media intelligence software. Almost all of this happens on social media so we have custom algorithms and formulae that acquire this stuff immediately."[76] That proved that such squirrelling away of obscure social posts was not always the organic process it often claimed to be. Out-of-context comments, usually on social media, were the downfall of untold numbers of Labour Party activists.

The treatment of Shah was only a sign of things to come.

---

76 *The Lobby - USA*, episode 1, timecode 06:55.

CHAPTER SIX

THE CRUCIBLE

A Black woman in her mid-sixties with greying dreadlocks sat waiting patiently, her left hand raised high in the air. The Jewish Labour Movement was nearing the end of its training session, "Anti-Semitism and Engaging Jewish Voters." It was one of many closed sessions arranged by party staff for Labour's 2016 annual conference in Liverpool. It had been introduced with the rule that questions could be asked if you raised your hand.

But Jackie Walker was being conspicuously ignored.

JLM's vice chairperson Mike Katz was clearly uncomfortable. He had stammered his way through a tense hour. Things hadn't gone to plan. A small group of left-wing Labour activists had come along to the discussion—mostly anti-Zionist Jews. It seemed to them that an anti-Corbyn Zionist group was taking over Labour Party training on anti-Semitism. The group had not heckled, interrupted, or shouted. But they did critically, if politely, engage with Katz.

"I'm Jewish, and I don't agree with the concept of a Jewish state," Walker's partner Graham Bash had said. "It gives me the right to live in Israel, whereas a Palestinian, who's been displaced has a lesser right than me." Bash was responding to a claim by Katz that it was "not appropriate" for party members to oppose the "basic right of Israel as a country to exist."

"That's a political question," Bash countered. "Are you really saying that it's not appropriate for us to have a political discussion? Or are you going further and saying that someone who shares my view is somehow anti-Semitic?"

Katz ignored his question and moved on.

Bash's friend Leah Levane stepped in next. "If you are saying, effectively, that Zionism is not open to debate as a concept, then that is really worrying," she said. "It takes away a lot of our armour to counter anti-Semitism."

Naomi Wimborne-Idrissi said that pro-Israel organisations were trying to "ban discussion about Israel-Palestine within the Labour Party and wider society." Wimborne-Idrissi is a well-known Palestine solidarity activist. A heckler cut her off, accusing her of talking "nonsense" and claiming that "nobody's trying to ban discussion about Israel-Palestine." Ironically, he only seemed to prove her point.

But probably the most contested part of the training was a definition of anti-Semitism pushed by Katz. It was September 2016, and the International Holocaust Remembrance Alliance's controversial definition of anti-Semitism had yet to be adopted by the British government (they did so in December 2016). So it had not become the national scandal for Labour that it would become in 2018.[1]

Instead, Katz put forward an older definition, practically identical to the IHRA's document. The European Union Monitoring Centre's "working definition," Katz claimed, was "the standard definition of anti-Semitism." The Jewish anti-Zionists voiced their disapproval. "Oh dear. We can't have that," Wimborne-Idrissi demurred.

Both documents were primarily aimed at protecting Israel. The list of alleged examples of anti-Semitism in both overwhelmingly concern Israel—seven out of eleven examples in each.[2] The worst such example cast criticism of Israel as a racist state as "anti-Semitism," with both documents forbidding "claiming that the existence of a State of Israel is a racist endeavour."

---

1   David Torrance, "UK Government's adoption of the IHRA definition of antisemitism," House of Commons Library, 4 October 2018.

2   The full IHRA definition is online at: "What is antisemitism? Non-legally binding working definition of antisemitism," International Holocaust Remembrance Alliance, undated (accessed 14 June 2022). A copy of the EUMC definition is still available online: "Fact sheet: 'Working Definition' of Anti-Semitism," Office to Monitor and Combat Anti-Semitism, US Department of State Archive, 8 February 2007 (accessed 14 June 2022).

The EUMC's document was widely discredited as long ago as 2011. In the end it was disowned even by the EU's racism monitoring centre.[3]

Katz seemed to know he was on shaky ground, so swiftly changed the subject. "I'm not going to go into the detail of this, this is meant to be a training session . . . we've actually not got a lot of time," he blustered. The JLM leader rushed through the rest of his presentation. He dodged further awkward questions by calling on friends in the room.

Adam Langleben, who introduced himself only as a Labour councillor in North London, was another member of the new JLM executive. Langleben claimed that Labour was now "directly hostile" to the Jewish community. He dismissed the earlier requests for open debate on Zionism, explaining that "some views are more mainstream than other views" and insisting that everyone in the room "needs to accept that." In what would become an obsessive theme pushed by Labour Party Zionists, he claimed that "there are mainstream opinions in the [Jewish] community and there are not-mainstream opinions." The idea seemed to be that such "minority opinions" could be dismissed wholesale.

Meanwhile, Jackie Walker had sat silently in the overwhelmingly white group. Earlier in 2016 her face had been splashed over the pro-Israel press as part of a smear by the Israel Advocacy Movement, a small anti-Palestinian group with a moderately large YouTube audience. Walker was also vice chairperson of Momentum, a group formed to support Corbyn's leadership. Now that she had raised her hand to speak, Katz was pointedly ignoring her. Glyn Secker, one of her comrades, could stand it no longer: "You're really not going to take the only Black Jew in the room?"

"Don't be pathetic," one of the hecklers sneered.

Katz relented. "Short contributions please," a Labour colleague fretted.

---

3   See the following articles by Ben White at the *Electronic Intifada*: "Don't mention the 'A' word: attack on freedom of speech turns into another own goal," 27 November 2011. "The chilling effect of a discredited definition of antisemitism," 1 December 2011. "Israel lobby uses discredited anti-Semitism definition to muzzle debate," 28 September 2012.

"Because we're going to be kept to time," Katz emphasised.

"I'll keep it very short," Walker said. I watched from the back of the room as Langleben took out his phone and began filming. Walker said that she had attended the training with an open mind but that "I still haven't heard a definition of anti-Semitism that I can work with"—an obvious reference to the EUMC definition which had been so vociferously contested that day.

The JLM later leaked Langleben's video to the media (in violation of basic principles of confidentially generally expected in anti-racist training groups). An edited version of the video released by the *Huffington Post* and the misleading way it reported on the event made it look as if Walker was denying the very *existence* of anti-Semitism. The reporting stated she had claimed to have *never* heard a definition of anti-Semitism she could work with. But that was clearly untrue. I reported on the event that same day, publishing my article even before the scandal broke out. It had been clear that Walker's comment concerned the only definition of anti-Semitism given in that room, saying she "hadn't heard a definition of anti-Semitism she could work with" during the training.[4]

Responding to earlier comments by Katz on Holocaust Memorial Day, Walker said: "Wouldn't it be wonderful if Holocaust Day was open to all peoples who experienced holocaust." This was a reference to her Facebook comments discovered by the Israel Advocacy Movement earlier in the year, in which she had described the transatlantic slave trade as an "African holocaust." This phrase is common among Black activists struggling for the recognition of the millions of dead caused by Britain's leading role in the transatlantic slave trade.

Yet Walker was shouted down. "It is! Yes it is!" someone in the room objected. "It is. It is. It is!" A mob-like atmosphere began to build.

Walker persisted: "In practice, it's not actually circulated and advertised as such."

As anyone doing a cursory check on the website of the organisation responsible for Holocaust Memorial Day would

---

4   Asa Winstanley, "Jewish activists criticize Labour anti-Semitism training," *Electronic Intifada*, 28 September 2016; Asa Winstanley, "Jewish anti-Zionist removed as Momentum vice chair," *Electronic Intifada*, 5 October 2016.

know, Walker was correct. While the annual event does in theory include remembrance of select genocides in more modern times, it quite specifically does not include the slave trade. Indeed, the Holocaust Memorial Day Trust, in a statement released later that day, tacitly conceded Walker's point. It wrote that the aim of the day was to "commemorate the Holocaust and *subsequent* genocides" (my emphasis). Their website made the same point, explaining that the day commemorates only the Nazi Holocaust and "subsequent genocides in Cambodia, Rwanda, Bosnia and Darfur."[5]

* * *

The ultimate upshot of the left-wing intervention was expulsion from the party for one of the anti-Zionist Jews. But it was not Glyn Secker, Naomi Wimborne-Idrissi, or Graham Bash that were pushed out (that would come much later, during Keir Starmer's anti-Corbyn purges). Only Jackie Walker was suspended from Labour and removed from her leading position in Momentum.[6] But the consequences for her personal life were far more serious than challenges to her membership of a political party. Her name was dragged through the mud on the national stage for years. Despite a three-year struggle by Walker and her supporters, Labour ultimately expelled her in 2019.[7]

It was Jackie Walker, more than almost any other individual in the Labour Party, who became the "left-wing anti-Semite" of the Israel lobby's fevered imagination. The hatred directed against her was even more intense than that against Ken Livingstone. This was

---

5 "What is Holocaust Memorial Day?" Holocaust Memorial Day website, undated (accessed 14 June 2022). See the oldest version of the page on the Internet Archive's WayBack Machine (24 April 2019). The page has now been reworded slightly. The current version reads "in genocides that followed" rather than "in subsequent genocides."

6 Asa Winstanley, "Labour suspends Jewish activist over 'African holocaust' post," *Electronic Intifada*, 5 May 2016.

7 Asa Winstanley, "Anti-racist Jackie Walker expelled from Labour," *Electronic Intifada*, 28 March 2019.

the case despite the fact she clearly had less power within Labour ranks. When the Israel lobby and the Labour right raged against what they termed the "high-profile cases of anti-Semitism," it was Livingstone, Walker and, later, the left-wing MP Chris Williamson who were most often cited. The party's bureaucrats compiled a dossier on Walker of more than 200 pages.

What had Walker actually done?

Before revisiting her story, we must address the elephant in the room. Walker herself is convinced, as a Black, Jewish woman, that the main reason for her exceptional mistreatment by the Labour Party—and even by some on the Labour left— was simply racism. She was subjected to extreme torrents of racist abuse online, incited by intense national media coverage. Since 2016 she has been smeared as some sort of British Louis Farrakhan, blaming "the Jews" for the slave trade while simultaneously dissimulating, and pretending to be Jewish in order to shield herself from accusations of anti-Semitism.

These were the parodies of the truth that became almost holy writ within the Labour Party, dogmas it was dangerous to challenge if you wanted to retain your membership. When you meet Walker in person, the mainstream media's horror story begins to evaporate. She first entered this story in May 2016 with her initial Labour suspension, which came at the urging of anti-Palestinian organisations. The *Jewish Chronicle* led the charge: "Labour suspended Ms Walker from the party after the JC brought her comments to the party's attention," the paper gloated.[8] This would become a wearingly familiar pattern. Hostile, anti-Corbyn media outlets would trawl social media, cherry-pick out-of-context comments by Labour activists and demand that party HQ condemn them. In far too many cases, Labour's disciplinary unit would respond by instantly suspending the activist concerned, seemingly without question.

After a grassroots backlash Walker was cleared. The suspension was rescinded only a few weeks later.[9] But the Israel lobby

---

8   "Labour suspends Momentum supporter who claimed Jews caused 'an African holocaust,'" *Jewish Chronicle*, 4 May 2016.

9   Asa Winstanley, "Labour 'anti-Semitism' witch hunt claims new victims," *Electronic Intifada*, 9 June 2016.

had marked her card and the story lingered. She became one of the "high-profile" cases. It seems a fair assumption that Walker had already been known to Mike Katz, hence his reluctance to allow her to participate in the discussion.

The group which screenshotted Walker's Facebook conversation about the African holocaust and fed it to the *Jewish Chronicle* was called the Israel Advocacy Movement. It puts out YouTube videos and other "influencer"-style content. It claims on its website to have had more than 24 million video views and 97,000 social media followers.[10] With 489,000 views, one of its most popular videos is an openly Islamophobic attack on Rashida Tlaib, the first Palestinian woman to enter the US Congress. Claiming to have exposed "the terrorist connections" of Tlaib, the video's thumbnail is a photo of the lawmaker and her brother with a masked Hamas fighter Photoshopped in.[11] But in 2016 the small group had been largely unknown. It had been founded only the year prior by Joseph Cohen, allegedly a former Marxist who, by his own account, got religion, converted to strictly Orthodox Judaism, and became an "incredibly proud Zionist." Speaking to the *Times of Israel*, Cohen made a stark admission. He had decided that "anti-Semitism wasn't the problem—[being] anti-Israel/Zionism is."[12]

Walker's Facebook posting had challenged the emerging narrative of an anti-Semitism "crisis" among Corbyn's supporters. *Jewish Chronicle* reporter Marcus Dysch threw in the claim that Walker had "claimed Jews were responsible for an 'African holocaust.'" This was, at best, a distortion of Walker's comments.

What she had actually posted was that as someone of mixed heritage, with Jewish ancestry on both her Black and white sides, "My ancestors were involved in" the African holocaust "on all sides." She stated that "many Jews (my ancestors too) were the chief financiers of the sugar and slave trade" in the Caribbean.

---

10   Israel Advocacy Movement homepage (accessed 14 June 2022).

11   "Rashida Tlaib's brother praises terrorists," Israel Advocacy Movement YouTube channel, 29 April 2019.

12   Jenni Frazer, "Pro-Israel 'lone warrior' stares down weekly anti-Israel protests in London," *Times of Israel*, 3 August 2015.

She was making the point that her ancestors had been both "victims and perpetrators" of the slave trade. The media coverage more often than not ignored the fact of Walker's Jewishness. Walker herself tells me that this was often down to racist ideas about Black people not being "really" Jewish.[13]

Walker has gone on the record many times to clarify that it would have been more accurate to write that certain Jewish people were "some of the chief financiers" rather that *the* chief financiers. But, as she told me in a new interview for this book, she never expected her personal Facebook page to be stalked by a pro-Israel group and exposed to public scrutiny. "I didn't think of myself as somebody," she said. "I was an activist, I wasn't a public figure. This was my personal Facebook page. I didn't give a toss who would read it."[14]

I asked her to talk more about her Jewish heritage on her Black Jamaican side. "It's funny, that's something I hardly ever get asked about," she said. Walker explained that her Jamaican family—who she declines to name for their own safety—descend from a "well known Jewish family in Jamaica, who came to the Caribbean, as far as we know, in the seventeenth century. They were amongst the original settlers." They were Jews from the Iberian Peninsula, almost certainly fleeing religious persecution. But as with virtually all Europeans in the West Indies at the time, they were involved in the slave trade, either as financiers or sellers of equipment and supplies to slavers, if not outright slave owners themselves.

It's an extremely sensitive subject involving extensive, unresolved, inter-generational trauma. I was reluctant to even raise it. But once I did, the floodgates opened. And it wasn't long before we addressed a sensitive topic: white slave owners in the West Indies often kept as mistresses the African women they enslaved, and rape was commonplace.

The population of Jamaica "has been generated by diversity, by rape, by ownership, by domination," Walker explained. "Virtually every Jamaican is a product of slave masters and

---

13 For a screenshot of Walker's original Facebook conversation, see Asa Winstanley, "How Jeremy Corbyn's enemies are gunning for Labour's ruling body," *Electronic Intifada*, 11 May 2016.

14 Interview with author, 28 January 2020.

slaves . . . our names are our slave masters' names for God's sake . . . who knows . . . what my family name might have been on my Black side, I became a Walker . . . That was the man who owned one of my female ancestors."

But there is another complication to this history: unlike white Christian settlers in the Caribbean, white Jewish settlers in the Caribbean would sometimes *marry* their slaves, rather than keeping them as mistresses.

"Jews in the Caribbean would actually marry African women," Walker explained. As a result, "their rabbis said those women were Jewish. And their children were Jewish . . . And that's where you got the mixture of population in Jamaica. So to say to somebody like me, you're not Jewish. It's such a weird thing to say. Because you're talking about a totally different context."

Walker was often attacked as not being genuinely Jewish. The idea seemed to be that she was somehow faking it for political reasons. But in Walker's view these ideas were just part of the common racist myths about Black Jews. This conspiracy theory was often bandied about on social media. High-profile Twitter account "GnasherJew" posted objecting to a 2020 newspaper article about Walker: "Why does this article claim that Jackie Walker is Jewish? Everyone knows that it's not true."[15] But even some on the left bought into this narrative.

"Give me a break," wrote Novara Media's Aaron Bastani. Walker "is as Jewish as I am. And I'm not Jewish."[16] As the JLM training scandal erupted, Bastani had immediately called for Walker to be expelled, apparently without checking the facts. "Even Corbynistas and Momentum supporters have said she should go," reported Guido Fawkes, citing Bastani.[17] When I asked him in 2022 if he stood by his 2016 comments, Bastani did not directly respond. Instead he told another Twitter user that he had "responded many times," and then made other comments

---

15   "GnasherJew" Twitter account, 10 September 2020.

16   Aaron Bastani, Twitter, 28 March 2018.

17   "Jewish Groups and Corbynistas Condemn Jackie Walker," Guido Fawkes, 29 September 2016.

appearing to double down on his attacks.[18] Over the years he has reiterated his view that Walker should have been expelled.

But an internal Labour report leaked in April 2020 shows even Blairite staffer Mike Creighton conceding that Walker's first suspension over the African holocaust Facebook discussion was "the weakest of the recent suspensions" and that Labour should take another look.[19]

In the wake of the JLM training session, Momentum boss Jon Lansman justified his removal of Walker from the group's steering committee by dismissing her objection that she was being targeted by a pro-Israel group which was seeking retribution for her anti-Zionist views. "None of these comments were related to Israel or Palestine. They have, however, made Jackie a focus of media attention," he claimed.[20] But Lansman was simply wrong. The context of the Facebook discussion shows that the debate was precisely about Palestine and the boycott of Israel. The full discussion thread shows that it had been sparked in the first place by Walker posting a Naomi Klein article calling for a boycott of Israel.[21] And the context of the JLM meeting (which I reported from) showed that Walker's intervention was sparked by Katz's promotion of a pro-Israel definition of anti-Semitism.

Walker's May 2016 readmission to the party had been met with extreme hostility from Labour's anti-Palestinian wing. Labour MP Michael Dugher, then an officer with Labour Friends of Israel, posted on Twitter to demand an "explanation" as to why "this person" was readmitted.[22] Joan Ryan, then Labour Friends of Israel's chairperson, also piled on.

---

18   Aaron Bastani, Twitter, 4 February 2022.

19   Harry Hayball et al., *The work of the Labour Party's Governance and Legal Unit in relation to antisemitism, 2014-2019* (London: The Labour Party, March 2020), page 363.

20   Jon Lansman, "A loss of confidence: the real reason why Momentum removed Jackie Walker," *Morning Star*, 7 October 2016.

21   Naomi Klein, "Enough. It's time for a boycott," *Guardian*, 10 January 2009.

22   Asa Winstanley, "Labour 'anti-Semitism' witch hunt claims new victims," *Electronic Intifada*, 9 June 2016.

The anti-Semitism "crisis" was settling into a pattern. It came in waves. It would rumble on in the background for months, then peak with a "high-profile" event such as the fabricated allegations in Oxford or the forcing out of Ken Livingstone. These peaks often seemed timed to coincide with elections. Walker's original suspension was imposed the day before the 5 May 2016 local elections. Ken Livingstone's 28 April suspension was also part of the lead up to that same election. It was widely seen as Corbyn's first major electoral test. Poor results would have led to more pressure for him to quit.

This second major phase of the manufactured crisis lasted roughly from February to June 2016, culminating in a coup attempt by a majority of Labour MPs against Corbyn. The coup was defeated and that September at conference Corbyn's re-election was formally announced.

It was against this background that this small group of non-Zionist Jews had decided to go to the JLM training session to challenge the pro-Israel group's narrative. Walker's re-admission had been a major defeat for those stoking the anti-Semitism crisis. There was a chance to fight back. As we've seen, the pro-Israel lobby were on manoeuvres that year at Labour conference: Joan Ryan, Shai Masot, Mark Regev, the Israeli embassy delegation as run by the JLM, and the mysterious £1 million in funding.

Most people didn't know about the covert Israeli influence campaign until Al Jazeera broadcast its documentary a few months later. But sharp activists were able to see its broad outlines even at the time. The only kind of resistance that could have succeeded against such skulduggery was a political counterattack. The JLM's attempted pushing of a Zionist "working definition" of anti-Semitism at the training confirmed the concerns of the left-wingers in attendance. But the backlash meant Walker was now suspended.

* * *

Mike Katz's attempt to rehabilitate the anti-Palestinian "working definition" was a harbinger of worse trouble to come. In 2018, the document would become a major flashpoint in Labour's civil war over Palestinian rights. The International Holocaust Remembrance Alliance (IHRA) definition was first formally set out in May 2016.[23] The very fact that Katz had made no reference to the group puts the lie to the claim by Zionist organisations that the IHRA document was the "international standard definition" of anti-Semitism. How could it have been the "standard" if even the JLM itself had never heard of it as late as September 2016? It was only in December 2016 that the British government formally adopted the definition, becoming the first government to do so.

Palestine solidarity activists had long been opposed to the EUMC definition, and it was only defeated after a long and bitter struggle. In 2011, University and College Union conference delegates passed a motion pledging to make no use of the EUMC definition, explaining that the document "confuses criticism of Israeli government policy and actions with genuine anti-semitism, and is being used to silence debate about Israel and Palestine on campus."[24]

There are multiple problems with both the EUMC and the IHRA versions of the "working definition." The most contentious of their "examples" of anti-Semitism is when both documents list: "claiming that the existence of a State of Israel is a racist endeavour" as anti-Semitic. The same point also claims that "denying the Jewish people their right to self-determination" in Israel is anti-Semitic. These examples potentially ban advocacy for a unitary, democratic state for both Israeli Jews and Palestinians between the Jordan River and the Mediterranean Sea. As Columbia University professor Joseph Massad has argued, the idea that Zionism represents "Jewish self-determination" in Palestine (a land which before the 1948 Nakba was overwhelmingly non-Jewish) is a myth. "Zionism is first and foremost a settler-colonial movement; this is not a national movement, for

---

23   Torrance, "UK Government's adoption of the IHRA definition of antisemitism."

24   "Business of the equality committee," Chapter 5 of the NEC's report, UCU Congress 2011: Monday 30 May. For context and analysis see "The Farcical Attack on the UCU For Voting Against Use of the EUMC 'Working Definition' of Antisemitism," Antony Lerman's blog, 2 June 2011.

example, by native populations that were trying to liberate their country from colonial forces . . . Zionism has never been a movement of self-determination. It never claimed to be. This is a new claim . . . This is not just what the enemies of Zionism have said; this is what Zionists themselves have said."[25]

There are many other problems with the IHRA definition. Another supposed example of anti-Semitism reads: "applying double standards by requiring of [Israel] a behaviour not expected or demanded of any other democratic nation." This is a very common Israeli government talking point. Israeli oppression—like any other form of oppression—has some unique features. Resistance to that oppression will therefore also have unique features. The idea of "double standards" in this context is therefore meaningless.

Another example of alleged anti-Semitism in the definition reads, "Accusing Jewish citizens of being more loyal to Israel, or to the alleged priorities of Jews worldwide, than to the interests of their own nations." The problem with this example is its calculated ambiguity. To say that all Jews are more loyal to Israel than to their own states is obviously anti-Semitic. But there do exist individuals in the world whose first loyalty seems to be to Israel. Some of them are even Jewish citizens of countries other than Israel. Therefore, it cannot be anti-Semitic to accurately report these facts.

Even some of the IHRA document's examples of anti-Semitism which are on their face uncontroversial seem calculated to launder pro-Israel lobbying, giving it a veneer of anti-racism. One reads: "Accusing the Jews as a people, or Israel as a state, of inventing or exaggerating the Holocaust." That sentence would work far better if the words "or Israel as a state" were removed. There's no need for those words except to insert the state of Israel into the document. Holocaust denial is an unambiguous example of anti-Semitism. If a Holocaust denier were to state that "Israel invented the Holocaust"—that would be a clear example of anti-Semitism. Such an anti-Semitic statement would be covered by a definition which read: "Accusing

---

[25] Interview with Nasim Ahmed, "The core of Zionism is settler-colonialism, not democracy," *Middle East Monitor*, 18 June 2019.

Jews of inventing or exaggerating the Holocaust"—due to the fact that Israel defines itself as the Jewish state. So any genuinely anti-racist document would not have need to mention Israel in such an example.

An even more problematic example of anti-Semitism in the document reads: "Drawing comparisons of contemporary Israeli policy to that of the Nazis." In the charged atmosphere of debate around the actions of the state of Israel, especially online, it is not uncommon for Israel to be accused of being as bad as the Nazis, or of carrying out similar crimes to the Nazis.

While such hyperbolic comparisons may well be inaccurate, it does not necessarily follow that they are then also anti-Semitic. This IHRA example flies in the face of occasions when *it is factually the case* that Israel has indeed carried out similar or identical policies to the Nazis. For example, Israel habitually commits the war crime of collective punishment against the Palestinians. The homes of the relatives of Palestinians accused of "terrorism" for having allegedly attacked Israeli soldiers or civilians are often demolished—even before there has been any charge or trial. It is a historic fact that the Nazis carried out similar war crimes in occupied Europe, sometimes using the pretext of an attack on Nazi soldiers.

The bogus example of anti-Semitism that prohibits "drawing comparisons" of Israeli "policy" to that of the Nazis also ignores something else: the fact that Zionist groups have, at times, allied themselves with anti-Semitic fascists, including Nazi Germany itself before the Holocaust. And such alliances continue today. As I revealed for the *Electronic Intifada* in 2018, the Israeli state is arming Ukraine's Azov Battalion—one of the world's most dangerous Nazi armed groups.[26] This is an example of objective material links between Israel and Nazis. Yet the effect of the bogus IHRA "working definition," as applied in practice, is to ban the reporting of such facts as "comparisons of contemporary Israeli policy to that of the Nazis." And documents sent from the

---

26   Asa Winstanley, "Israel is arming neo-Nazis in Ukraine," *Electronic Intifada*, 4 July 2018. Asa Winstanley, "Israel is still arming Ukrainian Nazis," *Electronic Intifada*, 21 April 2022.

Labour Party as part of its disciplinary process against members after the party adopted the "working definition" prove as much.

Both the EUMC and IHRA iterations of the "working definition" were part of a decades-long propaganda saga dubbed the "New Anti-Semitism." This campaign, led by the state of Israel and its friends, aims to redefine criticism of Israel as anti-Semitism. Anti-Semitism's common dictionary definition, "hostility towards or discrimination against Jews" was nullified. Instead, the Zionists argued, the "New Anti-Semitism" was hostility towards Israel and its actions—never mind how justified the opposition. The phrase has been promoted over the last two decades by Israel lobbyists like Irwin Cotler, a former Canadian minister.[27] But as Joseph Massad points out, the term goes way back to 1972. That year Israeli foreign minister Abba Eban (a leading Labour Zionist who began his career in the youth wing of JLM forerunner Poale Zion[28]) told a conference in Israel that "the New Left is the author and the progenitor of the new anti-Semitism . . . the distinction between anti-Semitism and anti-Zionism is not a distinction at all. Anti-Zionism is merely the new anti-Semitism."[29] Two years later the Anti-Defamation League continued this campaign with the publication of their book *The New Anti-Semitism*.[30] Since the ADL effort—and especially since 2000—there's been a whole glut of books with similar (or identical) titles.[31] (The ADL has long had a close working relationship with the Israeli state and its intelligence agencies.

---

27 Ali Abunimah, "Video: Canada activists disrupt top supporter of Israeli war crimes," *Electronic Intifada*, 5 June 2019.

28 Derek Taylor, *Solidarity and Discord: A brief history of 99 years of affiliation to the Labour Party* (London: Jewish Labour Movement, 2019), page 9.

29 Joseph Massad, "Pro-Zionism and antisemitism are inseparable, and always have been," *Middle East Eye*, 15 May 2019.

30 Arnold Forster and Benjamin R. Epstein, *The New Anti-Semitism* (New York: McGraw-Hill, 1974). The authors were senior ADL staffers and the book's copyright page assigns the rights to the group. For a critical review see Sharon Rose, *MERIP Reports*, No. 28, May 1974, pages 28-30.

31 For several examples, see Jerome A. Chanes, "Review Essay: What's 'New' – and what's not – about the New Antisemitism?" *Jewish Political Studies Review* 16:1-2 (Spring 2004).

In 2002 the ADL settled out of court when it was revealed that it had for years organised a spy ring to infiltrate leftist solidarity groups in the US, feeding the information back to Israel and apartheid-era South Africa.[32])

The 2017 paperwork expelling Moshé Machover is the first known mention of the IHRA definition in a Labour document. This suggests that—even before the public controversy the following year—there was an attempt by Labour's entrenched right-wing bureaucracy to cause problems for Corbyn, to embed reactionary doctrine, and to purge the mass membership.

As we'll see in a later chapter, the real tragedy is that these right-wing tools were later embraced even by the pro-Corbyn bureaucracy that took over in 2018.

* * *

The second major wave of the anti-Semitism "crisis" peaked at the end of April 2016—the lead up to May's local elections. Ken Livingstone had been suspended and Corbyn's team tried to defuse the situation. The day after Livingstone's suspension, the Labour leader ordered a party inquiry into anti-Semitism. It was to be chaired by lawyer and civil liberties campaigner Shami Chakrabarti. She issued her report after only two months.

Chakrabarti had only recently stepped down as director of Liberty, a human rights group and gadfly to the Blair government over its "anti-terror" curtailments on civil liberties. Her terms of reference were to investigate "anti-Semitism, Islamophobia, and other forms of racism" in Labour. But everybody knew this was a fig leaf. The report would indeed prove to be almost entirely about anti-Semitism. After a month of investigation, Chakrabarti concluded that "the Labour Party is not overrun by antisemitism, Islamophobia, or other forms of racism." But she claimed that there had been "an occasionally toxic atmosphere" and recommended banning the word "Zio" which she strongly

---

32   Mark Ames, "The Kings of Garbage, Or, The ADL Spied On Me And All I Got Was This Lousy Index Card," *Pacific Standard*, 3 May 2017.

implied (without showing evidence) had been used in Labour as a euphemism for "Jew."

Her report recommended changes to the party rule book, a moratorium on the "retrospective trawling of members' social media accounts and past comments," and removal from party staff of the power to suspend party members, giving it to Labour's elected National Constitutional Committee.[33]

But none of these changes was ever implemented.

The Israel lobby had mixed views on the report. The Campaign Against Antisemitism called it a "whitewash."[34] But the Jewish Labour Movement called it a "sensible and firm platform" and called for its recommendations to be implemented. Even the Board of Deputies of British Jews, a pro-Israel organisation, initially welcomed "aspects" of the report, while claiming that it was "a complete understatement" of anti-Semitism.[35] But only a month later, the Board appeared to have changed its mind, with their vice president also calling it a "whitewash." Labour Friends of Israel's MP Joan Ryan complained that "we wanted to see in that report clear lines drawn, where criticism of Israel becomes anti-Semitic," she said. "We did not get that, we were totally disappointed."[36] The Chakrabarti report was kicked into the long grass. The Labour Party establishment dragged its feet, and Corbyn's relaxed leadership style didn't force change.

But the Chakrabarti report is probably most remembered for a scandal surrounding the press conference held to launch it. It came at a time of near chaos in the Labour Party and in the country at large. A national referendum on the UK's membership of the European Union had, after a long and divisive campaign, concluded in a vote to leave. The week before, Labour

---

33   *The Shami Chakrabarti Inquiry* (London: Labour Party, 30 June 2016), page 1.

34   "The Chakrabarti Inquiry is a Vague, Meaningless Whitewash That Will do Nothing to Rid Labour of Antisemitism," Campaign Against Antisemitism website, 30 June 2016 (accessed 15 June 2022).

35   Asa Winstanley, "Defeating Labour's manufactured anti-Semitism crisis," *Electronic Intifada*, 26 August 2016.

36   Daniel Sugarman, "Corbyn's Chakrabarti peerage 'contempt,'" *Jewish Chronicle*, 27 June 2017.

MP Jo Cox had been murdered by a neo-Nazi activist, in revenge for her support for both Arab refugees and for the EU.[37] Amidst this poisonous national atmosphere, Labour's mostly right-wing MPs piled the blame on Corbyn for their defeat in the Brexit vote. But this wasn't some principled stance in favour of greater European integration. Always bitterly opposed to Corbyn, the MPs were simply seizing an opportunity to rid themselves of a troublesome left-wing leader, as well as the hordes of "Trots" and "cranks" they claimed he'd brought in.

There was a series of complicated overlapping coup plots. According to press reports, these had already been in the works for months. Blairite MP and Labour Friends of Israel supporter Margaret Hodge tabled a no-confidence motion and the Parliamentary Labour Party overwhelmingly voted for it. But Corbyn refused to resign, citing his democratic mandate from Labour members—then less than a year old.[38]

Chakrabarti launched her report only two days after the vote. The atmosphere at the press conference was frenetic. The corporate media acted like a pack of wolves, demanding to know *when* Corbyn would resign. They didn't seem to want to talk about the report, instead raging about Brexit and demanding Corbyn's departure.

In the question and answer session, a journalist and activist named Marc Wadsworth had come forward to speak. A veteran anti-racist, in the 1990s Wadsworth was prominent in the struggle to hold London's police force to account for institutional racism and the failure to investigate the murder of Black teenager Stephen Lawrence by a racist gang. Wadsworth introduced the Lawrences to Nelson Mandela, providing a high-profile boost to the family's campaign for justice. Wadsworth was also active in the push for Black sections in the Labour Party. The campaign

---

37   See the following articles by this author for the *Electronic Intifada*: "Labour Friend of Palestine Jo Cox slain," 16 June 2016; "How Jo Cox's alleged assassin was influenced by neo-Nazism," 23 June 2016; "Neo-Nazi assassin of Jo Cox claimed 'personal experience' of publishing," 23 November 2016.

38   Asa Winstanley, "After Brexit, Labour Friend of Israel launches coup against Corbyn," *Electronic Intifada*, 24 June 2016.

ultimately triumphed with the elections of Diane Abbott, Bernie Grant, and others.

Wadsworth had come to the Chakrabarti press conference as both a journalist and a campaigner. It was an unusual event. In addition to the "mainstream" corporate journalists, Labour activists had also been invited. The latter tipped me off and I went along to report.[39]

Outside the event, while handing out an activist press release that condemned Labour MPs for resigning from Corbyn's shadow cabinet, Wadsworth had run into the right-wing Labour MP Ruth Smeeth. It was their first ever encounter but the activist-journalist soon learned who she was. Wadsworth asked her name and, learning she was a Labour MP, openly criticised her for fuelling the coup attempts against Corbyn by briefing the right-wing media.

Inside it became clear that while Chakrabarti's mandate was to investigate "anti-Semitism and other forms of racism," she hadn't actually investigated any form of racism other than anti-Jewish bigotry. Called on to speak, Wadsworth made the point that, at an event supposedly about racism, he was one of the very few faces of colour in the room: "We really need to get our house in order, don't we?" he asked the meeting.

He then turned his attention to Smeeth: "I saw that the *Telegraph* handed a copy of a press release to Ruth Smeeth MP, so you can see who's working hand in hand."

Smeeth interrupted the activist. "How dare you!" she shouted. Stomping past a bank of TV cameras, the MP stormed out of the packed room. Footage of the intervention circulated widely online and was reported on news bulletins that evening. Smeeth faulted Corbyn for doing "nothing" while she was attacked by a Labour activist in the room. "Anti-Semitism at the launch of a report about anti-Semitism!" former *Sun* hack Kevin Schofield muttered as he watched Smeeth walk out of the room.[40]

---

39 Asa Winstanley, "Media concoct firestorm as Jeremy Corbyn launches anti-Semitism report," *Electronic Intifada*, 30 June 2016.

40 "Video: for transparency, #MarcWadsworth's actual words re Ruth Smeeth," *Skwawkbox*, 25 April 2018.

Contrary to later claims about Smeeth leaving the event "in tears," all the videos show her dry-eyed, angry rather than upset. One Sky News item showed the MP in the audience seated next to two other Labour right-wingers, Richard Angell (then director of Progress) and Jennifer Gerber (then director of Labour Friends of Israel).[41] Smeeth claimed in a statement posted to her website soon after that she had been "verbally attacked" by a "Jeremy Corbyn supporter who used traditional anti-Semitic slurs to attack me for being part of a 'media conspiracy.'"

Smeeth's statement was later deleted from her website. But by then the narrative that she had been attacked with anti-Semitic slurs at the launch of a report to combat anti-Semitism had already been widely reported. Two years later I discovered the deletion of the statement and dutifully reported it for the *Electronic Intifada*. Although the MP and her staff ignored my requests for comment, the text of the statement was re-posted to her website within days of my article's publication. (It was deleted once again later that year, seemingly for good.)[42]

Smeeth had good reason to delete the post—the idea that Wadsworth had said she was part of a "media conspiracy" was completely untrue. Importantly, he did not make any kind of anti-Jewish comment. In fact, he didn't refer to Smeeth's Jewishness in any way—he later clarified that he hadn't even know she was Jewish. Wadsworth replied to Smeeth's false allegations in a statement the same day, describing them as "poisonous slander." He said her claims played "into a Jewish media conspiracy theory that I utterly reject and have never espoused."[43]

---

41   "Ruth Smeeth Leaves Report Launch, June 16," video on Sky News website, 27 April 2018 (accessed 15 June 2022).

42   See: Asa Winstanley, "Labour Israel lobbyist deletes anti-Semitic 'conspiracy' claims," *Electronic Intifada*, 11 April 2018, and see also updates on the page. As of this writing (15 June 2022) the statement remains deleted and I can find no evidence it has been reposted by Smeeth elsewhere.

43   Marc Wadsworth, "I am not part of Labour's antisemitism problem," *Guardian* letters page, 5 April 2018.

Wadsworth's instincts about Smeeth "working hand in hand" with the right-wing press to overthrow Corbyn were totally correct. Only three days earlier Smeeth had played her own minor part in the coup attempt against Corbyn. She announced on Twitter "with a heavy heart" that she was resigning from a junior role in Corbyn's shadow cabinet.[44] It was timed to coincide with a series of resignations by dozens of hostile MPs, in a failed attempt to force him to resign. They came after the no-confidence vote tabled by Margaret Hodge and the firing of Hilary Benn, another right-wing shadow minister Corbyn had fruitlessly attempted to bring on board as part of his abortive "big church" approach.

But unlike Wadsworth and the others, as a journalist reporting on the UK's pro-Israel lobby, I happened to be pretty well acquainted with Smeeth's work.

I wrote a story about her in 2014, when she was selected as a Labour candidate. I did so because of two key facts, ignored by a media that would later pay her such close attention: she had worked as a spin doctor for the Israel lobby and had acted (wittingly or otherwise) as a secret Labour Party source for the US government.[45]

* * *

Over the next two years, Smeeth campaigned relentlessly to have Marc Wadsworth expelled. In 2018, Smeeth rallied a group of white MPs to accompany her to a hearing of Labour's disputes panel where she gave evidence against Wadsworth. His supporters later called this a modern-day political lynching.[46] The case undermined Corbyn's leadership and divided Labour's newly enthusiastic left-wing mass membership. Smeeth wasn't

---

44   Ruth Smeeth, Twitter, 27 June 2016.

45   Asa Winstanley, "Former Israel lobby spin doctor aims for seat in UK parliament," *Electronic Intifada*, 4 April 2014.

46   "How anti-semitism row MPs turned lynch mob," Jonathan Cook Blog, 26 April 2018. "Labour activist expelled after remarks to MP at anti-Semitism event," BBC News, 27 April 2018.

motivated so much by personal animus against Wadsworth as by a calculated political strategy. She was so dedicated to sabotaging her own party that she didn't seem overly concerned that her campaign ultimately came at the cost of losing her own Labour seat in 2019.

Journalists gave Smeeth sympathetic puff-piece interviews. She told London newspaper the *Evening Standard* that her critics were motivated only by racism. "I don't talk about Israel or Palestine," she claimed. "This is not about anything I've said on Middle-East politics. I don't participate."[47] This was, at best, incredibly misleading, as I knew from my prior reporting.

Smeeth was hired by lobbyists BICOM in 2005, the Britain Israel Communications and Research Centre, as director of public affairs and campaigns. A public relations industry publication reported at the time that she had arrived there from a position as head of government relations for Sodexho, a company providing support services to the military. BICOM's chief executive told the publication that Smeeth would help strengthen their relationships with the "Foreign Office, party leaders, think-tanks, and academia."[48] She worked for BICOM until 2007.[49] After a brief stint in public relations for Nestlé, she returned to the Israel lobby, joining the Community Security Trust for two years.[50] Although a registered charity tasked with documenting anti-Semitism, the CST also has a more clandestine mission: lobbying for Israel.[51] According to Antony Lerman, the founder of the Institute for

---

47 Charlotte Edwardes, "Ruth Smeeth: 'I've never seen anti-Semitism in Labour like this, it's normal now,'" *Evening Standard*, 20 September 2016.

48 "Smeeth exits Sodexho for pro-Israel lobby group," *PR Week*, 9 September 2005.

49 Leon Symons, "Israel research centre faces staff exodus," *Jewish Chronicle*, 20 April 2007.

50 Larry O'Hara and Heidi Svenson, "Pandora's Pox: How Far Right Labour Hijacked the Hope Not Hate Campaign," *Notes From the Borderland*, Issue 10, 2012, page 38.

51 Asa Winstanley, "Revealed: UK anti-Semitism watchdog charity helps lead Israel anti-boycott group," *Electronic Intifada*, 8 February 2013. Asa Winstanley, "CST denies it acted 'on behalf of Israel' in Salah plot," *Electronic Intifada*, 7 October 2011.

Jewish Policy Research, the CST even has ties with the Mossad, Israel's foreign spy agency.[52] The CST is another key part of the network of pro-Israel lobby groups that constantly pushed the "crisis" narrative on Labour.

After several abortive attempts, in 2014 Smeeth made her move into politics. She was selected as Labour candidate for the then–safe seat of Stoke-on-Trent North. Smeeth seemed an odd choice. She'd tried once already as Labour's candidate in nearby Burton, losing to the Conservatives by more than 6,000 votes in 2010. She finally managed to enter Parliament in 2015.

Far from cutting her Israel lobby ties while an MP, the register of MPs' financial interests reveals that Smeeth was given thousands of pounds in donations by two key BICOM figures: Poju Zabludowicz and Trevor Chinn.[53] The founder of Smeeth's ex-employer BICOM, Zabludowicz is the scion of an Israeli arms dealer and a billionaire property speculator.[54] Chinn is a retired motor industry tycoon who uses his wealth to support a raft of Israel lobby groups, including the Jewish Leadership Council and BICOM.

While the nearest US equivalent to BICOM—AIPAC—has increasingly become more partisan and affiliated with Trump and the Republican Party in recent years, BICOM from its outset was closely aligned with the Atlanticist, neoliberal wing of the Labour Party. They were always going to consider the left-wing, pro-Palestinian leadership of Jeremy Corbyn to be a threat. Smeeth and her pro-American tendency aimed to keep the party stubbornly pro-Israel and pro-NATO.

The extent of Smeeth's commitment to US empire was revealed by WikiLeaks in 2011. In one of the many classified US diplomatic cables revealed by whistle-blower Chelsea Manning, the US embassy in London secretly reported that "Ruth Smeeth (strictly protect)" had in 2009 given American diplomats inside

---

52 Asa Winstanley, "UK charity with Mossad links secretly denounced anti-Zionist Jews to government," *Electronic Intifada*, 21 December 2011.

53 Asa Winstanley, "UK Labour MP Ruth Smeeth was funded by Israel lobby," *Electronic Intifada*, 6 December 2016.

54 Asa Winstanley, "Is Israel lobby UK quitting battle for public opinion?" *Electronic Intifada*, 27 November 2013.

information about Gordon Brown, then the UK's prime minister. The intelligence concerned Brown's strategy on when to hold a general election and the confidential cable's author thought Smeeth's report important enough to note that "this information has not been reported in the press."[55] Smeeth declined to deny the cable's contents, claiming to the *Daily Telegraph* at the time of the WikiLeaks revelation that she had "no recollection of saying what has been attributed to me." But she confirmed contact with the US embassy, claiming she had had "a friend" who happened to work there. "I would not consider myself to be a source for the US government," she said.[56]

Soon after entering Parliament, Smeeth joined the Defence Committee—a group of MPs tasked with examining the policies of the armed forces. She remained active in the influential body until 2019.[57] She also signed up to the JLM and as a "parliamentary supporter" of Labour Friends of Israel. In 2016 Smeeth took part in an LFI delegation to meet Israel's then opposition leader Isaac Herzog, alongside UK Labour's deputy leader Tom Watson. The aim of the meeting was to "strengthen the bonds of friendship between our parties," LFI director Jennifer Gerber said at the time.[58]

Smeeth revealed the intensity of her campaign against Corbyn at a JLM conference in 2017. By then she had been elected as chairperson of the Parliamentary Labour Party, giving her high-level access to the leader in weekly meetings with Corbyn. Every week she used the meeting to harangue the leader about the "anti-Semitism" of his supporters. Smeeth boasted at the JLM conference that Corbyn was being made "incredibly uncomfortable." Fellow Labour right-winger John Mann also told the

---

55 "UK Political Snapshot: Gloomy Budget and a New Scandal Torpedo Brown's Poll Numbers," Confidential US Embassy, London cable to the National Security Council and Secretary of State, 24 April 2009. Published by WikiLeaks as 09LONDON956_a.

56 Christopher Hope, "WikiLeaks cables: Gordon Brown 'forced to scrap plan for snap election,'" *Daily Telegraph*, 4 February 2011.

57 Ruth Smeeth profile on UK Parliament website (accessed 15 June 2022).

58 Winstanley, "UK Labour MP Ruth Smeeth was funded."

conference that "Nothing destroys Jeremy Corbyn's soul more than the thought in his head that he could actually be tolerating antisemitism. This really hurts him—it disturbs him."[59]

* * *

Smeeth's intervention at the Chakrabarti press conference dramatically derailed Corbyn's attempt to draw a line under the crisis of anti-Semitism smears.

Over the next few years Smeeth became one of Corbyn's most vocal internal enemies. She constantly accused her own party of having a major anti-Semitism problem, claimed to be the victim of racist abuse at the hands of the left, and even said she wanted to "break and destroy" her opponents.[60] She demanded the expulsion of Marc Wadsworth and got her way. Her prominent role in this campaign led to her appointment as the Jewish Labour Movement's parliamentary chairperson in April 2019.[61]

The "crisis" gripping Labour led to a genuine climate of fear among members. Labour's membership had swollen to more than half a million thanks to Corbyn. Alarmed by the prospect of a left-wing ascendancy, the right-wing bureaucracy imposed punitive expulsions, suspensions, and "investigations." High-profile examples like Ken Livingstone and Jackie Walker were only the tip of the iceberg. The real goal was to expel broad swathes of the mass membership, and ultimately Corbyn himself.

Years later, in the Keir Starmer era, Labour's triumphant right-wing shadow chancellor Rachel Reeves made the strategy explicit. She told the *Financial Times* it was "a good thing" that membership was falling and that the resultant drop in income

---

59 Lee Harpin, "Ruth Smeeth: My 'hope' over Corbyn," *Jewish Chronicle*, 4 September 2017.

60 Jenni Frazer, "Ruth Smeeth at JLM conference: 'Only anti-Semites are weaponising anti-Semitism,'" *Jewish News*, 4 September 2017.

61 Joe Millis, "Mike Katz beats Ivor Caplin to become new Jewish Labour chair," *Jewish News*, 7 April 2019.

was a price worth paying to remove the "stain" of alleged anti-Semitism.[62]

Members fought back, founding a new group called Labour Against the Witchhunt. Comparisons to the Salem witchcraft trials of the seventeenth century and the McCarthy era of the 1950s were common currency among activists. American playwright Arthur Miller, writing his influential 1953 work *The Crucible*, explicitly sought to draw comparisons between those two malign historic phenomena. But after travelling to Salem to research the witch trials from original documents, Miller was worried his play would be a little too on the nose. He reminisced in 1996 that, "As the dramatic form became visible, one problem remained unyielding: so many practices of the Salem trials were similar to those employed by the congressional committees that I could easily be accused of skewing history for a mere partisan purpose." One such similarity was that "the best proof of the sincerity of your confession was your naming others whom you had seen in the Devil's company—an invitation to private vengeance, but made official by the seal of the theocratic state."[63]

The Crucible's flawed hero John Proctor—desperately defending his wife against false allegations of witchcraft—memorably asked: "Is the accuser always holy now? Were they born this morning as clean as God's fingers?" Confessing to the sin of witchcraft meant you were damned by your own word. But pleading your innocence also condemned you to death—it showed an unwillingness to repent a most grievous sin. There was no right answer. The starting point was always to assume the accusations were correct.

Labour's hunt for imagined "left-wing anti-Semites" established a similar train of circular logic. In this more secular witch hunt, the accuser too was sacrosanct. For those with a particular hard-line interpretation of identity politics, Zionism's mis-definition of anti-Semitism gained a sympathetic reception. This was illustrated in 2019 when Lara McNeill, the youth representative on Labour's ruling national executive took to Twitter to

---

62 "Reeves blames Corbyn for party's financial collapse – and says member exodus is a good thing," *Skwawkbox*, 20 January 2022.

63 Arthur Miller, "Why I Wrote 'The Crucible,'" *New Yorker*, 13 October 1996.

defend Corbyn from one particular allegation of anti-Semitism, calling it "demonstratively false."[64] Members of the Jewish Labour Movement's national executive committee lashed out at McNeill's tweet, with one calling it "institutional anti-Semitism" and "Jew baiting."[65] She timidly defended her post: "I'm not sure how it constitutes the scale of your accusations ... Am I not entitled to disagree with that?"[66]

"No. You're not Jewish," came the reply from JLM's international officer Izzy Lenga.[67] This encapsulated a dominant trend: if a Jewish person defines something as anti-Semitic it is therefore—by definition—anti-Semitic. But in practice this illogical principle only applied to pro-Israel Jews on the right who weaponised it against the left.

The best proof of the sincerity of the Labour penitent was to denounce others as anti-Semitic or admit to "the problem." "Do you agree that" a certain quote, social media posting, or unfortunate turn of phrase "is anti-Semitic?" became the new "Are you now, or have you ever been, a member of the Communist Party." As one activist put it, "this issue is now bigger than Corbyn. It is about where we stand on matters of intellectual and moral integrity; and most of all on the rights we accrue to an oppressed people and those of their oppressor. Future generations are watching and waiting for the stance that we take."[68]

As for Wadsworth, after a long ordeal and a two-year suspension he was expelled from Labour. Smeeth was pleased. Tellingly, her statement welcoming his expulsion did not mention anti-Semitism and did not repeat her false allegations about what Wadsworth had said at the press conference. "Abuse, bullying and intimidation have no place in our movement," she

---

64   Lara McNeill, Twitter, 16 October 2019.

65   Liron Velleman, Twitter, 16 October 2019.

66   Lara McNeill, Twitter, 16 October 2019.

67   At the time of access (15 June 2022), Lenga's Twitter account was set to private. But this tweet is still viewable on the Internet Archive's WayBack Machine: https://bit.ly/3NkMnqO.

68   John Wight, "The great antisemitism witch hunt: McCarthyism redux," Medium.com, 1 March 2019.

intoned solemnly.[69] Most members were outraged. Left-wing MP Chris Williamson condemned the decision, saying the expulsion "flies in the face of the evidence that was presented and offends against the principles of natural justice."[70] Even soft left MP Clive Lewis opposed the expulsion. He told one right-wing Labour critic that she should "go read a history book about what happens when an accusation equals evidence. It's not pleasant." Labour's crucible—the test of its moral character—was the increasingly frenzied accusations of anti-Semitism, where accusation was so often considered evidence. The accuser was indeed being treated as always holy.

It became depressingly clear to activists that Corbyn himself was also failing this moral test. He didn't speak out against the witch hunt. A source told me that Corbyn had privately expressed support for Wadsworth. But in public, he said nothing and did his best to publicly distance himself from the campaigner, despite having known him for decades as a fellow left-wing London activist. Grilled by a hostile Parliamentary committee about the Smeeth incident, Corbyn said, "The remarks made by Marc Wadsworth, which were along the lines that she [Smeeth] had been working hand in glove with the *Daily Telegraph,* were inappropriate and wrong."[71] Wadsworth felt betrayed. "It's affected me, my health, family and friends in a terrible way. I've faced awful racist abuse on social media and been threatened on public transport," he later said.[72]

An internal Labour report leaked in April 2020 shows that some of Corbyn's staff chased Labour's disciplinary unit for swifter action against Wadsworth and other "high-profile" activists falsely accused of anti-Semitism. "Could we have an

---

69 Asa Winstanley, "Activists outraged at Labour's expulsion of Black campaigner Marc Wadsworth," *Electronic Intifada,* 27 April 2018.

70 Chris Williamson, Facebook page, 27 April 2018.

71 House of Commons, Home Affairs Committee, Oral evidence: Antisemitism, HC 136, Questions 225–396, Witness [I]: Rt Hon Jeremy Corbyn MP, Leader, Labour Party, Monday 4 July 2016.

72 Sid Smith, "'My old mate Corbyn threw me under a bus . . . but he's no anti-Semite,'" *Metro,* 4 December 2019.

update on the current status of the cases of Ken Livingstone, Jacqui [sic] Walker, Tony Greenstein and Marc Wadsworth," wrote pro-Corbyn staffer Laura Murray, demanding a timetable on when "a final decision will be made on them. The Jewish Labour Movement [has] expressed frustration."[73] One contemporary Labour staffer told me Murray became "obsessed" with the alleged issue of "left-wing anti-Semitism." Murray later told Corbyn-sceptic *Guardian* journalist Owen Jones that she had grown to be "embarrassed" of working for the left-wing leader.[74]

Corbyn's enemies began to scent blood.

---

[73] Harry Hayball et al., *The work of the Labour Party's Governance and Legal Unit in relation to antisemitism, 2014-2019* (London: The Labour Party, March 2020), page 333.

[74] Owen Jones, *This Land: The Story of a Movement* (London: Allen Lane, 2020), page 211.

CHAPTER SEVEN

JEWS AND UN-JEWS

A spritely grey-haired woman trotted onto the stage with a spring in her step and excitement in her voice. Her speech was a highlight of Labour's 2017 conference in Brighton. She urged the delegates to beef-up Labour's policies on Palestine, calling for an end to Israel's occupation and settlements: "This is the very least we should be doing." But it was her concluding lines that earned the loudest cheers and a standing ovation.

"I say this as a Jew, as an anti-racist, and as a dedicated member of this revived socialist, internationalist Labour Party," she exclaimed. "And comrades, I'm not an anti-Semite!"

The crowd roared.

"Conference, this party does not have a problem with Jews!" The hall rose to its feet. It was another sign that the pro-Israel groups pushing the "Labour anti-Semitism" line were vastly outnumbered.

The woman was Naomi Wimborne-Idrissi, a veteran Palestine solidarity activist and Jewish anti-Zionist. The Corbyn phenomenon had brought her into the party. She later told me she had joined Labour "to participate in the movement."[1] That same evening, Wimborne-Idrissi joined her comrades at the most well-attended fringe of that year's conference: the launch of Jewish Voice for Labour. It was a new left-wing Jewish group. Unlike the Jewish Labour Movement, JVL didn't require dedication to Zionism as a condition of membership.

"Despite my grey hairs I am a virgin in terms of this conference: first-time delegate," Wimborne-Idrissi said. "I'm Jewish,

---

1   Phone interview with the author, 24 November 2020.

I come from a tradition of anti-racist and anti-colonial struggle, a socialist labour tradition of international solidarity with oppressed people."

She urged delegates to support a motion on Palestine, one which would insert criticism of Israel into Labour's next election manifesto (rather than the usual platitudes about a "two-state solution").

Wimborne-Idrissi pointed out that it had been 100 years since British politicians issued the Balfour Declaration, "when a British foreign secretary promised the land of Palestine to the Jewish people, my people." As a result, in 1948, "750,000 Palestinians were driven from their homes in what for them was a catastrophe that they call the Nakba. More than 450 towns and villages were destroyed." It is up to us as British citizens to take responsibility for this ongoing injustice, she said. "We call for an end to Israel's blockade on Gaza, an end to occupation and settlements."

Applause for Palestine at a Labour Party conference had become normal. Support for the Palestinian cause was hegemonic in the rank and file of the party. Only a few months before, Corbyn had come close to winning the general election. Surviving the 2016 coup attempt, and doing considerably better in the 2017 general election than anybody expected, Corbyn's leadership now seemed far less fragile.

Wimborne-Idrissi's heartfelt defence of Labour got her the biggest cheers, because the membership was sick of hearing the accusation of anti-Semitism. The smear had become the right's biggest weapon. Despite his successes, Corbyn's hold on the party machine remained tenuous. The best Labour election result in decades had bought him only a small breathing space.

The next day a motion was put forward to change the party's rule book. The Jewish Labour Movement wanted expulsions "where the victim or anyone else" considered any given statement to be anti-Semitic. Welsh Labour activist Darren Williams (a pro-Corbyn member of Labour's National Executive Committee) called the JLM motion "draconian." The change would have meant open season on the membership for the Israel lobby witch hunters.

A second member of the new Jewish Voice for Labour group spoke up. Leah Levane from Hastings and Rye Constituency Labour Party proposed a rule change to counter the JLM. She explained that they had been "worried about what was happening in the Labour Party with the suspensions" on the flimsiest pretexts. But behind the scenes, Labour's ruling NEC was brokering what it viewed as a compromise between the JLM's draconian motion and the alternative proposal promoted by Levane. Both were asked to drop their motions in favour of the NEC's version.[2]

Levane's delegation agreed. But she was still determined to put her point across. She used her short speech to promote Jewish Voice for Labour and pull back the curtain on the grubby backroom deal. "The NEC's clearly negotiated with the Jewish Labour Movement to come up with their rule change," she told delegates, criticising what she said was the NEC's lack of communication.

The loudest cheers came when Levane questioned the "Labour anti-Semitism crisis." She told the audience that, while the JLM had a right to exist, it didn't have the right to speak for all Jews. "They do not speak for me!" she insisted emphatically. Levane argued that the standing-room-only launch of Jewish Voice for Labour and the rapturous reception for Naomi Wimborne-Idrissi showed that "other Jewish voices exist."

To another standing ovation, Levane condemned the trend of using anti-Semitism as a stick to beat the left, to "make that accusation every time you criticise the despicable behaviour of the state of Israel towards the Palestinian people!"

Later, in his leader's speech, Corbyn demanded an "end to the oppression of the Palestinian people" and Israel's "50-year occupation and illegal settlement expansion."[3]

Palestine was the issue that year.

* * *

---

[2] For more detail on the various rule changes see Asa Winstanley, "Is the Israel lobby rewriting the Labour Party's rule book?" *Electronic Intifada*, 22 September 2017.

[3] Asa Winstanley, "Palestine was the issue at Labour Party conference," *Electronic Intifada*, 6 October 2017.

June's general election hadn't led to a Labour government, but it was still a political earthquake. Opinion polls and the political-media establishment both insisted Corbyn would be trounced. Sensing an opportunity to increase her parliamentary majority, Conservative prime minister Theresa May had called an early election. But her gamble backfired spectacularly. Not only did she fail to increase her (already very narrow) majority; she actually *lost* seats. This meant that no one party now had an overall majority—known in British political jargon as a hung Parliament. Labour's vote share surged to 40 percent, translating to a net gain of 30 seats. It was the first time the party had actually gained seats since 1997. In terms of vote share, the "unelectable" left-wing leader had outperformed every one of his Labour predecessors since Clement Attlee's landslide post-war win in 1945.[4] It began to look like Corbynism had stopped the rot. Labour's slide towards Pasokification could be reversed and the party might just escape the kind of wipe-out imposed by voters in Greece.

The capitalist press was grudgingly impressed. "The Labour Party now belongs to Jeremy Corbyn," declared the *Economist*.[5] Even *Jewish Chronicle* editor Stephen Pollard had to face up to the reality of Corbyn's achievements, admitting that "Like most pundits, I called the election completely wrongly." But he went to write that the 12.8 million people who had voted for Labour "scare me," implying that they were all anti-Semitic, or at least willing to tolerate Jew-hatred.[6]

Labour's grassroots was on a high that year. There was a new spirit of optimism and a hope that the anti-Semitism smears could be brushed aside. The issue hadn't played a major part in the Tory election campaign. While the witch hunt against the left had had a damaging impact on the Corbynite movement, its most prominent targets (Ken Livingstone, Jackie Walker, and

---

4   Asa Winstanley, "How Labour Friends of Israel tried to undermine Jeremy Corbyn," *Electronic Intifada*, 13 June 2017.

5   "The Labour Party now belongs to Jeremy Corbyn," *Economist*, 10 June 2017.

6   Stephen Pollard, "To the millions of people who voted for Jeremy Corbyn: you scare me," *Daily Telegraph*, 9 June 2017.

Marc Wadsworth) still hadn't been expelled. All three were suspended pending final investigation, but there was still a faint hope of exoneration.

The conference launch of Wimborne-Idrissi and Levane's new group Jewish Voice for Labour included some big names. It was addressed by Israeli historian Avi Shlaim, socialist filmmaker Ken Loach, and several others prominent figures. "It was the only meeting of the official fringe that people were talking about," journalist Alex Nunns told me. "There was a real buzz about it." (Nunns wrote *The Candidate*, the best book about Corbyn's rise to prominence in 2015, and was later hired as a speechwriter by Corbyn.) Also supporting were Tosh McDonald and Len McCluskey, two key trade union leaders. Both promised to advise their unions (ASLEF and Unite) to affiliate to JVL. The packed meeting room was euphoric.

JVL was established by veteran Jewish leftists to fight back against the smear campaign. They were tired of their own identity being used to bash the left. Their founding document explained that JVL opposes "attempts to widen the definition of anti-Semitism beyond its meaning of hostility towards or discrimination against Jews as Jews."[7] It wasn't established as an anti-Zionist group, but included anti-Zionist members.[8]

JVL was not primarily a Palestine solidarity group, but said it did support the right of activists to campaign for BDS and other forms of Palestine solidarity activism. Several of JVL's most prominent leaders are veterans of the Palestine solidarity movement. After being slandered for years by the pro-Israel lobby, JVL activists instinctively understood the reality of how anti-Semitism is used as a smear. Inasmuch as JVL raised awareness in the grassroots of the Labour Party, and even made limited inroads with the mainstream media, the group achieved some success. But it came at a heavy cost. By the Keir Starmer era, two-thirds of JVL's executive committee had been suspended,

---

[7] Asa Winstanley, "New Jewish group in Labour Party backs right to BDS," *Electronic Intifada*, 17 August 2017.

[8] Jenny Manson, "Jewish Voice for Labour is not an anti-Zionist group," *Guardian* letters, 28 September 2017.

expelled or otherwise disciplined as Labour members.[9] As early as June 2020, JVL stated that it was aware of at least 25 cases of Jewish party members being investigated for "anti-Semitism."[10]

Jewish anti-Zionists in Labour were habitually targeted by the "anti-Semitism" smear campaign. Their identity was no protection. Indeed, media coverage often stripped them of their Jewish identity altogether. They were denigrated by Zionists, told they were not "real" Jews. As we saw in the last chapter, this particularly nasty line of attack was used against Jackie Walker more than anyone else. A rumour consistently spread about Walker was that she was not "really" Jewish and had only begun to identify herself as such in recent times to protect herself against the "anti-Semitism" smear campaign.

In the new interview conducted for this book, Walker told me that she has always identified herself as Jewish, and that her mother from a young age in Jamaica always told her to be proud of her Jewish background. "It's very important to me," she said. "I think I have the most extraordinary heritage. You know, my ancestors have survived some of the most traumatic events in history. And that's astonishing. And something to be proud of."[11] This heritage comes from both sides of her family—from her white father, Jack Cohen (who was a Jewish communist from New York), and, as we've seen, also from her Jamaican mother, Dorothy Walker.

Online evidence supports Walker's claim that her Jewish identification predates the manufactured anti-Semitism crisis in Corbyn's Labour. Jews for Justice for Palestinians lists her as a new signatory in July 2014.[12] Copies of the original signatory

---

9   Naomi Wimborne-Idrissi, phone interview with author, 17 February 2022. See also David Hearst and Peter Oborne, "UK's Labour accused of 'purging Jews' from party over antisemitism claims," *Middle East Eye*, 12 August 2021.

10   "Jews accused of antisemitism," Jewish Voice For Labour website, 5 June 2020 (accessed 15 June 2022).

11   Jackie Walker, interview with author, 28 January 2020.

12   "Signatory Timeline," New signatories in July 2014 (55), Jews for Justice for Palestinians website (accessed 15 June 2022). That was the same month a major Israeli war began on the Gaza Strip.

page listed on the Internet Archive support this date. The group says it is part of the "struggle for justice for Palestinians by Jews from every background."[13]

But as we saw in the last chapter, even some on the left bought this. And the Lansmanite faction was disdainful of the new Jewish group. On one episode of his *All The Best* podcast, Momentum activist Max Shanly defended his mentor Jon Lansman from the influence of "a section of the old Jewish anti-Zionist left who were mainly in Trot groups in the seventies."[14] Lansman was hostile towards JVL right away. In one early meeting with Lansman, a JVL source told me, the group were stunned to find the Momentum leader recommending none other than the Jewish Labour Movement's Jeremy Newmark as someone they should work with. The Jewish Palestine solidarity activists already knew about Newmark's leading role in the Israel lobby and had for years been aware of Newmark's activities on behalf of the Israeli embassy. A source told me that JVL attempted to explain this to Lansman, supposing him to be ignorant of such facts. Lansman's response was a dismissive comment that Newmark was "not the worst of them."

Over the Corbyn years, there was an increasingly poisonous process in which the Jewishness of left-wing activists in the Labour Party was constantly ignored, sidelined, questioned, and maligned. At one event the JLM held to mark Hanukkah, Newmark made a thinly veiled swipe at the unwelcome new Jewish group. "We in JLM are the people who are the real Jewish voice of Labour," he said. The comment was directly addressed to Corbyn, present at the event as party leader.[15]

A disproportionately high number of Jews were targeted by the witch hunt. As anti-Zionist Jewish leftist Tony Greenstein explained on the *Electronic Intifada* podcast, "This is not

---

13   "Who We Are," Jews for Justice for Palestinians website, undated (accessed 15 June 2022).

14   "All The Best: Solidarity Forever," Novara Media, 4 July 2019.

15   "JLM Chanukah Party Speeches," Jewish Labour Movement website, 19 December 2017 (accessed 15 June 2022). See also Asa Winstanley, "Leader in Jewish group banned from Labour Party office," *Electronic Intifada*, 9 March 2018.

particularly surprising given that the Palestine solidarity movement has a disproportionately high number of Jews in it."[16]

Left-wing Jews opposed to the idea that Labour had a unique anti-Semitism problem were rendered as *Un-Jews*. The phenomenon was a symptom of the privileging of Israel by British political and media elites as a useful imperialist tool. Support for Israel is often alleged to be proof against anti-Semitism. But in practice, support for Zionism is often a mask for *very real* anti-Semitism.

Leading Christian Zionist John Hagee is a perfect example. The founder of Christians United for Israel, Hagee is a mega-pastor who once preached that Hitler was "a hunter" sent by God to chase the Jews to Palestine as a punishment for their sins. There could scarcely be a more anti-Semitic notion. Yet Hagee's anti-Semitism is rarely called out and he's openly courted by Israeli leaders. Israeli prime minister Benjamin Netanyahu has frequently appeared at CUFI events and in 2018 spoke alongside Hagee at the opening of the controversial new US embassy in Jerusalem. Hagee prayed the closing benediction.[17]

This malignant media narrative led to a ridiculous situation in which left-wing Jews were smeared as anti-Semitic (often by non-Jews) for criticising supporters of Israel. A frequent culprit of this was Joan Ryan, the chairperson of Labour Friends of Israel during most of Corbyn's leadership. One of many MPs implicated in a 2010 expenses scandal, Ryan was ousted in that year's general election. She returned to Parliament in 2015, just in time to undermine Corbyn from within the party. She was appointed LFI's chairperson that August—the same month Mark Regev was announced as the new Israeli ambassador. She was soon talking up her "deep concerns" over Corbyn's past. In an interview she indicated that the Israel lobby's "concerns" had less to do with real anti-Semitism and more to do with defending Israel. Labour needed to "win back the trust and confidence of the Jewish community," she claimed. She said LFI was

---

16 "Podcast Ep 15: Resisting the censors," *Electronic Intifada*, 22 February 2020.

17 Asa Winstanley, "Religious extremism is at the heart of US support for Israel," *Electronic Intifada*, 6 June 2018.

"adamantly opposed to boycotts and sanctions, which delegitimise Israel."[18] And yet criticism of Ryan was constantly delegitimised as "anti-Semitic"—though Ryan isn't Jewish—even when such criticisms came from Jewish leftists.

Such politicised limits on which Jews count as part of "the Jewish community" are nothing new. Marginalising anti-Zionist Jews has been a key goal of the Zionist movement from its outset. At the second Zionist Congress in 1898, the Zionist Organisation's founder, Theodor Herzl, placed "among our future aims the conquest of [Jewish] communities." Old representative organisations of the Jewish establishment—such as the Board of Deputies of British Jews—would be conquered and their anti-Zionism reversed. As academic Paul Kelemen explains, this was "the third 'conquest'" key to the Zionist movement. The other two "conquests" were focused on Palestine: the "conquest of land" and the "conquest of labour." The explicit goal of the "conquest of [Jewish] communities" shows that Zionism has never contained its aims to the land of Palestine alone and has always been a trans-national movement.[19]

One example of this was the sustained media frenzy about alleged anti-Semitism at Labour's 2017 conference. British-Israeli researcher and academic Jamie Stern-Weiner concluded that "virtually every allegation" of anti-Semitism that year concerned statements made by Jews. "In fact, not one of the specific allegations . . . withstands scrutiny," he wrote. "All either misrepresent events or impute anti-Semitism where none existed."[20]

At one conference fringe meeting, International Jewish Anti-Zionist Network activist Michael Kalmanovitz argued that "if you support Israel, you support apartheid. So what is the JLM and Labour Friends of Israel doing in our party?"

---

18   Marcus Dysch, "Don't vote for Jeremy Corbyn, urges new Labour Friends of Israel chair Joan Ryan," *Jewish Chronicle*, 10 August 2015.

19   Paul Kelemen, *The British Left and Zionism: History of a Divorce* (Manchester University Press, 2012), page 8.

20   "Labour Conference or Nuremberg Rally? Assessing The Evidence," Jamie Stern-Weiner's blog, 12 October 2017.

He said it was "time we campaigned to kick them out."[21] The press completely twisted this event. The *Sun* did not mention the fact of Kalmanovitz's Jewishness.[22] The *Guardian*'s coverage was also misleading, with Jonathan Freedland reporting from conference that Kalmanovitz's plea amounted to "Loud calls for the expulsion of Jewish groups," and he quoted a right-wing Labour MP as describing the situation as "redolent of the 1930s."[23] JLM chairperson Jeremy Newmark claimed Kalmanovitz had made "a thinly veiled call to purge Jews from" Labour.

Of course, this was all nonsense. If Kalmanovitz had genuinely been calling for the expulsion of all Jews from the Labour Party he would have been calling for his own expulsion. Ironically, the only calls for the expulsion of that particular Jew came from the right of party.[24]

Denial of left-wing Jews' Jewishness became ubiquitous and one of the main promoters of this phenomenon was Jon Lansman.

* * *

Jon Lansman was described by the *Times of Israel* as one of Labour's "key power-brokers."[25] Mainstream media often called on Lansman to represent the pro-Corbyn perspective. After Corbyn rose to prominence Lansman generated his own myth on the Labour left. Histories of how Corbyn won the leadership, such as Alex Nunns's book *The Candidate*, recount how Lansman

---

21 Asa Winstanley, "Has the Labour anti-Semitism smear been defeated?" *Electronic Intifada*, 7 November 2017.

22 Brittany Vonow and Natasha Clark, "Labour activists compare Israel supporters to the NAZIS and suggested debating Holocaust denial," *The Sun*, 26 September 2017.

23 Jonathan Freedland, "Labour's denial of antisemitism in its ranks leaves the party in a dark place," *Guardian*, 27 September 2017.

24 Asa Winstanley, "Jewish Labour Movement harassed Labour activists," *Electronic Intifada*, 4 April 2019.

25 Robert Philpot, "Jeremy Corbyn's biggest Jewish backer sows discord within UK Labour party," *Times of Israel*, 8 January 2018.

took turns with left-wing MP John McDonnell to stand outside the Labour whip's office to pressure, cajole, and (in one case) beg sceptical MPs to "lend" Corbyn their nominations so he could get onto the leadership ballot in 2015.

But by 2019, Lansman was coming under sustained criticism from the Corbynite grassroots, especially for his position on the anti-Semitism issue. One former colleague of Lansman's told me at the time that Lansman was "the person who has spectacularly screwed it up for us." The source said that he had "put the whole project in danger," and that on the issue of Labour anti-Semitism smears, Lansman had "actively encouraged attacks on [left-wing] MPs like Chris Williamson," one of Corbyn's most vocal supporters. Lansman would later go on to join right-wing Labour MPs in calling for Williamson to be kicked out.[26] This was part of a general attack by Lansman on the wider left-wing movement, my source said. Many Labour activists agreed that Lansman had encouraged the anti-Semitism smears. Discontent extended to Momentum's membership. The Camden branch of Momentum in March 2019 passed a motion calling for Lansman's removal as leader over his "inappropriate remarks about anti-Semitism, effectively siding with those who have made unfounded allegations."[27]

Lansman's criticism of those who refuted the "Labour anti-Semitism" narrative extended especially to Jewish activists. Lansman caused outrage by declaring that Jewish Voice for Labour was not "really" a true "part of the Jewish community." Lansman's argument was bizarrely circular. He pointed out that JVL opposed the notion that anti-Semitism was a major problem in Labour—a conclusion which Lansman alleged "every significant Jewish community organisation has arrived at about the Labour Party." Lansman seemed to be saying that JVL was not a "significant" Jewish group *precisely because* it disagreed with

---

26 Asa Winstanley, "How Jon Lansman joined Labour's witch hunt," *Electronic Intifada*, 7 October 2019.

27 "Camden Momentum calls for the removal of Jon Lansman from Momentum," Labour Against the Witchhunt website, 14 March 2019.

other Jewish organisations on the issue—a classic Catch-22 situation.[28]

In an email to JVL the group later made public, Lansman bitterly attacked it as "part of the problem and not part of the solution to antisemitism in the Labour Party."[29] Relations between Lansman and the left had not always been this bad. He initially recognised the fact that anti-Semitism was being weaponised as a political weapon against Corbyn's Labour. Recall that in May 2016, he wrote on his blog of a "frenzied witch hunt" partly fuelled by "the fundamentalist wing of pro-Israeli organisations."[30] Ground-zero of this fabricated crisis was Oxford University Labour Club that February, where those accused of anti-Semitism at Oxford had been close to Lansman.

But even earlier than Oxford there were signs Lansman was willing to give ground. Speaking to the *Jewish Chronicle* in January 2016 (the paper excitedly described it as "his first in-depth interview"), Lansman accused Ken Livingstone of having been "sloppy with his language on Jews and Zionists" in the past, although he said "I don't think he was anti-Semitic."[31] Only a few months later, Livingstone would become the most high-profile target of the witch hunt, leading to his suspension and ultimately his forced resignation. Lansman was livid at Livingstone's anti-Zionist comments. Rather than defend the ex-mayor he demanded Livingstone end his criticism of Zionism and leave politics "altogether."[32]

Lansman told the *Jewish Chronicle* that at age 16 he had worked on a kibbutz in the Naqab desert—one of the collective Israeli settlements that have been key military bases and are often built on the land of ethnically cleansed Palestinian villages. Initially

---

28 James Wright, "Momentum founder under fire after claiming left-wing Jews are 'not part' of the Jewish community," *Canary*, 19 June 2019.

29 "Jon Lansman and JVL," Jewish Voice for Labour website, 19 June 2019.

30 Jon Lansman, "A frenzied witch-hunt is not the way to combat antisemitism or any form of racism," *Left Futures*, 9 May 2016.

31 "Ex-kibbutznik who is Corbyn's left-hand man," *Jewish Chronicle*, 28 January 2016.

32 Winstanley, "How Jon Lansman joined."

"I saw myself as a Zionist," he told the paper. But after his kibbutz experience "I felt it less," he said. "Lansman says there is no reason why Zionist Labour supporters cannot find a place in the Corbyn Labour Party," the paper wrote. "I have Zionist friends in the party," Lansman explained.

A few weeks after he demanded Livingstone's "silence," Lansman told the *New Statesman* that "most Jews in Britain" see Zionism as "support for the existence of Israel as a Jewish state" rather than as a "pejorative" term.[33] So while not necessarily describing himself as a Zionist, Lansman seems have been pushing for pro-Zionist positions from within the Corbyn project early on. When I asked Lansman whether he still saw himself as a Zionist in 2019, he avoided a direct answer: "No, I don't describe myself as a 'left Zionist.'" I had not asked him if he saw himself as a "left Zionist."

Speaking to multiple left-wing grassroots Labour activists at the time, it was clear that, aside from the lack of democracy in Momentum, the main source of discontent with Lansman was Momentum's mishandling—even encouragement—of the manufactured Labour anti-Semitism crisis.

But there was evidence that as early as 2016, Lansman wanted Corbyn out and replaced as leader with his colleague John McDonnell. JVL activist Graham Bash revealed to me that Lansman had tried to have Corbyn replaced only months into his leadership of the party. He had approached John McDonnell with the idea in the spring of 2016, asking him to take over, but the latter said no.

Lansman denied my reporting of this but the BBC subsequently confirmed it: "I'm told that [Momentum's] founder, Jon Lansman, hopes that John McDonnell will become the next party leader," wrote political correspondent Iain Watson, only a few days into the general election campaign that would lead to Corbyn's political demise.[34] The following year, Lansman himself essentially confirmed Bash's account. According to

---

33   George Eaton, "Jon Lansman interview: 'There's no leader who would find it easier to win than Jeremy,'" *New Statesman*, 19 May 2016.

34   Iain Watson, "Jeremy Corbyn: Labour's accidental leader," BBC News, 14 December 2019.

Guardian journalist Owen Jones (who in 2016 also turned his back on Corbyn), "Lansman was disillusioned with the leadership. 'It was clearly dysfunctional,' he tells me. He even approached McDonnell to suggest he take over."[35] If Lansman had his doubts about Corbyn, and once privately called for him to go, what explains his brief support for Corbyn's leadership? Alex Nunns's book contains a key insight on this: Lansman simply saw Corbyn as a stopgap. Speaking to Nunns in the run-up to the 2015 leadership election, he explained his thinking: "Could we find someone who would be a caretaker leader," Lansman asked, "and then have another leadership election two years later?" He told Nunns that, "It was in that context that we began to think about people like Jeremy." Until then, Lansman recalled, the idea of Corbyn running for leader had "never entered my head." Corbyn wasn't on his list of "credible" candidates. Union activist Byron Taylor persuaded him otherwise.

"It's got to be Jeremy," said Taylor.

"Jeremy? Really Byron? Why?" Lansman replied.

"He's got all the right policies," Taylor argued. "Jeremy's the nicest man in politics. He hasn't got any enemies."

This point stayed with Lansman. "I never thought of it like that," he recalled to Nunns. "I'd never thought of looking for a candidate without enemies . . . That really sold me on the idea. That was when I started really arguing for Jeremy."[36]

But, by the spring of 2016, when Lansman was pushing for Corbyn to be replaced, it would have been very clear that Corbyn actually had many enemies. That partly explains Lansman's change of heart. The usual suspects from the Zionist movement were out to get Corbyn using "anti-Semitism" as a smear.

* * *

---

35 Owen Jones, *This Land: The Story of a Movement* (London: Allen Lane, 2020), page 112.

36 Alex Nunns, *The Candidate: Jeremy Corbyn's Improbable Path to Power* (New York: OR Books, 2016), pages 85-6.

Lansman's hostile attitude to JVL was in stark contrast to his friendly relations with the Jewish Labour Movement. He worked closely with the group, even, in 2018, addressing its conference, and speaking again at their Labour conference event later that September.[37] Lansman told the *Independent* back in 2016 that "I work closely with Jeremy" Newmark, the JLM's then chairperson.[38] Yet when Newmark was forced to step down after 2018's corruption scandal, Lansman declined to criticise him. When I asked him for comment on the affair he responded: "I don't want to comment on the internal affairs of a Labour Party affiliate of which I am not a member."[39]

Yet Lansman had used his platform at the September 2018 JLM conference to imply that Corbyn needed "training" on anti-Semitism. Reportedly drawing laughs from the audience, he said: "Everyone needs training and Corbyn has a commitment to lifelong learning."[40] Lansman later denied to me that Corbyn has said anything anti-Semitic: "Jeremy doesn't have an anti-Semitic bone in his body."[41]

According to Newmark, Lansman had told a Jewish charity in 2017 that he opposed BDS. This was one of Lansman's "classic left Zionist positions," according to Newmark.[42] I put Newmark's claims to Lansman and he responded that it was "untrue" to say he opposes BDS. "I do support boycotts of settlement goods and

---

37 Asa Winstanley, "Is Labour's Jon Lansman capitulating to the Israel lobby?" *Electronic Intifada*, 9 August 2018.

38 Ashley Cowburn, "Jon Lansman: Momentum chair would 'understand' Labour leadership challenge if party loses general election," *Independent*, 1 October 2016.

39 Jon Lansman, email to author, 9 February 2018. See also Asa Winstanley, "Labour's top Israel lobbyist accused of defrauding Jewish charity," *Electronic Intifada*, 9 February 2018.

40 Sienna Rodgers, "Momentum chief suggests Corbyn needs antisemitism training," *LabourList*, 2 September 2018.

41 Winstanley, "How Jon Lansman joined."

42 Jeremy Newmark, Twitter, 26 December 2017.

services," he wrote back.[43] The BDS movement, however, has never been limited to West Bank settlements alone.[44]

As we saw in chapter 2, Newmark was one of the Israel lobby operatives caught on camera in Al Jazeera's undercover series, *The Lobby*. He had candidly discussed his plan for subversion of Momentum and passing "intelligence" to ambassador Mark Regev. I asked Lansman, as the chair of Momentum, to comment on this. Apropos of nothing, he denied that "we have Israeli spies in Momentum."[45] This was a curiously defensive response, given that my questions had not accused anyone of being a "spy" of any description. The reference to "intelligence" was Newmark's own choice of words. Lansman himself had spoken of his working relationship with Newmark.

Lansman's relationship with the JLM only grew closer over time.

* * *

One of Corbyn's most implacable opponents, right-wing Labour MP Louise Ellman, had, over the years, played leading roles in both Labour Friends of Israel and the Jewish Labour Movement. As Gaza was being destroyed by Israeli aircraft in 2009, Ellman urged the crowd at a pro-war rally in Manchester to "stand together to stick up for Israel."[46] Although JLM leaders are quick to accuse those who describe them as being part of the Israel lobby of anti-Semitism, a deleted statement on their old website (quoting Ellman herself) stated that the goal of the group

---

43 Jon Lansman, email to author, 6 September 2019.

44 See "Know what to boycott," BDSmovement.net, undated (accessed 15 June 2022).

45 Winstanley, "Labour's top Israel lobbyist."

46 David Batty, Audrey Gillan and agencies, "Pro-Israeli protests in London and Manchester," *Guardian*, 11 Jan 2009. Ben White, "Zionists smear Amnesty over 'cocktail' joke," *Electronic Intifada*, 11 January 2013.

was to "lobby" for "Zionism."[47] Given that Zionism is the state of Israel's official ideology, and given JLM's own self-description it seems fair to describe the Jewish Labour Movement as being part of the Israel lobby. In October 2019—after years of undermining Corbyn—Ellman resigned from Labour citing alleged anti-Semitism in her local party and Corbyn's failure to deal with it. Ellman said she wanted Corbyn to lose the upcoming general election.

But sources in Ellman's local constituency party told me that Ellman's departure actually had nothing to do with anti-Semitism. She had been repeatedly criticised for her right-wing, pro-Israel views. Members said they were sick of her constant undermining of the leader. She was "politically crushed in Liverpool Riverside by ordinary members," a source said, and she "knew it was game over." Ellman had jumped before she could be pushed; she was facing calls to step down, and a no-confidence vote had been imminent. Most activists didn't want Ellman as their MP. Their opposition had nothing to do with the fact she was Jewish but rather was motivated by political differences. She was on the Labour right and strongly supported Israel; the constituency members were mostly on the left and supported Palestinian liberation.[48]

Ellman's allegations received widespread national media attention. Claims of anti-Semitism in Liverpool Labour had been slowly building for years and the issue was reported in the papers. One of the biggest media hits for this narrative was an episode of the BBC's *Panorama* programme in 2019, broadcast only a few months before the election. Ellman's claims formed a key plank of the film. It alleged widespread anti-Semitism in her local Riverside Constituency Labour Party. The MP's 2016 allegations against her own members had led to Labour imposing "special measures" on the local group, followed by a series of investigations and disciplinary action.

---

47 Home page, jlm.org.uk, undated. Website deleted, but copy available on the Internet Archive's WayBack Machine (oldest copy 10 February 2007).

48 Asa Winstanley, "Leading Israel lobby MP quits Labour," *Electronic Intifada*, 17 October 2019.

Ben Westerman, a Labour Party disciplinary staffer who is Jewish, appeared in the BBC film claiming to have been asked by a Liverpool member if he was "from Israel." He told *Panorama* of his shock to face anti-Semitism even at a meeting he was conducting against Labour activists accused of anti-Semitism. But the BBC had apparently not bothered to carry out even the most rudimentary verification. They did not seek comment from (or even name) the person alleged to have said this to Westerman. Soon after the BBC film was broadcast, a *Canary* investigation by journalist Joshua Funnell (based on an audio recording of the interview) severely undermined Westerman's claims. The recording showed that the activist in question, Rica Bird, had actually asked Westerman, "What [Labour] branch are you in?" and had not asked the loaded question "Where are you from?"[49] Crucially, she had said nothing about Israel. Bird later accused Westerman of being deliberately deceptive. "When he says, 'Where are you from? Are you from Israel?' – that's an absolute lie! I didn't say that."[50]

Funnell later told me that Westerman had never denied his findings, and that he had never responded to his report. The BBC also made no response, except to say they "stand by their journalism."[51] The *Panorama* programme neglected to mention the

---

49 Joshua Funnell, "Fresh testimony from Labour members could blow Panorama's antisemitism claims wide open," *Canary*, 19 July 2019.

50 Al Jazeera Investigations, *The Labour Files – The Crisis*, YouTube, timecode 00:09:55.

51 Joshua Funnell, interview with author, 12 March 2020. See also Al Jazeera's 2022 series *The Labour Files*, episode two of which compares the misleading *Panorama* account with Marks's and Bird's account, as well as their audio recording of the meeting. See *The Labour Files – The Crisis*, timecodes 00:07:10 - 00:11:10. When Al Jazeera's series aired in September 2022, Funnell reiterated on Twitter that Labour, Westerman and a colleague of Westerman's who had sat in on the meeting had still never responded to his requests for comment (at the time, Westerman had even changed his name on Facebook, apparently to avoid journalists). The BBC also "totally ignored the evidence," Funnell wrote, issuing a blanket statement in which they said they stood by their journalism but did not address the evidence their programme had been highly misleading. As of this writing (October 2022) *Panorama's* John Ware has authored two articles responding to Al Jazeera's series, both of which conspicuously ignore the Westerman

fact that both Labour activists talking to Westerman (Bird and her friend Helen Marks) were also Jewish—which would have been crucial context. "My father lost family in the Holocaust," Marks later told *Middle East Eye*. "It was like my own Jewishness simply didn't count—I was the wrong sort of Jew."[52]

Ellman's motivation for smearing the local membership was pretty obvious. Liverpool is a red city, with its parliamentary seats among the safest for Labour in the entire country. This was even more so the case after 2015, when a new mass membership flooded into the party as a result of Corbyn's leadership victory. An exhaustive series of secret documents, audio recordings, and statements by local members (collated by Jewish Voice for Labour) later revealed that Ellman had been desperate to stop members deselecting her as MP. Instead of admitting that the deselection was motivated by political differences, Ellman began accusing the membership of anti-Semitism.

Jewish Voice for Labour spent months talking to local members, examining documents, listening to recordings of meetings, and investigating the truth of what had happened in Liverpool. Shortly before Ellman resigned, they published their findings on their website, alongside a massive trove of primary sources. The left-wing group concluded that Ellman had waged "war on Riverside Labour Party," including against several local Jewish members, who were distressed to find themselves targeted by baseless anti-Semitism smears. JVL said members had been hit by wide-ranging, un-evidenced smears of anti-Semitism backed up with a mysterious dirty-tricks campaign. This included a mysterious audio recording which Audrey White (a local leftist and trade unionist) alleged had been doctored by an unknown

---

incident: see John Ware, "Al Jazeera's central allegation against my BBC programme can be easily debunked," *Jewish Chronicle*, 13 October 2022; and John Ware, "Rewriting history: Corbyn's Labour Party, antisemitism and 'Panorama'," *Article*, 18 October 2022. Responding to Al Jazeera, the Labour Party declined to comment on the Westerman case.

52 Richard Sanders, "'The wrong sort of Jew': How Labour pursued complaints against elderly Jewish opponents of Israel," *Middle East Eye*, 24 September 2020.

person or persons in order to smear her.[53] (In 2022 White was expelled from the party after publicly confronting Corbyn's successor Keir Starmer over what she said was a betrayal of his campaign promises to members.[54])

Central to the campaign was a widely circulated dossier on the "far-left" in Liverpool Labour. It was anonymously authored by someone who had apparently infiltrated the local chapter of Momentum. JVL's conclusions lined up perfectly with what I had been hearing for years. The dodgy dossier formed the foundation of the mainstream media's years of claims about "Labour anti-Semitism" in the city. A major story in *The Times* was clearly based on the document. It broke during the failed 2016 leadership challenge fronted by Owen Smith. *The Times* did not mention the dossier but quoted from it extensively. The paper described only "leaked documents" it claimed to have seen.[55]

The full dossier was released online later the same day by Guido Fawkes. It was titled, "An investigation into far-left infiltration of the Labour Party in Liverpool since September 2015," but included no disclosure of authorship.[56] Guido claimed it may have been compiled by "Labour Party moderates" and that the "forensic red-on-red black op" had "found its way to the press to diminish the party leadership." The document was indeed written in the same typeface the Labour Party uses for its internal documents, superficially adding credence to the claim it was authored by anti-Corbyn party officials (Labour HQ denied to Guido it was a party document).

It consisted of a scurrilous series of smears, tenuously conflating the then new left-wing group Momentum with

---

53 "Exclusive: The Riverside scandal," Jewish Voice for Labour website, 16 October 2019. For a summary see Winstanley, "Leading Israel lobby MP."

54 "Exclusive: Labour expels White after public criticism of Starmer – but tries to save Harpin by claiming backdated," *Skwawkbox*, 30 July 2022.

55 Lucy Fisher, "Leaked papers reveal hard-left tactics to deselect Labour MP," *The Times*, 15 September 2016.

56 "Leak: Labour Moderates Infiltrated Momentum," Guido Fawkes, 15 September 2016 (accessed 15 June 2022). The dossier originally embedded by Guido has now been deleted. I have attached a full copy to Winstanley, "Leading Israel lobby MP" for the sake of the historical record.

the Trotskyist Militant tendency which had made waves in Liverpool in the 1980s. But rather than being a crude fabrication, the dossier was quite artfully crafted, skilfully mixing lies in with a few decontextualised facts and a hefty dose of old-fashioned McCarthyism.

This is a common professional disinformation technique used by intelligence agencies, especially British ones. As Guido speculated, "Whoever carried out the extensive investigation must have had significant abilities and resources. This is not an amateur job." The document included extensive selections from private email discussion forums and meeting minutes from Liverpool Riverside Momentum. The author of the document also claimed to have infiltrated a closed Facebook group.

A major theme was the "far-left" membership's opposition to Ellman. "Liverpool Riverside constituency has seen the most Momentum activity in the city," the unknown author fretted. They claimed there were questions to be raised about "the nature of these [new] members and their motivations in joining the Labour Party." Ellman, the author wrote, had represented Liverpool Riverside "since her election to parliament at the 1997 general election"—when Tony Blair became prime minister. "Prior to this," it continued, "the seat was represented by Robert Parry, a hard-line left-wing politician . . . Over 20 members of Liverpool Riverside CLP have been reported to the Labour Party Compliance Unit for actively supporting and nominating other political parties as recently as 2015 and 2016." Assuming this figure was accurate, the author seemed to have access to sensitive private Labour Party data.

Along with red baiting, the dossier had a clear anti-Palestinian agenda. One of the key figures of the "hard left" it targeted was Jeremy Hawthorn, whom it stated "has been an active campaigner with Liverpool Friends of Palestine." According to the dossier, an unnamed group of three Labour members "has been routinely hostile towards Liverpool Labour MPs due to their stance of [sic] issues relating to the Israel-Palestine conflict . . . The crossover between Liverpool Friends of Palestine and Momentum activists is clear." The document also alleged anti-Semitism by these pro-Palestinian members against Ellman. What evidence did it give of such "racism"? The three unnamed members were said to have given out leaflets during the 2010 general election which asked constituents to "Remember Gaza" (the 2008-2009 Israeli war against Gaza) and "don't vote for Labour Friends of Israel."[57] But what the dossier conveniently ignored is the fact that Ellman had indeed played a leading role in Labour Friends of Israel.

It falsely claimed the activists' opposition to Ellman was motivated by her Jewish "background" and not by opposition to Israeli violence. The *Jewish Chronicle* spent years trumping up the story of opposition to Ellman, claiming without evidence that members were motivated by anti-Semitism. Eventually, the UK's press regulator found both these claims to be baseless. But by then the damage had been done.

In December 2019, the regulator ruled that the *Jewish Chronicle* had significantly misled readers in a series of "Labour anti-Semitism" stories about left-wing Liverpool activist and trade unionist Audrey White. In an unusually strong ruling, the often-toothless Independent Press Standards Organisation decried the newspaper's obstruction of their investigation as "unacceptable."[58] The *Chronicle* was later forced to apologise, admitting it had published "allegations about Mrs Audrey White" which were "untrue," and deleting the series of articles by Lee Harpin from its website. The paper paid out an undisclosed sum in libel damages.[59]

White had been one of the other "key figures" targeted by the mysterious Liverpool dossier. Amongst her supposed crimes was protesting against the Iraq and Afghanistan wars and being involved in Jeremy Corbyn's Stop the War Coalition. Again, the dossier mixed in outright fabrications with selective truths: it falsely claimed that White was "the daughter of Eddie Loyden, a hard-left, Militant supporting [former] Member of Parliament."

---

[57] See the dossier, page 8, which cites "Racist leaflets against Jewish candidates in Liverpool," *Jewish Chronicle*, 15 April 2010.

[58] Asa Winstanley, "Jewish Chronicle lied in reports on 'Labour anti-Semitism,'" *Electronic Intifada*, 2 December 2019.

[59] Asa Winstanley, "Jewish Chronicle to pay damages over anti-Semitism libel," *Electronic Intifada*, 21 February 2020.

In fact, White was not related to Loyden, who was not a member of Militant.[60] The reality was simply that Louise Ellman was a pro-Israel partisan of long standing, who often used her position in Parliament to further that end. As the *Jewish Chronicle* accurately summarised in 2014, "Ellman can always be called on to defend Israel" in the House of Commons.[61] As such, it was no surprise that the membership in Liverpool opposed her. It was fundamentally dishonest for Ellman to claim such opposition was rooted in anti-Semitism.

The MP's obsession with "Labour anti-Semitism" reached its peak in February 2019, during an interview with a BBC radio programme, when she accused Corbyn of nothing less than thought-crime. "Anti-Semitism is thriving under Jeremy Corbyn's leadership . . . Jeremy has a lot of those thoughts without registering that it is anti-Semitism," she claimed.[62]

* * *

The July 2019 episode of *Panorama* played a big part in destabilising Labour, only months before the election of December that year. Titled "Is Labour Anti-Semitic?" it relied heavily on the anti-Corbyn JLM for its narrative.

The lead reporter was John Ware, a reporter with a long and controversial record among Britain's Muslim community. Arzu Merali of the Islamic Human Rights Commission has described him as "someone who has made a career out of exceptionalising Muslims, their political activities, calls for equality and . . . general day-to-day doings, as things utterly alien, extraordinary

---

60 "Exclusive: The Riverside scandal," especially Appendix 10: Labour Party Compliance Unit interview with Audrey White, Riverside CLP.

61 The "JC Power 100" list of "the most influential figures shaping Jewish life in Britain," Numbers 100-51, *Jewish Chronicle*, 28 August 2014.

62 *The World at One*, BBC Radio 4, 28 February 2019. Clip available at "Jeremy Corbyn now accused of having 'antisemitic thoughts' by LFI Vice Chair, Louise Ellman MP," The Daily Politik YouTube channel, 28 February 2019.

and sinister."[63] The programme featured interviews with members of the Labour Party's Jewish community. Speaking straight into camera, they gave often emotional accounts of the anti-Semitic abuse they said they had received—one woman seemed on the verge of tears. Anyone not already familiar with those individuals wouldn't have been enlightened by *Panorama*. Few were given names or affiliations. Unsuspecting viewers were likely to have come away with the impression that they had not wanted to give their names for fear of further anti-Semitic attacks.

But far from being random Jewish members of Labour, most were actually JLM activists—predominantly from its executive committee. This was widely noted on social media at the time. It turned out that of 10 anonymous Jewish speakers claiming to have been on the receiving end of anti-Semitism in Labour, eight were current or recent senior JLM figures.

The first person to appear in the documentary was former Israeli embassy officer Ella Rose. By this time, she had become quite widely known by Labour activists, after appearing in *The Lobby* in 2017. *Panorama* did not reveal her role in the JLM's leadership, explain the group's partisan role in Labour's ongoing civil war, or even give Rose's name. As the film started so it went on. There was no concrete evidence of anti-Semitism. It featured a virtual *Who's Who* of Labour's manufactured anti-Semitism campaign, with the full involvement of JLM's young cadres.

Alex Richardson was another face familiar to Al Jazeera viewers. Richardson was parliamentary aide to Joan Ryan MP, Labour Friends of Israel's chairperson. By the time of the *Panorama* broadcast he was the JLM's membership officer. There was nothing given in the episode to disclose his name, his JLM leadership role, or his paid work for one of Parliament's most actively pro-Israel lawmakers. All these facts would have been directly relevant.

Undercover footage in *The Lobby* showed that Richardson was closely tied to the Israel lobby.[64] As we saw in chapter 4,

---

63 Arzu Merali, "The banality and boredom of anti-Muslim witchhunts. Or beware John Ware," *Middle East Eye*, 29 March 2018.

64 Asa Winstanley, "How the Israel lobby fakes anti-Semitism," *Electronic Intifada*, 14 January 2017.

his boss Ryan had been caught on camera faking an allegation of anti-Semitism against Jean Fitzpatrick, a Labour member and Palestine Solidarity Campaign supporter. It's unclear who exactly reported Fitzpatrick to Labour's bureaucrats, but there is evidence that Richardson was involved. Fitzpatrick was ultimately exonerated, but she was left under a cloud of suspicion. In the undercover footage, Richardson said that "Joan convinced me to report the one yesterday because I was made to feel uncomfortable." Yet he privately admitted, "nothing anti-Semitic was said."

After I had reported on this following the *Panorama* broadcast,[65] Richardson emailed me to deny fabricating anti-Semitism. He claimed that the Al Jazeera film had conflated two separate incidents and that the only complaint he had made at Labour conference 2016 "did not concern the incident featured in the film with Jean Fitzpatrick." The "entirely separate incident," he wrote, "did not allege anti-Semitism, instead it alleged harassment against an entirely different individual." But when I asked him to provide details of this allegedly separate incident, Richardson did not reply. He also failed to explain his comments as seen in the film speaking to "Robin" in which he appears to say of Fitzpatrick, "I kind of feel it was an anti-Semitic trope against Israel . . . although she didn't say Jews and she said Israel. It's definitely on the line . . . I suspect that this woman might be potentially banned [by Labour] because she did say something that was anti-Semitic."[66]

The Al Jazeera series also shows an email from Richardson asking Robin (who was of course there secretly filming the entire incident) to act as witness to Joan Ryan's complaint about "a lady, chatting to Joan" who "made an anti-Semitic remark."

To their credit, for once the Labour leadership pushed back. Corbyn said the *Panorama* episode had been inaccurate and Labour's press office said in a statement that the film was "not a fair or balanced investigation, it is an authored polemic, with

---

65   Asa Winstanley, "BBC's anti-Corbyn hatchet job fails to land blow," *Electronic Intifada*, 11 July 2019.

66   Asa Winstanley, "Labour Friends of Israel denies funding from Israeli spy," *Electronic Intifada*, 17 July 2019.

no political balance of interviewees" and "an overtly one-sided intervention in political controversy by the BBC." They even alleged that the filmmakers invented quotes and edited emails to change their meaning.

Many viewers were able to see through *Panorama's* distorted version of events. Jewish Voice for Labour complained that the BBC had not interviewed a single one of their activists. JVL activists would have given a very different picture of life in the party than the JLM. Almost 1,600 viewers made complaints to the BBC, but the broadcaster did not uphold a single one.[67]

The *Panorama* film was nominated in 2020's BAFTA television awards, making the final shortlist.[68] In October 2022, Ware settled a libel suit he had initiated against Jewish Voice for Labour. Their spokesperson Naomi Wimborne-Idrissi read out a statement in court accepting as "untrue" her previous assertion that "the BBC had taken action against Mr Ware in connection with allegations he has engaged in Islamophobia."[69] JVL later stated that "the apology issued in open court was not for what we had written or said about the *Panorama* programme. The agreed settlement did not require us to retract or qualify in any way our criticisms of the programme itself."[70]

* * *

All-encompassing phrases such as "the Jewish community," or "the mainstream Jewish community" were frequently bandied about during Labour's crisis of anti-Semitism smears.

The obsessive focus on the opinions of British Jews was at best short-sighted. Britain's estimated 300,000-strong Jewish

---

[67] "Complaints Report, 8-21 July 2019," BBC. A review of subsequent fortnightly complaints reports up to June 2020 shows that the BBC rejected them all.

[68] Jacob Judah, "Bafta nomination for Panorama investigation into Labour antisemitism," *Jewish Chronicle*, 4 June 2020.

[69] Tom Pilgrim, "Panorama reporter receives apology over defamatory radio comments," *Independent*, 4 October 2022.

[70] "Libel Settlement Clarification," Jewish Voice for Labour, 21 October 2022.

community has long been far more politically conservative than the American Jewish population—which votes overwhelmingly Democrat. By way of contrast, polling conducted just before the 2015 general election (before Corbyn became leader) showed only 22 percent of British Jews intending to vote Labour.[71]

But right-wing Jews in Labour who supported Israel and opposed Jeremy Corbyn's left-wing leadership project were consistently presented as if they were the only valid Jewish voices. Conversely, left-wing pro-Palestinian Jews were ignored and marginalised; they were even smeared as anti-Semitic and purged. Zionist organisations like the Jewish Labour Movement and the Board of Deputies of British Jews were presented as if they alone constituted *The Jewish Community*, or at least were the true representatives of that community.

Such a view was put forward in a candid admission by Stephen Bush writing in the *New Statesman*. "Full-throated support for the state of Israel would reassure many Jews about Corbyn's credentials," he wrote in the spring of 2018. In order to assuage their fears, Bush wrote, Corbyn should take a leaf out of the pages of Tony Blair and Gordon Brown who "always defined themselves in opposition to the anti-imperialist, anti-capitalist and anti-Zionist section of the left."[72] Speaking to *Panorama* reporter John Ware, Labour's Blairite director of complaints Mike Creighton said that, when asked how the party should respond to the "crisis," he had insisted Corbyn should give a speech, "particularly saying that Israel had a right to exist."[73]

The "anti-Semitism crisis" was always more about the Labour leader's lack of support for Israel than anything else.

In January 2020, after Corbyn had announced his resignation as leader following the previous month's election result, the Board of Deputies issued a set of demands on the new Labour leadership candidates. The "10 pledges" were an extraordinarily arrogant and broad-reaching set of conditions.

---

71 Marcus Dysch, "Huge majority of British Jews will vote Tory, JC poll reveals," *Jewish Chronicle*, 7 April 2015.

72 Stephen Bush, "This Passover has presented an uneasy dilemma for Britain's left-wing Jews," *New Statesman*, 5 April 2018.

73 Winstanley, "BBC's anti-Corbyn hatchet job."

Among the demands was that "prominent offenders" would "never be readmitted to membership." As part of this condition the Board specifically cited Jackie Walker and Ken Livingstone. Another condition was a ban on Labour contact with Jewish groups the Board deemed not to be its "main representative groups." Although they didn't name Jewish Voice for Labour, the implication was clear, as it specified that Labour contact with "the Jewish community" should never be made "through fringe organisations and individuals."[74]

All leadership candidates to replace Corbyn immediately agreed to these conditions.[75] The anti-Zionists were persona non grata.

---

74 "'Rebuilding will take more than mild expressions of regret' – The Board of Deputies launches its Ten Pledges for Labour leadership and deputy leadership candidates," Board of Deputies of British Jews website, 13 January 2020 (accessed 15 June 2022). The PDF of the actual 10 pledges appears to have been deleted from the Board's website, but is still available on the Internet Archive's WayBack Machine.

75 Asa Winstanley, "Labour's fake anti-Semitism crisis outlives Corbyn," *Electronic Intifada*, 16 January 2020.

CHAPTER EIGHT

THE TURNING POINT

"You're a fucking anti-Semite and a racist," the elderly Labour MP spat at Jeremy Corbyn. The erstwhile colleagues faced off in the House of Commons.
"I'm sorry you feel like that," the Labour leader replied. It was the summer of 2018 and a row over the definition of anti-Semitism was raging.[1] The Labour right and Israel lobby were piling on pressure for the party to adopt the IHRA's "working definition"—a strongly pro-Israel document which Palestine solidarity campaigners object to as it chills their legitimate free speech rights. The confrontation took place after another Brexit vote by MPs, behind the speaker's chair and "out of the range of TV cameras," *HuffPost UK* reported. According to the website, the other MP had told Corbyn "he didn't want people like her in the party anymore."[2]

The other MP was Margaret Hodge, the very same lawmaker whose no-confidence motion targeting Corbyn had triggered the failed leadership coup back in 2016. Hodge never denied the confrontation had taken place—she only claimed not to have sworn.

Corbyn's response seemed over-polite and characteristic of his failure to get to grips with the real crisis facing his party—the

---

1 Asa Winstanley, "New assault on Corbyn aims to ban criticism of Israel in Labour," *Electronic Intifada*, 20 July 2018. Benjamin Kentish, "Jeremy Corbyn called 'f****** racist and antisemite' by Labour MP Dame Margaret Hodge," *Independent*, 18 July 2018.

2 Paul Waugh, "Jeremy Corbyn Told by Veteran Jewish MP 'You're A F***ing Anti-Semite and a Racist,'" *HuffPost UK*, 17 July 2018.

rash of false, trumped-up, and exaggerated anti-Semitism allegations used as a political weapon against the left. Hodge's open attack on her own leader came as the biggest wave of the manufactured anti-Semitism crisis to date crashed into Labour. It raged through the whole spring and summer of 2018. Hodge was no neutral observer—she was a partisan of Labour's civil war and had been opposed to Corbyn from the start. A hardened right-winger, she was an ardent supporter of Labour Friends of Israel. Her support for Israel formed a key motivation for her opposition to the left-wing leader. She smeared Corbyn's support for the Palestine solidarity movement as inherently anti-Semitic.

* * *

Hodge held a series of relatively minor ministerial roles under the New Labour governments of Tony Blair and Gordon Brown. As a newly arrived MP in 1994, she had nominated Blair as Labour leader after the untimely demise of his predecessor, John Smith.[3] In the 2015 leadership election, she nominated continuity Blairite candidate Liz Kendall (who came last, winning a miserable 4.5 percent of the vote).[4]

Hodge's opposition to Corbyn's leadership was bitter and unyielding. It mirrored Blair's own position. Speaking to the pro-business Progress faction in July 2015, before Corbyn won his first leadership campaign, Blair advised that Labour members whose hearts were with Corbyn should get "a heart transplant." The ex-leader was frank. "Let me make my position clear: I wouldn't want to win on an old-fashioned leftist platform. Even if I thought it was the route to victory, I wouldn't take it."[5]

---

3 Rowena Mason, "Brief, brutal and very public: there's more to Margaret Hodge's grillings than dramatics," *Guardian*, 13 March 2015.

4 "Liz Kendall, candidate for Labour Leader," deleted page from Labour Party website, undated (available on the Internet Archive's WayBack Machine, copy dated 15 July 2015).

5 Jon Stone, "Tony Blair says he wouldn't want a left-wing Labour party to win an election," *Independent*, 22 July 2015.

Blair's intervention backfired, rallying more support for Corbyn. But the former prime minister's hostility to the idea of a left-wing Labour government set an example for his most die-hard followers. Blair had quit the House of Commons for a round of lucrative speaking engagements and thus had the freedom to openly criticise Labour's leftward swing in a way that other right-wing MPs found more difficult. They had to worry about being deselected by their local parties—difficult under party rules, but not impossible. Hodge was one such die-hard.

In the spring of 2016 Hodge had led an attempted coup. May's local elections had been a mixed bag for Corbyn's Labour. There were both gains and losses, and the schemers sharpened their knives. The press was full of rumours of a plot against the leader. MPs were expected to force him to resign, timing the coup around the upcoming referendum on European Union membership. The *Daily Telegraph* reported that "A plot to oust Jeremy Corbyn as Labour leader has emerged, with veteran MP Margaret Hodge said to have been persuaded to stand against him to spark a leadership contest." Although the article's prediction that Hodge would run herself as a "stalking horse before dropping out to allow moderate MPs" to take the field did not pan out, in most other respects the details of the plot reported in the *Telegraph* turned out to be true.[6] Hodge headed up the opposition to Corbyn after the referendum that approved Brexit the following month. Ten days before the referendum the paper reported more details. A group of Labour MPs, it wrote, believed they could "topple Jeremy Corbyn after the EU referendum in a 24-hour blitz."[7] Many Labour MPs were outraged at the referendum result. They attacked Corbyn, saying he hadn't done enough to support the remain campaign. An anonymous source

---

6   Michael Wilkinson, "Revealed: plot to oust Jeremy Corbyn by using veteran Labour MP Margaret Hodge to spark leadership contest," *Daily Telegraph*, 3 May 2016. See also Asa Winstanley, "After Brexit, Labour Friend of Israel launches coup against Corbyn," *Electronic Intifada*, 24 June 2016.

7   Ben Riley-Smith, "Labour rebels hope to topple Jeremy Corbyn in 24-hour blitz after EU referendum," *Daily Telegraph*, 13 June 2016.

told the *LabourList* website that the atmosphere among Labour MPs was "mutinous."[8]

On the Friday that the result of the referendum was announced, Hodge submitted a motion of no-confidence in Corbyn to her Labour colleagues, seconded by MP Ann Coffey. A "debate" followed at the Parliamentary Labour Party meeting the following Monday. But comradely discussion was thin on the ground. According to Corbyn's close ally Diane Abbott, the goal of the right-wing MPs in attendance was "to break him [Corbyn] as a man." MP after MP stood up to berate the left-wing leader in "the most contemptuous terms possible, pausing only to text their abuse to journalists waiting outside," Abbott recalled. Parliamentary sources described the scene as "a bloodbath, the worst I've ever seen"; "brutal," said another.[9] A non-Corbyn supporting MP had "never seen anything so horrible" and felt "reduced to tears."

The climax of the meeting was a lecture by Hodge herself. She advised Corbyn to ignore the democratic mandate he had won the year before. "This is not just about the party members," she said. To thunderous applause by her colleagues, Hodge intoned that "the most important contribution you can make to the Labour Party" would be to quit. But Corbyn left the room to join his supporters in Parliament Square. A large, enthusiastic "Keep Corbyn" demo had assembled in what turned out to be a successful effort to foil the coup.

The MPs voted overwhelmingly against Corbyn the next day. No less than 172 backed Hodge's motion demanding Corbyn resign. Only 40 backed the leader.

Parallel to Hodge's efforts, a second coup was being led from within the shadow cabinet by Hilary Benn, Labour's pro-war foreign affairs spokesperson. Son of left-wing icon Tony Benn, the younger Benn's politics lay far more to the right. The day

---

8   Conor Pope, "Mutinous Labour MPs to challenge Corbyn, *LabourList*, 24 June 2016.

9   Alex Nunns, *The Candidate: Second Edition*. As cited in "The Candidate: the summer coup - extract," CounterFire website, 23 November 2016.

after Hodge launched her own coup, Benn's plot came to light.[10] On the evening of Saturday, 25 June, the *Observer* broke the story that the shadow minister was planning to overthrow the leader by orchestrating a series of resignations from the shadow cabinet. To his credit, Corbyn sacked Benn immediately. The wave of resignations still followed, but their impact had been dulled.

The Parliamentary Labour Party motion orchestrated by Hodge had no standing under Labour rules. Corbyn refused to resign. On its front page, traditionally Labour-supporting paper the *Mirror* piled in with the rest of the press and called for Corbyn to "Go Now." But the paper inadvertently provided a morale boost to the Corbyn-supporting membership, with a double-page spread detailing how, although 46 Labour MPs had quit the shadow cabinet, "One refuses to walk." The central photo showed a man-of-action Corbyn pointing dramatically as he arrived in Parliament Square to address his supporters.[11]

After Hodge's 2018 outburst in Parliament, there was a short-lived attempt in the leader's office to take action against her. The party briefly launched an investigation into her conduct. A spokesman for Corbyn said that Hodge's public attack on the leader was "clearly unacceptable" and that the party would take disciplinary action. Hodge soon received a formal letter of investigation.[12] But the probe went nowhere.

Labour's new general secretary Jennie Formby claimed the investigation had been dropped after Hodge expressed "regret" to Labour officials. Labour's Chief Whip also issued her with a formal warning, according to Formby. But Hodge was defiant, vehemently denying Formby's claim she had backed down.[13] "She did not express regret . . . our client will not apologise for

---

10 Rowena Mason and Anushka Asthana, "Labour crisis: how the coup against Jeremy Corbyn gathered pace," *Guardian*, 26 June 2016

11 Roy Greenslade, "Why Jeremy Corbyn is not the Labour party's real problem," *Guardian*, 28 June 2016.

12 Hodge posted the whole letter along with her lawyers' reply on social media. Margaret Hodge, "Here is the letter I received . . . " Twitter, 23 July 2018.

13 "Margaret Hodge denies expressing regret. Formby: Chief Whip says twice that she did," *Skwawkbox*, 9 August 2018.

her conduct or words, as she did nothing wrong," her lawyers at Mishcon de Reya insisted.[14] Why Corbyn sacked Benn but took no substantive action against Hodge remains a mystery. Hodge was, after all, the originator of the first coup, not Benn. Due to Corbyn's "broad church" approach, Benn had been a member of the shadow cabinet and so could be fired from that role. Hodge had not. But she and Coffey could still have been disciplined by party officials. At the least, a public signal could have been sent out by Corbyn's surrogates. But no such action was taken, and Hodge and other implacably right-wing MPs remained free to sabotage the party from within.

It's likely that Corbyn's lack of action stemmed from a fear of further anti-Semitism smears should he make a decisive move against Hodge, who is Jewish. Hodge talked incessantly about her Jewishness, mobilising it as a weapon against Corbyn and the wider party membership.

Mishcon de Reya has longstanding links to the Israeli government. More famous as Princess Diana's divorce lawyers, the firm is often Israel's legal representative of choice in London. Its work for Israel has included some of the most high-profile attacks on the BDS movement in the UK. Probably the biggest was the years-long assault on the University and College Union (as we saw in chapter 2). Mishcon's deputy chairman, Anthony Julius, told me in 2012 that he had acted against that union *pro bono*.[15] This doesn't necessarily mean that Mishcon's representation of Hodge was a tie orchestrated by Israel. But the firm's history of making allegations of anti-Semitism to defend Israeli interests

---

14   Letter from Mishcon to Jennie Formby, 6 August 2018. Posted by Hodge to Twitter the same day.

15   Asa Winstanley, "How Israel's supporters are attempting to shut down boycott debate in UK unions," *Electronic Intifada*, 27 December 2012. The internal JLC report on Jeremy Newmark's alleged corruption obtained by the *Jewish Chronicle* in 2018 suggests that in fact Mishcon de Reya may have invoiced the JLC for "£20,000 . . . to cover their fees." It's perfectly possible that Julius himself still acted *pro bono* and that these fees (if they ever were finally paid) would have been to cover the time of the many other legal staff working on the case. See pages 10-11 of the report: "Jeremy Newmark - the evidence: Read the full report here," *Jewish Chronicle* website, 8 February 2018.

in the UK does help to explain why such a powerful firm would want to take on her case.

Having faced down the prospect of a very minor ticking-off, Hodge took to the airwaves to denounce the "cult of Corbynism." She even told one journalist that her situation in the Labour Party was similar to that of Jews under Nazi Germany. "On the day that I heard that they were going to discipline me, and possibly suspend me," she explained to Sky News, "it felt almost like—I kept thinking, what did it feel like to be a Jew in Germany in the '30s? Because it felt almost as if they were coming for me." The implication seemed to be that Corbyn was Hitler. "It felt to me like, 'Oh my God: are they doing this to me because I'm Jewish?'"

Michael Foster, a former Labour Party donor, had been suspended from the party for less, having called Momentum Nazi "stormtroopers."[16] Foster had demanded Corbyn "say the word Israel" at Labour Friends of Israel's 2015 reception.[17] Hodge also launched a denunciation of Corbyn's support for the Palestine solidarity movement. "It's a very fine line between being pro-Palestinian, the Palestinian cause, which he's always believed in, and being anti-Semitic," she claimed. "I think he's gone the wrong side of that line." The issue which had triggered Hodge's attack on Corbyn in Parliament in the first place was the IHRA definition of anti-Semitism. "Of course he's got to accept that definition, but even if he does that tomorrow, that will only be the start," Hodge had told Sky.[18]

The IHRA definition was increasingly insinuated into party structures by pro-Israel groups and arguments raged (as we saw in chapter 6). The document was utilised by Labour's right-wing bureaucracy to expel Moshé Machover in 2017, if only for a brief period. But by 2018 the Labour left began slowly conceding to the demand they should embrace the misleading document too. Before the national controversy that summer, Corbyn's office had

---

16 Asa Winstanley, "Pro-Israel donor suspended by Labour," *Electronic Intifada*, 13 September 2016.

17 Asa Winstanley, "Siege of Gaza must end, Jeremy Corbyn tells Labour Friends of Israel," *Electronic Intifada*, 30 September 2015.

18 Aubrey Allegretti, "Margaret Hodge: Labour investigation made me think about treatment of Jews in 1930s Germany," Sky News, 17 August 2018

already pushed out the line that it had endorsed the introductory part of the IHRA document (without commenting on the rest). This read: "Antisemitism is a certain perception of Jews, which may be expressed as hatred toward Jews. Rhetorical and physical manifestations of antisemitism are directed toward Jewish or non-Jewish individuals and/or their property, toward Jewish community institutions and religious facilities." The leader's spokespeople referred to this paragraph alone as "the definition," while declining to comment on the 11 "contemporary examples of anti-Semitism"—most of which brought Israel into the picture. But this attempt to divide the document was doomed to failure, partly because the IHRA itself repeatedly misrepresented the entire document (both the definition paragraph and the examples) as "the definition."[19] Nonetheless, the fact remained that both the definition and the "examples" formed part of a single page on the IHRA's website under the headline, "The working definition of antisemitism." The confusion seemed almost deliberate.

The thinking from Corbyn's team seemed to be that giving this particular inch would be enough to stop the Israel lobby taking a mile. But what they had missed was one simple fact: as far as the pro-Israel groups were concerned, the whole point of the "working definition" *was* the examples. And they were about to take far more than a mile. By July 2018, Labour's National Executive Committee had a pro-Corbyn majority. Jon Lansman was also now a member. After pressure to adopt the entire document including its examples, the national executive released a new interpretation of the IHRA's definition, which they set out as Labour's "Code of Conduct" on anti-Semitism. It endorsed

---

19 Despite the fact that senior IHRA spokespeople repeatedly claimed that the whole document, including the examples, was adopted unanimously by the entire May 2016 plenary of the IHRA, investigations in 2021 revealed this to be untrue. In fact, the Swedish and Danish representatives objected to the examples being rushed through, leading to the paragraph being separated, and voted through by the plenary as "the definition" alone. See: James Kleinfeld and Al Jazeera Investigative Unit, "IHRA 'misrepresents' own definition of anti-Semitism, says report," Al Jazeera online, 23 April 2021. I am grateful to Jamie Stern-Weiner for drawing my attention to this article.

most of the "examples" of supposed anti-Semitism, but set out its own interpretation of others. Inevitably, this wouldn't be enough to satiate the pro-Israel groups.

* * *

The engineered anti-Semitism crisis carried on, year in and year out. It refused to go away precisely because it was a *manufactured* crisis. For the right it was too useful a weapon. Just as the "crisis" seemed to be dying down, it would pop up again. On and on it went, in wave after wave after wave. For the grassroots Labour Party left, it often felt like being under siege, especially at its highest ebb in 2018. The entire weight of the British political establishment was bearing down on Corbyn and his supporters. The Israel lobby was committed to the strategy of throwing as much mud at the wall as possible and hoping that enough of it would stick. This tenacious strategy yielded results.

The only way that powerful vested interests can defeat popular movements of millions of people is by smashing their bonds of solidarity—divide and rule. The movement behind Corbyn was eventually worn down. While there were some earlier signs of this malign phenomenon, 2018 marked a key turning point and a moment of severe, irreversible defeat. The defeat was made all the worse by the refusal of much of the Labour Party left to even admit it was a loss. The summer of 2018 was an important step on the road to 2019's electoral defeat.

The "working definition" was an attempt to infiltrate a confusing, mis-definition of anti-Semitism into public life. It was a powerful weapon against the Palestine solidarity movement. The wearingly long summer of "Labour anti-Semitism" began as early as the end of March. It dragged on until the defeat of early September, with the full, formal adoption of the definition.

The whole furore was kicked off by an MP who had for years been a leading figure in the pro-Israel lobby—but who was rarely acknowledged as such. This was right-wing Labour MP Luciana Berger. After the Labour right's internal sabotage, their nightmare scenario had successfully been avoided—total election victory for Jeremy Corbyn's Labour Party in 2017. But they still reeled from his impressive gains. Local elections were coming up in May 2018. Opinion polling in January and February predicted major losses for Theresa May's Conservative party and triumph for Corbyn's Labour in London. The poll suggested the "best result for any party since 1968," the *Independent* reported.[20]

Something had to be done.

The biggest wave of the anti-Semitism "crisis" yet seemed deliberately calculated to tank the party's upcoming local election campaign. It was a years-long reactionary guerrilla campaign against the party. The vanguard of this band of contras-in-suits was the pro-Israel lobby. Luciana Berger kicked things off. She was now the "Parliamentary chairperson" of the Jewish Labour Movement in its new incarnation, after its September 2015 relaunch in coordination with the Israeli embassy. The role was a new position, with Berger established as the first to hold it. Although the old JLM had generally been led by Labour MPs, after the embassy-endorsed 2015 reboot, Louise Ellman made way for Jeremy Newmark as an essentially full-time professional chairperson. Bringing Berger onboard as "Parliamentary chair" created an honorary leadership role.[21]

The 2018 wave began with the disinterment of an obscure old social media post. Via Twitter, Berger posted a screenshot of a Facebook comment by Corbyn dating from back in 2012. The comment defended an artist who had painted a mural in East London, which was being threatened with removal by the council. The mural depicted a cabal of suited white men playing a giant game of Monopoly, with the board laid on the backs of darker-skinned exploited workers. It later emerged that the artist, a Californian who goes by the sobriquet Mear One, intended the figures to represent, in part, "the elite banker cartel known as the Rothschilds." Mear One denied any anti-Semitism in the mural, but that was the basis for its removal on the instruction of

---

20 Lizzy Buchan, "Theresa May to hold crunch talks as pollster warns of heavy losses in council elections," *Independent*, 27 January 2018

21 "National Executive Committee," page on deleted Jewish Labour Movement website (www.jlm.org.uk), undated. The earliest copy of this page on the Internet Archive's WayBack Machine to name anyone in this position is dated 1 March 2017.

Lutfur Rahman, the elected local mayor. Rahman, a left-winger expelled from Labour amid an Islamophobic media campaign predating Corbyn's leadership, explained his decision stating that whether "intentional or otherwise, the images of the bankers perpetuate anti-Semitic propaganda about conspiratorial Jewish domination of financial and political institutions."[22]

The Rothschild family are a banking dynasty of British Jews, with branches of the extended family in Germany and France. It is true that the word "Rothschilds" is sometimes used as a sort of code word by right-wing anti-Jewish conspiracy theorists. Nonetheless, it does not follow that any use of the word is necessarily anti-Semitic. For example, it is an uncontested historical fact that in the late nineteenth century, some leading members of the family provided key financial backing to the earliest Zionist colonies in Palestine. But, over the years, the family has included different opinions on the subject of Zionism and later on Israel. The attempt to collapse all this into an allegedly monolithic "Rothschilds" conspiracy for financial control of the world very much echoes classic anti-Semitism.

The word "Rothschilds" did not appear on the mural itself but was brought up by Mear One in a YouTube video explaining the meaning of his work. Furthermore, Corbyn's comment was based on a reproduction of the mural on Facebook that was of such poor quality that it was difficult to see what was being depicted. At worst the Facebook comment was a minor misstep by Corbyn. After Berger's Twitter post he apologised, saying he should have looked more closely at the image. But the media hysterics soared out of all proportion. The successful weaponisation of a six-year-old Facebook comment to sabotage the party (just as it was gearing up for local elections) dominated the airwaves for months. On BBC Radio 4's morning *Today* programme, Jewish Leadership Council chairperson Jonathan Goldstein attacked the Labour leader in no uncertain terms. "Jeremy Corbyn is now the figurehead for an anti-Semitic political culture, based upon obsessive hatred of Israel,

---

22 Asa Winstanley, "Jewish Labour activists defend Corbyn as Israel lobby attacks," *Electronic Intifada*, 26 March 2018. See also "Mear One—False Profits (London, 2012)," MearOneHD YouTube channel, 23 September 2012.

conspiracy theories, and fake news," Goldstein claimed. This was a revealing comment since the Mear One mural had nothing to do with Israel. That Goldstein focused on Corbyn's "hatred of Israel" was an insight into his group's priorities.[23]

Three days after Berger launched the row, a demonstration against the Labour Party and Corbyn was organised in Parliament Square by the Jewish Leadership Council and the Board of Deputies under the slogan "Enough is Enough." Some of those attending brought Israeli flags. Jewish Voice for Labour swung into action with a counter-demonstration, condemning the pro-Israel groups' efforts as "an attempt to influence local elections" in favour of the Tories.

Berger's apparent shock at the discovery of Corbyn's old Facebook comment on the mural was not supported by the facts. As dates on the image showed, the screenshot had first been taken in 2017. The story didn't gain traction until 2018, despite the *Jewish Chronicle*'s attempt to push it three years earlier.[24] The persistence of the Israel lobby had paid off. It now became a major national story and Corbyn began to retreat.

Much like in its coverage of Ruth Smeeth two years before, the entire corporate media conveniently omitted any mention of Berger's long history in the pro-Israel lobby. Her alleged "hurt and anguish" at discovering Corbyn's Facebook comment on the controversial mural was widely accepted as fact. Her generally right-wing stance and evident desire to sabotage Corbyn's electoral chances went largely without comment. Her political views were not taken into account.

There was an even stronger media omertà over the fact that Berger had for years been a pro-Israel partisan. Aside from her then current role in the pro-Israel Jewish Labour Movement, back in 2010 she had spent three years working as director and staff manager of Labour Friends of Israel.[25] In an interview with the *Jerusalem Post* in 2011, she revealed that she'd visited Israel

---

23 Winstanley, "Jewish Labour activists defend Corbyn."

24 Marcus Dysch, "Did Corbyn back 'antisemitic mural' artist?" *Jewish Chronicle*, 6 November 2015.

25 Luciana Berger, LinkedIn profile (accessed 1 April 2022).

more than 20 times and the paper described her as "an active supporter of Israel." One of the "hot topics" at the conference she was attending when she gave the interview was how to fight the boycott, divestment, and sanctions movement. "BDS has been raised in parliament," she told the paper. "It's a topic the new government is particularly aware of."[26] The UK government at the time was a Tory–Liberal Democrat coalition. Berger's comment was a perfect example of a politician in a supposedly left-wing party being happy to work with the right to oppose the campaign for equal Palestinian rights.

Berger's move from LFI to JLM showed once again that there was a revolving door between the two groups. It also shows just how incestuous the UK's Zionist movement really is. In a transcript of unused footage shot for Al Jazeera's series *The Lobby*, JLM's young new director Ella Rose explained how she got her "first ever work experience" thanks to Berger. She worked in her Parliamentary office prior to becoming president of the pro-Israel Union of Jewish Students.

Much like her later protégé Ella Rose, Berger had got her start in student politics. She was on the National Union of Students' executive between 2003 and 2005, a time when the organisation was thoroughly stacked with careerists who saw it as a pipeline to working for New Labour. Romantically linked by some papers to Tony Blair's son Euan, Berger has been accused by activists of benefiting from nepotism. The younger Blair was even forced to deny the link, issuing a bizarre statement from Labour headquarters in 2005: "Luciana Berger is not, and has never been, my girlfriend."[27] Despite being from Wembley (a suburb of North West London), she was parachuted into a safe Labour seat in Liverpool in 2010. Union officials complained the selection process had been fixed.[28] In a November 2016 Parliamentary debate, Berger celebrated the fact "that it was

---

26 Lahav Harkov, "UK MP: Encourage non-Jews to get involved in our issues," *Jerusalem Post*, 28 June 2011.

27 Cahal Milmo, "The NUS officer, the PM's son, and a love affair that never was," *Independent*, 21 April 2005.

28 Brendan Carlin, "Labour at war as Blair son's glamorous friend is chosen for safe seat," *Mail on Sunday*, 31 January 2010.

the Labour party that first expressed ... support for the creation of the state of Israel and advanced the Balfour declaration"— the infamous British colonial document which handed Palestine over to the Zionist movement.[29]

Despite all this, it is true that Berger was the subject of some disgustingly anti-Semitic threats from the far right, such as self-described Nazi John Nimmo. In February 2017 he was convicted for threatening Berger with a picture of a knife and a message that she would "get it like Jo Cox," and was sentenced to two years in jail.[30] Yet Berger and her supporters made a habit of implying that such horrific messages were the work of the left. According to researcher (and former Ken Livingstone aide) Bob Pitt, Berger "Consistently, and presumably intentionally, blurred the distinction between the abuse she has received from the left and from the far right" in order "to associate left-wingers with crimes that were in fact committed by fascists."[31] But as late as August 2016, in an interview with the *Observer*, Berger said she believed that "anti-Semitism exists more out of the Labour party than in it."[32] If Corbyn's Labour really had subjected her to anti-Semitic death threats, surely that interview would have been the natural time to raise them? Jewish Socialist Group activist David Rosenberg has argued that the timing of Berger and company's demonstration against Corbyn in Parliament Square was "transparently about damaging Corbyn in particular and Labour in general just weeks before those local elections."[33]

Pitt also concluded in his investigation that, "Perhaps the most notorious and widely publicised example of alleged left-wing anti-Semitism directed against Berger" was a

---

29 Hansard, Volume 617, Column 101WH, 16 November 2016: *Centenary of the Balfour Declaration*.

30 Sandra Laville, "Internet troll who sent Labour MP antisemitic messages is jailed," *Guardian*, 10 February 2017.

31 Bob Pitt, "Has the Labour left subjected Luciana Berger to hatespeak and death threats?" Medium.com, 20 March 2019.

32 Catherine Deveney, "Luciana Berger: 'I have been contending with issues surrounding my safety and security for years,'" *Guardian*, 28 August 2016.

33 David Rosenberg, "What do the Wavertree members want and what do they need?" Rebel Notes blog, 9 February 2019.

"myth"—one widely accepted by the mainstream media, as well as by at least one Tory minister. This was the idea that, as minister Michael Gove put it, "A Labour Member of Parliament needs armed protection at her own party conference" due to all the dangerously anti-Semitic Labour activists. While Berger had been given (unarmed) police protection in September 2018, as Pitt showed in his blog post, it was only given *outside* of Labour conference and not inside the delegates' hall. "Given the history of far-right threats against Berger," Pitt wrote, "it is obvious why the police would have decided she needed an escort while walking through the streets outside the conference area."

While the UK was being subjected to a "Labour anti-Semitism crisis" smear campaign, over in the Gaza Strip, Palestinian refugees were rising up to demand basic human rights. Only a few days after the Israel lobby's infamous Parliament Square demonstration, scores of Palestinians were shot dead by Israeli snipers. Unarmed civilian protesters began on 30 March to walk towards Gaza's boundary line with Israel. The Palestinian refugees were demanding the right to return to their homes in pre-1948 Palestine. The result was an Israeli massacre. Yet the Palestinians persisted, marching toward the fence every Friday until September 2019. The campaign was dubbed the Great March of Return.

Award-winning TV producer Richard Sanders later investigated the manufactured Labour "anti-Semitism" row. He could not find a British channel brave enough to broadcast his findings, and instead wrote them up in a series of articles for *Middle East Eye*.[34] "During 2018, at the height of the row," he wrote, "290 Palestinians, including 55 minors, were killed by Israeli forces [throughout historic Palestine] . . . Palestinians demanded their right to go back to ancestral homes from which they were driven in 1948. Most of those killed in Gaza were shot by Israeli snipers crouching behind sand berms several hundred metres away."[35]

---

34 Sanders eventually helped produce the 2022 Al Jazeera series *The Labour Files*.

35 Richard Sanders, "'The wrong sort of Jew': How Labour pursued complaints against elderly Jewish opponents of Israel," *Middle East Eye*, 24 September 2020.

Yet Berger could not bring herself to condemn the Israeli killers. Instead she urged "restraint," calling on unspecified parties to "halt the loss of civilian life. The voices of those in Israel who advocate for peace must not be drowned out."[36]

The weekly protests in Gaza lasted 18 months. More than 215 Palestinians were killed by Israel and 30,000 were injured—10,000 by live sniper fire, resulting in leg amputations and paralysation.[37] The day after the initial massacre Israel admitted responsibility, posting on Twitter that, "Everything was accurate and measured, and we know where every bullet landed." The tweet caused outrage and was soon deleted.[38]

The massacres were condemned the world over. But in Britain, even some who had previously supported the Palestinian cause were cowed by the frenzied atmosphere of "anti-Semite" witch-hunting which had now spread from Labour into wider society. Palestine Solidarity Campaign director Ben Jamal recalled to Richard Sanders that in past years, a significant minority of Labour MPs had supported their demonstrations, but that in 2018, despite the desperate situation in Gaza, "It became incredibly difficult to get any MPs to come along." Clearly many were afraid. On 14 May 2018 more than 60 Palestinians were killed by the Israelis in a single day. Only then, Jamal said, did 20 MPs from various parties attend a rally. "I remember commenting at the time," Jamal said, "at least now we know how many Palestinians have to be killed before people regain their moral compass."

The manufactured anti-Semitism crisis was having its intended effect.

* * *

---

36 Luciana Berger, Twitter, 15 May 2018.

37 Maureen Clare Murphy, "Israel's self-investigation shields its soldiers," *Electronic Intifada*, 26 November 2020.

38 Ali Abunimah, "Israel admits, then deletes, responsibility for Gaza killings," *Electronic Intifada*, 31 March 2018.

Meanwhile, the attitude of Israeli politicians toward Corbyn was openly hostile. When the Great March of Return started, Corbyn publicly condemned the Israeli massacres—something few other British politicians would do. But the anti-Semitism smear campaign was clearly having a negative effect. Corbyn stated that the killings were "appalling" but didn't call for any concrete measures to hold Israel to account.[39] This was in contrast with the summer of 2015 when he'd been the frontrunner in the first Labour leadership election, in an interview with me for the *Electronic Intifada*, he had committed his future Labour government to imposing a two-way arms embargo on Israel, meaning both sales of arms from Britain to Israel and sales of Israeli arms to Britain. He had even told me he supported the right of Palestinian refugees to return to their homes in present day Israel.[40]

As Israeli killings continued, Corbyn dialled up his tone in a longer statement posted to Facebook and read out at a PSC demonstration. But his commitment to an arms embargo had been watered down. He demanded instead that the UK government "review the sale of arms that could be used in violation of international law."[41]

Israeli prime minister Benjamin Netanyahu later attacked him on social media, calling for "unequivocal condemnation" of the UK Labour leader, claiming he had supported a Palestinian "terrorist" and made "comparison of Israel to the Nazis." Corbyn stood up for himself, hitting back with his own Twitter post within the hour: "Israeli PM @Netanyahu's claims about my actions and words are false," he wrote. "What deserves unequivocal condemnation is the killing of over 160 Palestinian

---

39 Abunimah, "Israel admits, then deletes, responsibility."

40 Asa Winstanley, "Jeremy Corbyn backs boycott of Israeli universities involved in arms research," *Electronic Intifada*, 2 August 2015. After delegates overwhelmingly passed motions supporting an end to the arms trade with Israel at two successive Labour conferences, to his credit, Corbyn's party did go into the 2019 general election committing to "suspend" arms to Israel and Saudi Arabia. See Asa Winstanley, "Labour would suspend arms to Israel," *Electronic Intifada*, 21 November 2019.

41 Jeremy Corbyn Facebook page, 7 April 2018.

protesters in Gaza by Israeli forces since March, including dozens of children."[42]

It was a rare moment. Corbyn was actually rebutting the anti-Semitism smear campaign, rather than just apologising for anti-Semitism. But it proved to be too little, too late. Netanyahu's very public attack was only one part of a coordinated campaign of psychological warfare against Labour. This campaign ultimately proved successful.

Despite all of Corbyn's peacenik talk about reaching across the divide and finding a "two-state solution," the Israeli Labor party's attitude towards Corbyn was no less hostile than Netanyahu's. Labor's leader at the time was former telecoms executive Avi Gabbay. He announced in April that Israeli Labor was suspending all relations with Jeremy Corbyn's office. In an open letter to Corbyn, which he posted on Twitter (seemingly coordinated with Labour Friends of Israel[43]), Gabbay condemned what he called the UK leader's "very public hatred of the policies of the government of the state of Israel" (a government, remember, which was at the time led by Netanyahu's hard-right Likud party). That past weekend, Corbyn had issued statements condemning the killing of unarmed Palestinian protesters as "an outrage." This seems to have been the "hatred" Gabbay was condemning. While covering up the realities of Israeli massacres in Gaza, Gabbay made it clear to Corbyn that he nonetheless supported the violence against Palestinian civilians. His letter stated that on "security" policies "the [Labor-led] opposition and [government] coalition are aligned."[44] While Labour Friends of Israel was trying to smooth over its image as being "pro-peace," a message from the leader of their Israeli "sister party" that they were in fact very much in favour of shooting unarmed Palestinian

---

42 Asa Winstanley, "Israel's bogus definition of anti-Semitism will unleash havoc in Labour," *Electronic Intifada*, 20 August 2018.

43 On Twitter, LFI actually posted their response statement to Gabbay's open letter twelve minutes *before* Gabbay's staff had even posted the letter to Twitter in the first place. LFI, Twitter, 10 April 2018, 3:15 PM (deleted tweet: copy on file). Avi Gabbay, Twitter, 10 April 2018, 3:27 PM.

44 Asa Winstanley, "Israel Labor party cuts ties to Jeremy Corbyn for supporting Palestinian rights," *Electronic Intifada*, 10 April 2018.

civilians may have seemed discordant. But ultimately it didn't matter. The letter got across the main attack line: Corbyn had failed to "address the anti-Semitism within Labour Party UK."[45]

Israeli political attacks were just one part of a wider push by the UK Labour Party's internal Israel lobby groups. The latest media assault at that time (the one Netanyahu was alluding to) revolved around a 2014 conference Corbyn had attended in Tunisia. The visit had been dredged up during the 2017 general election campaign. Corbyn had taken part in a wreath-laying ceremony to pay tribute to victims of a 1985 Israeli bombing raid on the Palestine Liberation Organisation's Tunis compound. The raid killed 60 Palestinians and Tunisians, including many civilians. But those facts were conveniently forgotten in most of the media coverage of the latest "scandal." It was another pressure point used by Israel and its lobby. They claimed Corbyn's visit amounted to support for Palestinian "terrorists."

Anti-Corbyn incitement peaked that summer with three pro-Israel newspapers (the *Jewish Chronicle*, *Jewish News*, and the smaller Manchester publication *Jewish Telegraph*) issuing identical front-page editorials denouncing Corbyn as an "existential threat to Jewish life" in the UK. The editorials claimed that Corbyn was an "anti-Semite" whose presence as leader has caused a flood of anti-Semitism in his party—it was a propaganda narrative pushed in an almost identical, coordinated fashion by the Israeli prime minister, Israel's opposition, and the UK's pro-Israel lobby.

* * *

The scandals over alleged anti-Semitism in Labour that summer had one main effect—the capitulation of the Labour leadership to the IHRA document. Labour adopted all eleven of its "examples" of anti-Semitism. The move came at the insistence of Momentum leader Jon Lansman and Corbyn's erstwhile ally John McDonnell. After initially backing the new NEC Code of

---

45   Ali Abunimah, "US, British lawmakers condemn Israel's 'horrific' massacre in Gaza," *Electronic Intifada*, 15 May 2018.

Conduct as the "gold standard" in anti-racism, Lansman did a U-turn. He began publicly lobbying for the full IHRA document. As part of this campaign he brought his Jewish Labour Movement contacts more into the open. In August 2018 it was announced he would be speaking at a one-day JLM conference the following month. Margaret Hodge, Wes Streeting, Ruth Smeeth, Luciana Berger, and Louise Ellman were among other pro-Israel stalwarts slated to appear.[46]

But adoption of the IHRA definition was ultimately the responsibility of Corbyn himself as party leader. In retrospect, the long, slow trickle of concessions Corbyn made to the Israel lobby in the face of the sustained "anti-Semitism" campaign made capitulation seem inevitable. As Labour and Palestine Solidarity Campaign activist Steven Garside put it at the time: "Corbyn seems to have conceded the Jewish Labour Movement's arrogant and chauvinist right to police the discursive boundaries of the conflict."[47]

There had been no absence of voices warning Corbyn about the grim consequences of adopting Israel's preferred definition of anti-Semitism. That August no less 84 Black, Asian, Arab, and other ethnic minority groups got together to sign an unprecedented open letter condemning the IHRA definition. It warned that adopting the document would add to the "silencing" of the Palestinian community in the UK, a phenomenon in which "the colonial history of the Palestinians is continually erased." They warned that this was "a dangerous breach of our own rights, and [those] of the wider British public: we must all hear the full story of the Palestinians in order to make sense of the current discussions about racism and Israel."[48]

Jewish thinkers and activists sympathetic to the Corbynist project also tried their best to warn the leadership of the dire

---

46   Asa Winstanley, "Is Labour's Jon Lansman capitulating to the Israel lobby?" *Electronic Intifada*, 9 August 2018.

47   Steven Garside, "Jeremy Corbyn must not back down on Palestine," *Electronic Intifada*, 24 August 2018.

48   "As BAME communities, we stand united against attempts to suppress our voices," *Independent* letters, 18 August 2018.

consequences. In a concise history of how the IHRA document was devised and promoted by the Israeli government and its affiliated lobby groups, Antony Lerman, the founder of the Institute for Jewish Policy research, wrote that the definition "was proposed deliberately to 'equate criticisms of Israel with hatred of Jews.'" Jewish Voice for Labour campaigned in local Labour Party groups against the document. They circulated a model motion calling on the NEC to "resist pressure to adopt the full list of examples attached to the IHRA definition of anti-Semitism and stand by its Code of Conduct."[49] This activism was backed by senior human rights lawyer Geoffrey Robertson QC, who concluded in a detailed legal opinion that the IHRA document was "likely to chill criticism of action by the Government of Israel and advocacy of sanctions as a means to deter human rights abuses" and did not even protect Jews from some of the worst forms of anti-Semitism.[50]

According to Owen Jones, Corbyn and his senior advisers Karie Murphy and Seumas Milne all opposed the IHRA examples, while NEC members Lansman and Rhea Wolfson (supposedly a left-wing non-Zionist, who ended up joining the Jewish Labour Movement) were both "determined" to pass the IHRA.[51] Corbyn adviser Andrew Fisher and Unite union leader Len McCluskey also pushed for the document (the latter doing so only reluctantly, accusing "the leadership of the Jewish community" of having "simply refused to take 'yes' for an answer").[52]

The NEC's adoption of the document was the cumulation of an intense summer of media invective, a massive Israeli and

---

49 "Model Motion in Defence of the NEC Antisemitism Code of Conduct," Jewish Voice for Labour website, 21 July 2018.

50 "IHRA definition of antisemitism is not fit for purpose," Doughty Street Chambers website, 31 August 2018.

51 Owen Jones, *This Land: The Story of a Movement* (London: Allen Lane, 2020), pages 238-40.

52 Len McCluskey, "Corbyn Has Answered Concerns on Anti-Semitism, But Jewish Community Leaders Are Refusing to Take 'Yes' For an Answer," *HuffPost UK*, 16 August 2018.

pro-Israeli disinformation campaign. But despite the monolithic British media embrace of the "Labour anti-Semitism crisis," the Labour Party grassroots itself remained stubbornly immune. Polling the same month Luciana Berger kicked things off showed that 77 percent of members believed that anti-Semitism in the party was being "deliberately exaggerated" or "hyped up" to damage Labour and Corbyn.[53]

As he did successfully during 2016's coup, Corbyn could have sought members' backing and openly rejected the IHRA document on the basis of its anti-Palestinian racism. He couldn't dictate the NEC's rules, but the body would have been helpless in the face of a declaration by the Labour leader that he would refuse to implement the misleading definition. Corbyn's defence of himself in the face of Netanyahu's hostility was sadly uncharacteristic. Much more such defiance would have been needed to defeat the narrative. But more often than not Corbyn folded. No matter how many concessions he made, it would never be enough. Margaret Hodge had made that clear in her Sky News interview.

Activist Steven Garside explained in a second article for the *Electronic Intifada* that conceding to the Israel lobby was a fool's game. It was a race to the bottom which could only lead to further concessions. "Thwarting the cause of Palestine in the party is for the Jewish Labour Movement and Labour Friends of Israel a war without end. It can only be repelled by a muscular, vigorous counter-narrative, one based on unqualified support for the Palestinian cause and emphatic denunciation of Israel's past and present crimes."[54] The muscular counter-narrative was never built.

There was a second battle inside the Labour leadership over the mooted Margaret Hodge disciplinary process. This time the strains between Corbyn and McDonnell were impossible to deny. Only days after the launch of the inquiry into Hodge's behaviour, McDonnell publicly called for it to be dropped,

---

53 Winstanley, "Israel's bogus definition of anti-Semitism."

54 Steven Garside, "How Israel's bogus definition of anti-Semitism shuts down free speech," *Electronic Intifada*, 12 September 2018.

claiming that "She's got a good heart."⁵⁵ The shadow chancellor pushed for a meeting between Corbyn and the unrepentant Israel lobbyist so they could kiss and make up. "I won't do it without an apology," Corbyn reportedly said. "It's never going to happen." Karie Murphy for her part insisted Hodge be disciplined. Ultimately nothing happened to Hodge and the inquiry was dropped.⁵⁶

As for Luciana Berger, despite the adoption of the IHRA document, early in 2019 she was one of the breakaway group of Labour and Conservative MPs that formed the "Independent Group." One of the group's financial backers was property tycoon and Israel lobby financier David Garrard. He had for years bankrolled Labour Friends of Israel's operations. Prior to 2015 he had also been a Labour Party funder. But after Corbyn's election win as leader, Garrard instantly halted his donations. He even called in a prior £2 million loan. But Garrard continued to finance anti-Corbyn, pro-Israel Labour MPs, such as Ian Austin and LFI chairperson Joan Ryan.⁵⁷ In what seemed like a coordinated action, in March 2018 Garrard quit Labour.⁵⁸ It was just more proof that Israel lobby financiers used their wealth to sabotage Corbyn's Labour Party from within.

Most of the Independent Group's former Labour MPs had associated themselves with Labour Friends of Israel—including Ryan herself, who quit Labour and joined the group the day after its formal announcement, citing what she called Corbyn's "demonization and delegitimization" of Israel.⁵⁹ If Corbyn had got rid of the saboteur right-wing pro-Israel MPs on his own initiative it's possible that things could have ended differently.

---

55   Andrew Sparrow, "Labour should drop action against Margaret Hodge, McDonnell says," *Guardian*, 23 July 2018.

56   Jones, *This Land*, page 242.

57   Asa Winstanley, "Israel lobby funders back breakaway British MPs," *Electronic Intifada*, 27 February 2019.

58   Thomas Conlin, "Labour Party donor Sir David Garrard quits party over 'blatant acts of antisemitism,'" *The Times*, 1 April 2018.

59   Asa Winstanley, "Joan Ryan, MP who fabricated anti-Semitism, quits Labour," *Electronic Intifada*, 20 February 2019.

As the "Independent Group" split showed, many ended up quitting anyway. The Independent Group failed to win any seats and was completely wiped out in the December 2019 general election.

But by lashing out against Corbyn in such a public manner, Margaret Hodge had set an important precedent which would soon be utilised to ruinous effect. Public figures were now free to slander Corbyn as an anti-Semite without fear of repercussion. Before Hodge's outburst they'd moderated such attacks. Although the leader had been incessantly smeared since the summer of 2015, accusers often seemed wary of being sued for libel. A careful reading of news reports between 2015 and July 2018 reveals that Corbyn was rarely accused directly of being personally anti-Semitic. The reason for this is quite simple: Jeremy Corbyn is not an anti-Semite and has never said or done anything anti-Semitic.

One early "Labour anti-Semitism crisis" smear story illustrates this point well. During the 2015 leadership election campaign, the *Daily Telegraph* falsely claimed on its front page that Corbyn stood "Accused of being an anti-Semite by one of Labour's most senior politicians." Ivan Lewis (a former New Labour minister) had in fact not quite said that—he'd actually only implied it. A close reading of Lewis's full quote further down in the piece showed that he said Corbyn had "Shown very poor judgment in expressing support for" unnamed persons Lewis alleged had engaged "in anti-Semitic rhetoric." The paper in its headline and lede mangled this quote to imply that Lewis (a former vice-chair of Labour Friends of Israel) had directly accused Corbyn of "anti-Semitic rhetoric," when he actually hadn't.[60] As I observed at the time, Lewis's statement was "carefully worded to associate Corbyn with anti-Semitism, while falling short of actually libelling him as an anti-Semite."[61] After a ruling by press regulator IPSO, the paper was later forced to issue a correction and the online version of its headline was altered.

---

60 Ben Riley-Smith, "Labour grandees round on 'anti-Semite' Corbyn," *Daily Telegraph*, 15 August 2015.

61 Asa Winstanley, "4 reasons the 'anti-Semitism' attacks on Jeremy Corbyn are dishonest," *Electronic Intifada*, 19 August 2015.

But a turning point had been reached. Hodge's foul-mouthed outburst had been allowed to stand. Thanks in part to the intervention of John McDonnell, Hodge remained unpunished. The Rubicon had been crossed. It was now too late to stop the rot and defeat was inevitable.

CHAPTER NINE

FALLOUT

A video posted online, Christmas Day 2019. Less than two weeks before, the general election had ended with Corbyn's defeat. A grinning man with a craggy face and a shaved head enters the frame. Captions appear as he sits. "We won," one reads. Corbyn "got finished," another.

Speaking to camera the man introduces himself as Joe Glasman from the Campaign Against Antisemitism. "I just wanted to take this moment on Hanukkah to say a purely personal thank you to every single person out there who actively resisted the anti-Semitism of Corbyn and the Labour Party and say: Well done, mazel tov!" Glasman exults: "A Hanukkah miracle has happened. The beast is slain!" As he says this, the word "slaughtered!" appears on screen. Glasman seems to be channelling the former Board of Deputies president who had called for Corbyn's "sacrifice" a few months earlier.

He continues with "Rabbi Joe's" sermon. Glasman compares Corbyn to Antiochus Epiphanes, a Seleucid king who suppressed Judaism in second century BCE Palestine. Antiochus's promotion of Greek culture and religion precipitated the Maccabean revolt in Jerusalem.[1] Glasman attacks Corbyn's Jewish supporters as "Jewish Voice for Stalin" and of being like the pro-Antiochus Jews who were "desperate de-circumcisers" and had learned "to wrestle naked in a desecrated Jewish temple."

---

1 Hans Volkmann, "Antiochus IV Epiphanes," Britannica.com (accessed 16 June 2022).

"Atheist, Marxist Jews were sent to undermine Jewish communities," he exclaims. "Now it seems that in modern Britain, you can be a good progressive and hate Jews." He warns that the "Greeks" will be back "for Jerusalem. So none of us should be ready to beat our swords into ploughshares just yet." But for now, we can rest, Glasman says. "Maccabees: at ease. They tried to kill us. We won. Let's eat." He explains: "We did it! By word and deed, by protest and tweet, by our spies and intel, by our fab celebrities and our anonymous volunteers . . . by interminable hours combing through tweets, by prayer . . . we metaphorically took the temple back."

The CAA claims to be an anti-racist group which protects Jewish life in Britain. But in practice it's an Israel lobby group. Its main goal since it was set up during Israel's war on the population of the Gaza Strip in the summer of 2014 has been to smear the Palestine solidarity movement and the left as anti-Semitic.[2] As such, Glasman's hostility was no surprise. But the sheer frankness of the video was staggering. When left-wing Labour activists discovered it soon after, Glasman thought better of his candour and set his post to private. But of course it was too late. Activists had already made copies.

My report for the *Electronic Intifada* was widely shared in January 2020 and it became one of my biggest stories of all time. It was so embarrassing to Glasman that he filed a copyright claim with YouTube, in an attempt to delete all copies of the video from the internet. He was only briefly successful. Although our copy was removed for two weeks while YouTube reviewed our Fair Use counterclaim, the Silicon Valley giant found in our favour. You can still view it online and—ironically—Glasman's censorship efforts only seemed to boost our views.[3]

* * *

---

[2] Tony Greenstein, "Campaign Against Antisemitism is a campaign against Palestinians," *Electronic Intifada*, 20 March 2017.

[3] Asa Winstanley "We 'slaughtered' Jeremy Corbyn, says Israel lobbyist," *Electronic Intifada*, 10 January 2020.

The Israel lobby's claim to have "slaughtered" Corbyn was a long time in the making. The final year of Jeremy Corbyn's leadership is a tale of missed opportunities and the decline of what old-time Labour left-wingers dubbed The Project.

The 2019 election campaign was quite unlike 2017's. There was less of a spark and diminished excitement among Labour activists. Corbynite enthusiasm had waned. Something was missing. In the view of many Labour activists I spoke to, that something was solidarity—Corbyn's solidarity with his supporters. They had backed him through the summer of 2016, when Margaret Hodge launched a coup. It's hard to imagine how he would have survived then without the membership's support. They had stuck with him too throughout 2017, defying the media's unanimous predictions of catastrophic Labour defeat in the general election. Labour's unprecedented 2017 election campaign would not have been possible without their support for Corbyn's popular, common sense manifesto, which had promised a radical change of direction in the country, after 40 years of neoliberal elite consensus.

The manifesto had fired up the party's new mass membership, which turned out in droves on the doorsteps, delivering an unexpected bloody nose to the Tories. According to one analysis, in 2017 Labour came within 2,227 votes of winning a chance to form a coalition government.[4] Without the efforts of Labour's bureaucracy and MPs to sabotage their own election campaign, it's likely Corbyn would have become prime minister.

The membership had also stuck with Corbyn through the tumult of the summer of 2018, when Israel and its lobby were in open warfare with the party. But doubts had begun to creep in. Why should the grassroots stick with the leader when the leader seemed so ready to sacrifice the troops? This rot had set in as early as 2016, when Ken Livingstone had been thrown under the bus. The Israel lobby got what it wanted but, characteristically, still demanded more. Most of the grassroots said little to criticise Corbyn's apparent green light. A massive internal Labour document on alleged party anti-Semitism, leaked in April 2020, says

---

[4] Harriet Agerholm, "Jeremy Corbyn was just 2,227 votes away from chance to be Prime Minister," *Independent*, 9 June 2017.

that Corbyn's office attempted in 2018 to bring Livingstone's disciplinary hearings forward, and John McDonnell offered to talk to the former mayor directly (seemingly to ask him to quit).[5] The sacrifice of Livingstone opened the floodgates. A steady trickle of high-profile pro-Corbyn Labour activists were suspended, expelled, or otherwise thrown to the wolves based on false allegations of anti-Semitism. As we've already seen, these included prominent Black and Jewish anti-racists like Marc Wadsworth, Jackie Walker, and Tony Greenstein. Wadsworth and Greenstein were expelled in 2018 and Walker was expelled in March 2019.

Looking back on 2019's fateful general election campaign a few months on, one local Labour activist reflected on the cumulative effect of this long war against the membership. A stalwart on the Labour doorsteps, Ed Poole had been a candidate for local councillor in 2018, a pro-Corbyn member in Enfield North—the North London constituency where Labour Friends of Israel's Joan Ryan ruled as MP until 2019. Through gritted teeth, Poole even campaigned for Ryan to win in 2017 on the basis that it would help Corbyn's national result. He did so even at the same time that Ryan was actively sabotaging her own election chances. Despite Ryan's best attempt to lose, popular enthusiasm for Corbyn's social-democratic reforms meant that she actually ended up *increasing* her majority. In early 2019 Ryan quit Labour for the short lived "Change UK" splinter faction. So she was no longer Labour's candidate for Enfield North in the election. But the damage had been done. Something was different on the doorsteps, as Poole recalled in a series of posts to Twitter.

"The four-year campaign against Corbyn took its toll," he wrote. "The Tories knew how to target people to get negative messages across and we failed to come up with any meaningful response to anti-Semitism or terrorist sympathiser accusations." The two most common reasons voters gave Poole on the doorstep for not wanting to vote Labour were the idea that, "They're all the same. Just in [it] for themselves" and what he recalled as

---

5   Harry Hayball et al., *The work of the Labour Party's Governance and Legal Unit in relation to antisemitism, 2014-2019* (London: The Labour Party, March 2020), pages 350-3.

the "hatred of Jeremy Corbyn, but they couldn't explain why. Neither of these responses were common in 2017."

Poole put this down to a long-term decline in Labour's vote since 1997 (Corbyn's 2017 campaign being the exception) as well as the party's failure to fight back against the anti-Semitism allegations. Years of controversy over Labour's shifting Brexit policy was also a big factor. In 2017 Corbyn's Labour had been the party of change, but that went out of the window between the two elections, Poole argued. "Perception of Corbyn went from being a breath of fresh air to being a typical politician flip-flopping for votes," he wrote. Corbyn's leadership was challenged from within and "his own MPs ran amok without consequences for years, lending credibility to every attack on him no matter how flimsy"—including on alleged anti-Semitism.[6]

Other anecdotal evidence from the front lines of Labour's doorstep operation reflected similar views. The manufactured anti-Semitism crisis had finally cut through to the electorate. It fit the wider narrative that Corbyn was an "extremist." Although most post-mortems of Labour's 2019 electoral defeat tended to put the blame primarily on Labour's Brexit policies, there's no doubt that the "anti-Semitism crisis" also played a big role. Polling data bears this out.

Michael Ashcroft is a billionaire former tax-exile, former deputy-leader of the Conservative Party and up until 2015 a member of the House of Lords—Britain's unelected upper chamber.[7] He runs a polling firm which is widely respected among Britain's political-media elite. In February 2020, he surveyed more than 10,000 British voters on the reasons for Labour's electoral defeat. While a leaked internal Labour review of the election blamed the Brexit controversy above all,[8] Ashcroft's data

---

6   Ed Poole, "Rambling Thread[.] The two of the most common..." Twitter, 11 February 2020.

7   "Rich List 2020: profiles 101-199=, featuring Sir Paul McCartney and Joanne Rowling," *Sunday Times* Rich List, 16 May 2020. Ewen MacAskill, "Lord Ashcroft used offshore trust to shelter wealth while Tory peer," *Guardian*, 5 November 2017.

8   Sebastien Ash and Gavin Stamp, "Lord Ashcroft: Tory pollster's analysis of Labour defeat sparks internal debate," *BBC News*, 11 February 2020.

seemed to pin the blame more on Corbyn himself. The most important reason for Labour's defeat given by voters in the poll was that "Jeremy Corbyn was not an appealing leader." Brexit came second. The figures showed that the years-long campaign against Corbyn over "anti-Semitism" (largely ignored by voters in the 2017 election) broke through in 2019. "Labour were divided" was the fourth most important reason given by voters. The anti-Semitism "crisis" was the main cause of Labour's internal divisions, outside the coterie of the party's MPs. Four years of witch hunts fed a constant stream of bad blood on the left. Former comrades, once united on the issue of getting Corbyn in as leader, were at each other's throats over who was and who wasn't an anti-Semite. Activists were kicked out of the party many had devoted so much of their lives to, often over nothing more than a badly worded—or simply just pro-Palestinian—social media post.

In joint fifth place of the most important reasons given by voters for Labour's loss was that "Labour failed to address the controversy over anti-Semitism in the party convincingly." This is ambiguously worded. That Labour had failed to "address the controversy" does not necessarily mean respondents agreed the "controversy" was valid or correct. Many were no doubt suspect of the "anti-Semitism crisis" narrative, while agreeing that Labour's response to it had been inadequate. This supposition is borne out by the Ashcroft poll's parallel survey of Labour Party members. This showed, yet again, that the vast majority of members rejected the manufactured Labour anti-Semitism crisis. Almost three quarters thought that "the issue of anti-Semitism in the Labour Party was invented or wildly exaggerated." The figure was even higher for Momentum members at 92 percent. Only 22 percent in Labour thought that "anti-Semitism was a real problem" in the party.[9]

The poll's findings amounted to a defeat for the Israel lobby. They had failed in their years-long mission to manufacture consent from Labour members to overthrow Jeremy Corbyn. But this was only a silver lining to an otherwise depressing

---

9   Asa Winstanley, "Poll: Labour members say anti-Semitism crisis 'invented,'" *Electronic Intifada*, 13 February 2020.

picture. The lobby, in alliance with the British establishment, the Labour Party right, and the Israeli state itself, had succeeded in convincing a significant chunk of the wider British electorate that there was probably no smoke without fire. The Israel lobby itself was in no doubt about who was responsible for Corbyn's defeat, as Glasman's Christmas Day boast about having "slain" Corbyn shows. The following month Ephraim Mirvis, Britain's notoriously pro-Israel chief rabbi, gave a rousing victory speech at AIPAC, the biggest annual pro-Israel conference in the US. Mirvis crowed that "Not only was Labour defeated, it was an emphatic landslide victory," and that he had "recognised that the weight of historic responsibility was on our shoulders, because a Corbyn victory would send a negative message right around the world." He urged American Jews to urgently combat the anti-Semitism he claimed was "prevalent to our left."[10] This was a not-so-subtle message to progressive US presidential candidate Bernie Sanders, who, despite describing himself as "pro-Israel," had had the chutzpah to recognise the seriousness of the Palestinians' cause.[11]

But none of this would have been possible without Corbyn and the Labour left's acquiescence. Capitulation was nowhere more evident than in Corbyn's willingness to allow his most dependable allies to be purged.

* * *

Working class Labour MP Chris Williamson (a former bricklayer) was one of Corbyn's few political allies in Parliament. Williamson had returned to the House of Commons in 2017, having lost his marginal northern seat in Derby two years prior. Before first entering Parliament in 2010 he had led the local council. Fired up by the Corbyn phenomenon in 2015 he moved increasingly to the left. Worryingly for the British establishment, Williamson also took this to its logical conclusion and began

---

10 "Rabbi Ephraim Mirvis Speech," AIPAC YouTube channel, 4 March 2020.

11 Asa Winstanley, "Don't let the smears that sank Corbyn tank Bernie Sanders," *Electronic Intifada*, 13 December 2019.

to embrace anti-imperialist politics. Much like Corbyn, he had warm words for the socialist government of Venezuela and was critical of Israel.

But Williamson was unique as the only Labour MP to publicly campaign against the manufactured Labour anti-Semitism campaign. It began as a passing comment in a *Guardian* interview. Williamson's commitment to full democratic selection of Labour's parliamentary candidates also rubbed the party establishment up the wrong way. He embarked on a "Democracy Roadshow" of local Labour parties around the UK, drumming up support for the strongly Bennite notion. Only a couple of months after his return to Parliament the Israel lobby asked for a meeting, Williamson recalled in a new interview conducted for this book.[12] Jewish Labour Movement leaders Jeremy Newmark and Adam Langleben visited him at his office. They were "upset" about comments he had made in a *Guardian* interview earlier that week, Williamson says.

"Proxy wars and bullshit," was how the MP had described "rows in the party" over Corbyn's handling of anti-Semitism, the paper reported. "I'm not saying it never ever happens but it is a really dirty, lowdown trick," he told the *Guardian*, "particularly the anti-Semitism smears. Many people in the Jewish community are appalled by what they see as the weaponisation of anti-Semitism for political ends."[13]

Williamson recalls that the two JLM activists said his comments had been offensive. The left-winger remonstrated that he had not wanted to cause offence, but defended the validity of his point. The duo had a specific ask: "What they were wanting me to do was to use them as a sounding board. So before I made any statements or anything like that, in the future, they wanted me to run it past them." Williamson says that, "It was a relatively friendly meeting. I guess they thought that having this conversation, that would quiet me down perhaps."

Despite the apparently friendly tenor of agreeing to disagree, only days later the JLM set about trying to depose the leftist MP.

---

12 Chris Williamson, interview with author, 27 April 2022.

13 Rowena Mason, "MPs should have no say over who leads Labour, argues shadow minister," *Guardian*, 28 August 2017.

At a packed JLM conference the following Sunday, right-wing MP Ruth Smeeth (who as we've seen was considered by the US embassy a source to "strictly protect") told attendees she was calling for Labour to take "action" against Williamson. "I've already raised it with" the head of Labour's group in Parliament, she said, "and I'll be raising it with the Chief Whip, and I'll be raising it with the leader of the Labour Party."[14]

Williamson never did quiet down. He rallied the grassroots left to fight back against the anti-Semitism smears. Absent any kind of strategy from Corbyn to fight back, the grassroots took matters into its own hands. But Williamson was isolated and vulnerable among Labour MPs. It took two years for the Israel lobby to get Williamson out but they eventually managed it. Early in 2019, the left-winger was suspended by general secretary Jennie Formby.

In an internal Labour Party report on "anti-Semitism" leaked in April 2020 (which gives a detailed, if one-sided account of the process by which Williamson was suspended), there is no indication that Jeremy Corbyn or his office were involved in Formby's decision to suspend the MP.[15] According to Owen Jones's account of Williamson in *This Land* (an often hostile post-mortem of the Corbynite movement), senior Corbyn aide Karie Murphy was a supporter while most other senior staff were against.[16] The allegation wasn't that Williamson had said anything anti-Semitic (he simply hadn't). Rather, Formby claimed he was guilty of a "pattern of behaviour" which she alleged was "reckless" and that "brought the party into disrepute." Formby complained that Williamson had supported campaign group Labour Against the Witchhunt, criticised pro-Israel MPs Ruth Smeeth and Joan Ryan, and "participated in a demonstration" and "gave television interviews" calling for Labour's ruling national executive not to adopt the IHRA's bogus

---

14 Lee Harpin, "Ruth Smeeth: My 'hope' over Corbyn," *Jewish Chronicle*, 4 September 2017.

15 Hayball, *The work of the Labour Party's Governance*, pages 825-30.

16 Owen Jones, *This Land: The Story of a Movement* (London: Allen Lane, 2020), page 253.

definition of anti-Semitism.[17] In other words, Williamson was canned for legitimate political speech. Comments Williamson later made at a local Momentum meeting about the party being "too apologetic," over its record on anti-Semitism were seized on as the pretext for his suspension. But Formby's email to the disciplinary unit contained in the report makes it clear that this was only one small part of the "pattern" of thought-crime.[18] Months before the arrival of a pretext, unelected Momentum leader Jon Lansman had told an audience at a Jewish charity that it was only a matter of time before Williamson did something "which will then have to be investigated."[19]

Two weeks before suspension Williamson was pulled in for a dressing down by Formby. "It was a fractious meeting. We didn't make much progress," Williamson recalls. "I think essentially, they wanted me to wind my neck in, to abandon the Democracy Roadshow, to not speak out about anti-Semitism." But Formby inadvertently revealed evidence there had been an organised campaign of bad faith complaints against Williamson. She said "she got more complaints about me than every other member of the Labour Party put together," Williamson recalls. The former MP says that despite the fractious nature of the Formby meeting, the general secretary conceded that the complaints against him were bogus. "She had acknowledged that they were nonsense," he recalls. "I said, 'Well, you know, the way you need to respond to them Jennie, is to tell them to fuck the fuck off' . . . And she responded, you know, fairly indignantly to say, 'Well, what do you think? We haven't pursued any complaints against you, have we Chris?'"

The real breaking point came days before his suspension. Williamson had agreed to a request from Jewish Voice for Labour to show a documentary called *WitchHunt* in a parliamentary meeting room. The film was a critical examination of Labour's manufactured anti-Semitism controversy. It drew links

---

17 Hayball, *The work of the Labour Party's Governance*, pages 826-7.

18 Hayball, *The work of the Labour Party's Governance*, page 827.

19 Simon Rocker, "Jon Lansman faces sceptical audience at Limmud," *Jewish Chronicle*, 24 December 2018.

between Israel and other right-wing racist regimes and centred Jackie Walker in its narrative.[20] The existence of the film caused uproar at a Parliamentary Labour Party meeting on 25 February 2019. The protest was led by Ruth Smeeth. Williamson says he had intended to stay away from the meeting, but had been asked by Corbyn's office to attend, "because Jeremy was going to be in attendance and it was supposed to be about Brexit." Williamson asked "the young lad who'd asked me to attend if he was sure they wanted me to be there because the PLP hate me. And he said, 'Oh, no, no, we need some friendly faces, it'd be good if you would be there and speak.'"

So Williamson went along. The hostile reception "didn't bother me in the slightest," he says. "I used to quite relish it if I'm honest, because I thought I was bulletproof. I thought there's no way they could do me [in] because I'm Jeremy's most loyal lieutenant." Williamson says he was happy to play the role of "a foil for Jeremy" because the hostility directed at Corbyn could instead be directed at himself. "I was more than happy to take that," he recalls. But almost immediately the meeting pivoted away from Brexit to anti-Semitism. Just before Williamson was finally called by a reluctant chairperson to speak, "Ruth Smeeth spoke and she said it'd been brought to her attention 'that one of our colleagues has booked a room to show the Jackie Walker film' is how she described it. 'I don't know who it is, but I can assure you I will find out,' was her menacing words." There was a sharp intake of breath in the room and Smeeth's supporters began loudly sneering, "Well done Chris!"

When the left-winger was finally allowed to speak, "It was just a cacophony. I mean, I was having to absolutely shout at the top of my voice to be heard." The media were assembled outside the doors listening in and gave a running Twitter commentary. Williamson pushed back, saying he agreed with Corbyn supporter Laura Smith who had accused the other MPs of creating a toxic atmosphere in the PLP. "I was just saying, you know, 'Listen to yourselves, listen to yourselves! I rest my case, Mr Chairman. Look at them!' . . . Of course they would hate it . . .

---

20 Asa Winstanley, "Watch the film Labour MPs didn't want you to see," *Electronic Intifada*, 17 March 2019.

I was like, 'Come on, I'll take you all on!' type of thing. Two days later of course, I was fucked: they'd suspended me."

On 27 February 2019, Formby suspended Williamson.[21] "That's what really hurt," he recalls, "because you've let those bastards win. And now there's no foil for Jeremy. No fucker else was prepared to stand up and take it like I was. I'm not saying I was any great shakes... [but] I was prepared to do that." In June 2019, a poll showed Labour members coming out overwhelmingly in Williamson's favour (61 percent).[22] The MP tweeted to express gratitude. He rallied his supporters to push for his re-admittance. Williamson's suspension meant he was marginalised and chastised. Labour rules state that anyone suspended as a member is barred from holding elected office—including in Parliament. So Williamson was no longer a Labour MP and was now sitting in the House of Commons as technically an independent. As long as he remained suspended, Williamson could not be Labour's candidate for the next election. With British politics in a state of turmoil since 2017's unprecedented general election (and with uncertainly over Brexit negotiations) another general election seemed constantly imminent. A reversal of Williamson's suspension would have to come soon if he was not to almost certainly lose his seat.

For a few days in June 2019, it seemed like just such a reversal had been won. A Labour disciplinary panel readmitted Williamson, letting him off with a warning.[23] His months of campaigning had paid off. While his supporters celebrated, Labour's establishment struck back. A massive list of Labour MPs signed a letter demanding party process be ignored and the left-winger expelled. "He has to go!" raged the normally circumspect Jon Lansman on Twitter.[24] Elected to Labour's ruling National Executive Committee the year before, Lansman's threat to get rid of Williamson was far from idle. After more

---

21 Winstanley, "Watch the film."

22 Asa Winstanley, "Labour grassroots want Chris Williamson back—poll," *Electronic Intifada*, 2 July 2019.

23 Winstanley, "Labour grassroots."

24 Winstanley, "Labour grassroots."

than three years of smears, Lansman had decided that Labour had "a widespread problem" with anti-Semitism since Corbyn became leader—despite previously arguing that there had been a "witch hunt" of the left on the issue.[25] Only a few days after the reversal, Williamson was suspended for a second time—on very similar trumped-up "charges" to those used in the first suspension. This second, "re-suspension" was later ruled unlawful by the High Court. But Formby's Labour got around this by simply suspending him a third time.[26]

Williamson remained suspended as the 2019 general election was called. With an election looming he had little choice. Either he'd give up his seat or he could at least go down fighting and run as an independent socialist candidate. He quit his Labour membership of 40 years and ran alone in Derby North. With little time to prepare an insurgent grassroots campaign, he lost to his official Labour rival, coming in last place.

* * *

The consequences of Labour's 2018 adoption of the IHRA's pro-Israel definition of anti-Semitism were far-reaching. So extreme was the obsessive support for the document that—in true McCarthyite style—opposition to the IHRA definition *alone* was supposed by the witch-hunters to be "evidence" of anti-Semitism. As only one example among many, Labour's suspension charge sheet against Chris Williamson cited his presence at a demonstration against the definition. The climate of repression caused by the toxic media coverage of the issue spilt over from Labour to the wider left. In August 2019 the Palestine Solidarity Campaign discovered after a freedom of information request that local government officials in East London had used the IHRA document as justification for banning a charity fundraiser

---

25 Asa Winstanley, "How Jon Lansman joined Labour's witch hunt," *Electronic Intifada*, 7 October 2019.

26 Asa Winstanley, "Court overturns Labour 're-suspension' of left-wing MP," *Electronic Intifada*, 10 October 2019.

benefiting Palestinian children—an annual sponsored bike ride called The Big Ride for Palestine.

That year the money was due to go to the Middle East Children's Alliance, a charity supporting children's mental health in Gaza. The council had refused organisers permission to use any of its parks for a rallying point to listen to speakers. "There is a real risk that the event could breach the IHRA's definition of antisemitism which the council has adopted," one Tower Hamlets council official wrote in the disclosed emails. Examples of such "antisemitism" cited by officials included the Big Ride's website where it criticised "the crimes of the Israeli state," as well as "the parallels between apartheid South Africa and the state of Israel" and "Israeli ethnic cleansing of Palestinians." It was a clear-cut example of how the IHRA definition is an inherently anti-Palestinian document. Labour's endorsement of the document had amounted to a wider attack on the Palestinian liberation struggle. Although the emails suggest that the decision was made by unelected officials, Tower Hamlets' elected council and local mayor were both Labour at the time. This fact clearly influenced their decision. The disclosed emails showed that the council secretly based their decision on the "furore within the Labour Party over anti-Semitism."[27]

The incident spoke to a wider issue: the Labour Party's attitude towards Zionism. Corbyn went from endorsing BDS and condemning Zionist hecklers before being elected leader, to later claiming that Zionists had played an "honourable" role in Labour. This was part of a series of concessions that began in the summer of 2018. The new line (articulated at first in a *Guardian* opinion piece and later in a more expansive new Labour web page titled "No Place For Antisemitism" the following year) was that "Labour is a political home for Zionists and anti-Zionists. Neither Zionism nor anti-Zionism is in itself racism."[28] The "No Place For

---

27   Asa Winstanley, "Anti-Semitism definition behind secret ban on aid to Palestinian children," *Electronic Intifada*, 12 August 2019.

28   Jeremy Corbyn, "I will root antisemites out of Labour – they do not speak for me," *Guardian*, 3 August 2018. "No Place For Antisemitism," deleted page on Labour Party website (oldest copy on the Internet Archive's WayBack Machine dated 21 July 2019—accessed 16 June 2022). For a

Antisemitism" web page was reportedly authored by Corbyn aide James Schneider (one of the cofounders of Momentum).[29]

* * *

The media's coverage of the Corbynite movement was always dire. But it was only on "Labour anti-Semitism" that Corbyn's team for the most part refused to fight back.

Apart from the *Jewish Chronicle* and *Jewish News*, the media campaign against Corbyn for "anti-Semitism" was led more than any other outlet by the *Guardian*. The paper was all the more effective in its sabotage of Corbyn precisely *because* of its liberal politics. It had often endorsed Labour in the past. The Tory papers had more obviously partisan reasons for undermining Corbyn. The *Guardian*'s opposition was motivated by deeper reasons: he presented a challenge to 40 years of neoliberal consensus among the political classes. But it was also the result of the paper's long-term political support for Zionism.[30]

Experts identified just how inaccurate the media's coverage of the Labour anti-Semitism "crisis" really was. Researchers from the Media Reform Coalition and Birkbeck, University of London concluded in September 2018 that the *Guardian*'s coverage on the issue amounted to a "disinformation paradigm." In an in-depth study of 259 newspaper articles and TV news segments on "Labour anti-Semitism" from 2018, researchers found 90 clear cut examples of misleading or entirely inaccurate reporting. They also found an overwhelming source imbalance, especially on television news, with those critical of Labour given "a virtually exclusive and unchallenged platform to air their views." Nearly half of *Guardian* reports on the controversy

---

detailed critical response to the page, see Liverpool Friends of Palestine, "Debating the nature of Zionism and the Jewish state," Jewish Voice for Labour website, 18 August 2019, and Phil Bevin, "Why did Labour's left leaders buy into Israel's lies?" *Electronic Intifada*, 20 December 2022.

29   Jones, *This Land*, page 248.

30   See Daphna Baram, *Disenchantment: The Guardian and Israel* (London: Guardian Books, 2004).

surrounding Labour's approach to the IHRA document featured no quoted sources defending the party or leadership.[31]

Although Labour activists often complained about right-wing media, the data shows that liberal media outlets were the most vociferous. According to the Media Reform Coalition's meta-analysis of the data on inaccurate and misleading stories about Labour and alleged anti-Semitism, the *Guardian* and BBC television were responsible for the top two number of inaccuracies. They concluded that proportionate to the volume of coverage, "BBC television still featured the highest rate of inaccurate reporting."[32]

This hostility endured over time. Data scraped from the *Guardian*'s website by Palestinian infographics expert Ahmed Barclay shortly after the 2019 election showed that between 2015 and 2019 the newspaper published 513 articles tagged with "Antisemitism" and "Labour" but only 62 tagged with "Antisemitism" and "Conservatives." There had been zero articles with any such combination in 2014.[33]

In the book *Bad News for Labour*, a group of media scholars came to similar conclusions. Greg Philo and Mike Berry commissioned polling and focus groups to gauge the voting public's opinions on the anti-Semitism controversy in the Labour Party. They compared the public's impressions of how much anti-Semitism existed in Labour (gleaned mostly from the media) to the actual facts of the anti-Semitism figures released by the party itself.[34] Perceptions were out of kilter with the real figures by a wide margin. "On average, those surveyed believed that 34 percent of Labour Party members had had complaints

---

31   Justin Schlosberg and Laura Laker, *Labour, Antisemitism and the News: A disinformation paradigm* (London: Media Reform Coalition, September 2018), pages 4, 10-12, 17.

32   Schlosberg, *Labour, Antisemitism and the News*, page 17.

33   Ahmad Barclay, "1/ THREAD. I had been planning . . . " Twitter, 22 December 2019. For a spreadsheet of the full data, see: https://bit.ly/3OdVYRL.

34   Greg Philo et al., *Bad News for Labour* (London: Pluto Press, 2019), pages 1-5. For a review see Asa Winstanley, "Bad news for Jeremy Corbyn," *Electronic Intifada*, 31 October 2019.

for anti-Semitism made against them," Philo and Berry wrote. The actual figure of complaints made at the time was less than 0.1 percent of Labour members (453 complaints in a party of over half a million). In other words, the public thought there were 340 times more complaints than actually occurred. Another report, published by Loughborough University researchers during the 2019 election campaign, came to a similar conclusion. It "indicated that newspaper coverage was overwhelmingly biased against Labour."[35]

Such facts and figures were repeatedly cited by grassroots party activists. But this made little impression on Labour's leadership. By 2019 even pro-Corbyn Labour MPs (as well as Corbyn himself) would gravely intone in response to such facts that "one case of anti-Semitism is one too many." In narrow terms, that response was one nobody could disagree with. But it entirely missed the point.

Why was the media coverage, when compared to objectively low levels of anti-Semitism, skewed by several orders of magnitude? Why was no corporate media commentator or Labour MP gravely intoning that "one case of anti-Black racism" or "one case of Islamophobia" was one too many? There was certainly no shortage of such allegations.

* * *

There was a variety of missteps by the Labour leadership in this period, but Corbyn's inadequate response to the manufactured anti-Semitism campaign ultimately proved fatal. Like his political ally in the US, social-democrat Bernie Sanders, Corbyn lacked a killer instinct. Ken Livingstone, by way of contrast, long maintained the political will to fight and win. This rewarded him with two terms in London's City Hall. Instead of throwing Livingstone under the bus for the crime of accurately recounting historical facts about Zionism's links to the Nazi regime, Corbyn

---

35 Jamie Stern-Weiner, "Labour's anti-semitism crisis – what caused it and how well was it handled?" *Morning Star*, 9 February 2020.

should have brought Livingstone on side. It could have been a winning combination.

Parallel to the Corbynist movement, there was a rise in independent left-wing UK media. Projects like the *Skwawkbox*, the *Canary*, and Novara embraced Corbyn (although the latter ended up promoting the "anti-Semitism crisis" narrative, aggressively denouncing Williamson, Livingstone, and Walker). The left-wing Labour leader should have embraced them in turn, at least granting them interviews on the topic and fighting back. Instead, his team seemed desperate for "credible" mainstream media coverage—despite how deeply distrusted the "mainstream" media really is by the British public.

Instead, Corbyn and McDonnell both made the baffling decision to grant major interviews to the anti-Palestinian paper *Jewish News*. The result was entirely predictable: bitterly hostile interrogations, hatchet-job articles, and more bad headlines.[36] Just whose bad advice were they listening to? It's hard to know for sure, but it appeared to be partly at the urging of Jon Lansman, who had pushed for Corbyn to "build bridges" with pro-Israel elements of "the Jewish community."[37]

Another opportunity missed by the left-wing Labour leader was in the courts. Corbyn sued for libel when he was falsely accused by a Tory MP of having been a Czech spy during the Cold War, winning the case easily and donating the damages to charity.[38] Yet he made no such attempt in the case of the manufactured anti-Semitism crisis. Why? There was no shortage of opportunities that would have made for stupendously combative headlines. Corbyn could have sued Margaret Hodge for calling him an anti-Semite. Although Hodge's initial comments

---

[36] Justin Cohen, "Exclusive Jewish News interview with Jeremy Corbyn: 'I'm not an anti-Semite in any form,'" *Jewish News*, 29 March 2018. The front page of the print edition blared "NOT GOOD ENOUGH." Justin Cohen, "Full Jewish News interview with John McDonnell: 'MPs shouldn't face deselection,'" *Jewish News*, 6 September 2018.

[37] "Ex-kibbutznik who is Corbyn's left-hand man," *Jewish Chronicle*, 28 January 2016.

[38] Jamie Doward, "Tory MP apologises to Corbyn for spy claim," *Guardian*, 25 February 2018.

had been protected by parliamentary privilege, she repeated them in an article for the *Guardian*, opening herself up to a libel case. Yet Corbyn did not defend himself, either legally or verbally. According to one *Middle East Eye* report, Corbyn rejected the advice of his personal lawyer at the time to sue Hodge. The Labour leader failed to even impose party discipline on an openly seditious MP. Corbyn's friend Geoffrey Bindman QC, a senior human rights lawyer, later criticised the Labour leader for his lack of action. "I like Jeremy tremendously," he told *Middle East Eye*. "But he has his faults. And part of his problem is he's too honest and too decent to be an ideal leader . . . And he never defends himself."[39]

Merseyside Pensioners Association secretary and Labour activist Audrey White showed a successful legal defence was possible. In February 2020, the *Jewish Chronicle* was forced to pay damages after libelling the left-winger with false allegations of anti-Semitism. As part of the settlement the paper issued an apology, admitting it had published "allegations about Mrs Audrey White" which were "untrue." It said it had agreed to pay White a sum in damages plus her legal costs. White told me her victory was dedicated to "every one of us under attack and vilified by this newspaper." A series of articles by the paper's reporter Lee Harpin in 2019 had put White at "the centre of bullying claims against Jewish MP Dame Louise Ellman"—then the member of Parliament for the Liverpool Riverside constituency. The libel settlement came after press regulator IPSO ruled that the articles were "significantly misleading." IPSO also slammed the paper for obstructing its investigation, calling its behaviour "unacceptable"—strong words from a normally hands-off industry regulator.[40]

Liverpool had been an important early focal point for the manufactured anti-Semitism crisis. A dossier on Liverpool activists, full of lies and half-truths, was leaked to the right-wing press (as we saw in chapter 7). As well as her links to the JLM,

---

39 David Hearst, "Geoffrey Bindman on Labour's antisemitism scandal: 'There has been political manipulation,'" *Middle East Eye*, 28 August 2022.

40 Asa Winstanley, "Jewish Chronicle to pay damages over anti-Semitism libel," *Electronic Intifada*, 21 February 2020.

Ellman briefly took over as Labour Friends of Israel chairperson when Joan Ryan quit in 2019. After the dodgy dossier, Liverpool Riverside was put into "special measures" by Labour HQ for at least 18 months. This restricted party democracy and prevented local members from meeting and freely debating. White later told me that these restrictions culminated in the forcible change of the local party to a delegate structure, a move which ultimately enabled the right to re-establish control, despite being in the minority of members.[41]

As well as White's victory, a later example of successfully using the courts was provided by academic and activist Philip Proudfoot. In April 2022, his lawyers announced that they had won a libel victory for their client over a tweet written by TV actor Tracy-Ann Oberman, in which she falsely claimed that Proudfoot had maintained a "Jew blocklist" on Twitter. Proudfoot was the founder and leader of the Northern Independence Party, a small left-wing group which Oberman had also claimed in the offending tweet was a "continuation [of] Corbyn."[42]

Such libel victories were significant. There were several other IPSO rulings and libel victories over the *Jewish Chronicle's* misleading coverage of "Labour anti-Semitism." Although White's libel settlement didn't come until after the 2019 general election, the IPSO ruling occurred during the election campaign itself.[43] Corbyn's office could have made use of that victory to show just how much of a lie the paper's stories about anti-Semitism really were—while providing a punitive warning to the hostile press. But it was too late. By that time Corbyn and his team had spent more than a year conceding to the narrative.

According to Owen Jones's 2020 book *This Land*, in October 2019 John McDonnell's growing influence on the Labour

---

41 Audrey White, text message conversation with author, 21 April 2022. See also Audrey White, "Riverside CLP Remains in Special Measures," *Labour Briefing*, 2 September 2017. Audrey White, "Neutralising the Red City - Silencing the Left," *Labour Briefing*, September 2021.

42 Asa Winstanley, "BBC actor eats 'humble pie' over Labour anti-Semitism smear," *Electronic Intifada*, 27 April 2022.

43 Asa Winstanley, "Jewish Chronicle lied in reports on 'Labour anti-Semitism,'" *Electronic Intifada*, 2 December 2019.

leadership culminated in a "palace coup."[44] Top Corbyn aides Karie Murphy and Seumas Milne (who had both at least tried to resist the path of capitulation urged by McDonnell) were sidelined. The shadow chancellor "was now effectively running the show," Jones reported. Long opposed to Corbyn's leadership,[45] Jones (a former researcher for McDonnell) approved of the coup, even lamenting it as a "tragedy" that McDonnell never formally "assumed the leadership" of Labour.[46]

Al Jazeera's 2017 revelations about the Israel lobby's interference in Labour were another missed opportunity. Corbyn could have announced his own inquiry into Israeli meddling in the party but failed to do so. Left-wing Labour activists Michael Kalmanovitz, Sara Callaway, and Moshé Machover wrote an open letter to general secretary Jennie Formby in the summer of 2018 arguing there was "now an urgent need for such an inquiry" and that "the overwhelming majority of members would welcome an investigation into any attempts by the Israeli government, or any other foreign power, to determine who represents their party . . . members and the public at large have a right to know."[47]

Corbyn's eventual embrace of the false "Labour anti-Semitism" media narrative constituted a series of own goals and his embrace of the Jewish Labour Movement was politically suicidal. The 2015 intervention (by Israel lobbyists such as Jeremy Newmark, known to work closely with the Israeli embassy) to revive the group as a key proxy was precisely targeted at Corbyn's political assassination. That the left-wing leader should actively support a group openly dedicated to his removal was an entirely avoidable mistake. The JLM incessantly

---

44 Jones, *This Land*, pages 276-8.

45 For detailed evidence, see Asa Winstanley, "How Owen Jones learned to stop worrying and love Zionism," *Electronic Intifada*, 21 March 2022, and Asa Winstanley, "How Owen Jones justifies Labour's purge of socialists," *Electronic Intifada*, 3 September 2021.

46 Jones, *This Land*, page 315.

47 For a link to the full letter see Asa Winstanley, "Israel's bogus definition of anti-Semitism will unleash havoc in Labour," *Electronic Intifada*, 20 August 2018.

opposed the socialist campaigner for his entire five years as leader, successfully played a major role in his departure, and celebrated when he left office. "Mazel tov to Keir Starmer," the JLM said in a statement the day the new right-wing leader took over from Corbyn. The group wrote that Corbyn's term had "without doubt been one of the darkest times for Jewish Labour members and supporters."[48]

Yet Corbyn had done his best to appease them, attending at least one of their events, granting their leaders regular meetings and privileged access, promoting the group as an integral part of the Labour Party, and even handing them an award in the name of Del Singh (a late Palestine solidarity activist, who—his family insisted at the time—would have been outraged).[49] In his embrace of the JLM, Corbyn had changed his tune. In the spring of 1984, he had been a sponsor of the Labour Movement Campaign for Palestine. In its platform, the group demanded the disaffiliation of Poale Zion (JLM's ideological forerunner).[50]

In his futile attempt to keep the JLM on side, Corbyn sacrificed his most important backers—the newly energised mass base of the Labour Party. This was the secret weapon that had kept him in office in 2016, as well as being a key factor in his 2017 electoral advance. The mass base never abandoned him. But slowly, Corbyn seemed to abandon some of his supporters. By expelling or forcing out key backers like Walker, Williamson, and Livingstone, Labour allowed a clear, demoralising message to be sent out to the mass base. Labour's organic membership influx halted and slowly began to reverse.[51] This helps explain the lack of energy in Labour's 2019 general election campaign, and thus ultimately part of why Corbyn was defeated. Labour's

---

48   "JLM Statement on the Labour Party Leadership Election," Twitter, 4 April 2020.

49   Olivia Alabaster, "Family of activist demand apology after award given to Jewish Labour Movement," *Middle East Eye*, 27 September 2017.

50   "When Jeremy Corbyn Supported a Democratic, Secular State & Breaking Links with Poale Zion (JLM)," Tony Greenstein's Blog, 21 May 2016.

51   Rowena Mason, "Labour membership falls slightly but remains above 500,000," *Guardian*, 8 August 2019.

war against its own members went into overdrive under Keir Starmer. He incessantly purged the party of Palestine solidarity activists and the left. In less than two years, Corbyn's successor managed to drive out an estimated 120,000–200,000 members, who were either expelled or quit in disgust.[52]

Corbyn's embrace of the Zionists under left-wing Labour's one-sided "broad church" inevitably led to more concessions. Instead of recognising Zionism objectively as the political ideology of a specific state (which is recognised by Amnesty International, Human Rights Watch, and all other mainstream human rights groups as an apartheid state), Corbyn's team bought into the modern Zionist strategy of whitewashing their reactionary ideology as an "identity." Liberal Zionists in particular frequently claim their alleged "identity" is integral to Jewishness. Although this trend could be understood as a cynical PR stunt, it is more serious than that. It is anti-Semitic, as it lays the responsibility for the racism of the Israeli state at the door of all Jewish people everywhere. Such blanket racism has been overwhelmingly rejected by the Palestinian liberation struggle yet has always been an integral ingredient of the Zionist movement.

External pressure led to Corbyn keeping Jewish Voice for Labour at arm's length while leader—despite the fact that JVL was not even anti-Zionist. As soon as it was established in 2017, JVL set about countering the "Labour anti-Semitism crisis" narrative and it even made some headway, building limited inroads with mainstream media. During the 2018 wave of the "crisis," JVL's eloquent spokespeople occasionally made it onto the airwaves. Thoughtful, friendly non-Zionist Jewish activists like Naomi Wimborne-Idrissi, Jenny Manson, and Graham Bash began to put forward the pro-Corbyn case and dispute the media consensus on "Labour anti-Semitism." Overall, they represented only a small candle of dissent in the stifling media darkness. Yet even this was too much for the Zionists, who incessantly denounced and complained about JVL. After

---

52   Asa Winstanley, "Labour blew $1.3 million pursuing 'anti-Semitism' leakers," *Electronic Intifada*, 11 February 2022.

a tenacious grassroots campaign, Wimborne-Idrissi was elected onto Labour's NEC in September 2022. The same night the election results were announced, three pro-Israel groups released a joint statement demanding she be marginalised and "kept off any committees" of influence.[53] She was suspended soon after and expelled that December.[54]

Despite JVL's efforts, Corbyn effectively ignored the group while he was leader, declining to take part in any of their meetings (although McDonnell did participate in one meeting with Manson, at which he refused to take questions about Palestine or the fabricated anti-Semitism crisis). This was another missed opportunity.

* * *

Probably the greatest single moral failure of Corbyn's leadership came in 2018 with the Hajo Meyer incident. Meyer was a Holocaust survivor who in 2010 had been the main speaker at a meeting chaired by Corbyn in Parliament. It was organised by the International Jewish Anti-Zionist Network. IJAN is a small group with branches in the US and UK. The 2010 meeting had been titled "Never again: for anyone." Meyer and the other speakers argued that the lesson of the Nazi Holocaust should be a universalist one: that we must act to prevent the horror of such unspeakable crimes being carried out against anyone. This would naturally mean campaigning to prevent Israel carrying out another act of mass ethnic cleansing against the Palestinians, like that they had perpetrated in 1948.

Meyer and the IJAN speakers were viciously harangued by the usual suspects. Former Zionist Federation official and convicted criminal Jonathan Hoffman was one of several disruptors escorted out of Parliament by police after verbally assaulting Meyer. Second disrupter Martin Sugarman "stunned everyone

---

53   Asa Winstanley, "Israel lobby fury as Jewish leftist elected to Labour's ruling body," *Electronic Intifada*, 2 September 2022.

54   "Labour expels Jewish NEC member Naomi Wimborne-Idrissi," *Skwawkbox*, 16 December 2022.

by giving the Nazi salute and shouting 'Sieg Heil'" on the way out of the meeting, witnesses stated.[55] The meeting was largely ignored in 2010. But the "mainstream" media took a very different attitude in 2018. *The Times* decided that a twisted version of events could form another useful attack on the Labour leader, claiming the meeting had "compared Israel to Nazism." Meyer had passed away in 2014, and so could no longer speak up for himself. John Mann denounced the event as violating "any form of normal decency." Apparently shocked, Labour Friends of Israel officer Louise Ellman told *The Times* that she was "appalled" and "exceedingly disturbed to hear that now there is evidence that Jeremy was actually at a meeting where these sorts of views were expressed. This report disturbs me greatly."

Activists who attended the meeting said that the impression Ellman gave to have only just learned about the event was highly disingenuous. In fact, she'd been at the meeting herself. Yet appearing on the BBC's *Newsnight* programme the same evening *The Times* printed its story, she was once again "appalled to read about the report that's now in *The Times*," even though she'd been quoted in that same *Times* piece, and clearly already knew of its existence.[56] Adri Nieuwhof, an anti-apartheid activist who had known Meyer personally, described the affair as "another manufactured crisis in order to pressure Corbyn because of his historic support for Palestinian rights."[57]

But instead of defending Meyer—a Jewish survivor of the Nazis' Auschwitz death camp—Corbyn distanced himself from the dead man and apologised for once offering solidarity. "Views were expressed at the meeting which I do not accept or condone," he told *The Times*. "In the past, in pursuit of justice for the Palestinian people and peace in Israel/Palestine, I have on occasion appeared on platforms with people whose views

---

55 Adri Nieuwhof, "How Israel lobby attacked an Auschwitz survivor to smear Corbyn," *Electronic Intifada*, 7 August 2018.

56 "Video: Ellman 'appalled' to find out Corbyn at 2010 Meyer event – that she personally attended," *Skwawkbox*, 1 August 2018.

57 Nieuwhof, "How Israel lobby attacked an Auschwitz survivor."

I completely reject. I apologise for the concerns and anxiety that this has caused."[58]

Another serious instance of backsliding was Corbyn's record on the BDS movement. When I interviewed him in the summer of 2015, he gave the impression of being broadly in favour of the movement to boycott Israel. He told me he supported a two-way arms embargo on Israel—a key demand of the BDS movement. He even said that there should be a boycott of Israeli universities that are "doing research into drones, taser weapons, or doing research into surveillance of the occupation in Gaza"—although he cautioned that the academic boycott was "complicated" to implement without inadvertently targeting anti-Zionist Israeli academics like Ilan Pappé.[59] While ending the arms trade with Israel is relatively uncontroversial, the academic boycott has been more intensively debated over the years. But the Palestinian Campaign for the Academic Boycott of Israel (or PACBI) in 2014 issued detailed guidelines on the academic boycott. The document makes it clear that the BDS movement targets Israeli academic *institutions*, and not individual Israeli academics (let alone dissidents like Pappé).[60] Asked at a meeting in the north of Ireland with grassroots Sinn Féin activists to express support for BDS, Corbyn was even more explicit: "I think the boycott campaign, the divestment campaign is part and parcel of a legal process that has to be adopted."[61] But after entering the Labour leader's office that all drifted away.

In 2017 Kate Osamor (a left-wing member of Corbyn's shadow cabinet) tweeted support for the BDS movement. Labour

---

58 Henry Zeffman, "Jeremy Corbyn hosted event likening Israel to Nazis," *The Times*, 1 August 2018.

59 Asa Winstanley, "Jeremy Corbyn backs boycott of Israeli universities involved in arms research," *Electronic Intifada*, 2 August 2015.

60 "PACBI Guidelines for the International Academic Boycott of Israel," Palestinian Campaign for the Academic and Cultural Boycott of Israel, 9 July 2014.

61 David Hirsh, "Jeremy Corbyn Supports BDS," Engage blog, 25 September 2015. A pro-Israel academic, Hirsh runs Engage to propagandise against the BDS movement. Nonetheless, this post includes the original video and timecode.

Friends of Israel's chairperson Joan Ryan angrily condemned Osamor, demanding she withdraw her support and claiming the BDS movement "seeks to demonise" Israel (a common Israeli government talking point). But instead of defending the movement, Corbyn's office told the *Guardian* that "Jeremy is not in favour of a comprehensive or blanket boycott. He doesn't support BDS."[62] Speaking to me at the time, Corbyn's spokesperson James Schneider tried to justify this climb-down from the leader's earlier pro-BDS positions, claiming that the *Electronic Intifada* interview "quotes stand." Schneider insisted that Corbyn still "supports targeted boycotts of those Israeli academic institutions involved in arms research and surveillance of the Palestinian population." Asked to explain the contraction between Corbyn's previous support for BDS and his spokespeople's latter-day denigration of BDS as a "blanket boycott" that he did not support, Schneider was not forthcoming.[63]

This was an unnecessary and immoral capitulation to Israel lobby pressure. It would have cost Corbyn very little to stand by the movement and by Osamor. Instead, he was discarding the very same Palestine solidarity movement which had played a part in his rise to power in the first place. Although Corbyn weakly defended Osamor as having a "right" to express her views, his capitulation was only one sign of worse to come. Many activists rationalised away such infractions of basic solidarity as the result of bad advisers. But the fact that this particular climb-down came at a time when Corbyn was probably at his politically strongest position (only a few months after the 2017 election) should have raised alarm bells.

"When one takes Corbyn's positions as a whole," one Labour activist wrote, "his critique of Zionism is evidently far from internally consistent or rigorous."[64] This was clear as early as 2015 when I interviewed him. When I pointed out that his

---

62 Rowena Mason, "Jeremy Corbyn does not support boycott of Israel," *Guardian*, 13 December 2017.

63 Asa Winstanley, "Labour shadow minister Kate Osamor backs Israel boycott," *Electronic Intifada*, 13 December 2017.

64 Steven Garside, "Jeremy Corbyn must not back down on Palestine," *Electronic Intifada*, 24 August 2018.

concerns about an academic boycott of Israel had already been very well addressed by PACBI, a Palestinian group, he conceded that he had not read their guidelines. It's a sign of movement weakness that one of the only MPs with any substantial form of connection to the UK's Palestine solidarity movement has not read such a key document.

Another early harbinger of Corbyn's self-defeating reversal on Palestinian rights was an anaemic video he made to support the Palestine Solidarity Campaign's 2017 demonstration to mourn 100 years since the Balfour Declaration. Corbyn remained a patron of the group (a sort of ceremonial position that many groups maintain to lend themselves institutional cachet). But in previous years he would have been actually leading the demonstration and addressing its rally, rather than just making a video. The message in the video had been dramatically watered down. Instead of calling for a reversal of this aspect of Britain's malign imperial legacy, Corbyn equivocated about what the openly colonial document meant to "both sides" of the "conflict."

In hindsight, Corbyn's backward trajectory on Palestine began almost as soon as he became leader. Only a few weeks in, he went to a Labour Friends of Israel event. For many years at Labour's annual conference, LFI had held a "reception," where politicians, lobbyists, aides and activists sipped Israeli wine and listened to Labour leaders extol the alleged virtues of Israel. Tony Blair had been a frequent speaker and even Ed Miliband went along in 2014, saying he was "proud to be a supporter of LFI" and that he was "a friend of Israel."[65] Arriving at 2015's conference in triumph, to a sea of enthusiastic grassroots supporters, Corbyn gave a victory speech. But he also accepted a last-minute invitation to address LFI. What would he say? Israel's lobbyists needn't have worried. Corbyn addressed a packed LFI ballroom and spoke only mildly critical words, expressing his hope that we "ensure the siege of Gaza, or the restrictions on Gaza, are lifted." That Corbyn expected an Israel lobby group to want to work in direct opposition to its stated aims was naive at best.

---

65 "Ed Miliband – 2014 Speech to Labour Friends of Israel," UKPol.co.uk political speech archive, 9 December 2015.

He was expressing a fundamental misunderstanding of the nature of political power.

"Sometimes," he said, "you have to be very critical of people for their abuses of human rights." Though he didn't name Israel as a human rights abuser, the implication was clear. But even timid criticism was too much for some in the audience. "Oi! Oi! Say the word Israel! Say the word Israel!" a man at the back of the crowd shouted. The heckler was later named as Michael Foster, a former showbiz agent and wealthy Labour Party donor.[66] The following year, as part of the summer of 2016's rolling series of interconnected coup attempts, Foster launched a failed legal action to block Corbyn from the ballot for re-election as party leader. A few months later he was suspended as a Labour member for comparing Corbyn's supporters to Nazis (a vanishingly rare example of Labour disciplinarily measures being applied to the right).[67]

The Israeli ambassador—usually present at LFI's reception—was absent that evening. Mark Regev was appointed as Israel's new ambassador to the UK at exactly the same moment it became clear that Corbyn would be the next Labour leader (the day before voting began in the summer of 2015).[68] Regev didn't arrive in the UK to take up his post formally until April 2016 so it's likely that the new ambassador was still formulating his strategy against Corbyn that evening.[69] But standing at the front of the crowd was another Israeli agent. Video of Corbyn's speech to LFI still available on YouTube shows that none other than Shai Masot had positioned himself right next to Corbyn all the way

---

66 Asa Winstanley, "Siege of Gaza must end, Jeremy Corbyn tells Labour Friends of Israel," *Electronic Intifada*, 30 September 2015.

67 Asa Winstanley, "Pro-Israel donor suspended by Labour," *Electronic Intifada*, 13 September 2016.

68 "Labour leadership: Cooper and Burnham bids ahead of September election," BBC News, 13 May 2015. "PM's spokesman said tapped as new ambassador to UK," *Times of Israel*, 14 August 2015.

69 "Ambassador Regev Arrives in the UK," Embassy of Israel, London website, 5 April 2016 (accessed 16 June 2022).

through his speech.[70] He sipped on wine and typed idly into his phone giving the impression of a man supremely uninterested in what was being said. Who was he texting? His colleague Regev? His handlers at Gilad Erdan's anti-BDS ministry back in Tel Aviv? We may never know. The video also shows another strange detail. The Israeli agent was flanked by two large security guards: men in dark suits even more uninterested in the details of Corbyn's speech. The video shows that they kept their backs turned to the new Labour leader the whole time, conspicuously scanning the audience, their heads moving from left to right.

The problem with Corbyn's approach to LFI was that he was treating a deadly enemy as if it were a friend. An organisation dedicated to the destruction of Palestine is never going to be friendly towards a politician who had close ties to the Palestine Solidarity Campaign—no matter which platitudes about "long-term dialogue" and "peace through negotiation" were used. Although Regev was absent, LFI's chairperson Joan Ryan stood on the dais next to Corbyn looking absolutely aghast at having to share a room with the man.

Corbyn's second (and as it turned out final) appearance at an LFI reception was still worse. This time at the 2016 Labour conference, Mark Regev turned up, standing at the opposite end of the platform to Corbyn. The Labour leader thanked Regev and Ryan, praising LFI "for their contribution in building awareness of the different dimensions of the Middle East conflict, and the crucial debate about how to achieve a peaceful long-term settlement." Corbyn also praised Shimon Peres, who was at that moment on his deathbed in Tel Aviv. A former Israeli prime minister and president, Peres was the financial architect of Israel's nuclear weapons arsenal and is held by Lebanese and Palestinians to be responsible for the 1996 massacre in Qana, Lebanon, which took place under his watch as prime minister.[71] Corbyn mentioned none of this and instead praised Peres

---

70 You can still watch the video at Winstanley, "Siege of Gaza must end."

71 Seymour M. Hersh, *The Samson Option* (New York: Random House, 1991), pages 29-30, 65-67. Ilan Pappé, "Shimon Peres from the perspective of his victims," *Electronic Intifada*, 28 September 2016. Robert Fisk, "Shimon

as "a giant of Israeli politics" and a "remarkable" Nobel Peace Prize winner.

None of this saved the Labour leader from being publicly humiliated by LFI and its Israeli accomplices that evening. Michal Biran (a member of the Israeli parliament for the Labor Party) berated Corbyn for his past remarks about Palestinian resistance movements: "Hamas are not friends. They are not freedom fighters," she chided. "They are anti-Semites, they oppress the Palestinian people." She described UK Labour as her own party's "sister" party—the same rhetoric the JLM had been promoting since 2015. "Michal Biran put Corbyn in his place at the Labour conference," one of her colleagues posted in Hebrew on Twitter. The tweet used a humiliating photo of Corbyn standing next to Biran as she read out her denunciations. Regev also lectured Corbyn, saying Labour shouldn't allow "hate speakers" in the party.[72]

Corbyn's genuflection at the LFI meeting was likely motivated by a desire to dampen down the "anti-Semitism crisis." By then it was in full swing. It had started at Oxford earlier that year and the various internal commissions and investigations had been reported, leaked, or covered up. Ken Livingstone had been suspended and so had Marc Wadsworth. Jackie Walker was suspended and then readmitted under popular pressure in May.[73] But she was about to be suspended again following events at conference. Corbyn addressed none of this directly, even while vainly trying to conciliate LFI. Instead he made what he hoped were the right noises: "The Labour Party is not a home for anti-Semitism in any form. I do not intend to allow it to be," he said. "People have come and talked to me, and others in my team, about the anti-Semitism that does exist in society, that has reared its ugly head in various places, and have helped to advise and inform us." This was never going to be enough for

---

Peres was no peacemaker. I'll never forget the sight of pouring blood and burning bodies at Qana," *Independent*, 28 September 2016.

72 Asa Winstanley, "Jewish Labour Movement worked with Israeli embassy spy," *Electronic Intifada*, 12 April 2018.

73 Asa Winstanley, "Labour 'anti-Semitism' witch hunt claims new victims," *Electronic Intifada*, 9 June 2016.

LFI. Corbyn's genuine attempts to tackle anti-Semitism were addressed to the wrong audience. His critics were not motivated by a genuine desire to fight racism against Jews but rather by a mission to depose him and the threat of the popular democratic socialist government he represented.

Also watching Corbyn at that final LFI reception was Jeremy Newmark, the later-disgraced chairperson of the Jewish Labour Movement. Undercover Al Jazeera footage records him smiling as he says of the Labour leader's speech: "I can kind of live with that for the time being, it will get us through another year."[74] The next year Corbyn didn't attend the LFI meeting, sending shadow minister Emily Thornberry (who openly described herself as a Zionist).[75] No matter how much Corbyn tried to pander, the Israel lobby always refused to take yes for an answer. Instead, they pocketed Corbyn's concessions and demanded more, and more, and more—until they finally got what they wanted with Corbyn's exit.

* * *

Al Jazeera's documentary laid bare the role that the Israeli state and its lobby played in manufacturing an anti-Semitism crisis in Labour during the Corbyn years. Pro-Israel groups worked in close cooperation with organs of the Israeli state to undermine the new leader and create a sense of constant crisis. That Zionist groups in the UK were working against Corbyn in coordination with the Israeli state was an uncomfortable reality for many in Labour to face up to. It was elided via denial, evasion and ultimately capitulation to the narrative. Some on the "respectable" left even denied that the "Israel lobby" existed at all. Israel's defamation campaign against its critics as "anti-Semitic" has been so successful, that some seem to consider even acknowledging the existence of the Israel lobby inherently anti-Jewish. Such denial of basic facts, ironically, can lead to an increase in anti-Semitism.

---

74   *The Lobby*, Episode 4, timecode 08:53.

75   See also Asa Winstanley, "Labour's foreign spokesperson Emily Thornberry endorses Israeli racism," *Electronic Intifada*, 14 December 2017.

Suppression of discussion of the real nature of the Israel lobby means that, in the absence of reporting and analyses of the material facts, people will begin to draw on alternative explanations, some of which may lead them in anti-Semitic directions.

Israel's psychological warfare campaign against Corbyn was often quite open. One of the most obvious examples of this, as we saw in the last chapter, was the incident in 2018 when prime minister Benjamin Netanyahu directly attacked Corbyn on Twitter. But it wasn't just Likud that pursued the Labour leader. Israel's opposition Labor Party (whose former leader, Shimon Peres, Corbyn had spoken so warmly of) was just as bitterly opposed. Only a few months before that, when Corbyn announced the Chakrabarti Inquiry into anti-Semitism, one prominent Israeli Labor lawmaker had called on Corbyn to resign. "Instead of setting up another ridiculous investigative committee," said Itzik Shmuli, Corbyn should "be ashamed of the anti-Semitic spirit and moral slump into which the Labor party entered under his leadership."[76] After Corbyn's 2019 election defeat, Shmuli openly rejoiced: "I never imagined that I'd be so happy about Labour's defeat."[77] Six months later, Shmuli's party had his own electoral mauling in Israel. The Labor lawmaker embraced defeat and joined the short-lived thirty-fifth government, led by right-wing prime minister Benjamin Netanyahu. It was far from the first time Israel's Labor Party had joined a government led by the Zionist right. The dominant party of government until 1977, Labor had been reduced to a pitiful three seats. Labour Zionism, it seemed for a time, was politically a spent force. But it remained a useful Israeli propaganda tool, one especially effective when used on gullible British leftists.

After Mark Regev's years of proximity to Netanyahu as his spokesperson, it's easy to forget that he was brought up in the Labour Zionist milieu in Australia. If the CAA's Joe Glasman could claim credit for having "slaughtered" Corbyn, then Regev's divide-and-rule politicking against the left was no less

---

76 Peter Dominiczak, "Chief Rabbi: Labour has a 'severe' problem with anti-Semitism,' *Daily Telegraph*, 4 May 2016.

77 Tamar Uriel-Beeri, "Jeremy Corbyn will not lead his party into the next election," *Jerusalem Post*, 13 December 2019.

responsible. He used this strategy to attack groups associated with Corbyn like the Palestinian Return Centre, filing a complaint that led to a formal investigation by the Commissioner for Standards, the UK's official parliamentary watchdog. The PRC had held a meeting in October 2016 to launch their campaign to call for the British government to apologise for the colonial-era Balfour Declaration. But the campaign was stopped in its first steps by Regev after media misreporting of the House of Lords meeting as having blamed Jews for the Holocaust. The parliamentary commissioner ultimately rejected Regev's claims that the host of the meeting, Jenny Tonge, had led an anti-Semitic event.[78]

In 2020, the PRC won £35,000 in damages plus legal costs from the *Mail on Sunday* in an out-of-court settlement. The *Mail* had serialised *Dangerous Hero*, an anti-Corbyn book by biographer Tom Bower. Both publications had falsely described the PRC as "known to blame the Jews for the Holocaust." Bower and his publisher apologised and withdrew the claim, removing it before publication of the paperback.[79] Corbyn and the Palestinians were vindicated once again. But the damage had been done. The Israeli ambassador and the Israel lobby had played a key role: the initial false reporting of the PRC meeting was based on a blog post by David Collier, an Israeli government–linked anti-Palestinian activist (see chapter 1) who was quite successful at feeding his narrative into the mainstream media.

The Israeli embassy played a key role, too, in working closely with the Jewish Labour Movement to promote the false anti-Semitism narrative. Right-wing Zionists like David Collier had limited utility in the context of the Labour Party. Zionists on the left were far more useful, as they could undermine the party from within. They maintained a close working relationship with the Israeli embassy. "We work with Shai [Masot], we know him very well," said Ella Rose, the JLM director who had been hired out of the embassy. This particular admission didn't

---

[78] Ali Abunimah, "Smears by Israel envoy rejected in UK Parliament probe," *Electronic Intifada*, 27 March 2017.

[79] Asa Winstanley, "Palestinians win damages over 'Labour anti-Semitism' libel," *Electronic Intifada*, 19 June 2020.

make it into *The Lobby*, but I later obtained the full transcript of the conversation.[80] It took place in September 2016, after Rose had formally quit the Israeli embassy post and taken up a job with the JLM. The fact that the JLM employee responsible for the group's day-to-day operations was on first-name terms with an Israeli embassy spy and explicitly stated that "we work with" him and "know him very well" suggests that the JLM has or had a very similar working relationship with the Israeli embassy to that which Labour Friends of Israel privately admitted. Recall that Joan Ryan also talked to Masot "most days." Sometime after the *Electronic Intifada* revealed Rose's working relationship with Masot, Rose stepped down as JLM director and moved on to the Holocaust Educational Trust. But she remained active with JLM and a member of its executive. In 2022 she was elected as a Labour councillor in North London.

In addition to the Israeli embassy and Israeli politicians, Israel's anti-BDS ministry was also leading the charge against Corbyn. Al Jazeera's undercover footage shows Masot saying that the Ministry of Strategic Affairs had tasked him with establishing a front company in London to work against Palestinian rights—a common Israeli intelligence method.[81] An Israeli consumer group later uncovered evidence that Masot was an agent for the Ministry of Strategic Affairs and had used the London embassy as cover. The group, Hatzlaha, obtained strategic affairs minister Gilad Erdan's official 2016 diary. The Hebrew document revealed that Masot had accompanied Erdan to a meeting in Parliament with the Conservative Friends of Israel. Yet when Al Jazeera's story broke in 2017, Erdan claimed Masot had "no connection to my ministry." The minister's web of lies was swiftly

---

80 Asa Winstanley, "Jewish Labour Movement worked with Israeli embassy spy," *Electronic Intifada*, 12 April 2018.

81 See Victor Ostrovsky and Claire Hoy, *By Way of Deception* (New York: St. Martin's Press, 1990), pages 133-6. Another example is in Andrew and Leslie Cockburn, *Dangerous Liaison* (New York: HarperCollins, 1991), page 105, which explains how an armed Mossad cell secretly owned Incoda (a beef exporter in Ethiopia) as a cover to run Israeli spies into Arab countries.

untangling. As we've seen, Masot had done everything in his power to undermine Corbyn.[82]

A further indication of the Ministry of Strategic Affairs's key role in the anti-Corbyn campaign came during that raging hot summer of 2018, when the IHRA definition was imposed on the Labour Party. Israel mobilised a million-dollar troll army (dubbed Act.IL) on social media platforms to undermine and attack Corbyn as an "anti-Semite." Before Act.IL was allegedly wound up in 2022, the global influence campaign claimed offices in three different countries and an online army of more than 15,000. Its stated mission was to "battle" the BDS movement and to "influence foreign publics." Via an app, the group (funded and managed by the Ministry of Strategic Affairs) issued "missions" to instruct its adherents to vote multiple times in online polls and flood comment sections. In exchange they were granted university scholarships and other "cool prizes."[83]

One such mission rallied the online army to make comments smearing Corbyn as anti-Semitic on a *Huffington Post UK* article, as well as up-voting similar comments. "You know it's all about them likes," the Israeli operators told the troops. "Jeremy Corbyn, the leader of the Labour Party in the UK, has been repeatedly criticized due to his ant-Israel [sic] remarks," the mission details explained. It referenced the Hajo Meyer meeting: "He's been under pressure to resign and later issued an apology. But anti-Israel remarks are often a way to hide anti-Semitism and there shouldn't be room for that in the Labour Party and nowhere else. Like and comment on Nancy's comment if you agree." Facebook user "Nancy" attacked the Labour Party and "those who use criticism against Israel to hide deeper anti-Semitic feelings."[84] The mission was an indication of a wider pattern,

---

82 Asa Winstanley, "Disgraced Israeli agent Shai Masot attended minister's secret London meeting," *Electronic Intifada*, 8 December 2017.

83 Asa Winstanley, "Inside Israel's million dollar troll army," *Electronic Intifada*, 12 June 2019. See also Asa Winstanley, "How Israeli spies are flooding Facebook and Twitter," *Electronic Intifada*, 25 June 2019.

84 Asa Winstanley, "Israel running campaign against Jeremy Corbyn," *Electronic Intifada*, 7 August 2018.

showing the deep involvement of Israel's intelligence agencies in Britain's electoral processes.

The idea that "criticism against Israel" was just a mask for anti-Semitism had increasingly taken root even on the Labour left. No matter how outrageously false the allegation or how far to the right the accuser, some on the Labour left insisted that *all* such allegations should be taken seriously. David Collier and the Campaign Against Antisemitism are on the right of the UK's Zionist movement. Yet their false allegations were often taken seriously, even by some pro-Corbyn journalists, those who did not object when, in December 2019, Benjamin Netanyahu's far-right deputy foreign minister Tzipi Hotovely intervened in Britain's general election to openly call for Corbyn's downfall. "This [election] very much troubles us," said Hotovely. "It is true that we as a country cannot say we support this-or-that candidate, but Corbyn is a real danger to Israel-Britain relations, and I know British Jewry are very worried about this possibility."[85] Israel's minister for intelligence and foreign affairs Israel Katz also intervened, telling Israeli Army Radio that "I hope the other side wins."[86]

After Corbyn's downfall, the ambassador's job was done. Mark Regev stepped down and was succeeded by Hotovely. A hard-right religious Zionist, Hotovely represents the most extreme wing of Netanyahu's Likud. She has dedicated much of her career to helping Israeli settlers to take over the West Bank at the expense of the Indigenous Palestinians. Her activism for the settler "sovereignty" movement was rewarded in 2020 with a promotion, when she was tasked with the founding of Israel's settlements ministry.

British Zionists objected to her London appointment. They worried she would "alienate" Israel's supporters and would be too crass for the refined "British ear." But once she was in office

---

85 "Israel 'very troubled' by Corbyn run in British election," Reuters, 12 December 2019.

86 Dan Williams, "Israel's foreign minister says he hopes Corbyn loses British election," Reuters, 5 December 2019.

they fell into line and Hotovely was kept in post by the coalition government that succeeded Netanyahu in 2021.[87]

* * *

After Corbyn's electoral defeat in 2019, Labour's civil war was conclusively won by the right. The Israel lobby was joyous. To add insult to injury, Corbyn's touted left-wing successor, Rebecca Long-Bailey, was trounced in the resulting leadership election (Corbyn's preferred successor, Laura Pidcock, had lost her seat to the Tories in the general election).

The new leader was Sir Keir Starmer, as thoroughly a part of the British establishment as could be imagined. "The Labour Party is under new management," he told prime minister Boris Johnson in Parliament soon after taking over. Before entering Parliament in 2015, Starmer had been the chief prosecutor for England and Wales. His five-year term in office spanned the Labour government of Gordon Brown and the succeeding Tory-Liberal Democrat coalition of 2010. Questions have been raised about Starmer's tenure at the Crown Prosecution Service. Journalist Matt Kennard documented for the Grayzone how Starmer in 2012 blocked the prosecution of Britain's spy agencies for their role in torture—often in alliance with American spooks. Kennard asked a series of questions to the new Labour leader, but his enquires were ignored.[88]

With Corbyn again marginalised on the backbenches, Labour was back in the hands of the British establishment. In no area was this more apparent than the re-imposition of pro-Zionist hegemony in the party—even before Starmer was crowned leader. The Jewish Labour Movement and Labour Friends of Israel organised a joint hustings to grill the candidates

---

87 Asa Winstanley, "Israel's next UK ambassador is a settler extremist," *Electronic Intifada*, 12 June 2020. Asa Winstanley, "At London Israel demo, calls to 'burn' Palestinian villages," *Electronic Intifada*, 1 June 2021.

88 Matt Kennard, "Five questions for new Labour leader Sir Keir Starmer about his UK and US national security establishment links," Grayzone, 5 June 2020.

in the new leadership race. The hot topic was Labour's alleged anti-Semitism crisis. TV news star Robert Peston chaired the well-attended evening at a North London synagogue, broadcast live on Facebook. All four leading candidates competed to outdo themselves with gushing declarations of loyalty to Israel. It was an extraordinary display of obsequiousness, unimaginable for any other foreign country. Emily Thornberry and Lisa Nandy enthusiastically declared themselves Zionists. Long-Bailey emphasised her support for the two-state solution, adding "so I suppose that makes me a Zionist." Initially, Starmer was slightly more nuanced. "I wouldn't describe myself in that way," he said, while reassuring the audience: "I sympathise with and I support Zionism." But speaking to *Jewish News* soon after, he quelled any doubts with a more emphatic declaration: "I support Zionism without qualification."[89] Each raced to outdo the others by bowing to the Zionist groups' demands—all on the pretext of fighting anti-Semitism. The ideological conformity of Labour's next leader to Zionism was assured.

Even more extraordinarily that evening, the candidates all denounced a statement made by Corbyn criticising Israel as anti-Semitic—even the alleged Corbynist, Rebecca Long-Bailey. It was easy for Peston to ambush Long-Bailey into agreeing with his claim that the 2018 statement by Corbyn had been an anti-Semitic "disgrace." He read out the statement without revealing its source. Long-Bailey said she agreed it was anti-Semitic. Then, when told that Corbyn had said it, she made a fool of herself by back-peddling. But it was too late. The crowd groaned at her disingenuousness. Once the frontrunner, Long-Bailey lost the leadership election decisively: her campaign never excited Labour's mass membership as Corbyn's had.

The statement that had entrapped Long-Bailey was this: That it should not be "regarded as anti-Semitic to describe Israel, its policies, or the circumstances around its foundation as racist because of their discriminatory impact" on Palestinians. Back in 2018 Corbyn had bravely fought a doomed rear-guard action inside Labour's NEC, attempting to convince the ruling body to

---

89   Jack Mendel, "Keir Starmer interview: I will work to eradicate antisemitism 'from day one,'" *Jewish News*, 14 February 2020.

adopt a qualifying clause which would have curbed the more egregiously anti-Palestinian parts of the IHRA definition. This had failed because Corbyn did not have the NEC votes. Now here in 2020, history was being erased. Corbyn's stand was being retrospectively tarnished as yet another example of his supposed anti-Semitism. "Jeremy Corbyn presented to the NEC a document . . . he wanted the NEC to approve, which would have said that that statement is not anti-Semitic," Peston told Long-Bailey, discarding any pretence of objectivity. "That was a disgrace wasn't it?" She blustered that she couldn't "remember the exact words." Nandy, meanwhile, had been so keen to denounce Corbyn that she instantly replied yes when Peston had asked her rival if the statement had been anti-Semitic. Thornberry also agreed. Starmer stayed quiet.[90]

Corbyn's leadership had represented a break with Labour's long, almost untrammelled history of support for the settler-colonial project driving out the Palestinian people. But now it was back to business as usual. Starmer won the election and promptly disposed of general secretary Jennie Formby. Her capitulation to the anti-Semitism smear campaign had all been for naught. She was replaced by former senior Tony Blair election adviser David Evans. "The Labour left has been thoroughly defeated, and the end of Corbynism is complete," the editor of right-wing Labour news site *LabourList* concluded.[91] Yet Starmer had only won over the membership by promising to continue Corbyn's policies but with a different presentation style.

Despite all other candidates revealing their major donors' identities, Starmer refused to do the same. The BBC's Andrew Neil challenged him: "Don't Labour members have a right [to know], as they decide whether to vote for you or not? They want to know where your money is coming from." Starmer conceded

---

[90] Asa Winstanley, "Candidates to replace Corbyn denounce him as anti-Semitic," *Electronic Intifada*, 15 February 2020. For video of the fuller version of the Peston quote, see "Jewish Labour Movement Leadership Hustings," JLM Facebook page, timecode 53:38, 13 February 2020, recorded live (accessed 29 April 2022).

[91] Sienna Rodgers, "With an ally in control of the party machine, Keir Starmer's victory is complete," *Guardian*, 27 May 2020.

that he was taking money from "individual donations," but refused to name the money men.[92]

It soon became clear why. One of Starmer's top four donors turned out to be leading Israel lobby financier Trevor Chinn—the same motor industry tycoon who'd bankrolled Israel lobby groups like BICOM and former Israel lobbyists like Ruth Smeeth. In February 2020 (two months before the leadership election result), Starmer's campaign received a £50,000 donation from Chinn. Yet it was not registered with Parliamentary authorities until five days *after* the vote. Although there's no suggestion of illegality, Labour members felt understandably deceived.[93] The Israel lobby cash secretly funding Starmer may help to explain why the new Labour leader had so quickly switched himself to a pro-Zionist stance—despite appearing on a PSC platform only a few years earlier. Running as an MP for the first time in the 2015 general election, Starmer spoke at a PSC meeting along with other electoral candidates, where a major topic was support for sanctions against Israel.[94] Palestinian British lawyer Salma Karmi-Ayyoub (who also spoke at the meeting) recalled to me that the future leader gave the impression that he supported BDS at the time, enough that PSC members likely supported him as a result. Yet Karmi-Ayyoub told me that Starmer was evasive and "said, 'Well, all the options need to be on the table and considered'—so he didn't 100 percent commit himself" to BDS.[95]

* * *

---

[92] The Andrew Neil Show, BBC Two, 4 March 2020. For a clip of the quote see BBC Politics, "Why has Keir Starmer. . ." Twitter, 4 March 2020.

[93] Asa Winstanley, "Israel lobbyist funded Labour's new leader," *Electronic Intifada*, 22 April 2020.

[94] "General election candidates urged to support sanctions against Israel," *Hampstead & Highgate Express*, 4 April 2015. Sabby Sagall, "Activists debate how best to win liberation in Palestine," *Socialist Worker*, Issue 2447, 31 March 2015. The Troublemaker, "When Labour leader Starmer stood up for Palestinian rights," *Socialist Worker*, Issue 2716, 4 August 2020.

[95] Salma Karmi-Ayyoub, phone interview with author, 25 April 2022.

In April 2020, only days after Starmer become leader, an internal Labour report on anti-Semitism was sensationally leaked to the press. It contained masses of Labour staff emails and WhatsApp group messages. At over 850 pages, the report was an exhaustively detailed apologetic for Jennie Formby's Labour leadership team. It contained proof that Labour's right-wing staff had worked to sabotage the party from within during Corbyn's 2017 general election campaign.[96]

But what the report also showed was the refusal of Formby and her staff to combat the anti-Semitism smears. Worse: it showed they actively participated. The report sought to blame right-wing Labour staffers for deliberately neglecting genuine cases of anti-Semitism as a convoluted form of anti-Corbyn sabotage. While there is some evidence to suggest this may have happened in a few cases, for the most part the report just perpetuates the Israel lobby's smears against wrongly accused Corbyn supporters. The authors went to great lengths to prove they were more effective purgers of Labour's membership than the Labour right.

As only one example, the report has an entire 10-page section devoted to attacking Jackie Walker. But Blairite staffer Mike Creighton admitted in messages recounted in the report that Walker's first disciplinary action was "the weakest of the recent suspensions" and advised Labour to take another look.[97] At the time, Creighton was experiencing pushback from the grassroots campaign to have Walker reinstated. But the "leftist" report authors actually fault Creighton for finally doing the right thing and push an "expert opinion" from Dave Rich of the pro-Israel group Community Security Trust. Rich's alleged concern for anti-Semitism is undermined by the fact that in his world, the "anti-Semites" are almost always Palestinians and their supporters. Yet the report's authors decry the "mishandling of Walker's

---

96   Asa Winstanley, "Leaks show how Labour sabotaged Corbyn," *Electronic Intifada*, 17 April 2020. The full report is Harry Hayball et al., *The work of the Labour Party's Governance and Legal Unit in relation to antisemitism, 2014 - 2019* (London: The Labour Party, 2020). It can be downloaded from archive.org and cryptome.org.

97   Hayball, *The work of the Labour Party's Governance*, page 363.

first disciplinary case" when Labour lifted her suspension and complain that the email from the CST "seemingly did not inform the questioning put to Walker."[98]

Others smeared in the document included Ken Livingstone, Marc Wadsworth, Chris Williamson, Jewish anti-Zionist Tony Greenstein, and this author. In places the report is faintly farcical. Any allegation of anti-Semitism whatsoever—no matter how blatantly false or politicised—was taken as deadly serious by Labour's new leftist witch-hunters. In one section, they complain that Labour's previous right-wing bureaucrats often let people off with a warning rather than refer them to the NEC.[99] An example of this terrible left-wing anti-Semitism? "A complaint was received alleging antisemitic remarks being made at meetings of Riverside CLP, where Louise Ellman, who is Jewish, was the Labour MP."[100] What the authors failed to acknowledge was the fact that this was one of the very same Liverpool constituencies where the "dodgy dossier" had falsely alleged that the simple act of campaigning for Palestinian rights was evidence of anti-Semitism (as we saw in chapter 7). The authors also claim my reporting of the fact that Louise Ellman was a Labour Friends of Israel officer amounted to an anti-Semitic "trope"—despite that being an incontrovertible and relevant fact (a fact which they of course did not dispute).[101]

The report's lead author was Harry Hayball, who'd been recruited in 2019 to work exclusively on anti-Semitism. He'd previously worked on the same topic for Momentum.[102] Hayball had met the Jewish Labour Movement to discuss "tackling anti-Semitism within the party and on the left," the report states.[103] Patrick Smith, a second staffer recruited as Head of Disputes under Formby, was even more extreme. Smith was

---

98   Hayball, *The work of the Labour Party's Governance*, page 364.

99   Hayball, *The work of the Labour Party's Governance*, page 237.

100 Hayball, *The work of the Labour Party's Governance*, pages 177-8.

101 Hayball, *The work of the Labour Party's Governance*, page 822.

102 Winstanley, "Leaks show how Labour sabotaged Corbyn."

103 Hayball, *The work of the Labour Party's Governance*, page 765.

a former organiser with the small Trotskyite sect Alliance for Workers Liberty, controversial on the British left because of its support for Zionism. In a 2013 article Smith described how he had quit the Palestine Solidarity Campaign some years prior, attacking its activists as "essentially mad."[104] The report adopts the smears wholesale, noting that Smith was "hired specifically because of his knowledge of anti-Semitism and the forms it takes on the left," while conveniently ignoring his past AWL membership.[105]

Even so, the report's leak proved embarrassing for Starmer. A secret document later obtained by the *Electronic Intifada* showed that the party spent at least £1 million on specialist lawyers and consultants in a fruitless attempt to scrub the report from the internet. The document confirmed my reporting that the report's lead author was Harry Hayball. It also named the other two main authors as Georgina Robertson and Laura Murray. In October 2021, senior Corbyn aides Seumas Milne and Karie Murphy, along with Hayball, Robertson, and Murray, all strenuously denied via lawyers that they had anything to do with the leak. The five said they had come forward because Labour was about to name them as the leakers, in a related case at the High Court which had been brought by a group suing the party over the leak. Despite accusing the leakers of "nefarious ambitions," the Labour lawyers in the secret document concede that the original leaked report raised "legitimate questions" about whether party officials "seriously misconducted themselves" by undermining Corbyn "and working to ensure that the party lost the 2017 general election," and that there was "a strong public interest in alerting the media" to the evidence of internal sabotage against Corbyn.[106]

Although some publications apparently acquiesced to Labour's legal threats, it was mostly a wasted effort. As of

---

104 Mark Fischer, "AWL: Failing the litmus test of loyalty," *Weekly Worker*, 7 November 2013.

105 Hayball, *The work of the Labour Party's Governance*, page 761.

106 Winstanley, "Labour blew $1.3 million pursuing 'anti-Semitism'."

this writing, the full report is still available to read at both the Internet Archive and whistleblowers' website Cryptome.org.

In an apparent attempt to take the heat off, Starmer announced an independent inquiry into the leak, led by senior barrister Martin Forde. Initially supposed to have been published later that year, the resulting Forde report was delayed for two years amid legal threats and an investigation by the Information Commissioner's Office. Forde and his team concluded that "some opponents of Jeremy Corbyn saw the issue of anti-Semitism as a means of attacking him" and thus "treated it as a factional weapon." In 2022, Forde's conclusions about the "weaponizing" of anti-Semitism against Corbyn made the issue far plainer to see. But with the Forde Inquiry's conclusions released during the summer months (when many journalists and politicians are on holiday), the report was mostly ignored by the very same media which had been so up in arms about "anti-Semitism" during Corbyn's leadership. Despite Forde's critical take, his report suffered from an artificial attempt at "balance" which was criticised by many on the left. The report bizarrely alleged that "both sides" had weaponised anti-Semitism, since "his supporters saw it simply as an attack on the leader."[107]

* * *

After Corbyn's electoral defeat the Labour left was routed. If the 2015 leadership win was a political revolution, then Starmer's 2020 takeover was a counter-revolution. The new leader acted with dizzying ruthlessness. His promise of unity meant leftist Rebecca Long-Bailey was briefly brought into his shadow cabinet. But he sacked her only a few months later. Starmer would go on to break all 10 promises he'd made to Labour members while campaigning for their votes.[108]

---

[107] Asa Winstanley, "Labour right guilty of 'weaponizing' anti-Semitism, inquiry finds," *Electronic Intifada*, 27 July 2022.

[108] Jeremy Gilbert, "Starmer has broken promises and gone to factional war. How will Labour respond?" *openDemocracy*, 9 May 2021. "Starmer

Only a few months after the JLM-LFI debate in which she had accidentally condemned Corbyn as an anti-Semite, Long-Bailey herself fell victim to the same witch hunt she'd promoted. Her crime was to approvingly post to Twitter an *Independent* interview with Maxine Peake in which the left-wing actress (mildly and in passing) criticised Israel. "The sacking represents the moment that Starmer decisively broke with the Corbyn era," *LabourList* gushed.[109] In the interview Peake had—apparently unknown to Long-Bailey—drawn links between the Black Lives Matter liberation struggle and the Palestinian liberation struggle. "Systemic racism is a global issue . . . The tactics used by the police in America, kneeling on George Floyd's neck, that was learnt from seminars with Israeli secret services," she said. Israel lobbyists reacted with fury, demanding swift action from Starmer. She was out on her ear.[110]

At a "business like" meeting, the Socialist Campaign Group of backbench Labour MPs raised a feeble objection. John McDonnell posted a petition to Twitter. Jon Lansman (who had organised Long-Bailey's failed leadership campaign) called the sacking an "overreaction." The Labour left was out in the wilderness once again. The party's right-wing political establishment was never again going to risk a repeat of an aberration like Corbynism. Less than two weeks later, another of Starmer's shadow ministers got in trouble for a comment on Twitter—a comment that had nothing to do with Israel and was far more problematic than Long-Bailey's entirely innocent tweet. MP Steve Reed had asked if Richard Desmond (a Jewish donor to the Conservative Party) was "the puppet master to the entire Tory cabinet." But Reed was a right-winger, and had been bitterly

---

attacks Johnson's broken promises – but broke ALL his leader campaign promises," *Skwawkbox*, 1 December 2021.

109 Sienna Rodgers, "Keir Starmer decisively breaks with the Corbyn era," *LabourList*, 25 June 2020.

110 Asa Winstanley, "Pro-Corbyn shadow minister purged after Israel lobby demand," *Electronic Intifada*, 25 June 2020.

hostile to Corbyn. There were no Israel lobby demands for his head and he stayed.[111]

Starmer soon imposed his stamp of authority. The day he came to power the new leader made a public show of meeting Labour Friends of Israel to discuss ending the party's policy on ending arms sales to Israel, and promised to intensify the purges.[112] That this meeting had to be held via video conference during the 2020 coronavirus pandemic was bitterly symbolic. His first act as "Labour" leader was not to address the material conditions of the working classes or (with the looming threat of millions of newly unemployed) lay out his plans to combat COVID-19. Rather his top priority was assuring the Israel lobby that they were back in the driver's seat. All the leadership candidates (and most of the candidates for deputy leader) had agreed to a list of 10 demands issued by Israel lobby group the Board of Deputies. Its conditions included guaranteeing Ken Livingstone and Jackie Walker would *never* be permitted to rejoin.

Starmer fulfilled his commitments to the Israel lobby with aplomb. Palestine solidarity activists were a particular target of a growing purge of the party's membership. Only weeks into his leadership, the party suspended Bristol university professor and Israel lobby expert David Miller, as well as Brighton PSC activists Becky Massey and Pam Page.[113] Four Liverpool anti-racists were suspended the following month after criticising a pro-Israel article written by their MP.[114] A few months later, the *Electronic Intifada* obtained documents revealing that purges of Palestine solidarity activists had been carried out under the direction of the Board of Deputies. "This is a political hit list," Massey said. Her name

---

111 Elliot Chappell, "Labour's Steve Reed apologises for 'puppet master' tweet," *LabourList*, 6 July 2020.

112 Asa Winstanley, "Keir Starmer hints at Labour retreat on Israel sanctions," *Electronic Intifada*, 24 July 2020.

113 Asa Winstanley, "New Labour purge against Israel critics," *Electronic Intifada*, 20 May 2020.

114 Asa Winstanley, "Labour purges defenders of Palestinians," *Electronic Intifada*, 16 June 2020.

appeared on the list along with at least 10 others.[115] The purge was part of an exodus of up to 200,000 members in the first year of Starmer's leadership. Neither was fame any protection. Left-wing filmmaker Ken Loach was expelled in August 2021.[116] Jewish Voice for Labour also noted how many of its own members were being kicked out: "Labour is purging Jews from the party."[117]

In December 2020 Labour published a new "action plan" on anti-Semitism which, among other things, established an "advisory board" to oversee it. Eight of the board's nine members had links to the Israel lobby, including five who were actual representatives of Israel lobby groups. These were: Marie van der Zyl of the Board of Deputies, Mark Gardner of the Mossad-trained Community Security Trust, Mike Katz of the JLM, Adrian Cohen of the JLC, and none other than Margaret Hodge (who was by then the JLM's parliamentary chairperson).[118]

Labour began making the party a safe place for the Israel lobby to return to dominating policy on Palestine. The JLM was invited to run compulsory "training" sessions for elected party officials on anti-Semitism. In these sessions the JLM was once again using anti-Semitism to launder its anti-Palestinian agenda. Footage of the sessions obtained by the *Electronic Intifada* in July 2021 showed JLM chairperson Mike Katz (who'd run the 2016 training session that got Jackie Walker suspended) instructing party officials to ban motions supporting Palestine rights. "If you're setting the agendas, there's lots of really important international issues going on out there," he said. "You don't have to have motions on Israel-Palestine on your agenda every single month."[119]

---

115 Asa Winstanley, "Revealed: the Israel lobby's Labour hit list," *Electronic Intifada*, 20 November 2020.

116 Asa Winstanley, "Labour intensifies purge of socialists, dissenting Jews," *Electronic Intifada*,19 August 2021.

117 "How Labour's claim of countering antisemitism has resulted in a purge of Jews," *Jewish Voice for Labour* website, 5 August 2021.

118 Asa Winstanley, "Labour hands more power to Israel's lobby," *Electronic Intifada*, 5 May 2021.

119 Asa Winstanley, "Take Palestine off agenda, says Jewish Labour Movement," *Electronic Intifada*, 9 July 2021.

Officials enthusiastically complied with the JLM's instructions to rig party meetings and prevent local outbreaks of democracy. In Brighton, a motion calling for Israel to "end its violation of the human rights of Palestinians" and for Britain to end arms sales to Israel was banned from the agenda after party officials baselessly claimed that the discussion could lead to "anti-Semitic behaviour."[120] Labour was so incensed with the *Electronic Intifada*'s report on the incident that their legal unit emailed me with an apparent threat to sue us should we not remove or alter our article. My editor Ali Abunimah replied that we would not be doing so unless Labour could show any factual errors in the piece. We heard nothing more.[121] Labour made similarly toothless threats to blogger Tony Greenstein.[122]

Labour also pushed failed JLM electoral candidates, such as Ella Rose, Izzy Lenga, and Liron Velleman. All stood for the party in May 2022's local elections, in which they were finally elected as councillors. The two women had both appeared in the infamous 2019 *Panorama* documentary decrying "Labour anti-Semitism." In 2021 a photo emerged of Lenga wearing an Israeli army uniform and carrying an assault rifle. Some years prior she had paid to take part in a paramilitary training programme in occupied Palestine.[123]

At Labour's 2021 annual conference, the Israel lobby celebrated its return to dominance. Although delegates overwhelmingly passed a motion explicitly condemning Israeli "apartheid" and reiterating the 2019 manifesto pledge to end arms sales to Israel, Starmer and his shadow foreign minister Lisa Nandy instantly signalled that they would undermine party democracy and ignore the motion. "We must bring people together,"

---

120 Asa Winstanley, "Labour bans Israel sanctions debate," *Electronic Intifada*, 25 June 2021.

121 Ali Abunimah, "Labour Party tries to intimidate The Electronic Intifada," *Electronic Intifada*, 2 July 2021.

122 Ali Abunimah, "Labour Party threatens to sue activist over criticism of Israel debate ban," *Electronic Intifada*, 28 July 2021.

123 Asa Winstanley, "Labour women's candidate Izzy Lenga trained with Israeli army," *Electronic Intifada*, 12 March 2021.

Starmer said in a video address to Labour Friends of Israel, "not drive them apart with boycotts." The motion didn't approach the "conflict" in a "balanced way," Nandy claimed. In an obviously stage-managed move, Starmer welcomed Louise Ellman back to the party. The veteran Israel lobbyist had quit ahead of 2019's general election, explicitly to scupper Corbyn's electoral chances.[124]

After returning the Labour Party to its anti-Palestinian roots, Starmer's main priority was to assure the media-political elite that things were back to normal.[125] For the Campaign Against Antisemitism, having "slaughtered" Corbyn was not enough. They demanded he be kicked out of Labour altogether. It wouldn't be long before they got their way.

* * *

In October 2020, the Equality and Human Rights Commission (the EHRC, an official watchdog) failed to find Corbyn's Labour guilty of "institutional anti-Semitism," despite a 17-month investigation.[126] Initiated while Corbyn was still leader, the probe came at the request of the Campaign Against Antisemitism and the Jewish Labour Movement. It accused two Labour members (including Ken Livingstone) of "unlawful harassment" against unspecified Jewish people.[127] "Our investigation has identified serious failings in leadership and an inadequate process for handling anti-Semitism complaints across the Labour Party," the report stated. But notably it didn't find the party guilty of

---

124 Asa Winstanley, "Israel lobby takes back the Labour Party," *Electronic Intifada*, 9 October 2021.

125 Asa Winstanley, "Keir Starmer tilts Labour sharply towards Israel," *Electronic Intifada*, 10 April 2020.

126 Asa Winstanley, "UK 'Labour anti-Semitism' probe finds only two 'unlawful acts,'" *Electronic Intifada*, 29 October 2020.

127 Asa Winstanley, "Ken Livingstone to challenge EHRC in court," *Electronic Intifada*, 14 January 2021. Asa Winstanley, "Legal analysis blows apart EHRC's 'Labour anti-Semitism' report," *Electronic Intifada*, 11 December 2020.

"institutional anti-Semitism," a baseless claim the JLM had been pushing for years. Although the JLM later played the phrase down after it became clear the EHRC could not use it, in their initial 2019 referral of the party to the watchdog, the JLM had insisted the EHRC "has the power (and we say the obligation) to force the Labour Party to acknowledge that it has become institutionally antisemitic."[128]

Geoffrey Bindman QC later slammed the EHRC's report, attacking one of its central claims as "legal nonsense." He told *Middle East Eye* in an interview that the initial complaints against Labour for anti-Semitism were "nearly all baseless, as the EHRC itself found . . . Harassment must relate to a protected ground—in this case race or religion. The complaints, of which there were 200 or more, were nearly all about criticisms of Israel related to Palestine. All but four were rightly rejected, as the remainder should have been." Bindman (who is himself Jewish) summed it up: "I think there has been political manipulation and the allegations were almost entirely bogus. There's antisemitism everywhere, but it was wrong to single out the Labour Party, to single out Jeremy Corbyn, to start an investigation into the Labour Party."[129]

The EHRC report caused a media sensation. The British establishment was still obsessed with demonising Corbyn. A month before publication, Labour sources briefed the media that it was "highly likely" the report would lead to Corbyn having the Labour whip removed—in other words he would be expelled from the Labour group in parliament. As the media's storm over the report's publication raged, and under pressure to comment, Corbyn defended his record. "As Leader of the Labour Party I was always determined to eliminate all forms of racism and root out the cancer of antisemitism," he wrote in a statement. But his apologetics got him nowhere. The crisis only escalated, in response to one line towards the end of what, overall, was a cautious statement.

---

128 "Antisemitism in the Labour Party: Closing Submissions on Behalf of the Jewish Labour Movement," Scribd.com, 5 December 2019, page 2.

129 David Hearst, "Geoffrey Bindman on Labour's antisemitism scandal: 'There has been political manipulation,'" *Middle East Eye*, 28 August 2022.

"One antisemite is one too many, but the scale of the problem was also dramatically overstated for political reasons by our opponents inside and outside the party, as well as by much of the media," he said. Of the EHRC's report he said: "While I do not accept all of its findings, I trust its recommendations will be swiftly implemented to help move on from this period."[130] It was a timid defence. But even that was too much. After a five-year campaign of incessant anti-Semitism smears, Corbyn was finally purged from Labour.[131] Starmer's new deputy-leader Angela Rayner (who years ago had posed as pro-Corbyn) condemned Corbyn's statement as "completely unacceptable"—even while conceding it was "true" that there was only a small number of cases of anti-Semitism in Labour. Rayner's bizarrely contradictory interview summed up the whole witch hunt in a nutshell: it was true that anti-Semitism was exaggerated, but it was unacceptable to say so.[132]

Corbyn was suspended as a party member pending investigation—the exact same wearisome process that had pushed out so many prominent Corbynites over the previous five years. Ironically, the party used the very same "fast track" expulsion rule (which had been brought in earlier that same year under Corbyn's leadership) to suspend Corbyn himself. At the time Labour claimed the rule would only be used to get rid of those accused of "extreme" or "high-profile" anti-Semitism (as we saw in chapter 7). But in practice the new rule was used for anyone.[133] For Jeremy Corbyn MP, loss of Labour membership had an important consequence. He was no longer part of Labour's group in parliament. Henceforth he was an

---

130 "My statement following the publication of the EHRC report," Jeremy Corbyn Facebook page, 29 October 2020.

131 Asa Winstanley, "Israel lobby slaughters Corbyn again," *Electronic Intifada*, 20 October 2020.

132 "Video: Rayner admits what Corbyn said was true – but it was 'unacceptable,'" *Skwawkbox*, 31 October 2020.

133 Tony Greenstein, "Collapse of [the] Corbyn project," *Weekly Worker*, 4 February 2021.

independent MP, just like Chris Williamson in the months prior to the 2019 election.

A Labour disciplinary panel readmitted Corbyn as a party member a few weeks later. But Starmer was adamant: he wouldn't restore the whip to his former colleague. Corbyn's partial readmission came after threats of legal action against Labour, combined with a massive membership backlash. But it also came after yet another concession. Apparently hoping he'd get the whip back, Corbyn released a new "clarifying" statement: "To be clear, concerns about anti-Semitism are neither 'exaggerated' nor 'overstated,'" it read.[134] It came to naught. Corbyn remained out in the cold.

Should a general election be held any time before the latest possible date in January 2025,[135] Corbyn will face the prospect of having to stand in Islington against an opposing Labour candidate.[136] As of this writing, there are rumours the MP could turn his new Peace and Justice Project group into a political party, or stand as an independent in the constituency.[137] But Corbyn has yet to announce any plans. He could be as old as 75 when the next general election is called. He seems unlikely to step back from the campaigning he's been devoted to throughout his life. But could he perhaps—like his mentor Tony Benn—retire from the House of Commons to have "more time to devote to politics"?[138]

* * *

---

134 Winstanley, "Revealed: the Israel lobby's."

135 James Strong, "The intention behind the repeal of the Fixed-term Parliaments Act is to strengthen the executive and the Conservative Party," LSE British Politics and Policy blog, 29 March 2022.

136 Anna Lamache, "Starmer signals Corbyn won't be Labour candidate," *Islington Tribune*, 18 February 2022.

137 Nick Clark, "Will a new left party challenge Keir Starmer?" *Socialist Worker*, Issue 2788, 14 January 2022.

138 Paul Waugh, "Benn retires to spend more time with his politics," *Independent*, 27 June 1999.

"The Israeli Ministry for Strategic Affairs will bring to Israel delegations from abroad in order to expose the truth about the state of Israel. We must go from defence to offence."

That's what strategic affairs minister Gilad Erdan said at an Israeli government conference held at the Knesset in 2016. As we've seen, his anti-BDS ministry was carrying out sabotage operations against the Palestine solidarity movement all over the world. Israeli Labor Party lawmaker Ayelet Nahmias-Verbin also spoke at the conference, thanking Erdan (a close ally of Prime Minister Benjamin Netanyahu) for his efforts to sabotage the BDS movement. Two years later, Nahmias-Verbin was dispatched to the UK, forming part of Erdan's "offence" operations. Speaking at a Labour Friends of Israel event she verbally assaulted Corbyn, calling alleged Labour anti-Semitism "deeply disturbing" and "shocking." She asked: "Mr Corbyn: what kind of leadership have you shown to root this out?" Corbyn's concessions had gotten him nowhere.

Regev lurked in the background as Nahmias-Verbin held forth. He no doubt approved of her use of the "language of social democracy," as he'd urged in the Al Jazeera footage. With Corbyn's removal as a Labour MP in 2020, Nahmias-Verbin posted triumphantly on Twitter in Hebrew: "Bye bye @jeremycorbyn. Justice is done. Proud I was part of this puzzle."[139]

One particular 2021 story illustrated just how dedicated to Israel Corbyn's successor as Labour leader had become: the hiring of a former Israeli spy onto his staff. As I revealed for the *Electronic Intifada*, Labour brought Assaf Kaplan on board to surveil social media chatter about the party, or "social listening," as the job description put it. Kaplan had been an officer in Israel's military intelligence agency for more than four and a half years, part of its notorious Unit 8200 cyberwar outfit.[140] Unit 8200 has a well-documented history of human rights abuses targeting the Palestinians for blackmail, extortion, and mass surveillance.

---

139 Asa Winstanley, "Israeli politician boasts about role in Corbyn's downfall," *Electronic Intifada*, 5 November 2020.

140 Asa Winstanley, "UK Labour Party hires former Israeli spy," *Electronic Intifada*, 19 January 2021.

Israel and its lobby no longer needed to infiltrate the Labour Party—Starmer had invited them into headquarters. "I am not sure if this is a good idea," left-wing former Labour minister Chris Mullin responded to the news of Kaplan's hire. "Is he still working for the Israelis or for the Labour Party?"[141] Mullin is the author of the acclaimed 1982 political thriller *A Very British Coup*, in which civil servants, the press, the City, and MI5 conspire to bring down socialist Labour prime minister Harry Perkins. Aware of very real threats to the project, pro-Corbyn Labour activists often took the novel as a warning to help rally in his defence.

Recalling the threat of a fair-means-or-foul "mutiny" led by senior military officers that greeted his 2015 election to the Labour leadership, Corbyn said that the *Sunday Times* story had "served as a warning to a lot of our supporters just what we were up against, in challenging the foreign policy establishment . . . Harry Perkins went through my mind."[142]

Unfortunately, Corbyn and his supporters had not been prepared for a very Israeli coup.

---

141 Ian Cobain, Oscar Rickett, Lubna Masarwa and Simon Hooper, "Anger grows within Labour over role of ex-Israeli military intelligence official," *Middle East Eye*, 22 January 2021.

142 Matt Kennard, "Exclusive: Jeremy Corbyn on the Establishment Campaign to Stop Him Becoming PM," *Declassified UK*, 22 June 2022. See the full video interview for his Perkins comment, timecode 00:02:30.

AFTERWORD

The witch hunt in the Labour Party was so intense and irrational that to call it out or to even question whether anti-Semitism was a genuine major problem in the party was in itself viewed as more evidence of anti-Semitism. This was a neat little bit of circular logic for the witch-hunters.

At the *Electronic Intifada*, we saw signs of this early on, as Labour Party bureaucrats implemented what was in effect a stealth ban on party members sharing our stories. This ultimately led to my own suspension from the party. I had joined during the 2016 coup, on the principle that the right-wing wreckers should not be allowed to overthrow the democratic election of Corbyn before he'd even had a chance to put his popular left-wing vision to the country in an election.

I was suspended in 2019 for tweeting (amongst other things) that the Jewish Labour Movement was a proxy for the Israeli embassy.[1] Despite the objections of the National Union of Journalists, I was also banned from reporting on Labour's annual conference in 2019, despite having been given a conference pass in both 2016 and 2018, and having reported on 2017's event remotely.[2] In fact, Labour's conference services unit initially approved my press pass for 2019 too, but this was revoked after a political decision by the party bureaucracy—which was by that point ostensibly less dominated by the Labour right and

---

1 Ali Abunimah, "Labour Party investigates Electronic Intifada journalist," *Electronic Intifada*, 11 March 2019.

2 Ali Abunimah, "UK journalists union urges Labour to restore Asa Winstanley's press pass," *Electronic Intifada*, 3 September 2019.

whose boss was ultimately Jennie Formby.[3] It's a sad fact that Formby presided over the decision to push me out of the party on false pretexts. She had previously been quite sympathetic, and had briefly been a target of the witch hunt herself, as we saw in chapter 3.

The result of all this capitulation was that Corbyn was out within less than two years. To paraphrase the late, great union leader Bob Crow, if Corbyn had fought back he might not have won. But by not fighting back he guaranteed a loss. I ended up quitting the party in early 2020 after Corbyn's demise. My resignation came in protest at the way Labour leaked my private data to the press in order to undermine me. But more importantly, I was objecting to Labour's blatantly anti-Palestinian policies. Their attempt to censor me was not personal. It was more an attempt to gag the Palestinians. I was not censored as just a journalist—I was censored as a journalist with proximity to the Palestinian cause.

Telling the truth had become incompatible with Labour Party membership.

---

3   Ali Abunimah, "Labour's poor excuses for revoking Asa Winstanley's press pass," *Electronic Intifada*, 20 August 2019.

APPENDIX

Interview with Ken Livingstone, BBC Radio London, 28 April 2016.[1]

Vanessa Feltz: Joining me on the line Ken Livingstone, former mayor of London. Good morning Ken.
Ken Livingstone: Hi.
VF: Hope you're well.
KL: Yes, yes. Nice day.
VF: You will have seen yourself written about in the *Telegraph* today, it's their editorial. It says: "Others are furious about the conduct of Mr Corbyn's friend and ally Ken Livingstone, who said Naz Shah's comments were not anti-Semitic." Now she's profusely apologised for them, said she made a mistake. If she's apologised for them, presumably she acknowledges they were anti-Semitic. Do you still maintain they were not?
KL: No, she's a deep critic of Israel and its policies. Her remarks were over the top. But she's not anti-Semitic. I've been in the Labour Party for 47 years. I've never heard anyone say anything anti-Semitic. I've heard a lot of criticism of the state of Israel and its abuse of the Palestinians, but I've never heard someone be anti-Semitic.
VF: She talked about relocating Israel to America. She talked about what Hitler did being legal. And she talked about the Jews rallying. And she used the word Jews, not Israelis or Israel. You didn't find that to be anti-Semitic?
KL: Oh it's completely over the top, but it's not anti-Semitic. Let's remember that when Hitler won his election in 1932 his policy then was that Jews should be moved to Israel. He was

---

1 Audio available at "Jeremy Corbyn denies crisis as Ken Livingstone suspended," BBC News, 28 April 2016 (accessed 17 June 2022).

supporting Zionism, before he went mad and ended up killing six million Jews. But the simple fact in all of this, is that Naz made these comments at a time when there was a brutal Israeli attack on the Palestinians. And there's one stark fact, which virtually no-one in the British media ever reports. In all these conflicts, the death toll is usually between 60 and 100 Palestinians killed for every Israeli. Now, any other country doing that would be accused of war crimes, but it's like we have a double standard about the policies of the Israeli government.

VF: You see some people will say there's a double standard operating in the Labour Party. That what's really a flagrant kind of anti-Semitism, a deeply embedded systemic anti-Semitism, is hidden behind a mask of anti-Zionism or criticism of Israeli foreign policy, but that's not what it really is. It's really, as John Rentoul, the political commentator for the *Independent* said on my programme, using a phrase that I would hesitate to use, but he used this morning, he said these are Jew-haters, long-term Jew-haters and they can use criticism of Israel as a cloak behind which to mask that sentiment.

KL: He's lying. As I said, I've never heard anyone say anything anti-Semitic. But there's been a very well-orchestrated campaign by the Israel lobby to smear anybody who criticises Israeli policy as anti-Semitic. I mean, I had to put up with 35 years of this, you know, being denounced. Because, back in 1981, we were campaigning saying the Labour Party should recognise the Palestine Liberation Organisation. We were accused of anti-Semitism but then, 12 years later the leader of the PLO's on the Whitehouse lawn shaking hands with the prime minister of Israel.

VF: How could it be therefore that you would think that it was alright for Naz Shah to mention Hitler at all? If her comments were anti-Zionist, or anti-Israeli-foreign-policy, why would that be part of the argument? Why would Hitler's name even come into it?

KL: I don't think she should have done that. I think, as I said, she was over the top. But we need to step back and look at the anger there is at the sort of double standards. We've just had a decade of painful sanctions against Iran. We invaded Iraq because we thought they were going to get nuclear weapons.

But Israel's had nuclear weapons for 40 years at least, and there's never any sanctions, never any complaint by anyone in the West. It's these double standards that make people angry.

VF: What do you think over the top really means? When I say, was it anti-Semitic, and you say no it wasn't, categorically no, anyone who says it was is a liar, but it was over the top—over the top of what?

KL: Well I mean, basically if you think of anti-Semitism and racism as exactly the same thing. And criticising the government of South Africa, which is pretty unpleasant and corrupt, doesn't make me a racist. And it doesn't make me anti-Semitic when I criticise the brutal mistreatment by the Israeli government—and let's look at someone who's Jewish, who actually said something almost similar to what Naz has just said: Albert Einstein. When the first leader of Likud, the governing party now in Israel, came to America, he warned emerging politicians, don't talk to this man, because he's too similar to the fascists we fought in the Second World War. Now if Naz or myself had said that today, we'd be denounced as anti-Semitic, but that was Albert Einstein.

VF: Lord [Michael] Levy, you know, a senior Labour peer, I think you'll agree, I spoke to him on the programme. And I said I'm going to be speaking to Ken Livingstone, what would you like me to say to him? And he said, in saying that what Hitler did was legal, in talking about moving all Jews from Israel to the United States—and of course there are more Jews in Israel now than in any other country in the world—Lord Levy says: Ken Livingstone, in saying that those things are not anti-Semitic, and I quote, must be living on another planet. Vanessa, will you ask him, is he living on another planet? And if he is, which planet is it?

KL: Well I mean, after Jeremy became leader I was having a chat with Michael and he said he's very worried, because one of his friends who is Jewish had come to him and said, the election of Jeremy Corbyn is exactly the same as the first step to the rise in power of Adolph Hitler. So frankly, there's been an attempt to smear Jeremy Corbyn and his associates as anti-Semitic from the moment he became leader. But the simple fact is we have the right to criticise what is one of the most brutal regimes that's going in the way it treats its Palestinians.

ACKNOWLEDGEMENTS

I owe a debt of gratitude to a large number of people.

First and foremost, this book would not exist without the support of the entire team at the *Electronic Intifada*. Genuinely independent, critical, investigative journalism, free from the shackles of corporate ownership, is a rare thing and should be treasured, nurtured, and generously funded. It was only because of the support of *EI* that I was ever able to do the reporting that this book is based on in the first place.

My thanks go to Ali Abunimah, *EI*'s executive director, co-founder, and leading editor and writer. Without his example, encouragement, and leadership through the entire period of this reporting, I would never have followed this exhausting story for as long as I did. Any credit due for my persistence on this story should therefore go to him equally. Ali guided me through the entire process of publishing and also played a vital role in finally finding a willing publisher. His book *One Country* (which I read in exile from Palestine in Jordan in 2009) was probably the most important book to influence my thinking about Palestine and marked a turning point in my life.

Thanks also go to Maureen Murphy, our brilliant senior editor, who first suggested this project, observing some years ago that I'd already done enough reporting on the subject to make up a book. The rest of the *EI* team all contributed over the years in many ways, whether it was editing and reading my articles, giving feedback, or just providing much needed encouragement and support. Nora, Dave, Tamara, Omar, Michael, and Leah, thank you: you all make me proud to work with you every day.

Many thanks to Joseph Massad, whose work has provided important intellectual scaffolding to this project and who gave some extremely helpful early advice. Thanks go to Max Blumenthal who read an early draft of the first chapters and gave some really useful feedback which shaped its development. His seminal work *The Management of Savagery* was a key influence. Abdel Bari Atwan gave enthusiastic praise for the book in an early draft and made great efforts towards publication, for which I am incredibly grateful.

Tony Greenstein's expertise on the fraught issue of Nazi-Zionist collaboration was an immense asset, and he gave generously detailed feedback and corrections which greatly improved chapters 2 and 5. Tony Lerman gave some incredibly useful feedback, which tightened the final chapter and provided some important corrections. Jackie Walker also read several chapters and provided useful corrections and feedback.

Max Geller was a constant source of encouragement and his editing ideas greatly improved chapter 1. Thanks to Ahmed Kaballo who read chapters and provided encouragement. Louis Allday kindly read and strengthened the final chapter. James Kleinfeld could never have touched the issue again for the rest of his life and would still have done more for the liberation of Palestine than most of us; but nonetheless he was a great source of support and read the whole manuscript, providing some important feedback. Alex Nunns generously read chapters and provided corrections and encouragement. Lowkey was a fantastic source of camaraderie and support. He insisted I find a real publisher and was livid on my behalf when for the longest time I couldn't. Many thanks also to Jamie Stern-Weiner and Rebecca Gordon-Nesbitt who both read the entire manuscript and provided important feedback and corrections.

Phil Rees gave essential support and so much of the reporting in this book wouldn't have been possible without him— diolch yn fawr. Thanks go too to Clay Swisher. The two Al Jazeera series they produced on the Israel lobby have already stood the test of time. I hope one day the network will actually broadcast the US one.

A special thanks to Roger Waters, who made the completion of this project possible and also offered vital moral support at a time when I was despairing of finding a publisher.

Many thanks to the entire OR Books team, especially Colin Robinson, whose skilled editing improved the manuscript immeasurably. OR is to be commended for getting behind this project when many others wouldn't. It also speaks volumes about the success of the "anti-Semitism" witch hunt that—even after two years of searching—I was unable to find a British publisher.

Thanks are also due to the countless numbers of ordinary Labour Party members and activists who have been my informants on this story over the years. Without their constant vigilance and solidarity, this book would have been threadbare. There are too many of you to name, but thank you.

Inevitably, I will have missed others who should be thanked too. Those I've named here are not responsible for any errors or omissions in the final book.

Finally, I'd like to thank my entire family, especially my daughter and my wife. The support of both was vital through the many long, weary years of following this story and writing this book. My brother-in-law also read some of the manuscript and was fantastically encouraging.

My wife in particular pushed me to keep going when I was almost ready to give up. B: I love you and I couldn't have done this without you.

EPIGRAPH SOURCES

Corbyn: "Jeremy Corbyn | Glastonbury 2017," Official Jeremy Corbyn Channel, YouTube, 24 June 2017, time code: 00:02:36. See also: Anoosh Chakelian, "'Rise like lions after slumber': why do Jeremy Corbyn and co keep reciting a 19th century poem?" *New Statesman*, 27 June 2017.
Mackenzie: W. J. M. Mackenzie, *History of the Special Operations Executive: Britain and the Resistance in Europe* (London: British Cabinet Office, 1948), pages 1153 and 1155. Unpublished original of the Public Records Office London: As cited in Daniele Ganser, *NATO's Secret Armies: Operation Gladio and Terrorism in Western Europe* (London: Routledge, 2004), page 39.
Johnson: Hansard, Volume 619, Column 148, 10 January 2017: *West Bank: Illegal Settlements*.

BIBLIOGRAPHY

Books

Agee, Philip. *Inside the Company: CIA Diary*. London: Penguin, 1975.
Blumenthal, Max. *The Management of Savagery: How America's National Security State Fueled the Rise of Al Qaeda, ISIS, and Donald Trump*. London: Verso Books, 2019.
Brenner, Lenni. *Zionism in the Age of the Dictators*. Atlanta: On Our Own Authority! Publishing, 2014.
Cesarani, David. *The Jewish Chronicle and Anglo-Jewry, 1841-1991*. Cambridge University Press, 1994.
Cockburn, Andrew and Leslie. *Dangerous Liaison: The Inside Story of the US-Israeli Covert Relationship*. New York: HarperCollins, 1991.
Curran, James and Jean Seaton. *Power Without Responsibility: Sixth Edition*. London: Routledge, 2003.
Ganser, Daniele. *NATO's Secret Armies: Operation Gladio and Terrorism in Western Europe*. London: Routledge, 2004.
Greenstein, Tony. *Zionism During the Holocaust*. Self-published, 2022.
Hersh, Seymour M. *The Samson Option*. New York: Random House, 1991.
Jones, Owen. *This Land: The Story of a Movement*. London: Allen Lane, 2020.
Kelemen, Paul. *The British Left and Zionism: History of a Divorce*. Manchester University Press, 2012.
Masalha, Nur. *Expulsion of the Palestinians: The Concept of "Transfer" in Zionist Political Thought, 1882-1948*. Washington, DC: The Institute for Palestine Studies, 1992.
Masalha, Nur. *Palestine: A Four Thousand Year History*. London: Zed Books, 2018.
Massad, Joseph A. *Islam in Liberalism*. University of Chicago Press, 2015.
Massad, Joseph A. *The Persistence of the Palestinian Question: Essays on Zionism and the Palestinians*. New York: Routledge, 2006.
Mayhew, Christopher and Michael Adams. *Publish it Not: The Middle East Cover-Up*. Oxford: Signal Books, 2006.
Miliband, Ralph. *Parliamentary Socialism*. London: Merlin Press, 1964.
Miller, Arthur. *The Crucible*. Penguin Modern Classics, 2000.
Mullin, Chris. *A Very British Coup*. London: Serpent's Tail, 2006.

Nicosia, Francis R. *The Third Reich and the Palestine Question*. London: I. B. Tauris, 1985.
Nunns, Alex. *The Candidate: Jeremy Corbyn's Improbable Path to Power*. New York: OR Books, 2016.
Ostrovsky, Victor and Claire Hoy. *By Way of Deception: The Making and Unmaking of a Mossad Officer*. New York: St. Martin's Press, 1990.
Palumbo, Michael. *The Palestinian Catastrophe*. London: Quartet Books, 1987.
Pappé, Ilan. *The Ethnic Cleansing of Palestine*. Oxford: Oneworld Publications, 2007.
Philo, Greg et al. *Bad News for Labour*. London: Pluto Press, 2019.
Segev, Tom. *The Seventh Million: The Israelis and the Holocaust*. New York: Hill and Wang, 1994.
Stern-Weiner, Jamie, ed. *Antisemitism and the Labour Party*. London: Verso, 2019.
Walker, Jacqueline. *Pilgrim State*. London: Sceptre, 2009.

Reports and pamphlets

The Shami Chakrabarti Inquiry. London: The Labour Party, 30 June 2016.
Hayball, Harry et al. *The work of the Labour Party's Governance and Legal Unit in relation to antisemitism, 2014-2019*. London: The Labour Party, March 2020.
Kanafani, Ghassan. *The 1936-39 Revolt in Palestine*. New York: Committee for a Democratic Palestine, 1972.
Reut Institute and Anti-Defamation League. *The Assault on Israel's Legitimacy*. January 2017.
Taylor, Derek. *Solidarity and Discord: A brief history of 99 years of affiliation to the Labour Party*. London: Jewish Labour Movement, 2019.

INDEX

Abbott, Diane 15, 184, 226
Afghanistan 12, 13, 216
Al Jazeera 46, 212, 230n
　The Labour Files (series) 212–3n
　See also The Lobby (series)
American Israel Public Affairs
　Committee (AIPAC) 1, 37
Anti-Defamation League (ADL) 122,
　180–1, 314
Ashcroft, Michael 252–3

Baime, Jacob 33, 121, 164
Bakr boys 99
Bash, Graham 166–7, 170, 207, 270
Bastani, Aaron 72n, 174, 175n
British Broadcasting
　Corporation (BBC)
　Panorama (documentary) 66, 110,
　211–3, 217–21, 296
BDS movement 1, 13, 29n, 33, 36, 58,
　69, 90, 111–2, 117, 124, 125n, 199,
　209–210, 228, 235
　See also Israel, Ministry of
　Strategic Affairs
　and Jeremy Corbyn 261, 273–7
　and Keir Starmer 288
　anti-BDS movements 43, 46,
　123n
Beckett, Jasmin 43, 44, 74, 86, 87–8,
　90, 92
Benn, Hilary 186, 226–8
Benn, Tony 15, 18, 72–3, 77
　Bennites 72, 77, 87, 255
Ben-Gurion, David 49, 53n, 157
Berger, Luciana 56, 119, 231–8,
　242, 244–5
Berry, Mike 263-4

Blair, Tony 12, 15-9, 20, 21, 23, 42n,
　44, 48, 55n, 120, 137, 181, 215, 221,
　224-5, 235, 275, 287
　Blairites 56, 63, 65, 66, 78, 91, 92,
　113, 175, 183, 221, 224, 289
Bindman, Geoffrey 266, 298
Biran, Michal 278
Bird, Rica 212–3
Board of Deputies of British Jews 9,
　64, 182, 203, 221–2
Brighton (city) 294, 296
　2017 Labour conference in
　160–1, 195
Britain Israel Communications
　and Research Centre (BICOM)
　1, 79, 187
Brown, Gordon 16, 17, 23, 48, 67, 120,
　189, 221, 224, 285
Bush, George W. 12, 17
Bush, Stephen 19n, 117, 134n, 221

Cameron, David 20, 109
Campaign Against Antisemitism
　(CAA) 1, 182, 248–9, 284, 297
Chakrabarti, Shami 84, 181
　Chakrabarti inquiry 84, 181–4,
　190, 280
　press conference for 182–16
Chalmers, Alex 74, 77–85, 87–8, 93–5
Chinn, Trevor 188, 288
CIA (US intelligence agency) 8, 51–2,
　83, 87
　See also Mike Pompeo
Cohen, Joseph 172
Collier, David 32, 33, 281, 284
Community Security Trust (CST) 1, 3,
　38–9, 130n, 187–8, 289–90, 295

Conservative Friends of Israel (CFI) 108–9, 126, 282
Conservative Party 16, 40, 65, 109, 112, 252, 293
  Theresa May's 232
Corbyn, Jeremy vii, 3, 5–19, 23-5, 29, 41–4, 47, 71, 83–8, 118, 133
  accusations of anti-Semitism 48, 61, 62, 70, 78, 82, 84, 131, 141, 163, 184, 193, 196
  Corbynism 3, 54, 63, 75, 92, 98, 163, 174, 176, 198
  media coverage of 14, 20–2, 32, 33–7, 73, 134, 171, 198
  coverage of connection to Raed Salah 38–41
  Peace and Justice Project 300
  Stop the War Coalition 12, 216
  support of Palestinian causes 27, 56, 160, 188, 197
Cox, Jo 57, 183, 236
Creighton, Mike 85, 175, 221, 289
Crossman, Richard 53

Dalton, Hugh 52–3
Deir Yassin massacre 34, 157
Duncan, Alan 108–9, 112, 126

Egypt 50, 53, 105
  Suez Canal 119–20
Elliot, James 74, 78, 82–95, 97
Ellman, Louise 54n, 56, 65, 106, 210–3, 215–7, 232, 242, 266–7, 272, 290, 297
Erdan, Gilad 111, 277, 282, 301
European Commission 22
Equality and Human Rights Commission (EHRC) 297–9

Fawkes, Guido 31n, 76, 88, 134–6, 140, 163n, 164, 174, 214
Feltz, Vanessa 138–41, 305
Fisher, Lucy 160n, 161, 214n
Fitzpatrick, Jean 113–6, 219
Fitzsimons, Lorna 80
Forde, Martin 292
Formby, Jennie 82, 227–8, 256–60, 268, 287, 289, 290, 304
Foster, Michael 229, 276
Freeman, Michael 111

Freiburg, Mark
  See Regev, Mark
Funnell, Joshua 212

Gabbay, Avi 240
Garrard, David 245
Gerber, Jennifer 185, 189
  See also Labour Friends of Israel
Glasman, Joe 248–9, 254, 280
GnasherJew (Twitter account) 174
Goldstein, Jonathan 233–4
Greenstein, Tony 142n, 145n, 146n, 148n, 149n, 151n, 194, 201, 249n, 251, 290, 296, 299n
Grinstein, Gidi 124–5
Guardian (newspaper) 13, 41, 42, 87, 125, 159, 194, 204, 208, 255, 261–3, 266, 274
Guru-Murthy, Krishnan 5–6, 14, 33, 41

Hagee, John 202
The Hague (city)
  See Kiswanson, Nada
Hague, William 11
Hamas 5, 6, 7, 33, 37, 42, 91, 101, 172, 278
Hassassian, Manuel 29–31, 117
Hayball, Harry 76n, 175n, 194n, 251n, 256n, 257n, 289n, 290–1
Hearst, David 42, 200n
Heffer, Simon 9
Herzog, Isaac 189
Hizballah 5, 6, 33, 91
Hodge, Margaret 223–9, 242, 244–7, 250, 265–6, 295
Hoffman, Jonathan 28, 33, 271
Holocaust 9, 80, 132, 141–7, 154, 155, 167, 169-70, 177, 178, 179, 213, 271, 281–2
  Auschwitz 9, 272
  International Holocaust Remembrance Alliance (IHRA) 167
Hotovely, Tzipi 284–5

Institute for Jewish Policy Research 243
International Jewish Anti-Zionist Network (IJAN) 203, 271

INDEX

IPSO 246, 266, 267
Iraq 12–3, 17, 40n, 216, 306
ISIS 17, 76n
Islamophobia 181, 220, 264
Israel
   Israel Advocacy Movement
     168, 169
   Israeli embassy (UK) 45–6, 57–8,
     62, 66, 77, 95, 97, 98, 106–9,
     110–3, 116–7, 120, 124, 176, 201,
     218, 232, 268, 281–2, 303
   Israeli Labor Party 50, 116–9,
     240, 301
   Israel lobby (UK) 3, 8, 9, 11, 21,
     30, 34, 36–7, 40, 44, 48
     Community Security Trust
       (CST) 38–39
     Parliament Square
       demonstration 234,
       236, 237
     East Jerusalem 42
     US embassy in 202
     Zion (as place name in) 49
   Ministry of Foreign Affairs 45
   Ministry of Strategic Affairs
     10, 31–3, 103, 108, 121–3, 282–3
   Mossad (intelligence agency) 6,
     188, 282n, 295
   Tel Aviv (city) 14, 120, 127,
     157, 277
   See also Zionism

Jamal, Ben 238
Jerusalem (city) 26, 27, 41, 120, 150
Jerusalem Post (newspaper) 234
Jewish Chronicle (newspaper) 21, 25,
   33–4, 36, 37, 40, 58, 62, 68, 71, 82, 92,
   94, 138, 171–2, 198, 206, 216–7, 234,
   241, 262, 266–7
   See also Pollard, Stephen
Jewish Labour Movement (JLM) 32,
   43, 47, 54, 66, 68, 74, 84, 89, 94, 99,
   111, 115, 117–9, 124–5, 127, 131–2,
   164, 166, 182, 194, 195–7, 209–11,
   221, 232, 234, 242–4, 255, 279, 281,
   285, 290, 297, 303
Jewish Leadership Council (JLC) 58,
   60, 64–5, 68, 124, 188, 233–4

Jewish News (newspaper) 33, 35, 36, 62,
   115, 164, 241, 262, 265, 286
Jewish Voice For Labour 67, 70, 195–9,
   205, 213, 220, 222, 234, 243, 257,
   270, 295
   See also Labour Party
Johnson, Boris 19, 47, 108, 125–6, 285
Jones, Owen 13, 125, 194, 208, 243,
   256, 267–8
Jordan 27, 53, 162
   Jordan River 26n, 177
   monarchy of 27

Kalmanovitz, Michael 203–4, 268
Kaplan, Assaf 301–2
Karmi-Ayyoub, Salma 288
Katz, Mike 65–6, 166–9, 172,
   175–7, 295
Kelemen, Paul 119–20, 148, 156, 203,
Kennard, Matt 7–8, 285
Kinnock, Neil 15–6
Kiswanson, Nada 123
Klein, Morton 104–5
Klein, Naomi 175
Klemperer, David 78, 80, 85, 95
Kopelowitz, Lionel 9
   See also Board of Deputies of
   British Jews

Labour Friends of Israel (LFI) 43,
   45–7, 56, 65, 71, 82, 97–8, 106–11,
   113–6, 118–20, 127, 131–2, 159, 175,
   183, 185, 189, 202–3, 210, 216, 224,
   234–5, 240n, 244–6, 267, 272, 275–9,
   282, 285, 290, 293–4, 297, 301
Labour Party
   National Executive Committee
     (NEC) 74, 82–3, 86–92, 137, 197,
     241–3, 271, 286–7, 290
   Young Labour 73, 74, 86–9,
     93, 118
Langleben, Adam 65, 168–9, 255
Lansman, Jon 75–6, 85, 92–5, 175, 201,
   204–10, 230, 241–2, 243, 257, 259–60,
   265, 293
Lawrence, Stephen 84, 183
Lebanon 277
   Al-Akhbar (newspaper) 106
Lenga, Izzy 192, 296

Levane, Leah 167, 197, 199
　　See also Jewish Voice for Labour
Lewis, Clive 62, 193
Lewis, Ivan 246
Lipman, Maureen 20–1
Liverpool (city)
　　2016 Labour conference in 100, 113, 115–7, 166
　　as base for Trotskyist group Militant 35, 215, 216
　　Liverpool Riverside 211, 266
　　Liverpool 'dodgy dossier' 214–6 266–7, 290
　　Liverpool Friends of Palestine 262n
　　Liverpool Labour 211, 212, 213–7, 235, 294
Livingstone, Ken 16, 59, 67, 120, 129–34, 136–43, 154, 158–60, 163, 164, 170–1, 176, 181, 190, 194, 198, 206–7, 222, 236, 250–1, 264–5, 269, 278, 290, 294, 297, 305–7
The Lobby (series) 31n, 33, 37n, 43, 45, 46–7, 55, 57, 62, 64–5, 89, 98, 100, 103, 106–15, 118–21, 125, 127, 164, 176, 210, 218–9, 235, 237n, 268, 279, 282, 301, 309
　　The Lobby—USA (series) 102, 104–5, 128
　　See also Al Jazeera
Long-Bailey, Rebecca 285–7, 292–3

MacDonald, Ramsay 51
Machover, Moshé 159–63, 181, 229, 268
Macpherson, William 84
Mann, John 59–60, 129–31, 133, 141, 143, 160, 162, 163, 189, 272
Manning, Chelsea 188
　　See also WikiLeaks
Manson, Jenny 199n, 270
Marks, Helen 213
Mason, Peter 47, 65–6
Masot, Shai 45, 46–7, 62, 98, 106–11, 113, 114, 116–8, 125–7, 176, 276, 281–3
Massey, Becky 294
Mayer, Martin 90
May, Theresa 19, 38, 126, 198, 232

Mayhew, Christopher 51n, 54
McCluskey, Len 73, 160, 199, 243
McDonald, Nikki 63
McDonnell, John 15, 30, 118, 134, 136, 207–8, 241, 244, 247, 251, 265, 267–8, 271, 293
McNeill, Lara 191–2
Meyer, Hajo 271–2, 283
MI5 and MI6
　　and Jeremy Corbyn 8, 41
Miliband, Ed 13, 17–8, 20–3, 24, 77, 275
Miliband, Ralph 21–3
Militant (group) 15, 215, 216–7
　　See also Liverpool
Miller, Arthur 191
Miller, David 294
Millett, Richard 9, 28–33
Milne, Seumas 41, 243, 268, 291
Mirvis, Ephraim 254
Mirwitch, Miriam 89
Mishcon de Reya (law firm) 228, 254
Momentum 62, 75–6, 93, 95, 101, 125, 168, 170, 174, 175, 201, 205–10, 214–5, 229, 241, 253, 257, 262, 290
　　The World Transformed (festival) 117
Morrison, Herbert 50, 156
Mullin, Chris 302
Murphy, Karie 243, 245, 256, 268, 291

Nahmias-Verbin, Ayelet 301
Nandy, Lisa 13, 136n, 286–7, 296–7,
Nazism
　　Nazi Germany 129, 140–8, 150, 157, 163, 179, 229
　　　　Eichmann, Adolf 155–6, 163
　　　　Haavara agreement 146–50
　　　　Hitler, Adolf 142–7
　　　　　　Ken Livingstone's comments on 130, 138–42
　　　　Mein Kampf 130, 145
　　　　Reinhard, Heydrich 146, 153, 161
　　　　Rosenberg, Alfred 144–5
　　Nazi-Zionist relations
　　　　Zionist militias
　　　　　　Haganah, the 26, 34, 51, 156–7

Irgun, the 26, 34
　Lehi, the 26, 34, 51, 157
　Polkes, Feivel 156–7
　Zionist Federation of
　　Germany (ZVfD)
　　150–1, 154
　　See also Zionism
　UK-based
　　Nimmo, John 236
　Ukraine-based
　　Azov Battalion 179
　　See also Holocaust
Netanyahu, Benjamin 50, 99, 118, 125, 138, 202, 239–41, 244, 280, 284–5, 301
　Likud (political party) 117, 121, 240, 280, 284, 307
　See also Israel
New Statesman (magazine) 117, 207, 221
New York Times (newspaper) 21, 79
Newmark, Jeremy 44–8, 54–71, 77, 84, 99, 101, 113, 116–8, 123–5, 132, 164, 201, 204, 209–10, 228n, 232, 255, 268, 279
　See also Rose, Ella, Jewish Labour Movement, *The Lobby* (series)
Nicosia, Francis 144–57, 158, 161
Northern Ireland 12, 136, 273
　Irish Republican Army (IRA) 12
　Sinn Féin 12, 273
Novara Media 72, 75, 86, 174, 265
Nunns, Alex 199, 204, 208

Osamor, Kate 273–4
Osborne, Darren 10

Palestine
　Gaza 20–1, 27, 35, 50, 70, 99, 123, 136, 138, 196, 210, 216, 237–40, 249, 261, 275
　Great March of Return, the 237–9
　Nakba, the 25, 34, 50, 135, 177, 196
　West Bank 27, 50, 70, 108, 113–4, 118, 162, 210, 284
Palestine Return Centre (PRC) 25, 27–9, 281

Palestine solidarity movement 3, 10, 13, 14, 24, 32–4, 41, 58, 61, 63, 78, 85, 89, 90, 108, 122–4, 162, 164, 167, 177, 195, 199, 201–2, 223–4, 229, 231, 249, 269–70, 274–5, 277, 294, 301
Palestine Solidarity Campaign (PSC) 13–4, 29, 34–5, 38, 91, 113, 117, 219, 238–9, 242, 260, 275–7, 288, 291, 294
　The Big Ride for Palestine 261
Pappé, Ilan 26–7, 273
Peake, Maxine 293
Peres, Shimon 277
Peston, Robert 286–7
Philo, Greg 263
Pitt, Bob 236–7
Poale Zion (group) 49–55, 120, 180, 269
Pollard, Stephen 21, 34, 35, 68, 198
Pompeo, Mike 8
　See also CIA
Poole, Ed 251
Proudfoot, Philip 267

Qatar 101–5, 127
　Doha 104, 105
　See also Al Jazeera

Rahman, Luftur 233
Rayner, Angela 299
Ravid, Barak 54n, 124
Reed, Steve 293–4
Regev, Mark 57, 62, 99–101, 124, 126, 176, 202, 210, 276–8, 280–1, 284
Reut Institute 101, 122–4, 314
Rich, Dave 289
Richardson, Alex 115, 218–9
Rose, Ella 43, 45–6, 55, 56–7, 64–8, 111, 116, 119, 218, 235, 281–2, 296
　See also Jewish Labour Movement
Rothschilds (family) 232–3
Royall, Janet 82–4, 93, 97
Rubin, Michael 43, 45, 97–8, 106–7
　See also Labour Friends of Israel
Ruppin, Arthur 149, 151–2
Ryan, Joan 36, 107, 110–1, 113–6, 132, 175–6, 182, 202–3, 218–9, 245, 251, 256, 267, 274, 277, 282
Salah, Raed 38–41, 187n

Sanders, Bernie 44, 254, 264
Sanders, Richard 237, 238
Saudi Arabia 101, 105, 239n
Schneider, James 262, 274
　See also Momentum
Secker, Glyn 168, 170
Shah, Naz 134–41, 163–5, 305, 306
Shanly, Max 72–8, 81–2, 85–8, 92–5, 97–8, 201
Shin Bet 42
Shmuli, Itzik 280
Slaughter, Andy 41, 117
Smeeth, Ruth 184–93, 234, 242, 256–8, 288
　See also BICOM
Smith, Owen 43, 66, 214
Smith, Patrick 290–1
Snelson, Anthony 59–60
Socialist Campaign Group 293
Souag, Mostefa 104–5
　See also Al Jazeera
South Africa 12, 36, 51, 137, 181, 261, 307
Starmer, Keir 11, 170, 190, 199, 214, 269–70, 285–97, 299–302
Strizzolo, Maria 108–9, 126
Sun (newspaper) 19, 20, 25, 184, 204
Syria 50, 53, 90, 99

Taylor, Byron 208
Trump, Donald 105, 188
Thornberry, Emily 127, 279, 286–7
Tlaib, Rashida 172
Thatcher, Margaret 15–9
Thatcherism 19–20
Times of London (newspaper) 37, 71, 88, 160–2, 214, 272–3
　Sunday Times 7, 302

Union of Jewish Students 42n, 43, 56, 66–7, 111, 235
　See also Berger, Luciana
Unison (union) 23–4, 61
Unite (union) 23, 82, 87, 90, 160, 199, 243
　See also Len McCluskey
United Arab Emirates (UAE) 101, 105
United Nations (UN) 26–7, 125
United States (US) 8, 17–8, 33, 36, 42, 46, 49, 62, 71, 104, 123, 127, 135, 140, 172, 181, 186, 254, 271
　McCarthyism era of 62, 191–2

US embassy (in London) 188–9, 256
US pro-Israel lobby 37, 164
Washington, DC 17, 102, 104, 105
University and College Union (UCU) 48, 58, 59–61, 67, 84, 91, 177, 228
University of Oxford 72–96, 98, 114–5, 136, 176, 206, 278
　Labour Club 73–5, 77–83, 86–92, 98, 206
　Ruskin College 73, 81

Vaknin-Gil, Sima 103, 123
　See also Israel, Ministry of Strategic Affairs
Velleman, Liron 43–4, 89, 192n, 296

Wadsworth, Marc 94, 183–7, 190–4
Walker, Jackie 168–75
Ware, John 212n, 217–21
Washington Post (newspaper) 8
Watson, Tom 71, 189
Webb, Sidney 50
White, Audrey 213–4, 216–7, 266–7
WikiLeaks 188–9
　See also Manning, Chelsea
Wimborne-Idrissi, Naomi 167, 170, 195–200, 220, 270–1
Williamson, Chris 67, 171, 205, 254–60, 265, 269, 290, 300

YouTube 40n, 233, 249
　comments on Corbyn's 2015 Channel 4 interview 7
　Corbyn's speech to LFI 276
　Al Jazeera channel 125
　Israel Advocacy Movement use of 168, 172

Zabludowicz, Poju 188
　See also BICOM
Zilberberg, Michal 118–9
Zionism
　Herzl, Theodor 151, 152, 203
　Zionist Organisation of America (ZOA) 104–5
　Zionist Association for Germany (ZVfD) 150–1, 154
　　Hechaluz (youth wing of) 154